MW00736551

ANCESTORS, POWER AND HISTORY IN MADAGASCAR

STUDIES OF RELIGION IN AFRICA

SUPPLEMENTS TO THE JOURNAL OF RELIGION IN AFRICA

EDITED BY

ADRIAN HASTINGS (University of Leeds)
MARC R. SPINDLER (University of Leiden)

XX

ANCESTORS, POWER AND HISTORY IN MADAGASCAR

EDITED BY

KAREN MIDDLETON

BRILL
LEIDEN · BOSTON · KÖLN
1999

This book is printed on acid-free paper.

Library of Congress Cataloging-in-Publication Data

Ancestors, power, and history in Madagascar / edited by Karen
Middleton.
    p.   cm. — (Studies of religion in Africa ; 20)
    ISBN 9004112898 (cloth : alk. paper)
    1. Ancestor worship—Madagascar.   2. Funeral rites and ceremonies-
-Madagascar.   3. Madagascar—Social life and customs.
4. Madagascar—Religious life and customs.   5. Madagascar—Politics
and government.   I. Middleton, Karen.   II. Series: Studies on
religion in Africa ; 20.
GN661.M2A52   1999
306'.09691—dc21
                                                                99-17591
                                                                CIP

Die Deutsche Bibliothek - CIP-Einheitsaufnahme

Ancestors, power and history in Madagascar / ed. by Karen
Middleton. – Leiden ; Boston ; Köln : Brill, 1999
    (Studies of religion in Africa ; Bd. 20)
    ISBN 90–04–11289–8
Studies of religion in Africa : supplements to the Journal of religion
in Africa. – Leiden ; Boston ; Köln : Brill
    Früher Schriftenreihe
    Früher u.d.T.: Studies of religion in Africa
Bd. 20. Ancestors, power and history in Madagascar. – 1999

ISSN 0169-9814
ISBN 90 04 11289 8

PRINTED IN THE NETHERLANDS

CONTENTS

ILLUSTRATIONS

CONTRIBUTORS

Maurice Bloch is Professor of Social Anthropology at the London School of Economics. His many publications on Madagascar include *Placing the Dead* (1971) and *From Blessing to Violence* (1986).

Jennifer Cole is Assistant Professor in Anthropology at Harvard University. She is the author of a number of articles on colonial and ancestral memory among the Betsimisaraka of the East Coast.

Sandra Evers is currently a PhD scholar at the Amsterdam School for Social Science, and has published several articles on stigmatisation and slavery in the southern Highlands.

David Graeber is Assistant Professor in Anthropology at Yale University, and the author of a number of papers on gender, memory, and power in Imerina.

Michael Lambek is Professor of Anthropology at the University of Toronto. He is author of *Human Spirits* (1981) and *Knowledge and Practice in Mayotte* (1993).

Pier Larson is Assistant Professor in African History at Johns Hopkins University. He is author of several articles on Malagasy Christianity and ethnogenesis in nineteenth century Highland Madagascar.

Karen Middleton is the author of several articles on the peoples of the Karembola in the Deep South.

Françoise Raison-Jourde is Professor of Modern History at the Université de Paris 7. Her many publications on Madagascar include *Bible et Pouvoir à Madagascar au XIXe siècle* (1991).

Karina Hestad Skeie is preparing a doctoral thesis at the University of Oslo on nineteenth century Norwegian missionaries to Madagascar.

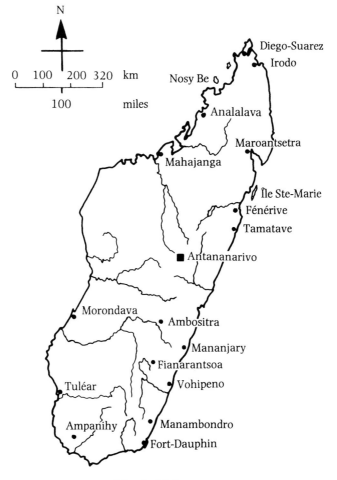

Map 1. Madagascar

Lesley Sharp is Professor of Anthropology at Barnard College, New York. Her publications on the Bemazava-Sakalava include *The Possessed and the Dispossessed* (1993).

Andrew Walsh is based at the University of Toronto where he has recently completed a doctoral thesis on the Antankaraña of Northwest Madagascar.

CHAPTER ONE

INTRODUCTION

KAREN MIDDLETON

During the early 1990s, when World Bank imposed structural 'adjust-
ment' was taking its toll on Madagascar and presidential elections
were under way, the greater part of Jennifer Cole's field diaries in
a Betsimisaraka village on the East Coast concerned speeches made
during sacrifices to the ancestors. Working at around the same time
in the southern Highlands, Sandra Evers was bemused to find 'owners' of a village drawing on ancestry and tomb membership to turn
other would-be settlers into 'slaves'. Meanwhile, in a valley in Imerina,
not many miles from the capital, where on a clear day the Hilton
Hotel seems close at hand, Françoise Raison-Jourde reflected on the
twists and turns of an intense intra-village conflict to gain control of
a tomb, which had spanned the colonial era, the neo-colonial government of Tsiranana, and the Marxist regime of the Second Republic.

To anyone familiar with the literature on Madagascar none of
this will be surprising since it has been so often said that what is
common to the peoples of this island is the extraordinary importance they all place upon ancestors (Mack, 1986). This preoccupation seems moreover to have been stubbornly enduring. During the
colonial period, French colonial administrators described Madagascar
as a 'civilization of death' (cf. Feeley-Harnik, 1991*a*). Then, following Independence in 1960, Madagascar figured in nationalist rhetoric
as 'land of the ancestors' (*Madagasikara tanindrazana*). Of course, the
latter has to be placed in the context of the 'invention of tradition' for
the purposes of nation-building in an island that prior to the colonial era had never formed one state. Yet the theme was apparently
also well-chosen in so far as it appeared to have strong resonances
with local practice throughout the island. Almost all the ethnographies published between 1970 and the early 1990s note in one way
or another that the key to power, fertility, and blessing in Madagascar
lies in the relationship between the living and the dead (e.g., Baré,
1977; 1980: 239; Bloch, 1971; Lombard, 1973; Feeley-Harnik, 1991*a*;
Kottak, 1980; Raison-Jourde, 1991; Sharp, 1993).

To say that the ancestors are important in Madagascar, then, is clearly to say something important about the organizing metaphors for Malagasy culture and cosmology. Indeed, one cannot but be struck at how prominently ancestors have continued to figure in the contemporary literature on Madagascar as compared, for example, with that on Africa, where, with a few notable exceptions (Lan, 1985),[1] scholarly interest in ancestors over the last twenty years has largely given way to a concern with other kinds of religious and ritual practice, especially, Zionist or millenarian cults (e.g., Comaroff, 1985; Fields, 1985; cf. McCall, 1995). The appeal of Christian cults and particularly of millenarianism to Black Africans has been attributed in part to the failure of 'traditional' ancestor-related practices to provide meaningful idioms for the interpretation and management of colonial and post-colonial experience (Poewe, 1978; Fields, 1985). In Madagascar, by contrast, similar movements sought to restore an ancestral order (Raison-Jourde, 1976; Ellis, 1985). Indeed, to voice protests at the way local ancestors have been appropriated by state authority, Malagasy have exchanged one set of ancestors for another rather than reject ancestors altogether (Althabe, 1965).

Yet these examples also indicate that to say that the ancestors are important in Madagascar is also to say very little in so far as it leaves the most important questions about ancestors unvoiced, viz., What part do ancestors play in the construction of identities in Madagascar past and present? What kinds of agency are vested in living people on account of powers that are vested in the dead? How does ritual around the ancestors engage with history? How do ancestors figure in everyday life? How have historical and social processes been shaped by a culture in which ancestors are prominent, and how has historical experience shaped ancestors in turn?

The essays in this volume draw on a wide range of ethnographic and historical materials to explore the significance of ancestors for changing relations of power, emergent identities, and historical consciousness in Madagascar. In many ways, the kinds of questions they ask about the meaning of ancestors for domestic, jural, political, and economic relations are those first posed in the classic Africanist literature e.g., Fortes, 1945, 1959, 1965; Goody, 1962; Middleton, 1964).

---

[1] Is it worth noting that this ancestor-oriented contribution to recent Africanist literature is based on a thesis that was supervised by a Madagascar specialist, Maurice Bloch.

The difference is that they ask these questions with all the theoretical insights since gained into the importance of embodied practice, the nature of social memory, the 'invention of tradition', the sociology of knowledge, the critique of 'social structure', and newer, more fluid understandings of the processes involved in the construction of identities.

Nonetheless, it is very apparent that these contemporaneous essays seldom take a common approach to the ancestors. From one essay, ritual focused on ancestors emerges as a 'cultural resource' which Malagasy deploy in the practical manipulation of others. In another, it is a creative practice that constitutes an 'imagined community'. For another writer, ancestors play a critical role in the construction of 'traditional authority' by linking those in power to a timeless, transcendent order, while for yet another they constitute more in the way of a 'social critique' or meta-discourse on history. Inevitably, one wonders to what extent these different approaches simply reflect ethnographic variation within the island, itself the product of different local ecologies and histories, and to what extent they derive from contrasting perspectives on key theoretical issues in anthropology, such as the interpretation of ritual and the nature of symbolic expression, a disposition on the part of the analyst to stress social conflict over consensus, or to employ or alternatively to reject the usefulness of concepts of superstructure and ideology. Musing on the diversity of approach, and the reasons for it, one wonders whether it is possible to go beyond platitudinous statements about the importance of ancestors in Madagascar to arrive at an island-wide understanding of what ancestors mean in relation to power and history. Or are Malagasy practices relating to ancestors so varied that it is not possible to make valid generalizations about this most basic of 'Malagasy' themes?

History and Power in Madagascar

Lying in the Indian Ocean, separated from Africa by the Mozambique Channel, Madagascar is a huge island, the fourth largest in the world. Some 1,600 km long and with a surface area of 587,000 km, its landscapes vary from the rainforests of the East coast through the savannah and steppe of the Highlands to the xerophilous flora of the Deep South (Jolly et al, 1984). With a current population of some 12 million people, this is also an island of great diversity in social and cultural practice. Political traditions, for instance, range from the nineteenth century kingdom of Imerina (Raison-Jourde, 1991), one of the largest indigenous states to have developed in precolonial sub-Saharan Africa, to peoples like the Tsimihety and the Vezo who have elaborated an egalitarian ethos in conscious rejection of hierarchy (Wilson, 1992; Astuti, 1995). In-between these two extremes, one finds a range of socio-political configurations, each with its own particular play upon hierarchy and equality (e.g., Beaujard, 1983).

For certain authors, the centrality of ancestors in Malagasy culture is closely related to the issue of the origins of the Malagasy (Southall, 1986; Mack, 1986), with some archaeologists appearing to suggest that the Proto-Malagasy carried a preoccupation with ancestors with them over the sea from southeast Asia (Vérin, 1967a). In fact, there are many competing theories about the origins of the Malagasy and the time of their arrival on the island (e.g., Deschamps, 1972; Kent, 1970; Kottak, 1980; Southall, 1967). The population is said to be a mixture predominantly of Indonesian and African elements with Indian and Arab influences; the Malagasy language, of which dialects are spoken throughout the island, is judged to be largely Malayo-Polynesian.

Of the religious traditions that have shaped contemporary Malagasy cosmologies and social practice, Islamic culture, brought by traders and immigrants since at least the tenth century, has had a profound and lasting impact throughout the island (Mack, 1986: 32–38; Vérin, 1986; Gueunier, 1994). This influence is well-documented in the case of theories and practices of divination, destiny, temporal and spatial categories and in the sacred manuscripts of the Antaimoro of the south east, although it is possible that Islamic practice may also have shaped Malagasy constructs of the person and authority. Today, however, the Islamic heritage is largely 'hidden' mainly because the Islamic elements have become local Malagasy cultural practice (Jaovelo-Dzao, 1993; Vérin, 1967b) and Islam is overtly practised as a religion only in some Islamised communities, mostly in the northwestern provinces of Antseranana and Mahajanga (Blanchy, 1990). Between 9 and 15 per cent of Malagasy identify themselves as Muslims, while Hindus and Buddhists comprise about 1 per cent of the population (Feeley-Harnik, 1997).

Although Christian missions were established from the sixteenth century, their greatest impact on Malagasy culture and politics began during the early nineteenth century, when missionaries were allowed to settle in the Highland kingdom of Imerina. So great was their impact in this region that by the time Madagascar was annexed as a colony by the French in 1896, Christianity had become the religion of the Merina state (Raison-Jourde, 1991). A number of excellent studies document how inextricably Christianity and Christian values became interwoven with beliefs and practices around ancestors in the Highlands (Bloch, 1971; Ellis 1985, Raison-Jourde, 1991). In the Deep South and the West, by contrast, evangelization has been more of a twentieth century experience. Thus, although today some 45 per cent of Malagasy are said to be Christians, roughly divided between Catholicism and Protestantism (Feeley-Harnik, 1997), Christian influence is far from homogeneous throughout the island. Of the various denominations (French Catholic, London Missionary Society, Norwegian Mission Society, American Lutherans, . . .) that have jostled for congregations in Madagascar, each has its particular history in relation to colonialism, Malagasy nationalism, and independence. To understand this chequered history, we need ethnographies exploring how the full range of Christian cultic practice, from the Seventh day Adventists to the *Fifohazana*, articulates with local constructs of ancestors and ancestral blessing in regions beyond the Highlands today (see Hübsch, 1993).

Identities and understandings of power in Madagascar have also been shaped by the various dynasties that rose and fell in different parts of the island between the sixteenth and nineteenth centuries. Hierarchical forms of political organization began developing in the sixteenth century. Most of these formations, notably the Sakalava on the West coast, and the Maroseraña in the Deep South, had characteristics typical of the traditional Southeast Asian state, that is to say, power was concentrated at the centre, fading at the margins, and the geographic extent of the kingdom was always in flux (Anderson 1990: 41). Others like the Betsimisaraka were probably no more than confederacies. The exception is the Highlands kingdom of Imerina which expanded throughout the nineteenth century until it ruled over two-thirds of Madagascar.

Although the peoples of Madagascar were brought into a single political and administrative structure for the first time under French rule (1895–1960), the long power struggles between Merina, Sakalava and French and British colonial powers that had preceded the declaration of a French Protectorate left their mark on relations between

Malagasy, especially between côtiers and Merina (Covell, 1987;
Esoavelomandroso, 1989). Differential access to education, administrative policies that varied by region, and, above all, the uneven development of the colonial economy, served to exacerbate these social
divisions during the colonial era. Attempts by the colonial administration to make the Merina dialect the standardized language of
Madagascar were resisted. Despite the official rhetoric of national
identity that accompanied independence, economic and political factors continued to promote antagonisms under the First Republic of
Tsiranana, the socialist revolution of 1975 and Malgachisation, into
the increasing poverty and deteriorating state infrastructure that has
characterised Madagascar in the 1980s and 1990s.

Given its immense size and complex history, it is perhaps no wonder that scholars have described Madagascar as a 'little continent'
or 'less an island than an archipelago' (Covell, 1987: 9). And yet
among Western academics as well as Malagasy nationalists there is
still a sense of a 'Malagasy culture' or 'pan-Malagasy themes' (Mack,
1986; Southall, 1986). Like all so-called 'culture areas', however,
Madagascar poses problems for the scholar: of acknowledging what
is held in common while not obscuring the very real differences that
exist. The study of ancestors exemplifies the difficulties. For while
practices around ancestors have been central to imagery of Madagascar, they also appear to vary significantly between Malagasy cultures,
and perhaps more importantly to have undergone transformations
over time. The challenge therefore is to find the fertile place between
platitudinous generalization and pointless particularism that places
ancestors in specific social, political and historical contexts while still
engaging in comparative analysis.

From Corpse to Tomb

In support of the idea of a 'pan-Malagasy culture', it is often noted
that all dialects of the Malagasy language have some cognate of a
common root (*raza, razana, razañe*) whose meaning is glossed in English
and French as 'ancestors' or 'ancêtres' respectively. Perhaps because
of the shared cognate rate, their translation has not generated the
intense debates, at least not among anthropologist and historians,
that one finds in the literature for comparable terms in African religions where the existence of different language families has led scholars to focus closely on the problems of translation, and in some cases

to elect to avoid cross cultural misunderstandings by using vernacular terms. Thus, while close attention has been paid to how the 'ways of the ancestors' (*fomban-drazana, lilin-drazañe*, i.e. 'custom', 'local cultural practice'), for example, vary throughout the island, curiously few scholars address the possibility that the range of cultural meanings among different speech communities of the terms we translate as 'ancestors' or 'ancêtres' may be broader than has been hitherto supposed.

In keeping with general trends in the anthropology of religion, analyses of ancestor-focused practices in Madagascar have moved away from concepts of 'ancestor worship' that characterised earlier western discourses (e.g., Mannoni, 1990). Thus, Feeley-Harnik (1991*a*) stresses that the work Sakalava perform for the royal ancestors is to be understood as 'service' rather than 'worship', while Bloch finds that the Merina model of ancestors has little in common with African models of ancestors (Bloch, 1971). We should be careful that such pronouncements do not mask important regional differences, however. Even for the Highlands, there appears to be some disagreement both as to the degree in which ancestors are conceptualised as individuals and mortuary ritual is aimed at deindividualising the dead (compare Bloch, 1971 and Graeber, 1995 on the Merina), and in the extent to which ancestors are held to be supernatural enforcers of the moral order (compare Bloch, 1971; Kottak, 1980: 214; Huntington, 1988). To grasp local conceptualisations of ancestral power, and the corresponding attitudes (dependency, endebtedness, awe, respect, homage, honour) that are required of the living, we need to make a closer study of the vernacular terms that describe their interactions. There may, for example, be significant contrasts in how Malagasy conceptualise the 'work' they undertake for royal ancestors and 'work' they perform for their own ancestors, even if both kinds of work are best glossed as 'service' rather than 'worship'. Acknowledging local and regional contrasts in Malagasy conceptualizations of 'work' and 'blessing' may be vital if we are to grasp the particular role ancestors play in local constructs of what Bloch and Parry term 'the political economy of fertility' (Bloch and Parry, 1982).

A considerable part of the anthropological literature on ancestors in Madagascar is devoted to the description of mortuary rites. This is because Malagasy funerals tend to be rich, elaborate, and extended, prompting comparisons with the 'double funerals' of southeast Asia.

At the same time, it has become almost a cliché to observe that the living generally expend more on tombs than on their own houses, a fact that is particularly significant given that Madagascar is among the poorest countries of the world. These elaborate and costly rituals are interpreted in the first instance to support the point made long ago for the African context, namely, that the dead do not automatically become ancestors. In the literature for Madagascar, the processes by which the dead become ancestors are very commonly seen to be linked with the way the extended mortuary ritual turns wet, polluting corpses into dry, hard bones, although Bloch also argues that the living begin to move towards ancestorhood through gradual processes of bodily maturation (1992*b*). At the same time, it has been suggested that, in the absence of elaborate eschatologies, the Malagasy experience their ancestors primarily in the context of these elaborate bodily practices focused on corpses and tombs (Huntington, 1988). In many parts of the island, Bloch points out, the term *razana* covers 'both our meaning of the word "ancestor" and our meaning of the word "corpse," especially after it has entered the tomb' (1989 [1985]: 218).

Without a doubt, anthropologists working on Madagascar have produced outstanding ethnographies that show how embodied practices focused on tombs and corpses are powerful media, not only for creating ancestors but also for constructing ideologies and identities for 'living people' (Bloch, 1971; Feeley-Harnik, 1991a). Even so, the dramaturgy of Malagasy mortuary rituals should not be allowed to obscure other important experiential dimensions of ancestral cults. For example, Cole (this volume) is able to present a densely woven account of Betsimisaraka interactions with their ancestors by focusing on sacrifice, and saying very little about funerals. For many parts of Madagascar, we need a theory of ancestors that moves beyond mortuary ritual to encompass the broader range of living in a social milieu which includes ancestors and explores the relationship of that experience to the construction and reproduction of historical consciousness and identity (McCall, 1995: 258).

The best-known mortuary practice is undoubtedly the *famadihana* practised by the Merina of the central Highlands, defined by most scholars as the practice of exhuming and periodically rewrapping the dead. Made familiar to the English-speaking world through Maurice Bloch's publications (1971, 1982), these rites inform the image most outsiders have of Madagascar as the 'island of ancestors'. The fact is, however, that not all Malagasy peoples practice burial, exhumation, and reburial. The very idea of exhumation is anathema to many in the West and Deep South.

Significant differences between Malagasy cultures also emerge if we compare those who apparently share the Merina practice of placing the remains of the dead in monumental stone tombs. According to region and other factors, such as whether the deceased is royalty or commoner, we find that tombs may be individual or collective. Corpses may arranged in families on shelves inside an existing structure or the tomb may be built for the individual deceased above the freshly dug grave. Tombs may serve to anchor people in an 'ancestral' landscape or they may be built to deflect the spiteful spirits of the recent dead (Middleton, n.d.). Tombs may be hidden in forests or put on public display. They may even topple into the world of the living when they are supposed to be out of sight (Astuti, 1995). Tombs may be the 'moral symbol of community', places where people seek ancestral blessing (Bloch, 1971) or they may be places that the living do their best to avoid. This is most likely when there are other sacred sites in or nearer villages—cenataphs, *hazomanga* stakes, holy houses, prayer posts—at which the living invoke the ancestors (e.g. Razafiarivony, 1995). In each case, the tomb has a particular spatio-temporal symbolic logic that can only be elicited by careful attention to local context. In the Sakalava monarchies, for example, the tomb derives its meaning through its articulation with *tromba* (possession by the spirits of dead kings) and relics (Feeley-Harnik, 1991*a*, 1991*b*; Sharp, this volume; Bloch, 1981) or, alternatively, ritual journeys that culminate in mast-raising ceremonies (Lambek and Walsh, this volume). Creating particular local cultural landscapes of sacred powers, both visible and invisible, tangible and intangible, these kinds of contrasts point to significant variation in Malagasy cosmologies of life and death. They also underscore the need to look more closely at how we translate the local terms we freely gloss as 'ancestors' or 'ancêtres'. Thus, for the Merina the term *razana* designates both 'corpse' and 'ancestor', but for Karembola of the Deep South the corpse and the dead in the tomb are known as *lolo*, and *lolo* are in many contexts contrasted with the *razañe*, the cool, generative ancestors who herd cattle in the sky to the east. In many ways, the term *razañe* is best glossed as 'the living dead'.

The risks in attempting a synthesis of Malagasy funerary symbolism are well illustrated in the book that was published to accompany an exhibition at the British Museum entitled *Madagascar, Land of the Ancestors* (Mack, 1986). Grouping the various kinds of mortuary practices to be found in Madagascar into three basic types, the author identifies their common denominator as the desire to generate a dry, non-polluted corpse (p. 85). Unfortunately, this approach not only glosses over significant cosmological differences that stem from regional variations in mortuary practice—for example, some Malagasy show considerable ambivalence as to whether ancestral fertility lies in the wet body rather than dry bones (Middleton, n.d.)—but also neglects what is most interesting to historians and anthropologists about rituals focused on corpses, namely, how they relate to broader social, historical and political processes.

Placing the Dead by Bloch represented the first serious attempt to describe the extraordinary 'custom' of the *famadihana* in a way that related it to a broader understanding of Merina socio-political organization. First published in 1971, the book made two important contributions to anthropology. First, against models of corporate descent groups that then dominated British social anthropology, it argued that the Merina deme (descent group), that played a pivotal role in Merina ideology, was essentially created during the *famadihana* as corpses were regrouped in monumental tombs. Secondly, in a context where anthropologists were just beginning to look at history, Bloch suggested that these mortuary practices had developed partly as a conservative response to social change during the colonial era, and especially of countering territorial dispersal (cf. Bloch, 1968).

In his later work, Bloch elaborated this understanding of ritual as being concerned with creating a world of 'immobilized', transcendent time into a broader theory of the role ritual and religion play in creating 'traditional authority'. In a well-known study (1986) tracing the history of Merina circumcision ritual over almost two centuries, during which the Merina state developed, was replaced by French colonialism, which in turn gave way to Independence, he sought to substantiate this thesis by demonstrating how, despite the extreme plasticity of its political and economic role, the symbolic core of the ritual remained essentially the same. This symbolic core was effective in legitimating traditional authority over time, he argued, because of its ability to link those in authority in this life with an ideal timeless order. Similar themes were developed in essays on the *famadihana* (1982) and the royal bath (1989 [1987]).

If the force and originality of Bloch's propositions about ritual and traditional authority gave Merina ethnography a readership that extended far beyond students of Madagascar, they also attracted a number of criticisms (Tambiah, 1985; Kelly and Kaplan, 1990: 125–126). Noting parallels with Kopytoff's (1971) much maligned article on 'Ancestors as elders in Africa', some critics suggested that the role Bloch ascribed to ritual in political economies had inherited the mantle of now defunct structural-functionalist models of ancestor-related beliefs and practices in traditional African social organisation. This charge was a little unfair, however, since Bloch did not argue for stasis in Merina historical processes nor did he equate the eternal world of ancestors with 'social structure' in the real world. Indeed, in so far as his approach stressed the reinterpretative power of ritual, it had rather more in common with the analytical subtleties of Anderson's (1991) 'imagined community'. On the other hand, the emphasis Bloch placed upon ritual as existing 'isolated in a heavy world between actions and statements' (1986: 188), together with his insistence that 'ritual transforms and reduces events so that they lose their specificity' (1986: 185), could not but obscure and weaken his earlier thesis that Merina ritual around ancestors had evolved partly in response to historical experience, making it easy to see why his approach to ritual came to typify for many the limitations of a synchronic approach (e.g., Comaroff and Comaroff, 1993: xv).

During the 1980s, the question of whether ancestors in Madagascar have undergone historical transformation in response to changing political and economic circumstances was taken up by Feeley-Harnik. Insisting that contemporary configurations of royal ancestors among the Bemihisatra Sakalava of Analalava (northwest Madagascar) can *only* be understood as historical products, she argued that the intrusion of Merina and subsequently French power beginning early during the nineteenth century brought shifts from ancestors in the relics at the *doany* to entombed corpses at the *mahabo*, along with shifts from male rulers to female ones (1984; 1991a). Challenging widely held and deep-rooted assumptions about 'Malagasy culture', she suggests that '[c]ontemporary Malagasy preoccupations with ancestors, attributed to age-old tradition, are a relatively recent development' (1991a: 3).

Although Feeley-Harnik's (1991) analysis of Sakalava royal ritual appears to contrast sharply with the 'ahistoricity' ascribed to Bloch, it should not be thought that there is no place for Bloch's problematic in her work. On the contrary, her argument that, by engaging in *menaty* ritual services for dead monarchs, Sakalava kept alive their sense of sovereignty in the face of foreign imperialism is not without parallels with Bloch's understanding of the *famadihana*. Where Feeley-Harnik and Bloch diverge most sharply is on the role ritual plays in creating 'traditional authority'.

Other anthropologists and historians also muse on the place of history in Malagasy ritual around ancestors. Some, it is true, are keen to distance themselves from the charge of 'ahistoricity'. Thus, for Sharp, *tromba* possession by royal spirits is a primary expression of Sakalava *mémoire collective*, explicitly incorporating references to modernity and history, and revealing an intense awareness of the effects of outside forces upon the local political economy (1995: 76). For others, the issue is more complex. While they see ritual around ancestors as intricately involved with history, they also feel the need to take account of the role 'ancestors' and 'the ways of the ancestors' frequently play in conceptualizing 'tradition', aware that in many cases it is the Malagasy themselves who saddle ritual around ancestors with the 'albatross of connections to "tradition"' (Kelly and Kaplan, 1990: 120). More often still, Malagasy cultural practice is constituted by highly contradictory symbolic operations in which ancestors are shown as both changed by historical experience and yet also to stand outside history (e.g., Lambek, 1998). Noting that ritual around ancestors may carry an 'out of time' dimension even as it encodes modernity, Cole and Middleton (n.d.) argue that ancestors have animated diverse academic imaginings of Madagascar, and constant reimaginings by Malagasy peoples of their lived worlds, precisely because they constitute a language that generates heterogeneous meanings. Disentangling the multiple, shifting ways ancestors figure in the social and political imagination will therefore call for considerable analytical subtlety, if a focus on ancestors is to facilitate rather than hinder our understanding of Malagasy historical consciousness (Jewsiewicki and Mudimbe, 1992: 9).

Reading 'ancestral' ritual as historical event

Given the attention Bloch's work has received in the wider literature on ritual and religion, it is curious how few anthropologists and historians working on Madagascar have examined his theories in the light of their own data. This is one reason why Larson's chapter in the present volume is so valuable. As a historian, Larson is con-

cerned to incorporate a historical perspective into his analysis of ritual. He explicitly contrasts his own approach to the Royal Bath of
1817 with Bloch's (1987) analysis. It is therefore instructive to see
what difference 'history' makes to their handling of the significance
of ritual around royal ancestors for power and agency.

Keen to demonstrate Malagasy agency in early cultural encounters with Europeans of expanding empire, Larson argues that the
entrance of Hastie, envoy of the British government in Mauritius,
into the capital of Imerina in August 1817 was choreographed by
Radama I, the Merina sovereign, to coincide with the ritual cycle
of the Royal Bath. The *Fandroana* of 1817 came at a tense moment
for Radama who was about to break the power of his father's coun-
sellors by conducting alliance with Britain and enacting the abolition of the export trade in slaves. Reading this particular performance
of the ritual against Bloch's (1987) analysis of the 'ideal' or 'generic'
Fandroana, Larson shows how Radama positioned his guest in the
ritual sequence, making symbolic inversions in the process, so as to
communicate his political intentions to the royal court. Thus, whereas
scholarly narratives have tended to situate Hastie's arrival within the
schema of British imperial expansion, Larson argues that the event
can be equally interpreted with reference to Radama's political agenda.

Larson's close study of the Royal Bath of 1817 constitutes a telling
critique of Bloch's theory of ritual, first, because it shows that there
are creative choices to be made within even the most formalised
rituals (cf. Csordas, 1987; Kelly and Kaplan, 1990) and secondly,
because it insists on looking at the dynamic of ritual as a specific
socio-historical event, notably in relation to the politics of international alliance. However, in so far as Radama emerges as an adroit
cultural broker manipulating key Merina symbols of ancestors, blessing, and fertility in pursuit of his political ends, Larson's reading
of the link between ritual and power is perhaps not so dissimilar
to Bloch's.

The question of whether ritual might be the 'special strategy' of
'traditional authority' (Bloch, 1989: 45) resurfaces when we learn
from other sources that a year or so earlier Radama had tried floating
his new diplomacy in another way. In the course of sealing blood
brotherhood with two envoys from Mauritius, he had shocked the
royal court by offering his kingdom to one in exchange for Mauritius
(Raison-Jourde, 1983: 36). Inevitably, one wonders whether Radama
subsequently embedded his message in rituals focused on royal

ancestors because he recognised that their 'highly formalised', 'repetitive' style of communication, 'marked by the way they imply no alternative', would make them less open to controversy (Bloch, 1986: 182). Did participants at the royal court find themselves in 'a kind of tunnel [. . .] where, since there is no possibility of turning either to right or left, the only thing to do is to follow' (Bloch, 1989: 41–42)?

In fairness, the case-study chosen by Larson is not best-suited to challenge Bloch's model of the role ritual around ancestors plays in creating 'traditional authority' in that it concerns royal historical agency seventy odd years before French colonial power annexed Madagascar. This was a time when indigenous elites, or certain factions within them, were often in a position to be able to manipulate 'tradition', together with alliance with strangers, to make political statements to their own advantage (cf. Raison-Jourde, 1983, 1991). Other scholars also consider the question of how ritual around ancestors bears on the abilities of Malagasy, individually and collectively, relative to one another and to outsiders, to act in and upon the world. While they almost all agree that local conceptions of agency are embedded in discourse and practice around ancestors, the ethnography they present is far from uniform. Some, in fact, present highly ambivalent readings of the role the 'language of the dead' plays in constructing 'the powers of the living' (Baré, 1977). For example, Feeley-Harnik argues that the shift from relics into corpses that occurred among the Sakalava Bemihisatra in response to the intrusion of foreigners was associated with a decline in the powers of the living monarch and the elevation of commoners and royal slaves (1991: 112–113). The reader may have certain reservations about this thesis, however, given the asymmetrical nature of Sakalava royal service, and the fact that many Sakalava monarchs were co-opted as colonial administrators, which meant that the distinction between royal service and forced labour and taxes for the colonial state was often blurred. The case against Bloch's understanding of ritual is made more persuasively through studies of more 'devolved' peoples, notably, Beaujard's (1983) monograph showing the complex balance of complementary powers between autochthonous commoners and incoming nobles that is achieved in ritual among the Tanala of Ikongo (cf. Raison-Jourde, 1983: 22–26).

Ancestors and Missionaries

At first glance, an essay on nineteenth century Norwegian mission-aries to the Vakinankaratra and Betsileo may seem out of place in a book concerned with ancestors. On closer examination, the chap-ter by Skeie meshes very well with its themes. To begin with, if ancestors in Madagascar have changed over the past two centuries, we can be sure that it will have been partly in the course of their encounter with missionaries of various Christian denominations. A key issue in the study of emergent 'Malagasy Christianities' concerns the extent to which Malagasy practices and cosmologies were trans-formed by Western agents in a 'process of profound acculturation', and the extent to which Malagasy themselves took the active part in the making of 'Malagasy Christianities' (Raison-Jourde, 1991; Larson, 1997). To make an informed judgement of these issues, we need *inter alia* clear accounts not simply of the doctrines and dog-mas that missionaries brought to Madagascar but also of how they lived their religiosity while there.

Drawing on the wealth of data that lies untapped in the Norwegian Missionary Archives at Stavanger, Skeie begins by highlighting a fun-damental ambivalence in Norwegian missionaries' understanding of the mission station. These houses were seen as 'light towers', whose construction symbolized the initiation of a Christian mission in a 'Pagan' environment. However, as soon as they had been built, mis-sionaries wanted to forget about them and move on to the 'real' missionary work of carrying the light into the darkness beyond. Relating this ambiguous conceptualization of the mission station to a more fundamental conflict in the missionaries' pietistic evangelism as to the relationship between the 'visible' and the 'invisible', or the 'tangible' and the 'intangible' worlds, Skeie shows how the contrast between 'real' and 'indirect' work was itself highly problematic for while Norwegian missionaries saw their work as a spiritual battle, daily missionary work was in fact highly corporeal and often tediously routinized.

Imagining their encounter with Madagascar in terms of bringing light to those who sit in darkness, the Norwegian missionaries saw evangelization as one way process in which the essentially malleable and passive Malagasy would be transformed. In practice, however, local Malagasy contexts impinged substantially upon their world. This leads Skeie contrasts the *outwards* movement of the missionaries, first

from Norway to Madagascar and then from the mission station to
missionize in the world beyond, with a counter *inward* movement
into the 'closed' world of the mission station, as they sought to
sustain the Gospel as an immutable, eternal truth. Yet even as the
mission station socialized missionaries into the values of missionary
culture in Madagascar, it encoded their permeability to external
influence, for no matter what they do to try to keep it out, 'Malagasy
fever' seeps inside the solid walls.

Focused on Norwegian missionaries, Skeie's historical ethnography
addresses many themes that are central to the study of Malagasy
ancestors: the complex interplay of passivity and activity in cultural
practice, the uncertain relationship between 'out-of-time' truths and
life-in-this-world, and the difficulties of negotiating a balance between
porosity and closure when constructing identities. The importance
of 'external' practice-based religiosity relative to inner 'invisible' belief
figures in Raison-Jourde's discussion of Merina discourses on the
destruction of the *Sampy* in the wake of the mass conversion of 1869
(this volume), and in the controversy between her and Larson (1997)
as to the place of orality and literacy among early Malagasy Christians. Skeie's sensitive unravelling of 'doing' and 'being' in Norwegian
missionary perceptions warns us not to create false dichotomies between 'European' and 'Malagasy' cultural practice. While embodied
practice is important in Madagascar, it never exists to the exclusion
of interior religious experience or philosophical and intellectual speculation. Moreover, different forms of knowledge may be variably
accentuated by individual members of any one 'society' (cf. Lambek,
1993).

Modernity and Tradition

One of the challenges for historians and anthropologists of Madagascar is to understand why royalty and royal ancestors from the pre-
colonial period continue to play such an important role in political
subjectivities in many parts of the island today (see articles in Raison-
Jourde, 1983). In her chapter, Sharp extends our understanding of
this phenomenon by focusing on succession in the urbanized Bemazava-
Sakalava kingdom of the north-west. Examining the lives of three
Bemazava rulers whose reigns have spanned the colonial and post-
colonial periods, she stresses the wilful 'modernity' which has char-

acterised this particular dynasty, often generating responses that defy local sense of 'tradition' and breach important local taboos. Insisting that such unorthodoxy should not be taken as evidence of 'decline' or 'crisis' in the Bemazava monarchy, Sharp suggests that the Bemazava should be understood as having collectively chosen to defy sacred mandate in an attempt to create a sense of identity and power within a kingdom that must exist within a larger nation-state (cf. Sharp, 1993).

Securing *succession* through radical ritual innovation is not without its paradoxes, however, especially since honouring the ancestors and their taboos is held to be as crucial to survival and power among the Bemazava as it is elsewhere in Madagascar. The consequent tensions are epitomized in the instatement of a new, young ruler who shows how modern he is, first by proceeding with the work of converting the royal palace into a disco hall, and secondly, and more seriously, by *not* completing his father's tomb. Such dereliction of filial duty, inconceivable to many Malagasy peoples, is particularly striking in a context where the first obligation of the *ampanjaka* is to carry out the funeral that will enable his predecessor to become a royal ancestor. Appearing to constitute rather more than yet another example of a play upon rules and their transgression that has been noted for Malagasy monarchies (Raison-Jourde, 1991), the young king appears to turn his back on the very roots from which his own power grows.

That a ruler should thus neglect his symbolic capital is puzzling precisely because it is generally the case that, even in the case of emergent class divisions, Malagasy actors still seek to 'naturalize' their advantage by drawing creatively on the power of the dead (see Raison-Jourde, this volume). One wonders what place, if any, there will be for 'royal ancestors' in the future Bemazava monarchy, and whether the followers of this dynasty will accept this 'modern' king or whether his taboo-breaking will encounter popular opposition, as did that of the nineteenth century Merina sovereign, Radama I? And what of the other powers that constitute the Bemazava monarchy? How, for instance, will the *tromba*, who embody the spirits of the royal ancestors, respond? Will they make what Raison-Jourde, writing of possession as popular protest in nineteenth century Imerina, has termed an 'appel contre le roi vivant à ses ancêtres' (1983: 48)? At present, there seems to be a striking degree of local consensus that radical ritual innovation will ensure Bemazava continuity. Whether this will eventually generate more profound transformations in local understandings of the role of monarchs and royal ancestors in the processes of social reproduction, only time will tell.

The Bemazava explicitly contrast their own 'modernity' with the 'traditional' orientation of the neighbouring Antankaraña dynasty whose king and followers make great play of their adherence to 'custom' as manifest in the performance of a ritual cycle which climaxes in the raising of the mast over the royal capital. Yet, as Lambek and Walsh show in their chapter, many of the elements that Antankaraña cast as 'tradition' are in fact the product of on-going processes of cultural innovation. (The best documented example of this kind of process is the way Protestantism came to be regarded as a truly 'Malagasy' ancestral 'tradition' in the Highlands in nineteenth century [Raison-Jourde, 1991; Bloch, 1971: 14–15; but contrast Ellis, 1985].) These examples highlight both the importance of paying attention to *local* constructs of 'tradition' and 'modernity' but also indicate the need for some measure of skepticism if the 'invention of tradition' (Hobsbawm and Ranger, 1983) is to remain a useful heuristic in historical and anthropological analysis.

Ancestors and Identity

Earlier I contrasted the enduring vigour of ancestors in the literature for Madagascar with the declining interest in ancestors and ancestor-related practices among scholars of African culture and society over recent decades. Arguably, one reason for this divergence is that in the literature for Madagascar the ancestors were never fastened to lineage theory as they were in the literature for the African mainland. Analyses of ancestor-related practices were a crucial component of structural-functional models of segmentary social organisation in Africa. With the waning of lineage theory in the 1970s, ancestors became a marginal issue for most scholars of African societies, although it has been argued that they remained very important in local peoples' lives (McCall, 1995). By contrast, unilineal descent group theory never took firm root in Madagascar ethnography: attempts to apply it to Malagasy social organization were dogged by the author's evident sense of ambiguity (e.g., Lavondès, 1967; cf. Southall, 1986). One of the achievements of *Placing the Dead* was that it pointed to a more processual understanding of descent identity by showing how the deme was an ideal created as corpses were grouped in the tomb.

More recently, this thesis has been taken up by Astuti (1995*a*) who argues that Vezo on the west coast south of Morondava draw a sharp distinction between the processuality of the world of living, who create their identity through activities performed in the present, and the dead whose identity is given as an essence inherited from the past. On this reading, descent or ancestor-oriented identities are no longer the primary idioms organizing the existence of the living because Vezo identity is 'performative'. Only the dead in the tomb are 'kinded', that is, grouped in a permanent and fixed order as ancestors. Generalizing for cultures throughout Madagascar, a number of scholars suggest that, in contrast to many African societies which primarily define people according to descent, Malagasy notions of the person are essentially Austronesian in that they are fluid and processual (Southall, 1986; Bloch, 1992; Astuti, 1995, 1998). Describing this process of becoming as 'cumulative kinship', Southall argues that 'what seems to be distinctive about all Malagasy kinship systems is not their qualities of cognation or agnation, but their emphasis on kinship and descent status as something achieved gradually and progressively throughout life, and even after death, rather than ascribed and fixed definitely at birth' (1986: 417).

In their chapter in this volume, Lambek and Walsh take up some of these issues by exploring the significance of ritual around royal ancestors for contemporary identities in Northwest Madagascar. Finding the depiction of social groups as discrete, bounded, reified entities problematic in the analysis of their data, they suggest that in the Northwest there is a logic of collective identity that is constituted less by categorization than by performance and less by exclusion than by inclusion. Focusing on the mast-raising ritual, which an estimated seven thousand people attended in 1987, they argue that Antankaraña identity (and indeed the Antankaraña polity) is created largely through popular participation in a ceremonial cycle.

Although Lambek and Walsh describe identity in the Northwest as fluid, inclusive, and performative, it is worth noting subtle differences between their ethnography and Astuti's model of Vezo 'ethnicity'. To begin with, history is a major form of symbolic capital in the Northwest region. In the year prior to the mast-raising, the Antankaraña king re-enacts a historical narrative by retracing his ancestors' steps. Thus, while Vezo deny the significance of history by insisting that anyone can become Vezo regardless of origin, history focused on royal ancestors plays a fundamental part in the construction of Antankaraña identity. And indeed the pre-eminence of royal ancestors over other possible idioms in Antankaraña constructs of their 'imagined community' would be puzzling if people themselves were to deny the relevance of historical subjectivities since dynasties *are* essentially idioms that make connections between the present and the past.

The greater value given to history in Antankaraña identity over Vezo identity not only highlights some of the difficulties in making general pronouncements on the relative place of performance ('doing') over essentialism ('being') in 'ethnicity' in Madagascar, but also suggests that 'performativity' can easily become a blunt tool if deployed indiscriminately. In fact, far from being uniform or homogeneous, the ways in which ancestors enter into on-going processes of creating, sustaining and transforming identities (national, 'ethnic', regional, and local) in the various regions of Madagascar are diverse, complex, and often highly nuanced. For example, the ritual cycle that creates Antankaraña identity itself encompasses lower-level ancestries (*karazana*, literally, 'kinds of people'), each with a particular work to perform. It also counterposes historical enmity to the Merina to alliance with the French. The very complex manner in which identities may be transacted in the course of even one ritual is finely illustrated in Feeley-Harnik's (1982, 1984, 1989, 1991) analyses of the reburial of the Sakalava king. She shows how a sense of Sakalava identity is created among commoners by uprooting them from their own ancestries, and drawing them through royal service into the body of the deceased, thereby making them into the 'king's men'.

Thus, while it is undoubtedly true that all Malagasy peoples 'are deeply engaged by the tension between malleability and fixity, indeterminacy and determinacy, processuality and stasis' (Astuti, 1998: 47), it is unlikely, given their variable political and historical experiences, that they will negotiate these tensions in the same way. Indeed, for a number of reasons, I would expect the clarity of the Vezo model, with its two sharply opposed kinds of identity, to be the exception rather than the norm. In most cases, grasping the shifting, multiple, context-dependent ways in which Malagasy peoples draw on essentialist and non-essentialist models to think about themselves in relation to ancestors and other alternative idioms of personhood will demand a multifaceted view of social dynamics in time and space (cf. Jackson, 1989).

Ancestors and Memory

The French *tricolore* and Antankaraña flags flying side by side over the royal capital are a reminder of the historical capacities of Malagasy monarchies for alliance with strangers (Raison-Jourde, 1983). Yet, as Lambek and Walsh note, the French are remembered as allies in contemporary royal ritual only by 'forgetting' those moments of humiliation when Antankaraña kings were made instruments of French colonial rule (indeed one was imprisoned for 15 days). Thus, like many historians and anthropologists today, Lambek and Walsh are concerned to show how remembering and forgetting are equally necessary to the construction of historical identities (cf. Lambek, 1996). In the process, they also convey the moral and political quandaries the historian or anthropologist may face when examining the 'fictions' that creative re-imaginings of the past may involve.

As might be expected of cultures in which ancestors are so important, the value of remembering is deeply etched in many Malagasy cultures, where it is seen as necessary to procreation and the regeneration of life. As Feeley-Harnik puts it, in remembering their ancestors, the living 'make them great' and the ancestors are held to reciprocate by blessing their descendants with fertility and prosperity (1991*b*: 126). At the same time, she notes the difficulties of striking a balance between remembering and forgetting: 'to separate from the dead is to live. To forget the dead is to die. But to recall them in ancestors is to walk a most difficult path between the two, brushing against death for life' (1991*a*: 45–46). Similar tensions between past and present, and between memory and violence, have been explored to powerful effect in the context of Merina mortuary rituals (Bloch, 1971; Graeber, 1995).

In her chapter on the Betsimisaraka of the East coast, Cole moves away from rituals focused on royal ancestors to explore how a more devolved people negotiate this balance. Focusing on cattle sacrifices, she directs our attention to a ritual which, while it probably constitutes the context in which ordinary Malagasy most frequently encounter their ancestors, has been largely neglected by historians and anthropologists in favour of more exotic rituals like royal baths. Drawing on narrative theory to extend Lienhardt's classic theory of symbolic action, she argues that the long speeches made prior to the slaughter of the cow are central to the local social imaginary because they provide Betsimisaraka with a powerful tool for reflecting on their position in the world, in relation both to one another and to more powerful outsiders with whom they are forced to contend. Indeed, although she finds parallels between the Betsimisaraka tomb and the Merina tomb in terms of their roles in creating the 'ancestral homeland' (tanin-drazana), her ethnography suggests that it is, in fact, preeminently in sacrifice rather than in funerals that Betsimisaraka confront the challenge of remembering the dead while also separating from them, of becoming 'standing-posts' to their ancestors while remaining alive.

Taken together, the essays in this book point to the need to move beyond statements that assert the importance of remembering in Madagascar to analyses that acknowledge and contextualize significant local differences in Malagasy cultural practice around memory. If, for instance, unlike Radama I for whom the ancestral past is primarily a resource to be manipulated in ritual to political ends, Betsimisaraka experience the memory of ancestral relationships as unbearably heavy and violent, this needs to be seen against their experience, first, of double colonization by the Merina and the French and secondly, of military reprisals following the 1947 rebellion (Cole, 1998). Likewise, the Bemazava appear to do rather more forgetting than other Sakalava monarchies, while the Vezo studied by Astuti appear to attach very little value to remembering. And the consensual memories apparently created in *all* the Sakalava royal ritual cycles contrast sharply with the contested readings of the past charted for a village in Imerina by Raison-Jourde (this volume).

Differences in the way memories are produced, kept, transformed and discarded are of course implicit in the different forms of burial practices to be found in Madagascar. Thus, while Bloch shows how *famadihana* and monumental tomb serve to create the ideal, regrouped deme rather than memorialise individuals (but see Graeber, 1995), in recent accounts of Sakalava royal spirit possession it is the individual medium who emerges as the culturally valued embodiment of historical memories in the shape of the individual spirits of individual monarchs (Sharp, 1995; Lambek, 1998). In each case, differential play upon remembering and forgetting has implications not only for how local ancestors are constructed but also for how those

constructions relate to power and identity. 'History' may be empow-
ering when deployed by the Antankaraña king in the 'most famous
village' in Madagascar, disempowering as in Ever's and Graeber's
chapters on slavery, or strangely ambiguous as in the case of workers for Sakalava-Bemihisatra royalty, who, in being cut off from their
own kin and ancestors, are deprived of their own history, while keeping alive a sense of Sakalava sovereignty by their engagement in
royal history. If, however, ancestor-related practices are media through
which people engage with the socially constituted past, providing cultural mechanisms to make and remake their social world (McCall,
1995: 258), then the ways in which ancestors are remembered or
alternatively forgotten in Madagascar are bound to differ, given how
variably Malagasy peoples have been situated *vis-à-vis*, and how
variably they have responded to, the various colonialisms they have
lived.

Violence and Ancestral Power

Describing the vulnerability Betsimisaraka feel in relation to the ancestors, ancestors who might be satisfied by what the living feed them
but then again may not, Cole's analysis of sacrificial narratives reveals
considerable ambivalence around ancestral power, a power which is
essential to the living as the source of blessing but also dangerous.
She draws a contrast to Merina ancestors who are portrayed as the
moral guardians of the community, bestowing blessing on their descendants (e.g., Bloch, 1971). Even those who explore the possibilities
of ancestral violence (Graeber, 1995), she suggests, report that most
Merina elders were very uncomfortable with the topic.

If the malevolent or amoral aspect of ancestors is reluctantly acknowledged in many parts of Madagascar, the fundamental ambivalence of power or *hasina* is a common theme (Delivré, 1974). It is
present in representations of sovereigns (and royal ancestors) as fierce,
cruel, and brutal (*masiaka*), 'greedy institutions', empowered both to
bless and curse (Feeley-Harnik, 1992: 56). It is present in the notion
of Divinity or a powerful Creator whose properties are beyond morality (Bloch, 1995; but see Kottak, 1980 for an alternative view). It is
also evident in the 'difficult' taboos and practices that surround commoner ancestors. In fact, ancestors throughout Madagascar probably share in this negative or amoral aspect in some measure (e.g.,

Astuti, 1995) but, perhaps for historical reasons, it is voiced more strongly and explicitly in certain local discourses than in others.

In his own work, Bloch has long been concerned to grapple with the ambivalence that lies behind Merina representations of ancestors as the source of blessing. *Placing the Dead* was partly concerned to explore the seeming contradiction that the tomb as the moral symbol of the community is also the place in which the living, notably, women, experience considerable horror as they are made to handle the corpses of kin. Likewise, *From Blessing to Violence* sought to reconcile Merina representations of circumcision ritual as a source of ancestral blessing with the violence the young boy undergoes. In his chapter in the present volume, Bloch sets out to explain another paradox, viz., that the Zafimaniry, an otherwise non-violent people, actively incite their young men to violence. He shows how this aggression is celebrated as a sign of the future vitality of the village but also frowned upon as amoral and antisocial because it leads young men not only to fight those with whom they share ancestors, but also on occasion to attack the holy ancestral house. Noting that the chief purpose of Zafimaniry rituals is to transmit the blessing of the ancestors and the elders to their descendants, but that vitality must be added to this blessing, a vitality that young boys, but not the ancestors, possess in abundance, Bloch argues that rituals effects a beneficial combination of these two antagonistic elements, first by capturing the wild vitality of boys and animals, and then transforming it into an element which, once consumed, vitalizes the whole community. This symbolic 'conquest' of young men, he suggests, also has material dimensions. Young men are deliberately coaxed to commit acts of violence against the sacred house of the ancestors, so that the product of their labour can be brought under control and 'eaten' by the elders in the shape of fines.

To understand this paradox, Bloch draws explicitly on his earlier analyses of power and ritual, analyses that began with his study of Merina circumcision ritual and culminated in his theory of 'rebounding violence' (1992a). At the same time, however, it is also a gentler, more allusive reading of power and powerlessness in and out of ritual, partly influenced by more recent readings of the tensions in Malagasy authority systems, readings that were themselves only made possible by his work (Graeber, 1995; Cole, in press). In fact, it could be said that, while Bloch is still concerned with showing how rituals become implicated in 'traditional authority', he experiences some difficulty in stabilising the 'passive' and the 'active' in his description of Zafimaniry social life. This is perhaps only to be expected given the differences between the essentially egalitarian Zafimaniry and the 'conquering', hierarchical ethos of the Merina whose nineteenth century expansionism was backed by organised violence.

Gender and Ancestors

Another context in which Bloch has explored the significance of ritual around ancestors for the construction of authority is that of relations between women and men. In fact, most of his work on Merina ritual has a gendered dimension. In a well-known essay on Merina secondary burials, for instance, he argues that the elders' authority as mediums of ancestral blessing depends on the created image of the eternal deme, which is itself achieved by 'an emphasis on the decomposition of the body, the pollution of natural birth, the guilt of sorrow and the attribution of all this to women' (1982: 223). Similar schema figure in his analyses of Merina circumcision ritual and the royal bath. At the same time, he appears to suggest that such schema hold true for all Malagasy rituals.

Bloch's ethnography for the Merina has been criticised for ignoring women's work in weaving the shrouds that were the focal point of secondary burials in the nineteenth century, and for persistently talking of Merina royal figures as 'he' or 'the king' (Bloch, 1986: passim) when for the most part queens ruled between 1828 and 1895 (Feeley-Harnik, 1989, 1997b: 161–162). More broadly, Sharp (1993) shows that Sakalava women achieve considerable influence as spirit mediums for royal ancestors (see also Feeley-Harnik, 1991), while a profound ambivalence among Karembola as to whether 'ancestral fertility' is associated more with the wet, decomposing body than with the dry bones in the tomb is linked to local configurations of gender, reproduction, and ancestry that differ markedly from the symbolic schema Bloch outlines (Middleton, n.d.).

Even so, it would be wrong to suggest that in Madagascar ancestors or practices relating to ancestors are ungendered. The problem rather is that gender as an integral and crucial dimension of Malagasy practices around ancestors is for the most part extremely complex. For example, terms like *razana* or *raza*, while not intrinsically

gendered, can be and often are gender marked. Ancestors can also
be gendered by the way they are remembered or alternatively forgotten during sacrifices or in genealogies, or by the different movements women and men make in marriage. Likewise, mortuary practice
varies within local communities according to gender, along with age,
ethnicity, class, religion and manner of the death. Also, the work
the living perform for the dead—mourning, tomb-building, handling
corpses—is often gendered, as indeed are tombs and cemeteries as
symbolic spaces, though rarely in a simplistic way. In short, the gen-
dering of local 'political economies of fertility' is extremely complex.
Even in Bloch's (1986, 1987) accounts of Merina ritual, the association of women with devalued entities like biological birth is coun-
terposed to their inclusion with men as gender neutral ancestors in
the tomb or eternal deme (contrast Graeber, 1995). Likewise, 'ancestral rules' as to whether Malagasy women can perform sacrifices, i.e.
invoke the ancestors, vary greatly, and not always in ways that are
obviously correlated with local constructs of ancestry. For instance,
despite the local emphasis on the 'unkindedness' of the living, the
sacrificial function is denied to Vezo women, a gender taboo which
places the Vezo surprisingly close to the Tandroy, Mahafale, and
Karembola peoples, among whom the dictum that 'sacrifice comes
through fathers' is vital to the production of agnatic descent identities for the living. Thus, while it may be true to say that gender is
relatively unstressed in Madagascar when compared to other cultural
traditions (Bloch, 1993), its exact significance relative to other factors (age, rank, descent) in determining agency and personhood *in*
and *out* of ritual appears to vary greatly (Huntington, 1988; Thomas,
1996). It is unlikely that we shall be able to formulate general propositions about gender symbolism in 'Malagasy' ritual around ancestors, and even less about its relation to power, authority, knowledge
and 'social value' achieved or granted in other domains, that are
valid for localized contexts, let alone for the whole island.

Power and Powerlessness

It is a well-known fact, and a common source of difficulty to European
and American speakers, that Malagasy language dialects are characterised by the prevalence of the passive voice. At the same time,
submission to the wisdom and ways of speaking handed down from

the past is often expected of speech-makers in many but not all parts of the island (Bloch, 1975). This is not to say, however, that the passive *are* passive. The Merina orator who stresses his formal submission to the ancestors may be actively exercising power or seeking to coerce others. The passive voice often masks the active voice.

It can be argued that a similarly deceptive play between passivity and activity often characterises Malagasy cultural practice around ancestors. This is clearly evident in the case of those who acquire a powerful voice by submitting to possession by royal spirits. It is also present in the idea found throughout Madagascar that rulers cannot exist without followers who are willing to participate in royal ritual (Feeley-Harnik, 1982). This paradoxical relationship between passivity and activity was put to good effect by Althabe (1967) when he argued that, in becoming possessed by royal ancestor spirits from other parts of the island, people on the east coast were able to voice their opposition to the elders who, as intermediaries for local ancestors, had been co-opted by the state.

In her chapter, Middleton documents the complex interplay of activity and passivity in and out of ritual among the Karembola of the arid south. She begins by showing how the *un*circumcised body, in evoking the memory of an 'ancestral' ritual Karembola no longer perform, constitutes a primary metaphor for their sense of powerlessness before foreigners in a 'modern' age. Relating these narratives to events of the early colonial period, she suggests that there are good historical reasons why Karembola should portray themselves as a broken people robbed of their capacity to act upon the world, when within the space of a few years a cactus pest completely transformed their lived world, profoundly altering their relationship to the colonial state. Underscoring the need, nonetheless, to look at the decline of circumcision ritual not simply as a negative but as a ritual performance in and of itself, she points out how its dramaturgy echoes key motifs in Feeley-Harnik's (1984) essay on the 'Political Economy of Death': the proliferation of mortuary symbolism in response to the intrusion of strangers, the sense of being caught in an interregnum, and of belonging to dead priests. To give expression to their sense of impotence in a 'modern' age, Karembola have elaborated the realm of the *lolo*—capricious, vindictive spirits of the recent dead—at the expense of the cool generative ancestors At another level, though, the story Karembola tell about themselves is more ambiguous because, as a body practice articulated to both past and present, *not* being circumcised also constitutes a kind of memorial practice whereby Karembola remain rooted in their past. Thus, while Karembola can hardly be said to have scripted the terms of their colonial encounter, they have sought to re-make themselves subjects of their own history, by simultaneously acknowledging and protesting the impact of strangers in local cultural idioms, albeit transformed.

Karembola ethnography also encodes an interesting analogy between the rising malice of the dead and the predatory nature of colonial power. This is a point taken up by Cole and Middleton (n.d.) in an essay exploring the link between ancestors and colonialism in Madagascar. Noting that local representations of colonial power often share in the ambivalence that characterises ancestral (and royal) power, they suggest that ritual around ancestors may have become powerful media for reflecting upon colonial experience partly by registering parallels as well as contrasts between the two.

Ancestors and Slaves

That 'slavery' is among the 'traditional' repertoire of meanings that inform Karembola narratives is perhaps not so surprising. A major factor in precolonial processes of state-building in Madagascar, it would be difficult to overestimate the impact that slavery and slaving has had upon Malagasy cultures and cosmologies. This is not to say that the Malagasy dialect terms we translate as 'slave' or 'dependent' (*ondevo, andevo*) carry identical meanings throughout the island, however. Their meanings and their articulation with local social processes have to be carefully specified for particular cultural and historical contexts. For example, Karembola symbolically create 'dependents' by giving wives to uxorilocal men, while in the Highlands, by contrast, slaves are precisely those whom one can never marry (Bloch, 1971; Evers, this volume). In almost cases, slavery is not simply a socio-economic status, but a political and ritual identity, created more often than not in the context of local cultural practice around ancestors. In many parts of Madagascar, 'ancestry' and 'slavery' are mutually constitutive because slaves are by definition people 'without ancestors' (Feeley-Harnik, 1982, 1991: 22, 57–58, 77).

In her chapter, Evers shows just how critical idioms of slavery are to the ongoing construction of rank and social status in parts of Madagascar today. Almost a century after slavery in Madagascar was formally abolished by the French colonizers, her field work uncovered villagers in the southern Highlands drawing on ancestry and tomb membership to turn themselves into *andriana* (nobles) and other would be settlers into 'slaves'. She then follows young 'slave' men to the towns, only to find that, while they may enjoy greater freedom to dispose of their labour, their inability to demonstrate links to tombs and ancestors limits their opportunities to marry and to realise their dreams.

The importance of Evers' ethnography is twofold. First, it shows 'slavery' not simply as a residue of Madagascar's past, but as a social condition that people seek actively to recreate in the present. This is a powerful way of marginalizing and subordinating others under the guise of keeping ancestral traditions alive. Secondly, the essay presents a useful balance to the rising hegemony of postmodern models of identities in Madagascar in so far as many of the migrants Evers describes do not experience identity as particularly fluid, inclusive, and performative. On the contrary, she demonstrates how very difficult it is for them to escape the determined efforts of other actors to cast the world in terms of 'essentialist' identities imagined in terms of ancestries and tombs. As Evers stresses, these are on going processes of social construction; we have no evidence whether or not people actually are *andriana* or 'slaves' by origin. The point, however, is that the person here is *not conceptualised* as being made through his or her lifetime but rather as being fixed by birth.

It is clear then that Malagasy models of personhood and agency are far from homogeneous. While some Malagasy peoples emphasise social inclusion—'strangers' have long adopted 'Sakalava' practices including respect for royal ancestors as a way of integrating into local networks of access to land and labour (Feeley-Harnik, 1991; Sharp, 1993; Lambek and Walsh, this volume)—others, like those studied by Evers, practice exclusion or rather include incomers only on condition that they are willing to accept and live their inferiority. Indeed, the extent to which ideas and practices concerning ancestors structure lived-in worlds also differs greatly. Among the Vezo studied by Astuti, ancestors seem to have very little bearing on the negotiation of interpersonal relations. For others, like the Betsimisaraka, the Karembola, and the villagers studied by Evers, ancestors are worked into the very substance of bodies and landscapes, becoming the *lingua franca* for the interpretation of the most mundane events. In the case of yet other Malagasy, like the followers of the various Sakalava monarchies, who move between royal sites, the provincial capital and surrounding villages, or who come from Antananarivo to attend the mast-raising ceremony every four or so years, the extent to which ancestors pervade identities and shape the experience of power encompasses social interactions in everyday contexts is less clear. In these cases, it would be useful to know more about the kinds of intercourse followers have with their *own* (non-royal) ancestors when not in royal service. It has long been recognised that a multiplicity of religious and social practices other than ancestor-based ones—from divination to friendship—play their part in shaping Malagasy lives. To document these other sources of knowledge and power that inform social relations in urban and rural communities (see Feeley-Harnik, 1991), and possibly provide local actors with alternative world views (cf. Synder, 1997), is especially important now because simplistic models of the dominance of ancestors and of timebound ancestral traditions in Malagasy social practice are being carried over into environmental discourses on Madagascar, where they are used to justify the appropriation of powers to manage local resources from local peoples by international agencies.

Evers' ethnography is complemented by Graeber's essay charting the attempts of descendants of former slaves in Imerina to escape the legacy of the past. As Graeber observes, it is difficult to imagine people for whom historical memory is more painful than those whose forebears were torn from their ancestral landscapes in previous centuries and taken to be slaves in Imerina. And yet, by exploring local narratives around contrasting types of burial and participation in *vazimba* possession cults, he shows how they are concerned to develop ritual idioms with which to reflect on their historical condition and to recover their power to speak. The narratives around burial are particularly interesting because they show Malagasy people contemplating alternative ways of making ancestors and identities through the connections they make between the present and the past. While most 'black people' seek to counter histories of placelessness and dispersal by being interred in their land of exile through the Merina idioms of tomb, deme, and land, local imagination is dominated by stories of those, who in conscious reversal of Merina practice, elect to secure a return to a (possibly imagined) origin in the Betsileo, by insisting that their children bury them in baskets from which, on the model of former Betsileo royal funerals, they will later emerge as snakes.

The chapters by Evers and Graeber underscore how often ancestors are drawn into social identities in ways that are linked to hierarchy. We know that in many parts of Madagascar in the past
ancestry and political authority were often closely bound together.
Sovereigns were pictured as giving ancestries to their followers (Baré,
1977) or at least ordering their relative rank (Raison-Jourde, 1983).
Accordingly, the low value that the Vezo studied by Astuti attach to
kindedness, and to history, can be linked to their wish to be free of
political control. From this perspective, a perplexing feature of recent
Malagasy ethnography (Feeley-Harnik, 1991; Sharp, this volume) is
how the various Sakalava dynasties have managed to rework their
erstwhile symbolic play on ancestry and slavery into rituals that
remained apposite and meaningful for an independent, indeed for a
while Marxist, Madagascar where all are deemed equal.

Bricolage and Social Competition

Several of the essays show Malagasy people drawing on fragments
of historical narratives (e.g., racist myths of origin, 'fraternity' with
colonial masters, the burial rites of Betsileo kings) as they reinterpret identities and re-order communities. 'Historical bricolage', and
its place in social competition, becomes the explicit theme of Raison-
Jourde's curious tale of Davidson's rise to eminence in a village not
far from Antananarivo. Showing how field enquiries made in one
location at intervals over twenty years can help unravel processes of
cultural innovation, Raison-Jourde follows Davidson and his family
over the decades as they move first to claim mastery of the hail
medicines, then guardianship of a 'royal' tomb, then to bar access
to *mainty* practitioners, and finally in the 1990s to invent *andriana*
identity for themselves. With a large part of the socio-political dynamic
involving actors misconstruing each others' intentions and agency as
they seek to realise contending projects, practice focused on ancestors is here less a symbolic language that conveys shared cultural
values than one lends itself to conflict and dissent.

   The chapters by Graeber, Evers, and Raison-Jourde all underscore the enduring power of tombs in the socio-symbolic landscapes
of the Highlands. At the same time, however, they reveal subtle shifts
in the way this cultural icon is deployed. In *Placing the Dead*, Bloch
showed how tombs play a major role in reconstituting peoples' connections with their ancestral homeland when they moved away.

People are lost to their ancestors if their corpses are not put in the family tombs. In Evers' essay, by contrast, established masters of the land seek to create local status differentials and unequal access to labour by evoking links to tombs that may or may not exist elsewhere. In Raison-Jourde's account, intra-village factions stake competing claims in the *hasina* or sacred power of a tomb in which neither will be buried and in which (initially at least) neither has ancestors. Finally, Graeber describes how descendants of ex-slaves are imagined to recover their ancestral origins and their agency to speak by refuting the value of entombment.[2]

It would interesting to explore further how these different nuances in the meaning of the tomb relate to economic factors. For example, Graeber tells us that *mainty* who own land tend to follow Merina burial practices, while Raison-Jourde is very clear that education and money has enabled Davidson to secure control over sacred places and ricelands. More generally, this points to the need to look more closely at how practices around ancestors relate to changing local political economies. While the link between ancestors and 'traditional' modes of production (land, labour, rice, and cattle) is well-documented, relatively few studies explore how 'work' for ancestors articulates with money, commodities, capitalism, and struggles for resources in urban contexts (Bloch, 1989; Feeley-Harnik, 1991). With increasing foreign debt and repeated devaluations of the Malagasy franc, these issues should be central to our analysis.

REFERENCES

Althabe, G.
    1969   *Oppression et libération dans l'imaginaire: Les communautés villageoises de la côte orientale de Madagascar.* Paris: Maspero.
Anderson, B.
    1991   *Imagined Communities.* London: Verso.

---

[2] Such contrasts *within* the Highlands inevitably raise the question of how well Bloch's (1971) classic model of the role of the tomb in creating 'ancestral land' (*tanindrazana*) applies *beyond* the Highlands. For instance, while a primary purpose of the regional associations formed by migrants in towns throughout Madagascar is to help meet the cost returning bones to 'ancestral land', it is my impression that emigrees from the Androy are often happy to establish tombs in new localities *once* there are sufficient kin *in situ* to perform the 'work' required to honour the dead (cf. Astuti, 1995; Sharp, 1993: 71). In this connection, it should be noted that in parts of the Deep South the term *tanen-drazañe* refers primarily to the location of the umbilical cords rather than the tomb (Middleton, 1995; Heurtebize, 1986: 252).

Astuti, R.
 1995 *People of the Sea: Identity and Descent among the Vezo of Madagascar*. Cambridge: Cambridge University Press.
 1998 'It's a boy'. 'It's a girl!' Reflections on sex and gender in Madagascar and beyond.' *Bodies and Persons. Comparative perspectives from Africa and Melanesia*, M. Lambek and A. Strathern (eds.). Cambridge: Cambridge University Press.

Baré, J.F.
 1977 *Pouvoir des Vivants, Langages des Morts. Idéo-logiques Sakalave*. Paris: Francois Maspero.

Beaujard, P.
 1983 *Princes et Paysans. Les Tanala de l'Ikongo*. Paris: L'Harmattan.

Blanchy, S.
 1995 *Karana et Banians: Les communautés commerantes d'origine indienne Madagascar*. Paris: L'Harmattan.

Bloch, M.
 1968 'Tombs and Conservatism among the Merina of Madagascar.' *Man*, 3, 1: 94–104.
 1971 *Placing the Dead: Tombs, Ancestral Villages, and Kinship Organization in Madagascar*. London: Seminar Press.
 1975 'Introduction.' In *Political Language and Oratory in Traditional Society*, M. Bloch (ed.). London: Academic Press.
 1981 'Tombs and States.' In *Mortality and Immortality: the anthropology and archaeology of death*, S. Humphreys and H. King (eds.). London: Academic.
 1982 'Death, Women and Power.' In *Death and the Regeneration of Life*, M. Bloch & J. Parry (eds.). Cambridge: Cambridge University Press.
 1986 *From Blessing to Violence: History and Ideology in the Circumcision Ritual of the Merina of Madagascar*. Cambridge: Cambridge University Press.
 1987 'The ritual of the royal bath in Madagascar: the dissolution of death, birth and fertility into authority.' In *Ritual, History and Power*, M. Bloch. London: Athlone Press.
 1987 'Descent and sources of contradiction in representation of women and kinship.' In *Gender and Kinship. Essays towards a unified analysis*, J. Collier and S. Yanagisako (eds.). Stanford: Stanford University Press.
 1989 'The symbolism of money in Imerina.' In *Money and the Morality of Exchange*, J. Parry and M. Bloch (eds.). Cambridge: Cambridge University Press.
 1992a *Prey into Hunter. The Politics of Religious Experience*. Cambridge: Cambridge University Press.
 1992b 'What goes without saying. The conceptualization of Zafimaniry society.' In *Conceptualizing Society*, A. Kuper (ed.). London: Routledge and Kegan Paul.
 1993 'Zafimaniry birth and kinship theory,' *Social Anthropology*, 1, 1b: 119–132.

Cole, J.
 1998 'The work of memory in Madagascar.' *American Ethnologist*, 25(4): 610–633.

Cole, J. and Middleton, K.
 n.d. 'Ancestors and Colonial Power in Madagascar.'

Comaroff, J.
 1985 *Body of Power, Spirit of Resistance: The Culture and History of a South African People*. Chicago: University of Chicago Press.

Comaroff, J. & Comaroff, J.
 1993 'Introduction.' In *Modernity and its Malcontents: Ritual and Power in Postcolonial Africa*, J. & J. Comaroff (eds.). Chicago: University of Chicago Press.

Covell, M.
    1987   *Madagascar. Politics, Economics, and Society.* London and New York: Frances
            Pinter.
Csordas, T.
    1987   'Genre, motive and metaphor: conditions for creativity in ritual lan-
            guage.' *Cultural Anthropology* 2, 445–69.
Decary, R.
    1962   *La mort et les coutumes funéraires à Madagascar.* Paris: G.P. Maisonneuve
            et Larose.
Delivré, A.
    1974   *L'histoire des rois d'Imerina: Interprétation d'une tradition orale.* Paris: Klincksieck.
Deschamps, H.
    1972   *Histoire de Madagascar.* Paris: Berger Levrault.
Ellis, S.
    1985   *The Rising of the Red Shawls. A Revolt in Madagascar 1895–1899.* Cambridge:
            Cambridge University Press.
Esoavelomandroso, M.
    1989   'Une arme de domination: le "tribalisme" à Madagascar (XIXe–milieu
            du XXe siècle).' In *Les Ethnies ont une histoire*, J.-P. Chrétien (ed.). Paris:
            Karthala.
Feeley-Harnik, G.
    1982   'The King's men in Madagascar: slavery, citizenship, and Sakalava
            monarchy.' *Africa* 52, 31–50.
    1984   'The Political Economy of Death: Communication and Change in
            Malagasy Colonial History.' *American Ethnologist* 11, 1–19.
    1989   'Cloth and the Creation of Ancestors in Madagascar.' In *Cloth and the
            Human Experience*, A. Weiner and J. Schneider (eds.). Washington D.C.:
            Smithsonian Institution Press.
    1991a   *A Green Estate: Restoring Independence in Madagascar.* Washington D.C.:
            Smithsonian Institution Press.
    1991b   'Finding memories in Madagascar.' In *Images of Memory*, S. Küchler
            and W. Melion (eds.). Washington: Smithsonian Institution Press.
    1997a   'Madagascar: Religious Systems.' In *Encyclopedia of Africa South of the
            Sahara*, J. Middleton (ed.). New York: Charles Scribner's Sons, Vol. 3,
            pp. 86–89.
    1997b   'Dying gods and queen mothers: the international politics of social
            reproduction in Africa and Europe.' In *Gendered Encounters. Challenging
            Cultural Boundaries and Social Hierarchies in Africa*, M. Grosz-Ngaté and
            O. Kokole (eds.). New York & London: Routledge.
Fields, K.
    1985   *Revival and Rebellion in Colonial Central Africa.* Princeton: Princeton University
            Press.
Fortes, M.
    1945   *The Dynamics of Clanship Among the Tallensi.* Oxford: Oxford University
            Press.
    1959   *Oedipus and Job in West African Religion.* Cambridge: Cambridge University
            Press.
    1965   'Some reflections on ancestor worship in Africa.' In *African Systems of
            Thought*, M. Fortes and G. Dieterlen (eds.). Oxford: Oxford University
            Press for the International African Institute, pp. 122–44.
Goody, J.
    1962   *Death, Property, and the Ancestors.* London.
Graeber, D.
    1995   'Dancing with corpses reconsidered: an interpretation of famadihana
            (in Arivonimamo, Madagascar).' *American Ethnologist* 22 (2): 258–278.

Gueunier, N.
 1994   *Les Chemins de l'Islam à Madagascar.* Paris: Harmattan.
Heurtebize, G.
 1986   *Histoire des Afomarolahy (Extrême-Sud de Madagascar).* Paris: CNRS.
Hobsbawm, E. and Ranger, T. (eds.)
 1992 [1983]   *The Invention of Tradition.* Cambridge: Cambridge University Press.
Hübsch, B. (ed.)
 1993   *Madagascar et le Christianisme.* Paris: Karthala.
Huntington R.
 1988   *Gender and Social Structure in Madagascar.* Bloomington: Indiana
       University Press.
Jackson, M.
 1989   *Paths toward a Clearing: Radical empiricism and ethnographic inquiry.*
       Bloomington: Indiana University Press.
Jaovelo-Dzao, R.
 1993   Richesses culturelles d'une civilisation de l'oralité (*Zanahary, Sampy,*
       Razana, influence ou rejet de l'Islam). In *Madagascar et le Christia-*
       nisme, B. Hübsch (ed.). Paris: Karthala.
Jewsiewicki, B. & V. Mudimbe
 1992   'Africans' Memories and Contemporary History of Africa.' *History*
       and Theory: Studies in the Philosophy of History, 32 (4): 1–11.
Jolly, A., Oberlé, P. & Albignac, R. (eds.)
 1984   *Key Environments: Madagascar.* Oxford: IUCNN/Pergamon Press.
Kelly, J. & Kaplan, M.
 1990   'History, Structure, and Ritual.' *Annual. Rev. Anthropology,* 19, 119–50.
Kent, R.
 1970   *Early Kingdoms in Madagascar, 1500–1700.* New York: Holt, Rein-
       hart, and Winston.
Kopytoff, I.
 1971   'Ancestors as elders in Africa.' *Africa* 43 (2), 129–42.
Kottak, C.
 1980   *The Past in the Present: History, Ecology, and Cultural Variation in*
       Highland Madagascar. Ann Arbor: University of Michigan Press.
Lambek, M.
 1993   *Knowledge and Practice in Mayotte: Local Discourses of Islam, Sorcery,*
       and Spirit Possession. Toronto: University of Toronto Press.
 1996   'The past imperfect: remembering as moral practice.' In *Tense*
       Past. Cultural Essays in Trauma and Memory, P. Antze and M. Lam-
       bek (eds.). New York: Routledge
 1998   'The Poiesis of Sakalava History.' *American Ethnologist* 25 (2): 106–127.
Lan, D.
 1985   *Guns and Rain. Guerrillas and Spirit Mediums in Zimbabwe.* London:
       James Currey.
Larson, P.
 1997   '"Capacities and modes of thinking": intellectual engagements
       and subaltern hegemony in the early history of Malagasy Chris-
       tianity.' *The American Historical Review,* 102, 4: 969–1002.
Lavondès, H.
 1967   *Bekoropoka. Quelques aspects de la vie familiale et sociale d'un village mal-*
       gache. Paris: Mouton.
Mack, J.
 1986   *Madagascar, Island of the Ancestors.* London: British Museum.
Mannoni, O.
 1990 [1950]   *Prospero and Caliban: The Psychology of Colonization.* Ann Arbor:
       Michigan University Press.

McCall, J.
    1995   'Rethinking ancestors in Africa.' *Africa* 65 (2): 256–270.
Middleton, J.
    1964   *Lugbara Religion: Ritual and Authority among an East African People.*
Middleton, K.
    1995   'Tombs, umbilical cords, and the syllable fo.' In *Cultures of Madagascar*,
              S. Evers & M. Spindler (eds.). Leiden: IIAS.
    n.d.   'Tomb-work, body-work: ancestry, gender and reproduction in the
              Karembola (southern Madagascar).'
Poewe, K.
    1978   'Religion, matriliny, and change: Jehovah's Witnesses and Seventh-day
              Adventists in Luapula, Zambia.' *American Ethnologist*, 5 (2): 303–321.
Raison-Jourde, F.
    1976   'Les Ramanenjana.' *ASEMI*, 7: 271–293.
    1991   *Bible et pouvoir à Madagascar au XIXe siècle. Invention d'une identité chrétienne
              et construction de l'État (1780–1880).* Paris: Karthala.
Raison-Jourde, F. (ed.)
    1983   *Les Souverains de Madagascar: L'Histoire Royale et ses Résurgences Contemporaines.*
              Paris: Karthala.
Razafiarivony,
    1995   Société et Littérature Orale Betsimisaraka d'Anosibe An'Ala: Pauvreté
              Matérielle et Richesse Culturelles. Thèse du Doctorat Nouveau Régime.
              Tome 1, Analyse. Institut des Langues Orientales, Paris.
Sharp, L.
    1993   *The Possessed and the Dispossessed: Spirits, Identity and Power in a Madagascar
              Migrant Town.* Berkeley: University of California Press.
    1995   'Playboy princely spirits of Madagascar: possession as youthful com-
              mentary and social critique.' *American Anthropological Quarterly* 68 (2): 75–88.
Southall, A.
    1967   'The problem of Malagasy origins.' In *East Africa and the Orient*,
              N. Chittick and R. Rotberg (eds.). London: Africana
    1986   'Common themes in Malagasy culture.' In *Madagascar. Society and History*,
              C. Kottak, J.-A. Rakotoarisoa, A. Southall and P. Vérin (eds.). Durham,
              N.C.: Carolina Academic Press, pp. 411–438.
Synder, K.
    1997   'Elders' authority and women's protest. The Masay ritual and social
              change among the Iraqw of Tanzania.' *JRAI* (N.S.), 3, 561–576.
Tambiah, S.
    1985   *Culture, Thought and Social Action. An Anthropological Perspective.* Cambridge
              MA: Harvard University Press.
Thomas, P.
    1996   Place, Person and Ancestry among the Temanambondro of Southeast
              Madagascar. Unpublished PH.D. Thesis, London School of Economics.
Vérin, P.
    1967a   'Austronesian contributions to the culture of Madagascar.' In *East Africa
              and the Orient*, N. Chittick and R. Rotberg (eds.). London: Africana.
    1986   *The History of Civilisation in North Madagascar.* Rotterdam: Balkema.
Vérin, P. (ed.)
    1967b   Arabes et Islamisés à Madagascar et dans l'Océan Indien. *Revue de
              Madagascar.*
Wilson, P.
    1992   *Freedom by a Hair's Breadth: Tsimihety in Madagascar.* Ann Arbor: University
              of Michigan Press.

CHAPTER TWO

A CULTURAL POLITICS OF BEDCHAMBER CONSTRUCTION AND PROGRESSIVE DINING IN ANTANANARIVO: RITUAL INVERSIONS DURING THE *FANDROANA* OF 1817*

PIER M. LARSON

Introduction: Western Indian Ocean Politics and Narrative Positioning

During the second week of August 1817 James Hastie, a British envoy to the Merina kingdom of highland central Madagascar, participated in an innovative and politically significant royal ritual.[1] The practices and festivities that accompanied that ritual—the *fandroana* or new year according to the lunar calendar of Arabic origin employed

* I would like to thank Jennifer Cole, Sheryl McCurdy, Karen Middleton and Amy Stambach for invaluable comments on previous drafts of this article. Abbreviations utilized in this article: *Tantara* = François Callet (ed.) *Tantara ny Andriana eto Madagascar: Documents historiques d'après les manuscrits malgaches* Deuxième Édition (Antananarivo: Trano Pirintim-Pirenena, 1981). *HOM* = William Ellis (ed.) *History of Madagascar, Comprising also The Progress of the Christian Mission Established in 1818 and an Authentic Account of the Persecution and Recent Martyrdom of the Native Christians* (London: Fisher, Son, & Co., 1838), 2 vols. MNA/HB/10/2/27–28 = Mauritius National Archives (Coromandel), Series HB, Volume 10, Number 2, pp. 27–28. LMS/1/2/C = Archives of the Council for World Mission (former London Missionary Society), Library of the School of Oriental and African Studies (London), Madagascar, Incoming Letters, Box 1, Folder 2, Jacket C. BL/MD/Add.Mss./18137/16r = British Library, Manuscripts Division, Additional Manuscript 18137, folio 16r.

[1] Highland Madagascar, central Madagascar and Imerina are employed synonymously throughout this article. Imerina once comprised only a small area around Antananarivo (before the very late eighteenth century), but now designates the entire modern Province of Antananarivo. I employ the modern definition of Imerina throughout this article. Similarly, by 'highland Malagasy' I designate the ancestors of people now known as Merina. The highland Malagasy kingdom in question, then, is conventionally known by the ethnonym of its people—the Merina kingdom. For a history of Imerina as toponym and Merina as ethnonym see Pier M. Larson, 'Desperately Seeking "The Merina" (Central Madagascar): Reading Ethnonyms and their Semantic Fields in African Identity Histories' *Journal of Southern African Studies*, 22,4 (1996). For a general introduction to the history of central Madagascar during the early nineteenth century see Mervyn Brown, *Madagascar Rediscovered: A History from Early Times to Independence* (Hamden: Archon Books, 1979), and Michel Prou, *Malagasy 'Un Pas de plus': Vers l'histoire du 'Royaume de Madagascar' au XIXᵉ siècle*, I, (Paris: L'Harmattan, 1987).

Plate 1. Portrait of Radama I, dressed in British uniform, by André Coppalle (1826), a French painter who lived for some time in Antananarivo. It was Coppalle who in his travel diary recorded Radama as saying that royal rituals were but bothersome 'political institutions fit to govern children of all ages'.

by the people of highland central Madagascar—were centered on the royal court (the *rova*, located in the highland capital of Antananarivo) and on the king, Radama I.[2] This article explores the political and cultural symbolism of Hastie's participation in the *fandroana* of 1817. I argue that Radama choreographed Hastie's participation in the ritual to invert customary ritual sequence and to thereby communicate to his subjects both his intentions for political alliance with Britain and his administrative independence as a young ruler who languished within the shadows of a popular predecessor and father, Andrianampoinimerina.[3] The significance of the culturally inventive *fandroana* of 1817 is most fully appreciated when situated within the context of politics in the western Indian Ocean during the first decades of the nineteenth century. Let us begin this inquiry, then, with the primary and secondary participants in the ritual.

An Irishman, Hastie was a sergeant in the British Indian army at Mauritius who came to the attention of that colony's governor, Sir Robert Farquhar, quite by accident when in 1816 he played a key role in dousing flames that threatened to consume a government house in Port Louis. Impressed by services Hastie subsequently rendered to him, Farquhar nominated the sergeant in mid-1817 as his ambassador to king Radama of highland central Madagascar. In his capacity as ambassador of Britain, Hastie was instructed to enter into an agreement with Radama, with whom Farquhar had only months before concluded a political alliance through a temporary envoy, to end the export trade in slaves to the Mascarene islands from central Madagascar.[4] Since Britain acquired the Mascarenes in

---

[2] Radama I reigned from 1810 until his death in 1828. I heretofore refer to him simply as Radama, distinguishing him from king Radama II, who ruled from 1861 until his assassination in 1863.

[3] For histories of Andrianampoinimerina, the founder of Radama's kingdom, see Jean Valette, 'Pour une histoire du règne d'Andrianampoinimerina (1787–1810),' *Revue Française d'Histoire d'Outre-Mer* 52,2 (1965), No. 187, 277–285; Hubert Deschamps, 'Andrianampoinimerina, ou la raison d'état au service de l'unité malgache' in C.-A. Julien (ed.) *Les Africains* (Paris: Editions Jeune Afrique, 1977), II, 77–97; Hubert Deschamps, 'Tradition and Change in Madagascar, 1790–1870' in J.E. Flint (ed.) *The Cambridge History of Africa* Volume 5 (Cambridge: Cambridge University Press, 1976), pp. 393–417. Histories of Radama conventionally begin in about 1816 with the British alliance and ignore Radama's early years of struggle for influence at his own court between 1810 and that time.

[4] The Mascarene islands were comprised of two principal islands, Mauritius and Bourbon (now Réunion), each lying some 900 kilometers east of the central coast of Madagascar. Since the first European occupation of the islands (there was no indigenous population) Madagascar was an important source of both food and slave

1810 from its rival, France, the trade in slaves which flourished from
both Madagascar and East Africa to the Mascarene islands had been
technically illegal but never effectively interdicted. Fearful that an
end to the importation of slaves would wreak havoc on Mascarene
economies, Farquhar was nevertheless under pressure from London
to end the trade.[5] Sending Hastie to Antananarivo to negotiate a
treaty with Radama to sever the flow of highland Malagasy slaves
at its source seemed a concrete anti-slaving measure that Farquhar
could justify to his superiors. An alliance with Radama proffered the
further merit of solidifying British alliance with a growing polity in
central Madagascar and edging the French, who maintained trading settlements along Madagascar's east coast, out of the western
Indian Ocean altogether.

Most scholarly narratives of the arrival of James Hastie in Antananarivo have tended to situate the diplomatic event within the foregoing familiar scheme of British imperial expansion.[6] The events,
however, can be equally and perhaps more convincingly interpreted
with reference to Radama's political strategies. Hastie's arrival in
Antananarivo represented a political triumph for Radama, for it
marked the fruition of a strategic political alliance he wished to conduct with Britain—then the dominant European imperial power in
the Indian Ocean—to rid himself of his predecessor's powerful advisors and to expand his kingdom across the island of Madagascar.

---

labor. For a history of the economic relationships between Madagascar and the
Mascarenes see Auguste Toussaint, *Histoire des îles Mascareignes* (Paris: Berger-Levrault
1972). For the slave trade specifically see J.M. Filliot, *La traite des esclaves vers les
Mascareignes au XVIIIe siècle* (Paris: ORSTOM, 1974).

   [5] See Anthony J. Barker, *Slavery and Anti-Slavery in Mauritius, 1810–33: The Conflict
Between Economic Expansion and Humanitarian Reform Under British Rule* (London:
Macmillan, 1996).

   [6] For examples of such narratives see *HOM*, II, 144–198; Jean Valette, *Études
sur le règne de Radama Ier* (Tananarive: Imprimerie Nationale, 1962); Hubert Deschamps,
Histoire de Madagascar (Paris: Berger Levrault, 1972); Hubert Deschamps, 'Tradition
and Change in Madagascar, 1790–1870' in *Cambridge History of Africa* Volume 5
(1976), 393–417; Ludvig Munthe, Charles Ravoajanahary and Simon Ayache,
'Radama I et les Anglais: les négociations de 1817 d'après les sources malgaches
("sorabe" inédits)' *Omaly sy Anio* No. 3–4 (1976), 9–102; Jean Valette, 'Radama I,
The Unification of Madagascar and the Modernization of Imerina (1810–1828)' in
Raymond K. Kent (ed.) *Madagascar in History: Essays from the 1970s* (Albany: The
Foundation for Malagasy Studies, 1979), 168–196; Michel Prou, *Malagasy un pas de
plus: le royaume de Madagascar au XIXe siècle*, (Paris: Editions l'Harmattan, 1987), 43–45;
Françoise Raison-Jourde, *Bible et pouvoir à Madagascar au XIXe siècle: invention d'une
identité chrétienne et construction de l'état (1780–1880)* (Paris: Karthala, 1991), 113–126;
Pierre Vérin, *Madagascar* (Paris: Karthala, 1994), 91–99.

When Radama ascended to the kingship in 1810 upon the death of
his father Andrianampoinimerina he was only fifteen. As he matured
he sought to extricate himself from the powerful commercial, military, and political interests of Andrianampoinimerina's well established advisors and army generals. Collectively known as the *namana*
(friends), these men ruled the realm during the first years of Radama's
kingship. They were the organizers and leaders of his armies, which
generated a large number of prisoners of war and expanded the
kingdom outward from Antananarivo. Partially because of their control over war captives who could be sold as slaves, the *namana* were
the primary highland Malagasy beneficiaries of the slave trade.
Andrianampoinimerina had granted them privileges in the slave trade.
After his death, they continued to expand their networks of king-
dom-wide influence through the capture and sale of more prisoners
and through strategic distributions of wealth derived from the slave
trade. If Radama were to thrust aside his inherited *namana* advisors
and replace them with counselors possessing less authority within his
dominions, he would have to erode the material basis of their influence by ending the slave trade. In this ambitious goal, Radama was
increasingly cognizant that Governor Farquhar of Mauritius could
be of significant assistance.

Even as a youth Radama was not unfamiliar with the complex
international politics of the Western Indian Ocean. A consummate
diplomat and well schooled in Mascarene culture and diplomacy,
Andrianampoinimerina had attended to Radama's practical education in European ways at the feet of the French slave traders who
had ventured into highland Madagascar well before Radama's
birth.[7] As a child Radama frequently conversed with these men of
commerce about the aims and positions of France and Britain in
his corner of the world. As Radama approached the age of twenty
in about 1814, he began to seriously consider a relationship with
Governor Farquhar of Mauritius. Farquhar himself was in the process
of gathering a variety of information about Madagascar, but at that
time his trade representatives on Madagascar's east coast shunned
Radama's diplomatic overtures.[8] When Farquhar later came under

---

[7] Gilbert Ratsivalaka has recently revealed that Andrianampoinimerina is likely
to have sojourned in Mauritius as a child. Gilbert Ratsivalaka, *Madagascar dans le
sud-ouest de l'Océan Indien (circa 1500–1824): pour une relecture de l'histoire de Madagascar*
Thèse pour l'obtention du doctorat d'état, Université de Nice, 1995, I, 153–155.
[8] Journal of Chardenoux, BL/MD/18129/157–76. The citation is from Jean

considerable pressure from London to stem the illegal flow of slaves into the Mascarenes, he eventually took Radama's bait. After dispatching two separate envoys in 1816 and early 1817 to explore Radama's intentions and to conclude an alliance of friendship, Farquhar sent James Hastie to Antananarivo in mid-1817 to negotiate an end to the export trade in slaves.[9]

Throughout the *fandroana* of August 1817 Hastie remained a guest of Radama and a confidant to members of the king's immediate family. Hastie's movements and activities from his entry into Antananarivo on August 7 to the end of the primary *fandroana* ceremonies on about August 11 were largely choreographed by Radama. The highland Malagasy king arranged Hastie's schedule to coincide with and meaningfully address the various cultural significances of the new year ritual. While Hastie became aware that something extraordinary was occurring during his first days in Antananarivo and cultivated his intimacy with Radama and his family to further British diplomatic objectives, his journal demonstrates that he failed to grasp precisely what the *fandroana* was or the significance of his participation in some of its ritual practices. Careful to 'conform' his diplomatic behavior to his own perception of 'their [highland Malagasy] customs,' Hastie was cognizant that his mission was a diplomatic success. Yet due to his ignorance of both the Malagasy language and the practices commemorating the highland Malagasy new year, the British envoy miscomprehended the deeper symbolic significance (for highland Malagasy) of his and Radama's activities in Antananarivo.[10] Someone explained to Hastie that the *fandroana* was like a

---

Vallette's published version of this journal: 'La mission de Chardenoux auprès de Radama Ier (1816)' *Bulletin de Madagascar* No. 207 (1963), 691–692. Evidence of Farquhar's early interest in Madagascar can be found in the collection of the Governor's papers relating to the history, culture, language, politics, economy and natural resources of Madagascar now located in the British Library Manuscripts Division (Additional Manuscripts 18117–18141—the Farquhar Papers).

[9] The preceding two paragraphs are based on chapter six of my forthcoming book: Pier M. Larson, *Identities of a Crisis: The Slave Trade, Gender and the Rise of Merina Ethnic Identity in central Madagascar, 1770–1822.* For a mid-nineteenth century narrative of these events consult *HOM*, II, 144–256.

[10] The foregoing conclusions are based upon what James Hastie wrote in his journal, an account of his perceptions and activities kept both for his own interest and for the purpose of documenting his activities in Madagascar for Governor Farquhar of Mauritius. James Hastie's journals from Madagascar were written in English. Copies of fragments of these journals, each covering a period of a few to several months, can be found in various places in the Public Record Office (London) among the dispatches of the Governor of Mauritius to the Colonial Office and in

celebration of Radama's birthday, which was how Hastie mistakenly described the ritual in his diary.[11] Largely unaware of the emic significance of his role in the *fandroana* of 1817, Hastie unwittingly played a ritually meaningful part in Radama's cultural stage management of international alliance.

The court celebration of the 1817 *fandroana* bears the marks of a proto-typical early modern cultural encounter: a meeting between Europeans of expanding empire and 'natives' at the periphery of the imperium.[12] While studies of such cultural encounters are frequently anchored in European-centered narratives, what is key to interpreting

---

the National Archives of Mauritius (Coromandel). The version of James Hastie's diary that covers the period of the *fandroana* of 1817 (this particular journal fragment runs from 6 August 1817 through 1 September 1817) is a French translation from an English language manuscript that I have been unable to locate (Gwyn Campbell footnotes an English language 1817 journal of Hastie in the Public Record Office, series CO/167/34, but I have been unable to locate such a journal in that volume or verify its precise dates: Gwyn Campbell, 'The Structure of Trade in Madagascar, 1750–1810' *The International Journal of African Historical Studies* 26,1 (1993), 118, n. 18). The French translation employed in this article was published by the Académie Malgache in 1903 for the interest of its members but without indication of who was in possession of the original manuscript: James Hastie, 'Le voyage de Tananarive en 1817: Manuscrit de James Hastie' *Bulletin de l'Académie Malgache* vol. 2, 3ᵉ trimestre (1903), 173–178. Quotations pertaining to dates other than 6 August 1817 through 1 September 1817 are from English manuscript versions of Hastie's diaries and are fully cited where employed. Hereafter specific pages of the 1817 journal published by the Académie Malgache are cited only where lengthy or particularly important quotations from it are placed in the text. For criticisms of the methods and procedures employed by the Académie Malgache to publish French versions of Hastie's English journals see Jean Valette, 'Etude sur les journaux de James Hastie (1816–1826)' *Bulletin de Madagascar* No. 259 (1967), 977–986, and Jean Vallette, 'Réflexions pour une édition des journaux d'Hastie' *Bulletin de Madagascar* No. 264 (1968), 472–474.

[11] Entry for 8 August 1817, p. 174. His informant may well have been one of Radama's two younger brothers who had spent several months with Hastie in Mauritius during 1817. These young men, Ratafika and Rahovy, are mentioned below in the text.

[12] Approaches to cultural encounter in European expansion take a variety of forms and operate through different paradigms. See, for example, Eric Hobsbawm, *The Age of Empire, 1875–1914* (New York: Vintage Books, 1987); Ranajit Guha & Gayatri Chakravorty Spivak (eds.), *Selected Subaltern Studies* (New York: Oxford University Press, 1988); Michael Adas, *Machines as the Measure of Men: Science, Technology, and Ideologies of Western Dominance* (Ithaca: Cornell University Press, 1989); Marshall Sahlins, *Historical Metaphors and Mythical Realities: Structure in the History of the Sandwich Islands Kingdom* (Ann Arbor: University of Michigan Press, 1981); Stuart B. Schwartz, 'Expansion, Diaspora, and Encounter in the Early Modern South Atlantic' *Itinerario* 19,2 (1995), 48–59; Stuart B. Schwartz (ed.), *Implicit Understandings: Observing, Reporting, and Reflecting on the Encounters Between Europeans and Other Peoples in the Early Modern Era* (Cambridge: Cambridge University Press, 1994).

the *fandroana* of August 1817 is that although Hastie was successfully pursuing British diplomatic policy, the cultural engagement was neither directed nor choreographed by Hastie but by his Malagasy host. If we are to understand what Radama's subjects felt their king was attempting to achieve by his hosting of Hastie during the *fandroana* of 1817, we must attempt to read the meanings of the encounter through their eyes. The task is beset with practical and theoretical difficulties. The only direct evidence concerning the *fandroana* festivities of 1817 is the diary of James Hastie. How can we purport to divine the significance of this cultural encounter for highland Malagasy if the only documents available to us are the writings of the British envoy, a man who did not speak Malagasy and who was visiting Madagascar for the first time?

The answer, of course, is that we cannot know exactly what the encounter meant for any highlanders in particular. On the other hand we can raise trenchant questions about what cultural significances Radama sought to invoke and what his subjects might have learned through Hastie's handling at the *rova* during early August 1817. This article is an interpretation of highland Malagasy political culture. While it is a study of cultural encounter at the highland Malagasy court as enacted during the *fandroana* in 1817, it is also a reflection upon the possible meanings of ritual politics internal to the Merina kingdom, of Radama's communication with his public. The inquiry additionally provides us with insights into the personal character of Radama and his disposition toward productions of royal ritual. The possibilities for exploring the above historical questions through the available evidence are counterintuitive. Although documentation for the 1817 *fandroana* is provided by Hastie, when the evidence is 'read' with reference to the symbolic structures of the *fandroana* we can learn more about the ritual predilections of Radama and about the cultural politics of international alliance than we can about the British envoy himself.

What I am proposing here is more than counterintuitive, it runs contrary to much modern cultural theory. Modern European propensities to observe, report, organize and represent the doings and sayings of 'native' others—to produce texts and discourses symbolized here by the writings of an imperial envoy—are commonly interpreted as techniques of imperial rule, of narrative appropriation. Such European produced knowledge, it is argued, is primarily representative of European-metropolitan-elite-dominant discourses and cannot be fruitfully employed to understand 'native' or subaltern consciousness with any integrity. This intellectual position is not universally held, of course, but it has gained considerable currency amongst postcolonial theorists, many scholars working in Foucaultian traditions, and proponents of cultural studies who work on issues of imperialism and colonization. Designed to draw scholars' attention to how histories of the 'other' are at the same time reflections of the historian's own consciousness, these propositions suggest that it is impossible to uncover the meanings and intentions of historical subjects in times and places other than one's own.

The relevant questions to raise concerning the project of ascertaining from texts produced by James Hastie what cultural meanings the *fandroana* of 1817 might have suggested themselves to highland Malagasy are *how* and *for whom* were imperial discourses (diaries) a powerful technology of rule? and *how* do we define, substantiate, and measure the 'power' or dominance of such discourses? The answers to these critical questions can move in various directions, and they depend largely upon which broader narrative or narratives one chooses to illuminate with the historical data at hand, or within which (or whose) historical narratives Malagasy and British actors are placed. The foregoing questions evoke persistent methodological problems that postcolonial theorists have appropriately termed an author's or a subject's 'positionality.'[13] What follows is a positioned attempt to utilize an imperial envoy's diaries along with some limited Malagasy language texts to set the *fandroana* of 1817 within a larger narrative of highland Malagasy cultural politics.

James Hastie's Narrative

Radama first encountered James Hastie in July 1817 at the eastern coastal port of Tamatave.[14] Hastie was accompanied by Radama's two half-brothers, Ratafika and Rahovy, who were returning to Antananarivo after having spent several months in Mauritius with Hastie

---

[13] Gayatri Chakravorty Spivak, 'Subaltern Studies: Deconstructing Historiography' in *In Other Worlds: Essays in Cultural Politics* (New York: Methuen, 1987), 197–221; Gyan Prakash, 'Subaltern Studies as Postcolonial Criticism' *American Historical Review* 99,5 (1994), 1475–1490.

[14] Unless otherwise noted, all information in this section comes from the previously cited Académie Malgache edition of Hastie's 1817 diary.

as a statement of diplomatic intent on the part of both Radama and the governor of Mauritius. Radama was himself at the east coast with an army attempting to submit the primary trade entrepôts of Foulpointe and Tamatave to his direct sovereignty. During late July and early August Radama, his half-brothers and their escorts, Hastie, and the highland Malagasy army struggled through Madagascar's eastern rain forest and into the highlands of Imerina. As the party drew near to Antananarivo, Radama hurried ahead of Hastie and his entourage. The British envoy approached the highland capital on August 5 and was greeted by a messenger from Radama who requested that he sleep in a small house at the bottom of the hill for two nights, after which he would be allowed to enter the city. To welcome Hastie below Antananarivo that day (August 5), Radama ordered that eleven guns be fired and offered the envoy a fattened ox. On August 7 a second messenger informed Hastie that he should enter the city that afternoon and be officially received by the king at exactly 3 o'clock p.m.—by Hastie's pocketwatch! This is significant for Radama had begun to coordinate his European diplomacy according to the mechanical clock. One of the gifts Hastie offered Radama in mid-1817 was a large chiming pendulum timepiece. British missionaries later explained Radama's reaction to the gift in the following terms.

> Amongst the presents sent to Radama by the governor of Mauritius, one of those which afforded him the most pleasure was a clock. It was at first a little deranged, and he could not conceal his chagrin on hearing it strike while the minute-hand was at the half-hour. While he was absent from the house, Mr. Hastie fortunately discovered the cause of the clock's going wrong, and rectified it; and when the king returned, his joy was unbounded. The clock was placed upon a block, at the distance of four feet from a fire large enough to roast a bullock. The monarch sat on the ground beside it for a whole hour, and, forgetful of his regal dignity, danced when it struck.[15]

Beyond Radama's personal fascination with the mechanical instruments of time measurement, the king employed European time-measurement as a cultural resource to lend innovative pomp to Hastie's arrival and, possibly, to put the British envoy at ease. But

---

[15] *HOM*, II, 173–4. This scene is also described, although with less color, in Hastie's journal, 9 August 1817, p. 175. Because none of the missionaries accompanied Hastie in 1817 this passage and others treating Hastie's sojourn in Antananarivo in 1817 printed in *HOM* (principally HOM, II, 159–201) most plausibly derive from some version of Hastie's journal, not an independent source or third party.

European time-measurement was juxtaposed against the longer-term understructure of the highland Malagasy lunar calendar. While Radama utilized his clock coordinated with Hastie's pocketwatch to choreograph the British envoy's entrance into Antananarivo, he timed that entrance to coincide with the last days of Alohotsy, the final month of the highland Malagasy lunar calendar. Because of this purposeful coordination, Hastie was to participate in the royal rituals of the new year during his first days and nights in Antananarivo.[16]

At 2:30 p.m. by the clock on August 7, the third to the last day of Alohotsy, cannon were fired from the heights of Antananarivo to notify Hastie to begin his ascent into the city. Winding his way toward the *rova*, Hastie passed through an impressive line of armed soldiers. He was preceded by Ratafika and Rahovy, both of them mounted on horses offered as gifts to the king by the British envoy. The arriving party found Radama in the *rova* seated on an elevated stage and dressed in an eclectic European outfit consisting of a scarlet coat, a military hat from Mauritius, blue pantaloons, and green boots. The king took Hastie's hand in a warm greeting, laughing heartily. Radama then commanded silence and presented a *kabary*, or speech, to those of his subjects crowded about. He 'brought to their attention all the people, particularly the English, who passed through their country to come and see him.' After the public reception, Radama and his entourage repaired to Hastie's personal quarters within the *rova* where Radama 'removed the most embarrassing parts of his clothing,' Hastie recalls, and while sipping brandy entered into an informal discussion with the British envoy concerning the state of roads in Imerina. Dinner was eventually served by twenty female servants. Radama retired to his personal quarters after sharing a bottle of imported white wine with Hastie and a few other Europeans resident at Antananarivo.

The next morning, August 8 and the second to the last day of Alohotsy, Hastie was awakened early to attend a distribution of 400 cattle from the royal court to the people of the kingdom. It was at this point that Hastie must have sought an explanation for the public proceedings at the *rova* because he notes here that the distribution was on occasion of the 'anniversary of Radama's birthday.' When

---

[16] Information for the first two paragraphs of this section comes from James Hastie, 'Le voyage de Tananarive en 1817: Manuscrits de James Hastie,' *Bulletin de l'Académie Malgache* 2, 2ᵉ trimestre (1903), 91–114. This journal fragment covers 19 July 1817 through 5 August 1817.

the distribution was complete, Radama accompanied Hastie to the British envoy's personal quarters within the *rova*. There Radama discovered that Hastie's servant was unsuccessfully attempting to hang a temporary division in the one-room house so that Hastie's bed would be hidden from the main space of the single room (although many royal houses in Antananarivo were double storied, none of the floors was partitioned into separate rooms). Realizing that Hastie was attempting to separate the space of his quarters into sleeping and public rooms in the European fashion, Radama called for his 'captains' to fetch bamboo and woven mats out of which a makeshift bedchamber could be partitioned. Pleased at Radama's intervention, Hastie himself supervised construction of the enclosure. Within two hours a private sleeping room of some twelve square feet had been set apart from the main public space immediately about the door.

Later in the day Radama and Hastie, along with several of Radama's advisors, employed considerable time and energy discussing slavery and politics in the western Indian Ocean. Having himself initiated the process of alliance, Radama was no doubt aware that Hastie carried instructions from Governor Farquhar authorizing him to enter into an agreement on behalf of Britain to end the export of slaves from Radama's dominions. In the meeting, Hastie reasoned (no doubt for the primary benefit of Radama's reticent advisors) that highland Malagasy slaves would offer greater ongoing benefit to Radama's kingdom and to their owners if they were employed in productive tasks within the island rather than exported from there across the sea. Radama replied that he had personally resolved to terminate the export of slaves from his kingdom but that contrary to the public climate in Europe the slave trade was generally considered an honorable business within his kingdom (i.e. he would face considerable opposition attempting to do so). Radama's revelatory statement of intent is reported by Hastie without further comment, yet it was of principal political significance and assists us in understanding Radama's management of Hastie during the 1817 *fandroana*. Radama's ritual choreography of Hastie at the *rova*, we can hypothesize, was scripted to publicly communicate the king's intentions for British alliance and an end to the slave trade, to comment upon what cultural impact such an alliance might hold for his people, and to test the public reaction to his new departure in royal politics. Known to Radama and his entourage, Hastie's intentions were not concealed from highland Malagasy who had for decades both endured the depredations of the slave trade and participated in it. Radama employed the remainder of his day receiving representatives from the various districts of his kingdom, a number of people Hastie reckoned at about 150. Each of them offered very small pieces of cut silver coin to Radama (the significance of this and other elements of the *fandroana* are discussed below).

On the last day of Alohotsy, August 9, Radama occupied most of his day receiving visitors and their offerings of money, as he had at the end of the previous day. Sometime during the day, Hastie attended to some problems with the pendulum clock that Governor Farquhar had sent to Radama. He also met with Radama long enough to present him with a compass and unfold for him some world maps upon which were indicated the principal kingdoms of the time. Like Radama, who sought to chart Hastie into the cultural and political consciousness of highland Malagasy by incorporating him into the various performances of the *fandroana*, Hastie would orient Radama within the political spaces of European cartography. 'I found it necessary [also] to conform to the customs of the country,' writes Hastie, 'and some time after he left me I sent to him a red outfit that I received of Pye [a British naval captain].' (Wearing red clothing was a privilege reserved for the sovereign and his family.) The evening of August 9 marked the end of the old highland Malagasy year and the beginning of the new one. Radama was preoccupied with ritual procedure as explained by Hastie:

> At the setting of the sun about 500 persons were admitted inside the Palace court [the *rova*]. I asked permission to watch the ceremony that was happening there and Radama soon consented. He undressed in one of his large houses and put on a piece of cloth of local manufacture, changed the black headband that he had about his head for a white one, and went to the house of one of his wives followed by 25 spear carriers and 10 men blowing on shells. Hot water had been prepared and two men began to clean him. As soon as the water touched him, he let out a piercing cry, which was repeated by the crowd outside. When his attendants began to rub him dry he again called out loudly, and that was also repeated. He then reclothed himself and exited while spraying his bath water on the assembled people. He stopped for a moment, commanded silence (which was observed), gave a short speech, sprayed still more water, and entered the house. The people having dispersed, the singers and the shell blowers rested.[17]

---

[17] Hastie journal, 9 August 1817, pp. 175–176.

Later that night Radama visited Hastie for two hours before retiring to sleep with one of his wives, 'which does not happen very often,' Hastie curiously noted.

On the morning of August 10, the first day of the new year, Hastie reports that Radama awoke at 7 o'clock and entered a house where he dressed himself in a scarlet cloth decorated with silver beads and returned to the doorway of the house in which he had slept. The ceremonies continued:

> The Palace court was filled with cattle. Radama sat himself on a mat and asked me to sit beside him. He said some words and a poor young heifer was brought. The king having raised his voice, it was immediately overturned by five strong men and its throat cut in an instant. Before the heifer finished bleeding, a large piece of its hump was cut off and all the cattle except 50 were pushed out of the court. I entered with him into the house where he slept and he sent for eight of his wives who came out: each woman made a fire at the tomb of each of his eight ancestors (the women had a bit of boiled rice on their heads) and roasted a piece of the hump. This finished, he returned again to his house and sat on the mat. Rice was boiled and a piece of the hump roasted. He ate of them in a silver plate and gave me some in a porcelain plate. He put some grains of rice on my head and said some words: their meaning was a prayer to the All-Powerful (who he called Eanrenemanetta,[18] or the perfumed) that I should not be sick in his country. He introduced his wives, 11 in number. He had 12, but one had died, and he accompanied me then to see the houses. I returned with him and ate a morsel of the roasted hump with the skin attached. It was very good. . . . He was very tired and retired into a small house where he usually sleeps. I stayed with his wives, who were all beautiful and accompanied them inside several houses. They performed the same ceremony with me that the king had at noon; my head was covered with rice. In some houses we ate boiled blood and liver without salt: it did not taste good but I conformed to their customs. While entering the palace court, the oldest of the wives said to me that the king had placed her under my guard and that in the evening she was to visit at my quarters. I consented and they each savored a glass of cognac with even greater pleasure than all the things they had eaten.[19]

With these words Hastie ends his description of the ceremonial festivities of the *fandroana*. Later that day Hastie occupied some time with Radama discussing politics at Madagascar's east coast and attending

---

[18] Modern orthography: Andriamanitra.
[19] Hastie journal, 10 August 1817, pp. 176–177.

to some sick horses belonging to the king. The gift of 300 cattle that Radama informed Hastie on August 13 he would send to Governor Farquhar and the bull fights that the king presided over two days later were probably also part of the gift giving and celebration that accompanied the new year, but Hastie does not link these events to the rituals performed at the *rova* some days earlier.

Establishing an Interpretive Framework: The Symbolism of Fandroana

Hastie's narrative of the 1817 *fandroana* is the earliest known written account of the ceremony, which like other rituals of highland Malagasy royalty probably originated as a domestic or corporate kin rite but was later appropriated by royalty. By the late nineteenth century the *fandroana* had evolved into a grand cultural production at the *rova* and was described in writing by both foreigners and highland Malagasy. Anthropologist Maurice Bloch has employed an extensive compilation of such written accounts (most of them originating from the period after 1860) to construct a model of the ritual sequences of the *fandroana* and to propose an interpretation of the rich symbolism that structures them.[20] While Bloch's account and interpretation of the *fandroana* problematically collapses multiple historical performances into a composite ritual that was never performed exactly as described, it presents historians with an opportunity to 'read' Hastie's narrative of the *fandroana* of 1817 against the possible meanings of an 'ideal' *fandroana* and thereby to assess the extent to which it 'played' with ritual symbolism. Bloch's ideal *fandroana* serves as a template, a menu of symbolism and cultural resources that we can conceptualize Radama as having drawn upon in 1817 as he elected to organize the ceremony in a particular manner and to ritually position Hastie within its sequence of performances. The following paragraphs summarize Bloch's interpretation of the *fandroana*, drawing attention to those performances relevant to understanding Hastie's movements in Antananarivo while omitting others; readers interested in greater detail are referred to the text of Bloch's article.

In English *fandroana* translates as 'the bathing' and refers to the

---

[20] Maurice Bloch, 'The Ritual of the Royal Bath in Madagascar: The Dissolution of Death, Birth and Fertility into Authority' in David Cannadine and Simon Price, (eds.) *Rituals of Royalty: Power and Ceremonial in Traditional Societies* (Cambridge: Cambridge University Press, 1987), 271–297.

primary royal ceremony of the new year, the sovereign's bath in
warm water at the royal court as the old year gave way to the new.
According to Bloch, at the simplest level the *fandroana* was a classic
highland Malagasy ritual of blessing, signified by the sovereign's act
of spraying the *fandroana* bath water on people assembled in the royal
court yard. He writes:

> The word blessing is here a translation of the Malagasy word tsodrano
> which literally means to blow on water, since the most ordinary bless-
> ing, from a father to his child, as well as the most elaborate, as here,
> involves the scattering of water onto those blessed.[21]

A complex of associated rituals and performances, the *fandroana* was
structured into two primary contrasting segments. The first segment
corresponded to the end of the old year, the last days of Alohotsy,
and the second to the beginning of the new year, the first days of
Alahamady. These two segments and the chronological arrangement
of their related ceremonies are depicted graphically in Figure 1,
which is adopted with permission from Bloch's article.[22] The enactment of *fandroana* ceremonies at the turning of the year invoked a
symbolic opposition between the ending of the old year during the
'weak' and generally unpropitious month of Alohotsy (commonly
associated with decline, degeneration and death) and the beginning
of the new one during the 'strong,' fertile, life-giving and propitious
month of Alahamady. The first day of Alahamady was considered
the most auspicious day for a sovereign's birth, and this is probably
why the 1817 *fandroana* was explained to Hastie as a celebration of
Radama's birthday (it is highly unlikely that Radama was born on
the first day of Alahamady).[23]

The *fandroana* was normally announced in a formal declaration
some two weeks before the end of Alohotsy. By royal decree all
incomplete work was to be concluded and no new projects commenced. Alohotsy was a month of decline, unpropitious for the initiation of new enterprises. No unfinished project was to be carried
over into Alahamady. By similar reasoning, no animal was to be

---

[21] Bloch, 'Ritual of the Royal Bath,' 284.
[22] Bloch, 'Ritual of the Royal Bath,' 293. I have omitted Bloch's designation of
'funeral,' 'blessing,' and 'resolution' sequences from the illustration because they are
not relevant to the present argument.
[23] Because of the day's salutary associations, Andrianampoinimerina, Radama,
and Prime Minister Rainilaiarivony all claimed to have been born on 1 Alahamady.

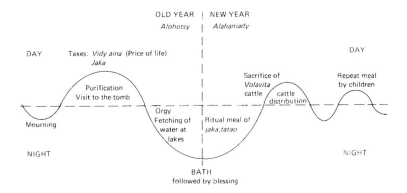

Fig. 1. Simplified diagram of the Royal Bath, after Bloch (1987: 293)

slaughtered until the first day of the new year, and all funerals were prohibited during the festivities. Additionally, both the convening of markets and complete bathing of the body were forbidden for they implied the fulfillment of cycles, one weekly, the other daily. The night before the last full day of Alohotsy people publicly and loudly mourned their dead. The next day they similarly gathered at family tombs to pay their respects to the dead. During that day, the last of Alohotsy, people presented symbolic taxes called the *vidy aina* (the 'price of life') to the sovereign. Finally, on the eve of the new year a symbolic social disorder was produced by human actions during the *alin-dratsy* (the bad night) in which sexual activity across social lines was tolerated where normally it was more vigilantly regulated. This was a night of 'orgy' that symbolically vanished with the dawning of the new year and the royal regeneration of order. Ideally the sovereign's bath would take place at midnight, just as Alohotsy gave way to Alahamady, social chaos to social order.[24]

Here Bloch's account faces a contradiction and requires modification. In 1817, as at other times, the sovereign's bath took place just after sunset on the last day of Alohotsy, not at or after midnight. This produced a sort of ritual middle ground between the two segments of the *fandroana*, for the last night of Alohotsy—after the sovereign's bath—was also the *alin-dratsy* when men and women could seek lovers of different social statuses and enjoy that normally

---

[24] 'Then, in the middle of the night, came the bath itself at the very moment of the turn of the year.' Bloch, 'Ritual of the Royal Bath,' 280.

forbidden sexual encounter with impunity. The *alin-dratsy* was the last phase of the social chaos sequence that was to disappear in the morning as everyone returned home to their respective social and domestic units. The evening of the bathing (August 9 to August 10) can therefore be seen as a time of transition between the two primary phases of the *fandroana* in which chaos reached its climax, so to speak, while the fresh order symbolically brought by the sovereign's bath began to take hold, banishing the vestiges of social chaos only with the rising sun on 1 Alahamady (10 August).[25]

As the contrasting second segment of the *fandroana* cycle (I return here to Bloch's interpretation), the new year was inaugurated with the royal bath and the blessing of representatives gathered inside the *rova*. Water for the sovereign's bath was fetched from specified lakes by youths 'whose parents are still living.'[26] As the sovereign disrobed and touched the water, he or she yelled *masina aho* (may I be sacred), which when heard by those assembled at the court to witness the occasion was responded to with *masina hianao* (may you be sacred).[27] At the conclusion of the bath, the bathing water, or *rano masina* (sacred water), was sprayed by the sovereign upon the assembled as a blessing. The bathing and blessing sequence was later repeated in individual households by those senior kin who had attended ceremonies within the royal court yard. Human and agricultural fertility and order secured for the kingdom through the king's bath were thus symbolically extended from the *rova* to domestic units across the realm. At the dawn of the new year, all were to return home to their proper social stations, including slaves to the households of their masters and those who had enjoyed the *alin-dratsy* with illicit lovers to their respective spouses of allowable social status. In contrast to

---

[25] In this way the ritual symbolism of the new year paralleled the symbolism of the rise of a new king. Historical traditions hold that on the evening Andrianampoinimerina felt his death to be near he issued orders for Radama to be confined in the royal house called *Masoandro* (the sun) inside the court at Antananarivo. Only at daybreak, after a night of mourning, did Radama emerge from *Masoandro* to reign as a new sun over the kingdom. See *HOM*, I, 100.

[26] Unmarried adolescents, conceptualized as those who are in between generations, vital yet lacking domestic commitments. See Maurice Bloch, *From Blessing to Violence: History and Ideology in the Circumcision Ritual of the Merina of Madagascar* (Cambridge: Cambridge University Press, 1986), 56–57.

[27] *Masina* is a word of complex and multiple significances. For a critique of the historiography of *masina* and its substantive, *hasina*, see Pier M. Larson, 'Multiple Histories, Gendered Voices: Remembering the Past in Highland Central Madagascar' *The International Journal of African Historical Studies* 28,2 (1995), 305–309.

the previous night of 'orgy' across social lines sexual order was restored, as was social order with the resumption of markets, funerals, bathing and butchering.

Following the royal bath and its domestic replications,[28] a special ritual meal called *tatao* consisting of boiled rice, milk and honey—culinary symbols of sweetness, fertility and order—was usually prepared for and eaten by the sovereign and within individual households across the kingdom. Elders customarily placed grains of *tatao* rice upon the heads of their subordinates as symbols of their authoritative blessings and prayers for fertility. As food, *Tatao* was accompanied by *jaka*, a mixture of fresh beef and dried beef preserved from the preceding *fandroana*. At daybreak, the sovereign released masses of gift cattle from the *rova* into Antananarivo's joyful streets and sacrificed a *volavita* heifer within the palace enclosure (*volavita* refers to a specific and symbolic body color-marking). Spatially, the ritual focus of the first day of Alahamady was upon the tombs of ancestors, where women sojourned to pray and to burn the hump fat of the butchered *volavita* heifer (like water, fat signified wealth and fertility, both of which were conceptualized as tangible outcomes of social order). Ceremonies performed at ancestral tombs during the first day of Alahamady were symbolically contrasted to the public mourning conducted two evenings earlier. The chaos and loss of death were juxtaposed with the life and fertility that social order and properly remembered ancestors obtained for the living. The *fandroana* ritual of the new year was a key performance articulating a highland Malagasy ideology of royalty. The core elements of that ideology included a depiction of the sovereign as the ultimate source of social order and fertility, and a naturalization of those royal powers through a conceptual linking of political power to the inevitable rhythms of nature.

'Reading' the Fandroana *of 1817*

Several of the ritual sequences described by Maurice Bloch are present in Hastie's account of the August 1817 *fandroana*; others are not. This may be due either to the fact that Hastie was not aware they

---

[28] Bloch suggests (p. 282) that this occurred the same night following the sovereign's bath but in practice it usually took place during the following day, the first day of Alahamady.

were occurring or because they did not take place. Royal development of the *fandroana* was still underway in 1817 so it is not surprising that all the sequences described by Bloch from documents
relating to the late nineteenth century do not appear in Hastie's
narrative. At the same time we would not expect Hastie, especially
on his first visit to highland Madagascar, to have been aware of
the complex happenings and preparations associated with the *fandroana*. Nevertheless, if we take Bloch's graphic model for the *fandroana* (Figure 1) and transpose onto it the historical events as reported
by Hastie (Figure 2), we can identify considerable similarity between
the historical *fandroana* of 1817 and Bloch's ideal *fandroana*.

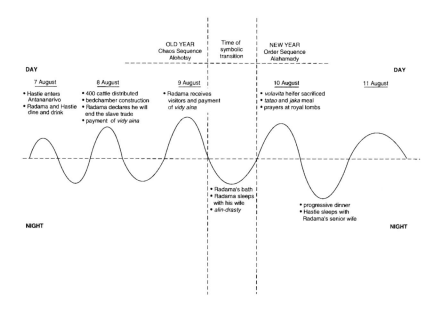

Fig. 2. The historical *Fandroana* of 1817

The visitors that Hastie observed occupying much of Radama's time
during the last two days of Alohotsy were no doubt coming to render their *vidy aina*, for they were offering the small sums of money
(typically a *voamena*) characteristically presented to the sovereign during the days preceding the bath. The bulk of Hastie's narrative as
it intersects with the composite account of *fandroana* produced by
Bloch describes the principal ceremonies of the sovereign's bath on

the eve of the new year: the sacrificing of the heifer, the release of masses of cattle from the royal court yard into the town, the *tatao* ritual meal, the placing of rice upon heads, and the prayers offered by Radama's wives at the tombs of the sovereign's deceased prede-cessors. In its broad outlines, the *fandroana* of 1817 substantially repro-duced the recognizable symbolic structures of the late nineteenth century.

The silences, deviations, and embellishments in the choreography of the 1817 *fandroana* as compared to Bloch's ideal *fandroana*, how-ever, call attention to the potential cultural and political meanings of this particular performance. Some of those differences are not especially important. For example, Hastie observed some 400 cattle being distributed from the *rova* on the morning of August 8, the sec-ond to the last day of Alohotsy. Such a distribution was not a remark-able feature of *fandroana* performances later in the century and is not therefore described by Bloch. We can surmise that the king provided cattle to his people from which the *jaka* meat eaten during the rit-ual meal following the sovereign's bath was obtained. It is possible, therefore, that despite a theoretical cessation of butchering during the last weeks of Alohotsy, beef to be employed in the festivities was slaughtered during the first part of the ritual cycle. On the other hand, the cattle distributed on August 8 may have been somehow linked to the gift cattle released to the people of the kingdom from the *rova* on August 10.

What was most unique about the *fandroana* of August 1817 was Hastie's presence and intimacy with the royal family. Radama timed Hastie's entrance into Antananarivo for maximum public exposure, epitomized by the pomp with which the British envoy describes he was received in Antananarivo. The political import of such a recep-tion certainly did not escape the 'captains' of Radama, the *namana*, who stood much to lose by the alliance Radama desired with Britain. Recall that many *namana* were merchants who had been favored by Andrianampoinimerina with privileges in the export slave trade and who continued to enjoy their commercial interests during the first decade of Radama's reign. If Radama's political intentions toward the British were unclear on August 7, his profession to a party of *namana* and to Hastie during the evening of August 8 that he would sign a treaty to end the trade in slaves from Imerina must have con-siderably clarified his position. From what we know of the porousness of the walls that surrounded the *rova*, Radama's revelations could not have remained privy only to an inner circle.[29]

It was within the expectant atmosphere of Antananarivo at the turn of the new year, 1817, that modification of ritual symbolism in the performance of the *fandroana* assumed potent political meaning. The ritual innovations—performances out of sequence or, effectively, inversions of ritual sequence—were presaged by Radama's hospitality and conviviality during the private hours he spent with Hastie. In the accepted fashion of European diplomacy, Radama lubricated social deliberations with bottles of (imported) brandy and white wine. This venerable ritual of alliance in an emerging globalized political culture represented a significant departure from the court procedures of Andrianampoinimerina, who had prohibited both the production and consumption of alcohol within the kingdom.[30] Under Andrianampoinimerina's regime of teetotalism Radama and his brothers had learned to sip wine and *eau de vie* on the sly with the slave traders who visited their father's court.[31] Perhaps under the excuse of a foreign diplomatic encounter and an emerging adulthood, Radama was consuming spirits within the *rova* itself. By savoring cocktails within the comfort of the royal court, Radama was symbolically contrasting himself to Andrianampoinimerina, registering his newfound adulthood and suggesting an independent political philosophy.

The first significant sequence inversion in *fandroana* performance commenced serendipitously on August 8 as a result of Hastie's discomfort with the arrangement of his domestic space. When Radama noticed Hastie attempting to separate a private bedchamber from the single-roomed space in his royal quarters, he called for bamboo and woven mats to be fetched and commanded his 'captains' to conduct the labor themselves. This incident represented more than an amusing cultural encounter, for it transpired during the first sequence of the *fandroana*, the period of decline at the end of Alohotsy during which no new projects or productive labor were to be under-

---

[29] Many people moved in and out of the walls of the *rova* daily. The tremendous influence that 'private' events within the *rova* could have for the people of the kingdom is perhaps best illustrated by the 'secret' baptism of Queen Ranavalona II and Prime Minister Rainilaiarivony in 1869. Details of the baptism became widely known, and the event touched off a mass of conversions to Christianity during the ensuing months. Raison-Jourde, *Bible et pouvoir à Madagascar*, 296–306.

[30] *Tantara*, 673, 760, 932.

[31] B. Hugon, 'Aperçu de mon dernier voyage à ANCOVA de l'an 1808,' BL/MD/Add.Mss./18137/16r.

taken. What was more, the persons commanded to conduct the work under Hastie's supervision were not described as court servants but rather as the 'captains' of Radama—most likely *namana* themselves![32] Here we find Radama far from a scrupulous observer of his father's ritual traditions and court etiquette. He suffered the esteemed advisors of his father, men whose political situation was already precarious, to undertake the potentially harmful labor of ritual sequence inversion for him. These insights into Radama's manipulation of symbolic politics on the fly help to explain why he was so effective at communicating his political intentions, on the one hand, and why the cultural feeling that later mobilized against him ran so deeply, on the other.[33]

A second inversion in the proper ritual sequence of the *fandroana*, one of capital importance, was premeditated by Radama. Like the first inversion, the second bore a symbolic significance of which Hastie appeared oblivious. I am referring to Hastie's progressive dinner with Radama's wives inside the *rova* during the first day of Alahamady and the visit that night by Radama's senior wife—very probably Ramavo, the future Queen Ranavalona I—to Hastie's personal quarters under instructions from Radama. The sequence inversion derived from the timing of Hastie's libidinous intimacy with Radama's wives precisely when the symbolic order of the kingdom was to be reinvoked by the sovereign during the second half of the ritual sequence. This reinvocation of order required that the bath and other ceremonies be performed at the *rova* and that sexual relationships across social lines—and in this case we can surmise even

---

[32] Hastie employs the term 'captain' in his journal to refer specifically to Radama's highest military officers. See, for example, Hastie's entry for 7 August 1817 where the British envoy explains that Brady, a British officer serving Radama, was no longer a soldier but had been promoted to a 'captain.' (Brady was considered a 'general' of the army and was in charge of training elite troops in European military techniques.) Later in the entry for that day, Hastie indicates that the deliberations about the slave trade in the western Indian Ocean took place in Hastie's quarters, which were full of people, 'among which were all his captains.' It is clear from this passage that by the term 'captains' Hastie meant to distinguish Radama's highest officers and counselors from lower level members of his entourage.

[33] A particularly poignant example of opposition to Radama's cultural politics occurred when in mid-April 1822 thousands of women from Avaradrano protested Radama's decision to shear off his plaits and wear his hair short in the European military fashion. Radama put an end to the protest by shaving the hair of several women he identified as protest leaders, having them publicly executed, and leaving their bodies to be devoured by wild dogs. See Larson, *Identities of a Crisis*, chapter seven.

more so across language and national lines—come to an end and
that all domestic unit members repair to their respective households.[34]
The potential meaning of the sequence inversion becomes clearer
when we examine the sexual chaos-to-order sequence of the new
year more closely.

Conspicuously absent from Hastie's description of the 1817 *fandroana* is specific mention of the activities of the *alin-dratsy*, the ritual
event during the first half of the *fandroana* that Bloch describes as an
'orgy' and that typically occurred during the last night of Alohotsy.
One presumes that the activities of the *alin-dratsy* occurred quietly
beyond Hastie's observation. With its connotations of sexual excess
rather than sexual intercourse across social lines, 'orgy' does not
properly describe the activities of the *alin-dratsy*. In Malagasy language narratives the *alin-dratsy* is described as both an *andro tsy maty*
(literally 'day-of-no-death') during which the social rules governing
sexual intercourse were suspended and transgressors, if they remained
discreet, could not be prosecuted (i.e. would not 'die'), or as a *valabe* (literally a 'vast [rice] field' or 'unpartitioned [rice] field') in which
social distinctions were effaced by the erasure of water retaining
boundaries.[35]

English Translation	Text of *Tantara ny Andriana*
Day-of-no-death, the day of bathing, says old Mister R. Everyone does as they please, except that which is against the government law that makes guilty.	*Andro-tsy-maty*, ny andro androan-drano, hoy rangahy R, samy manao izay tia'ny, afatsy ny lalam-panjakana mahameloka.
All prisoners are excepted from this.	Ny migadra rehetra afaka amy ny izany.
The 'vast field' almost becomes a reality on that day-of-no-death. Every-	Ka saikia manao valabe amy ny io androtsimaty io: dia mahazo man-

---

[34] European slave traders who traveled and conducted their business in Madagascar
commonly entered into sexual and commercial relationships with Malagasy women,
often called *vadim-bazaha* (European spouses). It was not the fact of sexual contact
that was remarkable about Hastie's tryst with Radama's senior wife, but the timing of that relationship during the *fandroana*, the differing social and national statuses of the sexual partners (in that ritual context), and the fact that it is the only
documented case in which the wife of a highland Malagasy king ever bedded with
a foreigner.

[35] All quotations from this document below are from *Tantara*, 167–168.

one can go to whom they wish on that day, the *havanandriana* can go to the *hova*, the *hova* can go to the *andriana* and even to the *andevo*—that is what is called the 'vast field.'[36] But it is a hidden 'vast field' that no one observes with their eyes; they follow the unseen bad with their hearts.

The water in a marsh makes a 'vast field.' If the water is drawn off, the [social] analogy becomes apparent. There are borders, elevated divisions, mud with which to make the barriers for shunting fish into carefully placed nets. So what lesson can we learn from the land? The government is not lawless and anarchical, it makes things go in their order, it binds every descent group. Each person takes their own part, because each takes [accepts] that which characterizes their descent group. That is what keeps the land from becoming a 'vast field.' Everything has a purpose. Those who have problems with each other are shown to the knowers of the law and the judges.

[Paragraph elided]

This is what makes the 'vast field' hidden away from watching eyes. They follow the unseen bad with their hearts. As for the 'vast field,' it is not the land that becomes a 'vast field,' but the people who break social taboos by sleeping with those who are not of the same ancestry as themselves, that is what makes it a 'vast field.' As for the 'vast palace' [another term for the *alin-dratsy*], it

deha amy ny izay tia'ny aleha ny olona rehetra amy ny io andro io, ny havanandriana mahazo mandeha amy ny hova, ny hova mahazo mandeha amy ny andriana na ny andevo aza, k'izany no atao hoe *valabe*, kanefa valabe *takona*: tsy misy mpijery ny maso, dia mpanaram-pò amy ny tsy hita ny ratsy.

Vala be ny rano an-keniheny, ary raha misintona ny rano dia miseho ny ohatra: misy valavala, misy valamparihy, misy valam-bovo anaovana tanam-bovo: ary aiza izany fahazavana ny tany? tsy atao rabantsahona ny fanjakana, fa ampandehanina amy ny tsipiriana, ampitadidina isampirenena, samy maka ny anjara'ny tsy ampifanandohina fa samy maka izay tandrify ny tera-drazana; izany no tsy mahavalabe amy ny tany, fa manana tonia ny avokoa ny zavatra rehetra. Fa izay mifanolana aterina amy ny mpahalala ny fitsarana sy ny mpitsara[.]

[Paragraph elided]

Izao no anaovana ny valabe takona tsy misy mpijery ny maso, dia manaram-po amy ny tsy hita ny ratsy. Ary ny valabe: tsy ny tany no valabe, fa ny olona manao otafady mandry aman'olona tsy mitovy razana amy ny, izany no mahavalabe azy. Ary ny lapabe: lafimpatana tsy ampy andriana izay malalaka iaraha-mandry, dia atao hoe lapabe ny filaza ny fandriana, 'hianareo an'indrana ary

---

[36] *Andriana, havanandriana, hova* and *andevo* were each distinct social classes or castes of highland Malagasy who were—ideally—not to intermarry or to have sexual interrelationships.

is like the side of the hearth without enough *andriana* [i.e. nobility],
anyone sleeps in the area that is open,
and we call such a common bed the
'vast palace,' 'you on the east side
and us on the west side.'

atsinanana, izahay aty an'indrana
andrefana.'

[Paragraph elided]

[Paragraph elided]

And according to old Mister—'When
the day-of-no-death arrives: the bad
things are not spoken of, whether
people can sleep with others' spouses,
for example, or whether they can
sleep taboo (*mandry fady*). There is a
clarification in the words used to describe it in the past: as the custom
of 'the-heart-not-enduring.'[37] Whether
the black and the white sleep,[38]
whether slaves and the nobles sleep,
they follow the words of the kings
and the people of old, and they say
day-of-no-death, heart-not-enduring.
This is the origin of the heart-not-
enduring: it is not only the eating of
food that is the heart-not-enduring.
Those who desire each others' countenances must unite, that is what
makes it said that the day is the 'day-
of-no-death,' and those who transgress at that time are not lectured.

Ary hoy ity Rangahy—'Ny nisehoany
ny andro tsy maty: tsy mba itene-
nana ny zava-dratsy, na azo maka
vady n'olona na azo mandry fady.
Misy fahazavana ny teny lazainy ny
tao aloha ho fomba ny fo-tsi-aritra:
na ny mainty sy ny fotsy mandry,
na ny andevo sy ny andriana mandry,
dia manaraka ny teny n'andriana sy
ny olona teo aloha, dia milaza andro-
tsy-maty: fo tsy aritra, izao nisehoany
ny fo tsy aritra; tsy dia ny fihinanan-
kanina hiany no fo tsy aritra: fa izay
mifaniry tarehy, dia tsy maintsy miray,
izany no ilazana androtsimaty ny
andro, dia tsy anaovana kabary izay
manota.

[Paragraphs elided]

[Paragraphs elided]

---

[37] The phrase 'heart not enduring' here refers to the weeks of prohibition on
slaughtering livestock during the last part of Alohotsy. Although most highland
Malagasy did not regularly eat beef during the early nineteenth century, the ban
was considered a symbolic and physical deprivation that the heart could scarcely
endure, to be contrasted with the generosity of the sovereign with the gift of beef
during the morning of the first day of Alahamady. The narrator here draws a parallel between deprivation of rich foods as part of the *fandroana* ritual sequence and
deprivation of cross-social group sexual appetite that can only be fulfilled during
the *alin-dratsy*.

[38] The color symbolism in this sentence refers to the common association of people of low status (principally but not exclusively *andevo*, slaves) with black and those
of high status (principally *hova* and *andriana*) with white.

Hidden [sexual] stealing, hidden sleeping, hidden loving when no one is looking or seeing: these are what make the day-of-no-death. For those who transgress the law, if they are seen, they are bound by the law and condemned by it. But the followers of the heart, on the other hand, the hidden, they sleep without being illigitimate. Taking something that is not one's own, wealth not from one's own feet and hands, and tearing what belongs to someone else, if one is not seen at this, it is called day-of-no-death. But if one is caught by people doing this, one jumps over the protected [i.e. forbidden] grass, it is within the law as agreed upon by the sovereign and the people. They [who do so] travel the road that will kill them, for the land has rulers and the government has a lord.

'Mangalatra takona, mandry takona, fitia takona tsy misy mpijery tsy misy mpahita, izany no anaovan'azy andro-tsi-maty; fa izay mpanota amy ny lalàna, raha hita: dia anaty ny lalàna, dia maty ny lalàna; ary ny mpa-narampò kosa, ny takona, mandry tsy mifankaheny, maka zavatra tsy hari'ny tsy harin-tongotra tsy harin-tànana fa mandriatra ny an'olona dia raha tsy hita amy ny'zao, dia milaza ny andro-tsi-maty; ary raha azo n'olona amy ny zao izy, dia man-dingana ny ahitra arovana, anaty ny lalàna nifanekaheny ny Mpanjaka sy ny ambanilanitra, ankaharany ny la-làna hahafaty azy izy, fa ny tany manana andriana ny fanjakana misy tompo ny.'

These passages from the *Tantara* stress that the permissiveness associated with the *alin-dratsy* was specifically limited to sexual liaisons ('the heart-not-enduring'; 'those who desire each other's countenances must unite') and that the liaisons themselves were to be conducted with discretion, not flaunted before the public eye ('it is a hidden "vast field" that no one observes with their eyes'; 'they follow the unseen bad with their hearts'). The passages confirm the symbolic importance of the *alin-dratsy* as a *mise en relief* of the distinctions highland Malagasy drew among different social categories of ancestry ('the people who break social taboos by sleeping with those who are not of the same ancestry as themselves') and of the social ideology that sustained such distinctions ('So what lesson can we learn from the land? The government is not lawless and anarchical, it makes things go in their order, it binds every descent group').

It is curious in light of this symbolism that on the night of the *alin-dratsy* in 1817—the evening of August 9 to the morning of August 10—Hastie remembers Radama to have retired to sleep with one of his wives rather than with some socially forbidden lover. With a paucity of evidence and given the fact that the evening of August 9 represented the overlapping time of transition between two opposing

symbolic segments, it is difficult to interpret this action with preci-
sion. We might argue that the sovereign was himself exempted from
the permissiveness of the *alin-dratsy* and therefore constrained to
sleep with one of his own wives during that night, as he would normally have been supposed to do. On the other hand, Hastie notes
that Radama's choice of bed partner that night represented something out of the ordinary (it 'does not happen very often'), a curious
remark for him to make (having just recently arrived in Antananarivo) and the closest Hastie came in his journal to supplying any
evidence about the *alin-dratsy*. It could be that Radama chose to participate in the chaos symbolism of the *alin-dratsy* by laying with a
wife with whom he did not normally sleep or whose ancestry was
most dissimilar to his, and yet there was no reason to believe that
any of his wives was considered illegitimate. Could it be, on the
other hand, that Radama was purposely inverting the sequence of
the *alin-dratsy* by sleeping with the permitted rather than the forbidden? Or was he simply choosing not to participate in the *alin-
dratsy* or comment upon the chaos sequence and merely slumbered
at the side of one of his lawful wives on the night after his bath
restored sexual order to the kingdom?

While answers to the foregoing questions will likely elude us,
Radama's arrangement of an intimate evening between Hastie and
his senior wife must have spoken to highland Malagasy with greater
clarity because it was timed to coincide with the first evening of the
new year (10 August), which was unambiguously inside the social
order segment of the *fandroana*. The symbolism of order associated
with the first night of the new year, 1 Alahamady (10 August), required all domestic members to be properly distributed within their
publicly recognized households and for sexual activity to conform to
principles of descent order and social status. Yet on the evening of
1 Alahamady (10 August) Radama abandoned Hastie to all eleven
of his wives and retired into a house within the *rova* while the con-
vivial party progressed from royal house to house (these were apparently the houses of Radama's wives) partaking of a local delicacy,
blood-boiled liver, and sipping cognac. While Radama presumably
slumbered alone, Hastie bedded with the king's senior wife. It was
a ritualized scandal, for it flipped the chaos and order sequences of
the *fandroana*. Let us return to the *Tantara* texts to more fully appre-
ciate this inversion of ritual sequence. The following passages refer
to the transition in the *fandroana* from the old year and the *alin-dratsy*
(the chaos sequence) to the new year and the necessity of returning

to one's household (the order sequence) simply as 'the bathing' or 'the bathing of the people.' Recall that 'the bathing of the people' was performed the morning after the sovereign's bath within individual households and that it brought domestic members back from a night of social-sexual license.[39]

For the customs of the ancestors of old [i.e. the *fandroana* customs] have a name: there is a day called the 'day of purchasing' for there are none who do not return home.[40] Whether people have offended, whether a spouse has run away, one does not disregard the bathing of the people, for the 'bad night' arrives and everyone awakes and runs away again in the morning, afraid of the place where living is not endured; the 'relationship' is no longer endured so it is parted from:[41]

Fa misy anarana ny fomba ny ntaolo taloha, fa misy atao hoe andro vidina, fa tsy misy tsy mody any an-trano; na olona manankeloka, na vady misintaka, tsy manary fandroan'olona, fa avy ny fanaovan'alin-dratsy miaramifoha ka mandositra indray izy raha maraina, atahorana toerana tsy zaka ny fonenana, efa tsy zaka intsony ny fanambadiana ka ialana:

If the bathing is disregarded on the day of purchasing, according to the rulers of old, it will be counted among the twelve crimes, among the crimes that killed one according to the transgressions of old.

'Raha toa manary fandroana amy ny andro vidina, hoy ny andriana taloha, atao ko isa ny heloka 12, isa ny mahafaty azy amy ny heloka tsy tiany ny teo aloha.'

These *Tantara* texts are remarkably articulate about the importance of observing 'the bathing of the people' through a return of wayward spouses and other individuals to their socially recognized households. In light of this sensitivity to the sexual-social ethic of the

---

[39] These passages are among the 'elided paragraphs' in the texts presented above.

[40] I translate *andro vidina* here as the 'day of purchasing,' for the phrase (properly translated 'the purchased day') most likely refers to the fact that the last day of Alohotsy was, as we have seen, the day during which highland Malagasy rendered small payments of silver called *vidy aina* (the price of life) to the sovereign. It is likely that the orthography *vidina* employed here simply assumed the deemphasized 'a' sound inserted between the final 'i' and the 'n' in *vidiana*. The most likely interpretation here is that the author is emphasizing that it is following the day of paying *vidy aina*, the last day of Alohotsy, that lovers must return to their socially recognized domestic units.

[41] The Malagasy word translated as 'relationship' here is *fanambadiana*. While *fanambadiana* today designates the legal marital relationship between a man and a woman, its nineteenth century connotations were considerably less tied to legal definitions and referred more to a range of loving and cohabiting relationships.

fandroana, the otherwise unremarkable action of Radama leaving a court visitor to be entertained by his wives assumes especial significance. Retiring alone while arranging for Hastie to publicly visit his wives on the first night of the new year (it is ambiguous from Hastie's journal language but the progressive dinner may have taken place outside the walls of the *rova*),[42] Radama organized a party maladapted to the symbolic and practical requirements of the ritual. When 'read' against the symbolic structures of an 'ideal' *fandroana*, the progressive party arranged by the king invoked the sexual disorder sequence a full day after Radama had performed the bath and restored order to the kingdom. It was a notable inversion of ritual sequence, an innovation. Yet Radama had not abandoned the ritual expectations his subjects anticipated from him, he had merely performed the *fandroana* in an innovative fashion. Through his ritual choreography Radama had held the equivalent of a modern press conference, informing his subjects of late breaking diplomatic news. Hastie's intimacy with Radama's wives—and his senior wife in particular—was a ritually meaningful 'sign in action.'[43] It is unlikely that Radama's purpose in organizing the sequence inversion was simply innovation for the sake of demonstrating a disrespect for royal ritual. It was a creative public demonstration of how seriously he sought an international alliance and revealed how generously he intended to entertain foreign envoys at his court. The alliance with Britain would turn certain of Andrianampoinimerina's recently invented customs on their head and entail transformations, or inversions, of existing cultural practice. It was no coincidence that Hastie's participation in the 1817 *fandroana* scripted the envoy's intimacy with highland Malagasy royalty, for despite his nationality Hastie soon became Radama's most trusted and familiar advisor.

Radama's choreography of the 1817 *fandroana* can also be read as a cautious means by which Radama continued to publicly float his new politics of international alliance and his plans for replacing the

---

[42] At the conclusion of the progressive dinner, Hastie writes: 'While entering the palace court, the oldest of the wives said to me that the king had placed her under my guard and that in the evening she was to visit at my quarters.' By 'while entering the palace court,' Hastie may either be referring to entering a certain part of the *rova* from Radama's wives' houses also inside the enclosure, or he may mean that the party entered the *rova* after having spent the afternoon-evening outside of it. It is unlikely that all of Radama's wives lived within the *rova*.

[43] Sahlins, *Historical Metaphors and Mythical Realities*.

namana with his own advisors and military leaders (a sort of political inversion). Although we have little evidence of resistance beyond the close circle of the *namana* to Radama's new politics in 1817, it is clear from Hastie's reports and from those of British missionaries who lived in Antananarivo beginning in 1820 that the young sovereign faced widespread popular opposition to many of the transformations he effectuated between 1820 and his untimely death in 1828.[44] Radama was cognizant of these challenges and was particularly skillful at finding a way to test the political waters before proceeding with his initiatives. Micromanagement of ritual symbolism such as that of the 1817 *fandroana* was part of Radama's public communication and royal politics. Unafraid to apply force when publicly challenged (as by the women who opposed his newfangled haircutting practices in April 1822), Radama nevertheless preferred to proceed in his transformations of highland society and politics without soliciting the open disapproval of his public. In the end Radama stripped the *namana* from his entourage, a success attributable to his skill at navigating treacherous waters with cultural tact and political dexterity. Along with Hastie, he replaced the *namana* with European and Malagasy counselors, most of whom had little political standing within central Imerina. By doing so Radama matured into a reign of his own. He was successful not because he abandoned highland Malagasy cultural traditions for a bourgeois modernity but because, like his father, he skillfully employed highland Malagasy cultural symbolism and ritual to set his politics firmly within a highland Malagasy cultural logic.

'The King Himself is But a Ceremony': Radama and Highland Malagasy Culture

Both French and English historians have interpreted Radama as a Malagasy sovereign particularly keen for things European. In this understanding of the young monarch, the cultural choices facing Radama have been perceived as 'all or nothing' prospects in which the king chose to replace outmoded highland Malagasy practices with modern European ones. This historiographic tradition began to crystallize even before the death of Radama in 1828 and emerged

---

[44] Larson, *Identities of a Crisis*, chapter six.

from the writings of the king's European admirers and contemporaries who saw in Radama an instrument by which they might
'civilize' (i.e. Europeanize) the highland Malagasy. The portrait they
painted of Radama was one of a ruler openly skeptical of much
highland Malagasy religious and cultural practice. Some concluded
that Radama had abandoned his cultural heritage, claiming that he
disbelieved and even despised fundamental highland concepts of
kingship, blessing, and fertility. After a seven-month residence at Antananarivo, for example, LMS missionary David Jones commented
optimistically in one of his letters that

> Radama says that he does not believe in the superstitions and foo-
> leries of his people, but that he conforms to some of them as they are
> the customs of the country over which he is king, and that he does
> not wish to encourage them by any means; also that it is very difficult
> to make his people to leave off divination, polygamy &c., &c. at once:
> but that these things will be done away by degrees as their minds are
> enlightened; and says he, I hope that a great change will be seen
> among my people in twenty years longer.[45]

André Coppalle, a French painter who lived for some time in Antananarivo, noted in his travel diary that Radama cynically commented
one day that royal rituals were but bothersome 'political institutions
fit to govern children of all ages.'[46]

Drawing upon the same evidence, nineteenth and twentieth century scholars have similarly portrayed Radama as a progressive
monarch struggling against the religious, social, and cultural traditions of his people to install a western-style modernization.[47] The
Tantara ny Andriana, an edition of Malagasy language historical and
ethnographic texts collected by a French Jesuit priest in the mid-
nineteenth century, even suggest that Radama did not believe in the
power of the *sampy*, or royal talismans. Criticized one day by the
keeper of *sampy* Rakelimalaza, Radama is recounted to have been
furious and to have publicly shouted that only he was *andriamanitra*
(god) and not the *sampy*.[48]

There is a grain of truth in this historiographic tradition. Although
the international sophistication of Andrianampoinimerina is seldom

---

[45] David Jones to Rev. George Burder, Antananarivo, 3 May 1821: LMS/1/2/C.
[46] A. Coppalle, *Voyage à la capitale du roi Radama 1825–1826* (Tananarive: Association
Malgache d'Archéologie), 1970, 56.
[47] See citations in note 6.
[48] Tsy misy andriamanitra fa izaho no andriamanitra, hoy izy. *Tantara*, 1104.

appreciated by *malgachisants*, Radama was more interested and adept than his father was in conducting himself among the intellectual and material cultures of Europe. As a result of Andrianampoinimerina's international training of Radama and the young man's frequent inter-actions with French slave traders at his father's court, Radama was at ease and predisposed to adopt elements of the increasingly glob-alized culture of enlightenment Europe, especially if such adoptions would effectively contribute to his quest for personal power. Radama did make occasional comments to his European acquaintances ques-tioning the logic of highland cultural and religious practices, but his abandonment of things Malagasy has been overdrawn. While Eu-ropean missionaries, merchants, and political emissaries wanted to claim a sense of shared bourgeois rationality with Radama or to see him as an instrument of their designs for the so-called 'civilization' of Madagascar, Radama had his own aims and a domestic con-stituency to please, negotiate with, and rule. Despite his assistance to British missionaries as a condition of the political alliance he con-cluded with Governor Farquhar's agents, for example, and his desire to claim the technology of writing for his army, Radama never expressed a personal interest in Christianity. Throughout his reign, Radama consulted frequently with diviners (the *sikidy*) and healers at his court.[49] He was careful to perform royal rituals at the appointed times, demonstrated by his elaborate thanksgivings at the tomb of his father at Ambohimanga on 12 January 1818, as reported by Hastie who accompanied him on that occasion.[50]

Hastie similarly reports that Radama responded to the ritual expec-tations of a king at times of crisis by distributing charms (*ody*). This, for example, he did in early 1818 when a smallpox epidemic rav-aged Antananarivo and its environs.[51] The *tangena* poison ordeal that Radama supposedly abolished was in fact employed at the king's orders away from European eyes.[52] A history of royalty and religion

[49] See, for example, Journal of Barnsley from 12 December 1821 to 30 June 1822: MNA/HB/7/87/205. Barnsley's entry for 11 January 1822 indicates that he (as temporary British envoy to Antananarivo) attempted to see Radama that day but that Radama was busily engaged with diviners all day long. See also *HOM*, II, 251.
[50] Journal of James Hastie from 14 November 1817 to 19 May 1818: Entry for 12 January 1818: MNA/HB/10/2/19–23.
[51] Journal of James Hastie from 14 November 1817 to 19 May 1818: Entry for 9 January 1818: MNA/HB/10/2/19–23.
[52] Journal of James Hastie from 14 November 1817 to 19 May 1818: Entries for 17 February 1818 and 18 February 1818: MNA/HB/10/2/27–28.

during highland Madagascar's early nineteenth century must therefore consider the nature of Radama's participation in rituals of royalty rather than his abandonment of them. For Radama, as for his
father, ceremony was a defining feature of kingship. Emissaries of
the London Missionary Society resident in Antananarivo after 1820
conceded this fact when they observed of the young monarch in a
collective publication that he believed 'no ceremony should be deemed
a trifle, since the king himself is but a ceremony.'[53]

Radama was an adroit cultural broker, a man in the social middle who sought new directions for his kingdom in alignment with
European imperial powers. At the same time he was constrained
to employ cultural languages and symbols that his subjects understood. Despite a common perception to the contrary, this was not
a role altogether foreign to his father Andrianampoinimerina. Usually
conceptualized as a traditionalist who would admit of no European
influence among his people, the founder king was the most successful of highland Malagasy rulers of the late eighteenth century at
attracting and retaining alliances with Europeans from Madagascar's
east coast and in modifying royal ritual. If in comparison to Andrianampoinimerina Radama was cynical about rituals of royalty, he was
equally skillful at employing them to strategic purposes as his father
had been.[54] Radama seized and transformed the available ritual
symbolism of his day. By doing so he was not abandoning Malagasy culture but creatively charting elements of the European cultures closing in about him into highland Malagasy consciousnesses.
These cultural initiatives were understood—although not necessarily
approved—by his subjects. Radama foundered in highland Malagasy
opinion following the British alliance not because he tampered with
immutable highland Malagasy cultural traditions nor because he
brokered Malagasy and European cultures, but because he cleverly
and effectively communicated an increasingly exploitative and unpop-
ular politics through royal ritual symbolism.

---

[53] *HOM*, I, 101–2.
[54] For the little we know, Andrianampoinimerina could have been of similar personal disposition toward royal ritual. For excellent studies of Andrianampoinimerina's
innovation and management of royal ritual see Gerald Berg, 'The Sacred Musket:
Tactics, Technology, and Power in Eighteenth-Century Madagascar' *Comparative
Studies in Society and History* 27,2 (1985), 261–279, and Gerald Berg, 'Sacred Acquisition:
Andrianampoinimerina at Ambohimanga, 1777–1790' *Journal of African History* 29,2
(1988), 191–211.

CHAPTER THREE

BUILDING GOD'S KINGDOM. THE IMPORTANCE OF THE HOUSE TO NINETEENTH CENTURY NORWEGIAN MISSIONARIES IN MADAGASCAR*

KARINA HESTAD SKEIE

Introduction

In his seminal essay on the Kabyle house, Bourdieu shows the intimate connection that exists between the house, its inhabitants, and the wider society.[1] He argues that in architecture, furnishing, and decoration, as well as through the organization of space, the house objectifies cultural schema and values fundamental to the social context in which the house exists. However, the house is more than a material and symbolic expression of these categories and values. According to Bourdieu, it is simultaneously a primary locus for their reproduction.[2] By moving in the house world, and between the worlds inside and outside the house, people internalize these schema as their taken for granted world—as habit, both in a mental and a bodily sense.

Drawing upon Bourdieu's work on the Kabyle house, this essay examines the importance of the house to nineteenth century Norwegian missionaries to Madagascar. It focuses on Norwegian missionaries in the Vakinankaratra and Betsileo, the two highland regions south of the capital Antananarivo where the Norwegian mission concentrated its efforts.[3] Examples from their Norwegian contemporaries in other regions of Madagascar will be drawn upon where relevant.

* *Acknowledgements*: This is the first publication from an ongoing Ph.D. project funded by the Norwegian Research Council. My sincere thanks to Karen Middleton for her constructive suggestions. Thanks also to Maurice Bloch for discussions of the house material, to Rita Astuti, Jennifer Cole, Rolf Welde Skeie, and professors and fellow students at the Faculty of Arts, University of Oslo, for reading and commenting on earlier drafts. I, however, am responsible for any shortcomings.
[1] Pierre Bourdieu, 'The Kabyle House or the World Reversed' (1970) in *The Logic of Practice* (Oxford 1990), pp. 271–283.
[2] Pierre Bourdieu, *Outline of a Theory of Practice* (Cambridge 1977).
[3] In this paper I use the term 'highlands' interchangeably with 'Vakinankaratra' and 'Betsileo'.

To judge from the archival material, the work of building God's kingdom in highland Madagascar was to a surprising degree centered around the construction of buildings,[4] not merely churches, schools, and assembly places but also the houses in which the Norwegian missionaries would live. While the 'mission station' eventually comprised at least a church and a school in addition to the missionary's dwelling, it was often realised in the first instance around a combined school and dwelling, built by the missionary himself. Until a church was built, a room in this building was also used for Sunday services. This building was not only the first physical manifestation of the Norwegian mission's presence in a Malagasy locality to the Norwegian missionaries and their audience in Norway. It was also recognized by the local Malagasy peoples, by the government in Antananarivo, and by mission organizations of other nationalities and denominations, as a sign of their determination to stay. Wherever they settled, the Norwegians created 'Station districts', each with a missionary residing in a mission station at its centre, surrounded by an ever growing number of satellite churches and schools. Constantly travelling out from his station, the missionary would lead mission work in the district.

Despite its centrality, the Norwegian missionaries did not define the dwelling as part of the 'real missionary work'. The house belonged to the 'external' or 'indirect' aspects of their task, aspects which were related to but distinct from the 'direct' or 'real' work of spreading 'the Word'. This distinction corresponded to a distinction between 'the external' and 'the spiritual', or the 'visible' and the 'invisible', in the missionaries' religion. In Norway, the relationship between what was spiritual and invisible, on the one hand, and what was external and visible, on the other, seems to have been largely taken for granted. In the missionizing context in Madagascar, however, it became somewhat of a theological problem for missionaries. I will show why it was essential for the missionaries to define themselves as preoccupied with 'the spiritual', and how the dwelling played an important part in creating and maintaining this imagery.

---

[4] I once commented upon the prominence of buildings and their construction in the nineteenth century missionary material to missionary Kjetil Aano, at that time editor of the Norwegian Mission Magazine. He told me that a survey had revealed this theme to be by far the most prominent in the Mission Magazine over the previous decade.

While Bourdieu's theory concerns the house in a familiar world, this paper concerns the house in a context of a cultural encounter. Bourdieu's thesis is nevertheless relevant in two ways. First, it alerts us to the ways in which the house carried the Norwegian missionaries' culture and values, and structured their lives and work in a very concrete sense. At the same time, the complex dynamic Bourdieu proposes between the house and the world beyond directs our attention to the ways in which the house, on account of being placed in the Malagasy socio-cultural world, became implicated in the negotiation and transformation of Norwegian missionary culture and values.

In exploring the role of the house in this cultural encounter, I have drawn on historical sources that tell us about life on the mission station. The classification of the dwelling and everything associated with the dwelling as only indirectly relevant to the missionary task was underlined in a gendered division of labour between the missionary couple: she took care of the world inside the house so that he could spend his time and energy on the 'real' task outside the house. This is one reason why the material from male missionaries, who are most substantially represented in the NMS archives, primarily describes life outside the mission station, where the 'real missionary work' took place.[5] My primary source for the lived world inside the mission station is missionary wife Anna Caroline Amalia Christine (Lina) Haslund's ten year private correspondence to her family in Stavanger.[6] Lina and her husband, Johan Christian Haslund, are central figures in this paper because the material from them regarding life on the mission station is particularly rich.

Lina Haslund's information can be considered representative in so far as her role as wife and mother corresponded to the situation of most Norwegian missionary wives in Madagascar. The details in her

[5] This chapter is based on 1) NMS archives, Stavanger, Hjemmearkivet (abbreviated NMS/Hjemme), boxes 34–40, Konferansereferater and boxes 131–141 Innkomne brev, and 2) Theodor Olsen's personal diaries, Bok 1 (1891–1892), Bok 2–3 (1892), Bok 4 (1894, 1896) (abbreviated NMS/Diary/Olsen 1–4). I thank Pier Larson for generous permission to use his 'Catalog of Madagascar holdings contained in the Hjemme-arkiv of the NMS' and 'Lists of documents contained in the Larson catalog of the Madagascar holdings of the Hjemme-Arkiv 1866–1899', and Nils Kristian Høimyr and Randrianirina Phillipe for their generous permission to use the printed transcript of Theodor Olsen's diaries.

[6] The letters were donated to the NMS archives in 1971 and 1980. One of the donors had received them from a descendant of Lina Haslund's brother, Isak Isachsen.

letters also tally with the information given by male missionaries in
their personal diaries or in more formal letters to the mission leaders in Stavanger, as well as with photographs of other Norwegian
mission station interiors. By the time Lina Haslund arrived in Madagascar, more than 10 years after the Norwegian pioneers, issues
regarding housing had probably become part of the largely taken
for granted structure of missionary life in the highlands.

I begin with a brief history of the Norwegian mission in Madagascar
and an outline of the nineteenth century Norwegian missionaries'
home background.

The Norwegian Mission to Madagascar

The substantial missionary effort in Madagascar made by the London
Missionary Society (LMS) is well known.[7] Less well studied is the
impact of another Protestant mission to Madagascar, that of the
Lutheran Norwegian Mission Society (NMS).[8] Commencing in 1866,
and still active today, Norwegian missionary engagement on the
island has been extensive. Indeed, as the French historian Raison-
Jourde notes in her exhaustive work *Bible et pouvoir à Madagascar au
XIXe siècle*, the Norwegians have left so profound a mark in the
Vakinankaratra and Betsileo that any history of Christianity in inland
Madagascar not considering their contribution remains incomplete.[9]

The Norwegian mission to Madagascar was inaugurated primarily
because the NMS needed a field likely to provide quick positive
results. Their first mission field, Zululand-Natal, had proved to be
'exceptionally hard and unpromising', and the mission leaders were
anxious to retain the growing interest of an increasingly affluent Norwegian population.[10] Their timing proved to be excellent. In 1869,

---

[7] See Bonar Gow, *Madagascar and the Protestant Impact. The Work of the British Missions
1818–1895* (London 1979); Françoise Raison-Jourde, *Bible et pouvoir à Madagascar au
XIXe siècle. Invention d'une identité chrétienne et construction de l'État* (Paris 1991).

[8] The only publication in English to date is Finn Fuglestad and Jarle Simensen
(eds.), *Norwegian Missions in African History*, Vol. 2, Madagascar (Oslo 1986).

[9] Raison-Jourde, *Bible et pouvoir à Madagascar*, p. 13.

[10] Fridtjov Birkeli et al., *Det Norske Misjonsselskaps historie. Madagaskar Innland, Vest-
Madagaskar, Øst-Madagaskar* (Stavanger 1949), p. 19. Madagascar had been known
to Norwegians since the 1830s through articles in the Mission Magazine about the
work of the LMS. Also, the NMS had started to build a mission ship, and therefore was looking for a field, close to the existing mission in Zululand-Natal, that
could be reached by sea.

within three years of the first Norwegian missionaries' arrival, the Merina queen and her Prime Minister were baptized, and 'the worship', as Christianity was called, became the state religion for all loyal subjects in the areas under Merina control.[11] While the Norwegian missionaries were grateful for the large number of Malagasy who filled their churches and were baptized, the fact that 'the worship' was 'the Queen's religion' also meant that many aspects of how Christianity came to be practised in the Highlands collided with their own understanding of conversion as something individual and spiritual, a transformation of the inner self. Yet the Norwegian missionaries had to be associated with Merina state Christianity in order to get pupils in their schools, people in their churches, and permission to preach in the many assembly houses.

The first Norwegian mission stations were founded in Betafo, (Ant)Sirabe, and Masinandraina in the Vakinankaratra. This and Betsileo were to become the primary regions for Norwegian mission effort. From 1874 the NMS began work in Tulear and Morondava on the West Coast,[12] from 1888 on the East Coast (Vangaindrano), in the Bara region (Ihosy), and in the far South (Fort-Dauphin),[13] and from 1892 in Ambohimanga, in the forest region. However, the Norwegian mission in these regions was far less successful than in the highlands.

Before the French occupation in 1895, education was a major part of Norwegian missionary work, especially in the Vakinankaratra and Betsileo, where the Merina government from 1881[14] tried to enforce compulsory schooling. In addition, there were teachers' colleges in Masinandraina and Fianarantsoa, and a Lutheran Seminary for training Malagasy pastors which was started in Antananarivo but later moved to Fianarantsoa. From the 1880s, Malagasy personnel—teachers,

---

[11] For details, see Gow, *Madagascar and the Protestant Impact*; Raison-Jourde, *Bible et pouvoir à Madagascar*; Stephen Ellis, *The Rising of the Red Shawls* (Cambridge 1985).

[12] The movement to the West coast in 1874 had resulted from a disagreement with the LMS. The LMS claimed the capital and 'a large circle around it' as their 'field'; the NMS disputed this claim (Fridtjov Birkeli: *Politikk og misjon. De politiske og interkonfesjonelle forhold på Madagaskar og deres betydning for den norske misjons grunnlegging 1861–1875* (Oslo 1952), p. 141).

[13] This field was handed over to a (Norwegian) American Mission Society after two years, and the missionaries, first and second generation Norwegian immigrants to the USA, were transferred to the new society.

[14] Although the Merina government had made school attendance compulsory in 1876, the law of 1881 was more radical (Fuglestad and Simensen, *Norwegian Missions in African History*, pp. 102–103).

evangelists and pastors—had a major hand in daily missionary work. The first three Malagasy Lutheran pastors were ordained in 1883,[15] and by the 1890s there were more Malagasy pastors than Norwegian missionaries in the Malagasy Lutheran church.[16]

Medical work or 'the work of mercy' (*Barmhjertighedsarbeidet*)[17] became a separate branch of missionary work from 1876. It came to include two hospitals, a medical school run in cooperation with the LMS, work among the leprous, and two institutions for raising Malagasy children in a Christian environment, in which women were to play a major role.[18] Medical assistance also went hand in hand with congregational work for most Norwegian missionaries; some theologians became much sought after lay doctors.

A rapidly growing missionary movement is an important feature of nineteenth century Norwegian society, which was undergoing wide-ranging social change. A period of economic prosperity led to better communications, improved schooling, and greater urbanization.[19] In both urban and rural areas an emerging middle class 'had the necessary surplus of money, time and energy to subscribe to missionary publications, attend meetings, and contribute to a national organization'.[20] Jointly founded by Moravians, Haugians and state church clergy in Stavanger in 1842, the NMS was a private organization fully dependent on financial contributions from its local affiliated societies. By the turn of the century, it had developed into one of the broadest popular movements in Norway, which partly explains Norway's exceptionally large number of active missionaries relative to its population size.[21]

---

[15] The Franco-Merina war (1883–85) helped bring about the ordination of Malagasy pastors because it forced the Norwegian missionaries to abandon their stations for a while (Birkeli et al. *Det Norske Misjonsselskaps historie*, pp. 118, 120).

[16] *Ibid.*, p. 121.

[17] *Ibid.*, p. 128.

[18] Line Nyhagen Predelli, 'Contested Patriarchy and Missionary Feminism. The Norwegian Missionary Society in Nineteenth Century Norway and Madagascar.' Unpublished Ph.D. dissertation in Sociology, University of Southern California, Los Angeles 1998.

[19] Einar Molland, *Norges kirkehistorie i det 19. århundre*, bind I, (Oslo 1979), pp. 10–11.

[20] Jarle Simensen (ed.), *Norwegian Missions in African History*, Vol. 1 (Oslo 1985), p. 15.

[21] *Ibid.*, p. 13. In 1885, the NMS fortnightly journal *Norsk Missionstidende* had 10,000 subscribers in a population of around 1,9 million, giving it a larger circulation than any newspaper in the country at the time (Jarle Simensen, 'The Norwegian Missionaries' Image of the Malagasy' in Rian et al. *Revolusjon og Resonnement. Festskrift til Kåre Tønneson på 70–årsdagen den 1. jan. 1996* (Oslo 1995), p. 141).

The majority of Norwegian missionaries to Madagascar were recruited from the south-western regions of Norway, where the missionary movement was strongest.[22] These were areas where teetotalism
and pietistic Christianity had a firm foothold. Arne Bugge Amundsen
argues that the pietist awakenings of the nineteenth century can be
seen as a movement away from a hereditary collective piety towards
an increasingly individual and personally experienced type of religiosity.[23] The Haugian movement[24] emphasized the Christian ethic
and moral responsibility in this world, combining this with the creation of circles of Haugian 'friends', which functioned as networks
for social and economic improvement. The Moravians' pietism, which
became the stronger influence from the 1840s and 50s, was inter-
confessional from the outset and had extensive international contacts.
Their religion was more emotional and 'Evangelical'; the subjective
experiences of sinfulness and salvation were emphasized.[25] From the
1850s clergy in the State church were profoundly influenced by an
awakening which moved them closer to the lay movements' religious
outlooks. Thus, the NMS was firmly based within the Norwegian
Lutheran state church which also kept the Haugian and Moravian
lay influences largely within its membership.

To Bring the Light of Salvation to Those Who Sit in Darkness

The prescript of the NMS states that the purpose of the mission is
'to take the Gospel of Good Tidings farther and farther beyond the
borders of the homeland, to those who still sit in darkness not knowing the Light of Salvation.'[26] This highly visual image of the encounter

---

[22] Many candidates came from families of farmers, cotters, artisans or petty traders
on the south-western coastline between Bergen and Nedesnes (Simensen, *Norwegian
Missions in African History*, p. 19, pp. 27–28).

[23] Arne Bugge Amundsen, '"The Living Must Follow the Dead". In Search of
"The Religious Person" in the Nineteenth Century', in *Arv, Nordic Yearbook of Folklore*,
53 (1997), pp. 107–130.

[24] Haugianism named after its founder, Hans Nielsen Hauge, a farmer's son, was
a revivalist lay movement of Norwegian origin, which gained many followers from
the 1790s, especially among prominent farming families.

[25] Kristin Fjelde Tjelle, 'Kvinder hjælper Kvinder. Misjonskvinneforeningsbeve-
gelsen i Norge 1860–1910'. Unpublished Master thesis in history, University of
Oslo, 1990, p. 6.

[26] Jørgensen (ed.), *I tro og tjeneste. Det Norske Misjonsselskap 1842–1992* (Stavanger
1992) p. 27, my translation from Norwegian.

between light and darkness was extremely potent in mission interested religious milieus.[27] With strong Biblical roots, it conveys both
conviction in the power of the Christian Gospel and the urge to
missionize. Many of the Norwegian missionaries were recruited from
Evangelical movements in which salvation followed intense experiences of sinfulness and abandonment by God, often conjoined with
very strong fears of death and hell. For those who had experienced
how conversion might transform utter despair into peace, a sense of
obligation to spread the 'Good Tidings' was a powerful motive for
becoming a missionary.[28]

To bring God's light to those in darkness was a spiritual battle,
in which the missionaries saw themselves as engaged in a fight against
the King of Darkness' grip on peoples' souls.[29] This was more serious than a battle between life and death; it was a battle between
eternal life and *eternal* death. Yet this spiritual battle also had clear
bodily and material implications. Not only did it lead the Norwegian
missionaries to journey to and settle in Madagascar, but once there
missionary work had to be carried out on two fronts: the spiritual—
through the preaching and teaching of 'God's holy word'—and the
bodily and the material—through the creation of an infrastructure
of dwellings, schools and churches from which the missionaries could
work to create an environment where 'Christians' could grow in
knowledge and faith. Some missionaries depict themselves as gar-
deners sowing the word of God in the Malagasy soil.[30] It was necessary to prepare the ground beforehand so that the seed would
germinate and grow. God's Kingdom therefore had both internal
and external aspects; it was at one and the same time spiritual and
corporeal. Yet in another sense the spiritual side of missionary work
was God's realm, as only God could make the seed grow. As mor-
tals, the missionary could only see, describe and work on the external aspects, and conclude from these the work's internal worth.

---

[27] I explore this imagery further in 'Beyond Black and White. Reinterpreting the
Norwegian Missionary Image of "the Malagasy"' in *Encounter Images in the Meetings
Between Europe and Africa* (The Nordic Africa Institute, forthcoming).

[28] See Simensen, *Norwegian Missions in African History*, chapter 1.

[29] NMS/Hjemme/Box 136/Jacket 14/Minsaas, Fihasinana 5 Aug 1885.

[30] NMS/Hjemme/Box 39B/Jacket 1/Einrem, Midongy 12 Jan 1898; Box 134/
Jacket 10/Lindø, Soatanana 27 Oct 1877; Box 135B/Jacket 8/Minsaas, Fihasinana
23 Feb 1882; Box 136/Jacket 5/Haslund, Tsaraindrana 28 Jan 1884; Box 139/Jacket
8/Thorbjørnsen, Manambondro 16 May 1890.

The Mission Station

The Norwegian missionaries called their dwelling the 'Mission Station' (*Missionsstationen*) or simply the 'Station', terms which connected the house inextricably to missionary work. Webster's dictionary defines 'station' as:

> 1. a place or position in which a person or thing is assigned to stand or remain or is standing or remaining. 2. the place at which something stops or is scheduled to stop: a regular stopping place, as on a railroad. 3. the building or buildings at such a stopping place. 4. the district or municipal headquarters of certain public services. (. . .) 5. a place equipped for some particular kind of work, service, research or the like. 8. Mil. a. a military place of duty. b. a semi-permanent army post. (. . .) 10. Formerly (in India) the area in which the British officials of a district or the officers of a garrison resided.

In calling their dwellings 'stations' the Norwegian missionaries probably followed an established terminology from other countries and other mission fields, which perhaps in turn had been taken over from a military-colonial context. The connotations of 'station' for the Norwegian missionaries nevertheless fit the definitions in Webster's dictionary. To settle in a location was to 'occupy a place' (*besette et Område*). The correlation between this and missionizing as spiritual warfare is evident. Since it was the Malagasy who were the 'target', population density was a crucial factor in deciding where to place a station. Places chosen were those where the missionary could most easily reach a sizeable population.

Each missionary was 'placed in' (*plassert*) or 'appointed to' (*bestemt*) a particular locality by the mission leaders in Stavanger and/or by decisions taken jointly at the annual meetings of missionaries in Madagascar. From the moment they were selected for the lengthy missionary school education to the time they were allocated, the missionaries saw the hand of God at work. If their 'vocation' (*Kall*) was 'from God', He would work through all the decisions to reveal his will. Thus, upon reaching the appointed place in Madagascar, the missionary saw himself as a representative (*Udsending*, literally, 'out-sent') of the NMS and the mission congregation in Norway, but above all of God. The station became his post of duty until he was relieved or given another posting or died. This sense of 'the calling' (*Kallet*) and of submission to God's will no doubt sustained the missionaries in the face of disappointments and hardships. Some felt

that their entire life had been a longing and a preparation for the
moment when they could begin 'the holy missionary work' (*Den hel-
lige Missionsgjerning*).

Both the Norwegian missionaries and local and central Malagasy
political powers looked upon the setting up of a dwelling as a declaration of their intent to stay. Competition between the various
British, French and Norwegian mission societies also meant that in
areas where several organizations had interests, it was considered
important to build stations and churches in order to 'secure' and
'occupy' a particular district for the mission society. The Merina
government for its part wanted to regulate where foreign missionaries could settle. In Vakinankaratra and Betsileo, no foreigner was
allowed to set up a dwelling without permission from the authorities
in Antananarivo. In general, however, the Merina government was
favourable to and even wanted the missionaries to work in areas
under its control. This was not always the case in the other regions of
Madagascar where Norwegian missionaries took up missionary work.

Until they could build their own dwelling, Norwegian missionaries in the highlands lived in rented houses. These tended to belong
to the most prominent people in the local community, often a Malagasy noble (*Andriana*), and were usually but not always grander than
other houses in the neighbourhood. This association with *Andriana*
at the outset linked the missionaries to the highest strata, and continued, at least indirectly, when the missionaries moved into their
'proper dwellings'.

Like other Europeans at the time, the Norwegian missionaries had
a strong preference for constructing their dwellings on hilltops. The
reason for this preference was generally pragmatic: malaria or 'Malagasy Fever' was perhaps the most serious health problem the missionaries faced, and in areas 'with fever', they, like their European
contemporaries, believed hilltops were healthier than places with less
change of air. However, the landscape where the Norwegian missionaries placed their stations also had a cultural logic of its own.
In the highlands, hilltops were associated with holiness and power.
Johan Christian Haslund's description of the construction of Ambohimahamasina station in Southern Betsileo illustrates how dramatic
the resulting conflict of interests could be:

> As a site [for school and dwelling] I had chosen a small hill with
> evenly falling slopes close to the village. However, the problem with

this hill, on which I for several reasons wanted to build, was that it was, or rather had been, a holy site; on its top lay a quite large holy sacrificial stone and beside it was erected a high stake, whose top was decorated with some carved embellishment. Elderly people, whom I have spoken to, said that before the Queen started to pray and commend the people to do the same, this hilltop was a place for public sacrifices, where large numbers of people in the south came together to eat and bring the gods their sacrifices. On such yearly occasions a number of oxen were slaughtered here on the hilltop, and the oxen's blood was spilled over the sacrificial stone as a kind of propitiatory sacrifice. I had already several times requested the local leader to give me this hilltop to build on. However, I had not succeeded in getting his permission, since he feared that people in the village as well as in the surrounding area would die, either of heat or of cold or of hunger if he were to permit such destructive abomination of the ancestors' holy place. I did not let him in peace, however; the place's holiness merely strengthened my desire to erect precisely there a sanctuary for the living God, from which—by God's grace—a warming beam of light would shine, enlightening the surrounding darkness.[31]

Through the intervention of 'an influential Malagasy' (he gives no details), Haslund eventually obtained permission to destroy the holy site at Ambohimahamasina (literally: 'at the hill which makes holy'), and build his mission station in its place. Closely watched by the Malagasy workmen, the local leader and his household, Haslund himself swung the ax that gave the holy stake its 'fatal wound'. The sacrificial stone became a cornerstone in Haslund's house. 'It was more suitable as cornerstone than as a sanctuary'. 'Thus it can truly be said that I have founded my school house on a fallen Pagan sanctuary'.

The desacration of a Malagasy holy site in order to replace it with a mission station appears to have been exceptional. Not all hilltops were sacrificial places. Yet the story is highly revealing of how the missionaries thought of their mission as toppling Pagan idols, and replacing them with a more enlightened way of life. No wonder this passage from Haslund's letter was reprinted in the Mission Magazine.[32]

In the highlands, the Norwegian missionary houses were built of local material: sundried (red) earth bricks, the roof usually covered with grass. The walls inside and out were covered with a mixture

---

[31] NMS/Hjemme/Box 134/Jacket 4/Haslund, Ambohimahamasina 23 Nov 1876.
[32] NMT No 4, April 1877, pp. 137–138.

of earth, cowdung, water and sand, before they were chalked white.
Durability and solidity appear to have been two factors in the choice
of building material. In the coastal and forest areas, the missionaries rejected the local grass and cane houses in favour of prefabri-
cated wooden houses sent out from Norway on the mission ship.[33]

The Norwegian mission station was more than a dwelling for the
missionary and his family; it was the material expression of the mission society's presence in Madagascar. They were large constructions
not only because the missionaries liked to keep an open house for
missionary colleagues and their families but also to signal power and
influence. Coming from a young nation on the periphery of Europe,
and working alongside and partly in competition with powerful mission organizations from imperial countries, the Norwegian missionaries and their mission society were concerned about their social
status. Judging from the more military aspects of missionizing terminology, size also signified domination, an aspect which was reinforced by the preference for siting mission stations on hilltops.

While there are very few detailed descriptions of Norwegian mission station architecture, the photographs we have of their exteriors
suggest that they tended to be highly modern by Norwegian standards, and more in keeping with contemporary architectural trends
in Europe than Norwegian style.[34] They had rooms for different purposes: office, bedrooms, living rooms, storage rooms and a kitchen.
In addition, most stations had a separate 'kitchen house', in which
the Malagasy servants slept. With time, other buildings were added,
not only a school and a church, but also barns and perhaps a small
carpentry workshop. Among the Norwegian middle- and upper classes
at the time, as in Europe, the internal division of space by function,
combined with the gradual differentiation of buildings, reflected the

---

[33] Asked by the mission leaders about the possibility of building clay houses in
the coastal areas, Thorbjørnsen argued that it was not local practice because of the
climate, and did not mean that people there were less civilized than in the highlands (NMS/Hjemme/Box 139/Jacket 8/Thorbjørnsen, Manambondro 27 Feb 1890).

[34] Adjustments were made to local conditions. For instance, the roof had to cover
the walls to prevent the sundried bricks from dissolving in heavy rain because it
was too expensive to build the foundations of stone (NMS/Hjemme/Box 132/Jacket
3/Engh, Betafo 9 Feb 1870). I am indebted to Arne Lie Christensen for his assistance in assessing the architectural style of the Norwegian mission stations. One
problem has been that many stations (e.g. Betafo) changed over time as storeys or
sections were added, making it difficult to match the original, rather unclear floorplan
with the photographs and descriptions.

increasing segregation of people by gender, age and social class.[35] In Madagascar, the category of race was added to the others, for example, the Malagasy servants slept in the kitchen house. In the milieux where the majority of male Norwegian missionaries were recruited, however, this kind of segregation (i.e., of the farmer and his workers and servants) did not take place until the turn of the twentieth century.[36] For most missionary men, the mission station therefore represented a very visible step up the social ladder.

Another missionary describes how:

> The Station has a large, lovely garden full of (. . . .) the loveliest roses, heliotropes, reseda and some rare red flowers, bibas trees with ripe fruits, peach trees still in flower. In the middle of the garden lies a small pond surrounded by kalas. From the pond, water is led down to the kitchen garden. A low wall with small, white linking posts, almost surrounds the garden. In the middle (. . .) are three small pavillions which look very pretty indeed.[37]

Expressing a modern sense of order and beauty,[38] in which 'civilization' triumphed over nature, the mission station garden also differentiated external and internal space in a new way. It expanded the sphere of the house, creating a distance between it and the world beyond. This was underlined by the wall or fence that bounded the people inside the mission station from the Malagasy outside.

The modern European architecture of the Norwegian mission stations in Madagascar connects them firstly to the LMS missionaries,[39] and secondly, to Malagasy people of means. The station which Cameron built for missionary J. Pierce carries the key features of the so-called Swiss architectural style.[40] The fact that the Norwegian station houses were built with fireplaces according to English custom

---

[35] Until the nineteenth century, houses in Norway had largely developed through adjustments and additions to existing buildings. The 'Swiss' style, which gained most ground from the mid-nineteenth century onwards, constituted both an aesthetic and a social program (Arne Lie Christensen: *Den norske byggeskikken. Hus og bolig på landsbygda fra middelalder til vår egen tid.* Pax forlag A/S, Oslo 1995, p. 282).

[36] Christensen, *Den norske byggeskikken*, p. 20.

[37] NMS/Diary/Olsen/Book 1, Friday 28 August 1891.

[38] Christensen, *Den norske byggeskikken*, p. 284.

[39] While I have been unable to establish whether the Norwegian missionaries hired LMS trained slaves as builders, they would have found prevailing European architectural styles in Madagascar familiar and suited to their requirements. I am indebted to Arne Lie Christensen for this point.

[40] I thank Arne Lie Christensen for this observation.

supports the theory of British influence.[41] According to Sibree, houses
of sun-dried bricks were introduced by Cameron,[42] and quickly copied
by those Malagasy who could afford it for their own dwellings. These
were also made bigger, with verandahs, and windows and doors all
around. The interior was divided into a living room and two sleeping chambers.[43] The houses which Norwegian missionaries describe
from Vakinankaratra and Betsileo, however, more resemble Sibree's
description of 'a Malagasy house of the poorer class'.[44] Their simplicity and spatial logic contrasted markedly with the Norwegian mission stations.

The House Interior

Like the majority of her fellow missionary wives, Lina Haslund was
one of the 'brides' who came out on the mission ship to marry their
fiancés in Madagascar. Students at the missionary school were not
allowed to marry and then had to stay two years in the field before
they could fetch brides. Mission leaders were able to impose this
strict rule because the missionary school financed the students' education and subsistence.[45] The majority of students came from lower
class families, and had no other opportunity for higher education.
By contrast, missionary candidates with an academic education, i.e.
candidates who had financed their own education, were allowed to
marry prior to going to Madagascar.

Throughout the nineteenth century and well into the twentieth

---

[41] Lina Haslund to her parents and siblings, Ambohimahamasina 1 Nov 1876
and 4 July 1880.

[42] James Sibree, *Madagascar and its People*, (London 1870), pp. 208–209.

[43] *Ibid.*, pp. 208–209. See Gow, *Madagascar and the Protestant Impact*, p. 65, and
NMS/Hjemme/Box 134/Jacket 2/Egenæs, Ambohimasina 15 March 1876.

[44] These houses were rectangular, usually made of a mixture of cowdung and
clay, and always oriented from south to north, with a window and a door on the
west side. Inside, the house consisted of one room where all the family slept and
ate; the domestic animals were kept in the southern end of the room at night. The
hard-beaten clay floor was sometimes covered with straw mats, similar to those on
the walls. The ceiling was usually black with the smoke from the hearth, slightly
north-west of the central pole (Sibree, *Madagascar and its People*, pp. 203–204; Raison-
Jourde, *Bible et pouvoir à Madagascar*, pp. 86–88; Lars Dahle, *Madagaskar og dets beboere*
(Christiania 1876–1877), pp. 165–166; Maurice Bloch, *From Blessing to Violence. History
and ideology in the circumcision ritual of the Merina of Madagascar* (Cambridge 1986), pp.
38–39.

[45] See Simensen, *Norwegian Missions in African History*, p. 26.

century, the Norwegian missionaries married only Norwegian women.[46] Some married single female colleagues, but the majority, like Johan Christian Haslund, got their 'brides' from Norway.

While many of the missionary wives also worked outside the home, teaching Malagasy women handicrafts, hygiene and principles of child care,[47] their primary role was without doubt to run the house and raise the children, and help and encourage the husband in 'his often difficult missionary work'. I interpret the fact that the women who came out as brides were given no formal education in the Malagasy language as a very clear signal from the mission organization that their place was *in* the house rather than outside.

Like the majority of brides, Lina brought several boxes of dowry. There were duvets, pillows, linen, glasses, vases, lamps, pictures, plates, bowls, meat and coffee grinders, pots and pans, everything required to create a good Norwegian home in Madagascar. She even brought a selection of familiar vegetable and flower seeds for the garden: radish, purslane, parsley, carrots, peas and sweet peas, reseda, snapdragon, sunflowers and dahlias.[48] The majority of seeds germinated and grew well in the Malagasy soil, Lina reported home.

Lina describes the furnishings and decoration of the living room in some detail. Confirming the central place her family in Norway occupied in her thoughts, the 'main wall', facing as one entered, was decorated with 'dear family portraits' and a picture of her 'dear family home'. In the lower corner, a clock stood on a shelf which her husband had worked. The glass had broken in transit, but this 'does not matter much' because the clock still worked. 'It is so nice to listen to its cosy and homely ticking.' Decorating the wall leading to the couple's bedroom, over a buffet, which a Malagasy carpenter made to Christian's specifications, were pictures of their spiritual heritage: one of the Mission school and two of Stavanger cathedral, interior and exterior. Although the buffet 'is a pretty piece of furniture', Lina immediately points out its practicability, with storage space, drawers, and lockable cupboards. On the other side, 'all our prettiest books, shining with their pretty, gilded bindings' stood on 'a pretty bookshelf', which her husband had made and given her

---

[46] As far as I know, there have been three marriages between Norwegian missionaries and Malagasy, the first in the 1970s, a second in the 1980s, and the third in 1997. Two of the marriages were between Norwegian women and Malagasy men.

[47] See Predelli, 'Contested Patriarchy and Missionary Feminism.'

[48] Lina Haslund to parents and siblings, Ambohimahamasina, 3 Feb 1877.

for Christmas. A mirror hung in the upper corner of the main wall. The organ was to be placed under the mirror as soon as it arrived. In front of the window, with a chair on each side, stood a sewing table, a birthday present from Christian. In the middle of the room was a new table they had had a Malagasy carpenter make.

The fact that the living room is the only room Lina describes in detail suggests that it was the main room in the house. A room for work and pleasure, the sewing table is a visible reminder that Lina constantly mended and sewed clothes for Christian, the children, and herself. It is also clear from her letters that the living room rather than the kitchen was the room for meals, and for receiving and entertaining guests, as was the case among the middle and upper classes of Norwegian society.[49] Judging from her dowry, Lina appears to have come from a rather wealthy family. Although Christian came from the same social stratum, missionary wives generally came from a higher social background than their husbands.[50] An upwardly mobile group, the missionary school education had made the missionary men appropriate marriage partners for middle and upper class Norwegian women.[51]

Lina repeatedly emphasises how important it was to both of them that everything should be 'pretty', 'cosy', and in 'good working order'. The nice but functional furniture are all markers of modern, middle-class tastes. A certain amount of decoration helped to create a sense of well-being and prosperity and 'elevated the mind'. Too much decoration, however, was inappropriate; it was the useful which embellished a house.[52]

There is nothing in this living room to indicate that it is a room in a house in Madagascar. Norway is present through portraits and pieces of furniture as well as through the basic values and decorative taste. In her first letter to her parents, Lina remarked that they were using a *lamba* (a length of cloth that Malagasy wear) as a temporary table cloth. After the dowry boxes arrived, however, this had been replaced with a Norwegian tablecloth.

---

[49] Arne Lie Christensen (personal communication).

[50] The majority of NMS women came from the families of ministers, higher or middle ranking public officials, master craftsmen and builders, ship- and factory owners, and medical doctors (Predelli, 'Contested Patriarchy and Missionary Feminism').

[51] Simensen, *Norwegian Missions in African History*, p. 31; Predelli, 'Contested Patriarchy and Missionary Feminism'.

[52] Arne Lie Christensen, *Den norske byggeskikken*, pp. 282–284.

'Norwegianness' was further underlined in their food. For breakfast and supper the family ate bread, coffee and tea, sometimes with boiled egg and cold meat[53] or home made cheese.[54] For dinner: steak, saddle of pork, turkey, duck, hen, and chicken-, beef-, sago- or rice-soup. The missionary wives exchanged cake recipes, along with advice as to which Malagasy ingredients produce the best results. Thus, Lina described making waffles from manioc flour, egg, sugar and buttermilk.[55] On one occasion she even tried to make *kumle* (potato dumplings), a dish served with variations along most of the Norwegian coast, but because 'they did not turn out right', she asks her mother to send out some rye flour next time she sent her a box on the mission ship.[56]

Because meat and vegetables were cheap in the highlands, missionaries could afford a better life style in Madagascar than most people of their class in Norway. Prior to Lina's departure from Norway, Christian writes to reassure his future parents-in-law:

> Matters of the house is not something the missionaries speak much about, because there are so many important issues that occupy our interest, and partly because one does not want to aggravate weakly-minded mission friends at home. When the missionaries out here have settled, their situation is at least as comfortable and good as that of the majority of rural pastors at home. As far as food is concerned, one would have to be rich in Norway to be able to live as well as here. For that matter it is not hard to live here, while other things make it hard enough.[57]

While Lina and Christian's life-style was shared by most of their colleagues in the highlands, it contrasted with how some of the Norwegian missionaries on the East coast lived.[58] Standards of living, as well as the degree of 'Norwegianness' missionaries were able to recreate on their mission stations, largely depended on their proximity to

---

[53] Lina Haslund to her parents, Alakamisy 1 Nov 1876.

[54] Lina Haslund to her parents, Alakamisy 3 Feb 1877.

[55] Lina Haslund to her parents, Alakamisy 1 Nov 1876 and 3 Feb 1877.

[56] Lina Haslund to her parents Alakamisy 17 Feb 1879. Over the years, Christian and Lina had things sent from Norway with the mission ship on a fairly regular basis. In return, they sent Malagasy gifts to family and friends in Norway.

[57] Christian Haslund to Mr and Mrs Isachsen, Fihasinana 26 Dec 1875.

[58] NMS/Hjemme/Box 140A/Jacket 13/Joh. Smith, Antananarivo 1 April 1893; Box 140A/Jacket13/Thorbjørnsen, Fianarantsoa 25 May 1893; Box 140A/Jacket 17/Bjertnæs, no place, no date; NMS archival photographs of the living rooms at Antananarivo and Sirabe.

Antananarivo, where commodities could be bought at the main market or ordered from abroad through the NMS 'depot'. Since transportation greatly increased their cost and all Norwegian missionaries
received the same salary regardless of locality, the differences between
them could be substantial. Lina's elaborate meals contrast sharply
with those of missionaries on the East coast living largely on the
same diet as the Malagasy people around them: rice, coffee and the
occasional chicken. While Lina describes how all the good food makes
her strong, the East coast missionary complains that the poor nurture is bound to weaken their health.[59]

Bodies and Boundaries

Cleanliness and order were two fundamental values in Norwegian
missionaries' homes. In Lina's letters, this issue is strongly connected
with the need to create boundaries between an ordered, clean Norwegian world inside the house and a correspondingly dirty and dangerous Malagasy world outside. The domestic servants appear to
have been the only Malagasy people with whom Lina was in daily
contact, and her relationship to them was ambiguous. Although she
describes them as 'nice', 'kind' and 'loyal', she also complains of
difficulty in making them understand what they were required to do.
It was not like having servants 'at home', i.e. in Norway, where they
knew how to wash the floor and make Norwegian food without having to be taught. Although language problems probably played some
part in her frustrations, at least in the beginning, Lina also seems
to have wanted her Malagasy servants to be and think like Norwegians.

For Lina, the main problem with the domestic servants, 'as with
the Malagasy in general', is their 'great degree of uncleanliness'.[60]
In order to see more clearly when they get dirty, Lina makes them
wear white uniforms; besides, 'white suits them best'.[61] Even so, she
has to show them over and over again how to 'clean the house properly', constantly checking whether they actually do as they are told.[62]
Yet she also describes in detail how the Malagasy women she hired
to do her laundry manage to get everything nice and clean, despite

---

[59] NMS/Hjemme/Box 140A/Jacket 17/Bjertnæs, no place, no date.
[60] Lina Haslund to her parents and siblings, Ambohimahamasina 3 Feb 1877.
[61] Lina Haslund to her mother, Ambohimahamasina 17 Feb 1879.
[62] Lina Haslund to her parents and siblings, Tsaraindrana 20 Feb 1881.

washing the laundry in cold water in the river (without putting it to soak) and drying it on the ground. Lina credited the strong 'Malagasy soap'. Drawing on Douglas' argument that 'dirt' is 'matter out of place',[63] I would argue that Lina's concern with Malagasy unclean-liness both manifests her sense of moral superiority and differentiates her houseworld from the 'Malagasy' world outside. That it is the domestic servants who constitute a group of great ambiguity is not surprising. As Malagasy they belong to the outside, yet their work brings them inside the mission station. Continually transgressing the boundaries, this marginal group constitutes a visible threat to the structures of the missionary world.

Significantly, there was more to the domestic servants' 'unclean-liness' than what was visible on a white uniform:

> We are always exposed to dangers and hardships while being down here [on earth], however, I think this can be said in a more profound sense about life out here where one is surrounded by Paganism and darkness, illness and destitution. Yes, life out here has many seamy sides. One of the worst for me is nevertheless the terrible illness with which the people are so imbued. It gives one constant cause for worry, but even more so when one has small children. Alas! how often do I not worry that our sweet little Agmund will be infected thereof, which could easily happen through the servants in food and drink, clothes and (wash)cloth if God did not protect both him and us.[64]

'The terrible illness', too terrible to be named, is syphilis. According to the missionaries, the Malagasy are 'imbued' with this terrible ill-ness on account of their promiscuity (i.e., immorality). Again and again, they complain that sin against the sixth commandment was the most frequent reason for church discipline; one missionary claimed this was the Malagasy people's 'Sisyfus' stone', which prevented them from developing into mature Christians.[65] In the missionaries' eyes, the prevalence of the disease demonstrated the need for their work in Madagascar, but its sexual overtones also added to the secrecy and fears. While unmarried missionaries' sexuality (i.e., their bodily boundaries) was strongly monitored through rules and prohibitions, married missionaries' sexuality, including related issues like preg-nancy, was surrounded by silence. As the Norwegian wife was there

---

[63] Mary Douglas, *Purity and Danger* (London and New York [1966] 1989).
[64] Lina Haslund to her mother, Ambohimahamasina 8 July 1878.
[65] NMS/Hjemme/Box 138/Jacket 5/Egenæs, Ambohimasina 22 Jan 1888.

to take care of all her husband's needs, the house world was expected to protect against syphilis.

Like AIDS in the twentieth century, syphilis led to a more general fear of bodily contact with Malagasy people. The missionaries' children, characteristically another marginal group, were thought to be especially vulnerable.[66] Lina refers to stories circulating among the wives of how Mrs. Egenæs became suspicious of 'their trusted and much beloved nursemaid', 'whom they had thought free of the illness'. Upon demanding to 'see her underneath from top down', she had turned out to have 'the worst sores and abscesses that could be imagined'. It was 'a miracle' that the child had not been infected by the nursemaid 'he had loved so much'. Mrs. Egenæs had stated that, from that day on, no girl would come into their service before she personally had examined them (*beseet dem*) stipped top down.[67] Such stories no doubt served to reinforce existing fears and suspicions. Missionary wife Agnethe Lindøe, Lina reports, was convinced that 'if the Lord had not protected us', they all would easily have been infected through the water scoop in the kitchen from which 'so many kinds of people, who (. . .) come in there, drink'. ('This is difficult to prevent, since we are not always present ourselves.') 'I daily pray the Lord to protect us from all the harm and danger which especially in times like these surround us; and you must do the same for us', Lina's letter to her mother continues.

The Norwegian missionaries' discourse on the supposed promiscuity of the Malagasy was partly carried out as a discourse on the Malagasy house: things were bound to go wrong when animals, men, women and children were crowded together in one room for the night.[68] At the same time, the Norwegian missionaries felt able to evaluate peoples' spiritual condition by the cleanliness of their houses,

---

[66] Growing up with Malagasy nursemaids and playmates, the missionaries' children quickly learned the language and customs. This made some parents fear that, despite their efforts to raise them as 'Norwegians', 'the Malagasy air' would 'permanently damage' the childrens' minds, unless they 'were torn away in time from the Malagasy soil' (Christian Haslund to his father-in-law, 14 April 1885; NMS/Hjemme/Box 137/Jacket 15/Selmer, Soraka 12 Sept 1887). Notions that children were more susceptible to tropical disease, and by extension, to social contamination, seem to have been widespread among European colonialists (Ann Laura Stoler, 'Rethinking Colonial Categories: European Communities and the Boundaries of Rule', *Society for Comparative Study of Society and History*, 31 (1989), pp. 149–150).

[67] Lina Haslund to her mother, Ambohimahamasina 8 July 1878.

[68] NMS/Hjemme/Box 132/Jacket 3/Egenæs, Ambohimasina 16 Sept 1870.

their bodies, and their clothes. Thus, the missionaries thought that their presence had had a good side effect when greater quantities of soap were sold at the markets and when Malagasy began to build houses with more than one room.[69] Yet while they wanted the Malagasy to copy the basic structure of the mission station, especially when building substations,[70] it is unclear to what extent they were meant to copy its size and standard. Too big a house with too many commodities was not a good thing, especially not for a Malagasy Christian.[71] The Malagasy are so preoccupied with the material, the missionaries frequently complain, if only they could be as interested in the spiritual.

At the same time, there was always the danger that the Malagasy world might impinge upon the Norwegian missionaries themselves. Upon staying the night in a colleague's home, Olsen remarks that the housekeeping appeared to be 'less soigné', and in another reference to the same couple, that they had become somewhat 'barbarized'.[72] Such developments threatened to reverse the missionaries' imagery of evangelization as a one way process in which they would bring enlightenment to Malagasy people. Thus, Lina's obsession with cleanliness can be seen as a double boundary marker, both marking the moral difference between the mission station and the Malagasy world beyond, and proving that she and her family were able to resist the latter's barbarizing influence.

Yet no matter what the missionaries did to protect their world from its surroundings, the invisible yet omnipresent malaria or 'Malagasy fever' seeped in. The uneasy security of the house set high on the hill became claustrophobic as the fever penetrated its solid walls, infecting the inhabitants, one after the other, with its burning poison. Occasionally the fever held the missionaries hostages in their bedrooms for weeks. It is heartbreaking to read Lina's letters on this subject. Initially, both she and Christian hope that children are less susceptible to the fever than adults, only to recognize the symptoms of malaria in their ailing child. Thinking that fever could be transmitted through breast-feeding, Lina weaned their baby son, only to find him burning with the 'evil' fever the moment he was weaned.

[69] NMS/Hjemme/Box 134/Jacket 2/Egenæs, Ambohimasina 15 March 1876.
[70] NMS/Hjemme/Box 137/Jacket 5/Haslund, Tsaraindrana 16 Feb 1886.
[71] NMS/Diary/Olsen/Book 4, Friday 5 Oct 1894.
[72] NMS/Diary/Olsen/Book 1, 19 Aug 1891; NMS/Diary/Olsen/Book 4, 22 April 1895.

On some of the mission stations so many fell seriously ill or died
from fever that the station was judged 'unhealthy'.[73] Certain missionaries thought that, once the fever 'got in them', it would return
at regular intervals. Others claimed to have developed a resistance
after extended exposure, implying that the experienced missionary
was less susceptible to the fever than a recently arrived one.[74]

Relationships Between Houses

Apart from the domestic servants, the only room in the mission station where Malagasy people were let in on a regular basis was the
missionary's office. The office belonged to the 'outside', to 'real missionary work'. While many Norwegian missionaries learned to cher-
ish and deeply respect many of their Malagasy pastors and teachers,
they appear never to have moved freely in and out of each other's
homes.[75] On the rare occasions when trusted Malagasy co-workers
penetrated further, this is mentioned in the missionaries' letters as if
it were the exception rather than the rule. Lina Haslund once tells
how one of Christian's trusted co-workers comes into the bedroom
to pray for him during a severe fever attack.[76] Another missionary
records how he and his wife have made it an annual event to invite
the newly examined graduates of the seminary at Ivory, Fianarantsoa,
into their house. For this one evening, they remove all chairs and
tables, and 'according to the good custom of the countryside', enjoy
a typical Malagasy meal of rice and meat, sitting on mats laid upon
the floor.[77] Rather than invite the students into their Norwegian
world, the missionary couple convert their living room into a 'Mala-

---

[73] Five Norwegians died on Fianarantsoa mission station within a year, three of
them children (NMS/Hjemme/Box 39A/Jacket 4/Johnson, Fianarantsoa 15 Jan
1897). Fever also haunted the new mission station in Morondava (NMS/Hjemme/Box
135B/Jacket 7/Jakobsen, Fianarantsoa 9 Sept 1882).

[74] NMS/Hjemme/Box 140B/Jacket 14/Thorbjørnsen, Mananjara 8 June 1897.

[75] The batchelor Nilsen-Lund may have been an exception. Nursed by 'the
Christians' when ill (NMS/Hjemme/Box 140A/Jacket 19/Nilsen-Lund, Ambato-
finandrahana 15 July 1894), he also, apparently as a matter of course, invites a
total stranger, a Bara, to stay the night in his house (NMS/Hjemme/Box 140B/
Jacket 18).

[76] Extracts of Lina Haslund's private letter to her parents reprinted in NMT. 18
Sept 1886, pp. 351–360, 352.

[77] NMS/Hjemme/Box 38/Jacket 9/Jakobsen, Fianarantsoa 14 March 1895.

gasy' world, legitimizing this by observing that countryfolk in Norway also sometimes sit on the floor.

Equal to this strong opposition between 'the Norwegians' and 'the Malagasy' is the connection *between* the worlds of the Norwegian mission stations. Lina's most highly cherished social contact was with fellow missionary wives. Almost unanimously, if in different ways, she and the missionaries underline the close and good relationships between the Norwegians, who go freely in and out of each other's houses, almost as if they belonged to one big family. Missionary wives 'were with each other all without distinction, as if they were home in their own house (. . .) just like sisters'.[78] The male missionaries consistently used sibling terminology to refer to each other: 'Brother Johnson', 'Brother Valen', etc. Religious differences among the Norwegians must have appeared minor relative to those that came between the Norwegians and the Malagasy or missionaries of other denominations and nationalities. Yet the combination of the sibling terminology *with* the family name also spells out the createdness of this closeness, and suggests hidden tensions in this egalitarian community based on Christian brotherly love.

Outside the Mission Station

While the missionary wife 'held the fort' in the relatively safe, clean and ordered world of the mission station, the male missionary moved away from the house in order to carry out 'the real missionary task' in the Malagasy world 'outside'. This 'real missionary work' is often depicted by the missionaries as a kind of *spiritual* trial. It is not immediately evident, however, in what sense this was so. Judging from the missionaries' own descriptions, daily missionary work was highly corporeal and to some extent tediously routinized.

Within a few years of starting up, the typical Norwegian missionary in the highlands ran a large parish from his mission station. He was more or less constantly on the move about the district, teaching and preaching in the villages and negotiating permission from local authorities to create congregations and schools. As these grew in number, he would supervise and lead various kinds of construction

---

[78] Lina Haslund to her mother, Alakamisy 1 Nov 1876.

work. In addition, houses for Malagasy mission workers had to be
built around the station district; assembly houses were erected by
the local people as part of their *fanompoana*, their duty to work without pay for the Merina queen. The missionaries also taught children
and adults how to read and write; literacy, together with some knowledge of the Lutheran dogmas, was usually a prerequisite for baptism. As the work expanded, the missionaries would spend several
days a week educating their Malagasy teachers, evangelists and
pastors, and travelling about the district to supervise their work.
Thus, before long most Norwegian missionaries in the highlands
were primarily dealing with converts and school children (along with
local leaders and state officials), rather than the Malagasy population at large.

At first, however, the missionary had contact with all kinds of
people. On long journeys he would spend the night in Malagasy
homes, although his hosts would usually sleep elsewhere. In any case,
he always brought a portable bed and linen, sometimes also food,
so that, even as a visitor in Malagasy people's homes, he tried to
be self sufficient and adjusted the surroundings to suit his own requirements.

The missionaries recognised only a small proportion of the work
they did as 'real missionary work'. Construction work and dealing
with Malagasy officials, for example, was considered 'external' (*ydre*)
or 'indirect' work. Although necessary, it was not seen as part of the
'real task' (*den egentlige Gjerning*) of speaking and teaching 'the Word'.
Teaching Malagasy children and baptismal candidates to read and
write was part of the 'real' task because as Lutherans the Norwegian
missionaries believed each individual should have direct access to the
word of God. Teaching the Malagasy to sing Christian hymns also
counted as 'real' missionary work, while seeing the sick and distributing medicines was 'indirect' work, unless the missionary had been
sent out to work as a doctor. It is clear from their reports that 'external' work preoccupied the missionaries as much as 'real' work, and
that at least some of them found this frustrating. During the initial
phases of starting up missionary work in a place, almost all their
time would be spent on 'indirect' tasks.

The manifest corporeality of their work posed theological difficulties
for the missionaries. They recognised that investment of resources
in the visible organization of God's kingdom in Madagascar was
both necessary and worthwhile. Indeed, we could say that they sought

to reach the 'invisible', Malagasy people's hearts and minds, by creating a visible infrastructure of dwellings, churches, and schools in which they could teach and preach 'the Word'. But in the end what really counted was the individual's inner state. Thus, while the missionaries could not help but constantly look for 'external' signs of spiritual transformation in their Malagasy converts, they always mistrusted what they saw.

This tension can be illustrated through the kinds of complaints missionaries made about Malagasy converts. The missionaries believed that a moral Christian life followed from a true inner conversion. Yet in practice they found that Malagasy converts had to be *taught* Christian moral behavior, ranging from which 'Pagan' rituals and customs they should not observe, 'how Christians mourn', to codes of dress and cleanliness. Time and again, the missionaries report baptizing candidates who had shown clear signs of having grasped the eternal truths, only to be disappointed to find that these individuals did not grow as Christian moral beings in the ways the missionaries had expected. Missionaries were uncertain whether this meant that the conversion had not been 'of God' in the first place or whether a tender plant had been subsequently corrupted by the unfavourable Malagasy environment.

In this sense, the missionaries' intense efforts in the work of visible construction were constant reminders to them of their own inadequacy. Regardless of the number of churches and schools they built, or the size of the congregations they drew, God's kingdom would be built in Madagascar only to the extent that it was built in Malagasy peoples' souls. The missionaries felt strongly that whatever they did, their efforts were fundamentally inadequate because the 'real' work was done by God.[79] Only He could make 'the Word' germinate and grow in peoples' souls.

Yet in another sense it was by living their *inadequacy* to the task that the missionaries' work became 'real missionary work'. Fever and other hardships were systematically interpreted as God's way of testing the sincerity of their 'calling' and of moulding them into vessels of his divine agency. By revealing their inadequacy, God demonstrated that human vessels, although important, were not irreplaceable.

---

[79] While protests of inadequacy were 'required' of missionaries as expressions of piety, a reading of their letters suggests that it would be wrong to dismiss these simply as rhetoric.

Thus, in the last instance, the 'spiritual trial' that the missionary underwent in the world 'outside' the mission station can be read as a constant battle for his *own* salvation rather than a battle for Malagasy souls.[80]

Inside and Out

I have indicated how the basic values and cultural schema exposed in the Norwegian mission station corresponded to Norwegian middle class values, but that this was not the home background of the majority of the Norwegian missionaries. For most male missionaries, the lived world of the mission stations scattered in the Malagasy landscape continued a process of social elevation which the missionary school education had begun.

Likewise, the Norwegian culture created on and between these stations was not simply a mirror image of Norwegian culture in Norway. The missionaries always referred to Norway as 'home' and to Madagascar as 'out here'. Yet, after a while they had to create their 'Norwegianness' from a collective nostalgia for a beloved and distant homeland. Creating and maintaining a 'Norwegian' environment required considerable effort, and this was effort invested in *material* things (furniture, decoration, dress and food). Moreover, Norwegian culture recreated on the mission stations in Madagascar came to mean something different than it did in Norway,[81] because, as with the Kabyle house, the meaning and values of the mission station were created partly through a dynamic interaction between the 'inside' and the 'outside'. This explains how missionaries might well return to Norway as strangers, despite having lived like 'Norwegians' in Madagascar for one or more decades.

The same material symbols that created and sustained their identity both as individuals and as a group also separated the missionaries from the Malagasy. Defining the 'Malagasy' as unclean,

---

[80] When Maurice Bloch first suggested this idea to me, I dismissed it as unlikely since my understanding was that missionaries worked first and foremost for the salvation of others.

[81] Stoler calls colonial cultures 'unique cultural configurations' and 'homespun creations' ('Rethinking Colonial Categories', pp. 136–137). The manioc waffles brilliantly catch this hybridity. In Madagascar the missionaries would eat manioc *waffles* and remember the taste of waffles in Norway. Back in Norway, however, at least some would eat waffles and become nostalgic for *manioc* waffles.

promiscuous (i.e. immoral), and bearers of contagious illnesses helped to connect the Norwegian missionaries together. Racial differentiation did more than simply 'fix and naturalize the differences between We and They'; it was also 'part of how people identify the affinities that they share'.[82] That these racial divisions became sharper once the missionary married does not necessarily mean that the Norwegian women were more racist than their men. For other colonial contexts it has been argued the presence of European women often 'justified policies already in motion to tighten the European community, and to control those European men who blurred the naturalized categories'.[83] In fact, just after the turn of the century, one Norwegian missionary requested but was refused permission to marry a Malagasy woman. He was not allowed to return to Madagascar until he had married a Norwegian woman.[84]

The main reason missionaries gave for not living in 'Malagasy houses' was that they needed 'proper dwellings' in order to maintain their long term 'health'.[85] Reading the missionary wife's letters, however, it is clear that avoiding sickness meant maintaining boundaries between the Norwegian world inside the mission station and the Malagasy world outside in the broadest sense. In order to fulfill their calling, the missionaries needed to maintain the *social* person that had left Norway.[86] A 'proper dwelling' provided a prime locus for the reproduction of the values and principles that were fundamental to the missionary and to missionary work. The culture was literally 'in the walls' of the mission stations. Newly arrived missionaries were silently and invisibly enculturated into the axioms of the missionary world in Madagascar as they took over the station from experienced ones.

Maintaining an ever present connection with Norway through their houses became vital to their work of preaching the word of God in Madagascar because it gave the missionaries a measure against which

---

[82] Stoler, 'Rethinking Colonial Categories', pp. 134–161.

[83] Stoler, *ibid.*, p. 148.

[84] Line Nyhagen Predelli, personal communication.

[85] NMS/Hjemme/Box 133/Jacket 8/Walen, Tulear 11 June 1875; Box 133/Jacket 8/Jakobsen, Ranompasy 22 Sept 1875; Box 134/Jacket 1/Lindo, Ranompasy 13 Nov 1875; Box 134/Jacket 2/Minsaas, Fihasinana 27 Jan 1876; Box 138/Jacket 13/Gahre, Ihosy 31 Oct 1889.

[86] For a telling example of what happened when missionaries failed to establish boundaries, see NMS/Hjemme/Box 140A/Jacket 17/Bjernæs, no place, no date.

they could guarantee the Gospel as an eternal truth. Thus, the movement *outwards*, initially from Norway to Madagascar and then from
the mission station to missionize in the world beyond, which pre-
dominated in the missionaries' imagery of their work, coexisted with
an *inward* movement as missionaries sought protection in the bounded
world of the missionary house.

This raises the question of whether and to what extent the missionaries' own religion was changed through its encounter with Malagasy culture, perhaps just as the 'Norwegian' culture they recreated
in Madagascar became different from Norwegian culture in Norway.
Certainly, the relationship between the internal and the external,
largely taken for granted in a Christian country, became more problematic for the missionaries. To what extent these difficulties revealed
underlying and unresolved tensions in their own religiosity, and to
what extent they were inherent in the process of translating Lutheran
precepts and practice into Malagasy socio-cultural contexts is difficult
to say. Arguably, the greater importance of 'doing' corresponded to
'Malagasy' understandings of religiosity.

I have alluded to how attractive the mission station must have
been to Malagasy people as the embodiment of rank and material
prosperity, not least through its connection with *andriana*. That most
Malagasy people never saw the interior of the mission station probably did not prevent them from imagining the commodities inside;
besides, the domestic servants no doubt carried away stories of what
was there. In any case, the connection between missionaries and
money was both immediate and direct. Raison-Jourde has argued
that the LMS missionaries' extensive building work, and their willingness and ability to pay the rising costs of labour and materials,
directly contributed to a massive inflation between 1873 and 1875.
In this way, Christianity or 'the worship', as embodied by the missionaries, came at least partly to be associated with material prosperity and wealth. No wonder, then, that many Malagasy approached
the Norwegian missionaries to ask for monetary and other material
contributions, only to be reproached for having failed to grasp the
true meaning of the Gospel and for valuing the material over the
spiritual.

Despite the striking materiality of life on the mission station, the
missionaries did not see themselves as either rich or immersed in
material things. The clear primacy given to the spiritual and internal over the material and external in their religion made the lived

world of the station 'invisible' to them. Although missionary work often turned out to be highly corporeal, these aspects were always subordinated ideologically to the 'direct' task of preaching the holy word of God. Indeed, it was precisely because the missionaries needed to create and maintain a picture of themselves as preoccupied with 'the spiritual' that the materiality of the lived world of the house had to be made invisible. Yet in another sense, the materiality of the house world played a key role in transforming the missionaries' daily toil into 'real mission work'.

This hierarchical logic in turn had gendered implications. So long as the house and the world outside were clearly separated, the missionary could class the highly corporeal and material aspects of the mission station as his wife's business, thus reinforcing the imagery of himself as preoccupied with 'the real missionary work'. The more visible the task, the less important it was held to be. Just as the lived world of the station was made invisible to the missionary, so too the key role of his wife in the missionizing enterprise was overlooked.

Yet placing the mission stations in the Malagasy landscape inevitably entangled them and their inhabitants in a web of meanings far beyond what the missionaries had intended, let alone could control. For example, missionary work often involved breaking sacred taboos stemming from the ancestors and from the past. The house on the hill and the missionary's presence could therefore be harbingers of misfortune and sickness for the Malagasy—as Haslund's first station at Ambohimahamasina, built on a desacrated ancestral place, indeed turned out to be. Within three years of his triumphal destruction of the sacrificial stake, the mission station and the Malagasy houses around it lay abandoned. In 1879 the area had been stricken by a fever epidemic, and people died in thousands. Lina and Christian Haslund barely survived, but had to bury their two small children by the station. Many Malagasy people no doubt interpreted this as a manifestation of ancestral wrath.

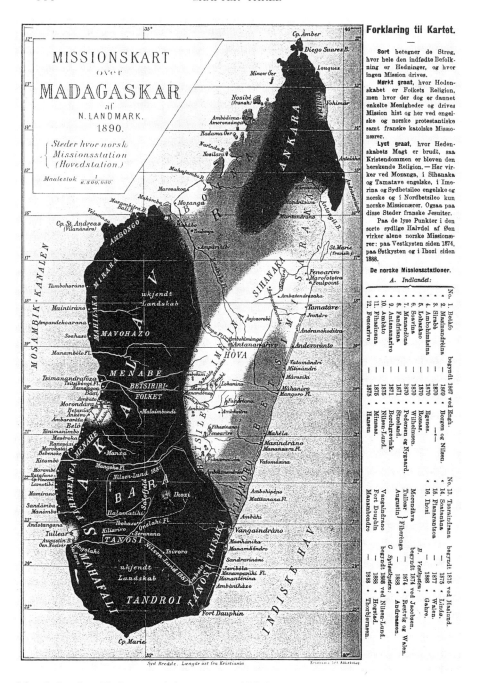

Map 2. Landmark's famous missionary map of Madagascar, 1890. The bright areas indicate geographical areas 'where the mission had been successful'. The dark areas indicate 'Pagan areas'. The map proved to be very persuasive in gaining support in Norway for the mission cause. Source: *Det Norske Misjonsselskap 1842–1942*. Vol. IV. (Stavanger 1949), p. 144. NMS Archives.

Plate 2. Betafo Mission Station, 1893. Photo: Johan Smith. NMS Archives. Pictures of NMS mission stations in Madagascar featured in the missionary magazines published in Norway rather more often than pictures of Malagasy people or scenes from everyday Madagasy life. As 'material proof' of the presence of the NMS in Madagascar, these images were very powerful in recruiting support for the movement back home.

Plate 3. Missionary Rosaas' livingroom, Antsirabe Mission Station, 1903. NMS Archives.

CHAPTER FOUR

ROYAL DIFFICULTIES:
THE ANXIETIES OF SUCCESSION IN AN
URBANIZED SAKALAVA KINGDOM*

LESLEY A. SHARP

I. *Introduction*

Overview

At the far western end of the beach at Ankify in northern Madagascar
stands an imposing structure: resting upon a concrete platform as
high as a man's chest is a large, two story, rectangular building. It
is oriented, lengthwise, from east to west, with two main entrances,
one facing north, the other south. Its exterior has been freshly painted
a brilliant white, and the tall windows and doors that line each floor
are protected by hinged wooden shutters tinted a pale blue. Its roof
is peaked and colored a deep brick red. Three tall, rounded doorways mark the northern entrance; from here, four steps lead down

* *Acknowledgments*: This newer version of this article integrates a few revisions
deemed necessary in response to political shifts that have occurred at the national
level since the article first appeared in 1997. I wish to thank the following people for
their comments and helpful suggestions at various phases of this project: in Madagascar, Maman'i'-Franck, the Ralaizonias, 'Arab,' Jean-Baptiste and his wife, Mme.
Fatima Ashimo and M. Cassam Ali, the Ely Hoafys, Mr. Said Mohamed, Mr. Claude
and his staff and, of course, Tsiaraso Victor III and his wife, and Tsiaraso Rachidy
IV; in the United States and Europe, N. Rothschild, S. Gravronsky, S. Kenyon,
K. Middleton, H. and C. Rideout, L. Gezon, F. Raison-Jourde, M. Mbodj, and my
colleagues in the Columbia Seminar on Identities, Representation, and Institutions.
  The data reported here were collected during three seasons of research in
Madagascar, spanning the (northern) summer months of 1993, 1994, and 1995,
building on earlier research in 1987. An association with L'Institut des Civilizations,
under the helpful guidance and direction of its Director, Jean-Aimé Rakotoarisoa,
made this research both possible and enjoyable. Funding was generously provided
by the American Philosophical Society, an Academic Grant from Butler University
and a grant from the Joint Committee on African Studies of the Social Science
Research Council and the American Council of Learned Societies with funds from
the National Endowment for the Humanities and the Ford Foundation. This article
is dedicated to the memory of Andriamanaitriarivo—*izaho koa nanaitry be; misaotra
zanahary sy dadilahy.*

to a small, free-standing arch a few meters away. It, too, is painted white; drawn in red upon its crest is a small star nested within a crescent moon, which together form a prominent symbol of the local Bemazava-Sakalava dynasty.[1] A red inscription frames this symbol. Written in French, it reads: 'Palais Royal,' or the 'Royal Palace.'

If one stands before the northern entrance one may gaze out upon the Indian Ocean, through a throng of small, stilted one- and two-roomed dwellings of *ravinala* palm, as well as coconut trees, slender outrigger canoes, and one or two larger fishing boats. Beyond the beach lies the grand offshore island of Nosy Komba; in the distance can be glimpsed another named Nosy Be. Making an about-face, the observer may then look beyond the building's dark interior and through two southern doors to see a simple, yet elegant, privately-owned seaside villa nestled beneath a forested cliff side, and another even larger one perched above.

The Palais Royal has been standing for only a little over seven years. Although it is decorated in the royal colors of red and white, and is roughly oriented northeast in order to face the sacred direction of the ancestors, this structure is, nevertheless, in many ways a cultural anomaly. For one, it breaks serious local taboos (*fady*), since it has been placed deliberately upon the ruins of a former ruler's palace. Furthermore, its architectural design bears little resemblance to other Sakalava royal dwellings, so that it more closely resembles a colonial office building than a ruler's home. The village at Ankify beach is also known as 'Andoany,' indicating it is a seat of royal power, yet the building itself is seldom referred to in Sakalava as the *doany* ('royal compound') or even *zomba* ('royal residence').[2] Instead,

---

[1] The ethnographic present here is late 1996. The Sakalava are the fifth largest sub-group of Malagasy speakers, their territory encompassing most of Madagascar's western coastline. The oldest Sakalava dynasties in the south have been documented as far back as the sixteenth century; in response to disputes over succession new dynasties moved progressively northward. This article focuses on the newest and most northern of these kingdoms, the Bemazava. For the sake of clarity, throughout this article I will use the term *Bemazava* to refer specifically to the kingdom that is based in Ankify, the town of Ambanja, and the surrounding Sambirano Valley. *Sakalava*, on the other hand, will be applied as a general term of ethnic affiliation for the people of the west coast.

[2] More specifically, *zomba* refers to the actual royal residence, whereas *doany* refers to the residence or palace as well as the surrounding households of royal guardians. These terms are applied in different ways throughout Sakalava territory (see, for example, Feeley-Harnik 1991: 595). As will be made clear below, today, in northern Bemazava territory, the *zomba* is located in the heart of the town of Ambanja, whereas the remnants of older *doany* are over fifteen kilometers away at Ankify.

the French name of 'Palais Royal' is the favored referent. And, oddly, as the careful observer will notice, the full color scheme of the building—blue, white, and red—is reminiscent of a foreign rather than simply Sakalava royal power, for these are the colors of the flag of France. Finally, regardless of its name, the Palais Royal shows little evidence of being inhabited. The current ruler, Tsiaraso Rachidy IV (r. 1993–), holds exclusive rights to its use, although he only occasionally enters it. When he wishes to enjoy the seaside, he stays next door at his cousin's comfortably furnished villa. Currently, the vacant Palais Royal is used as a dance hall for seasonal *bals* or discos.

This Palace defies a host of rules or 'customs' (*fomba*) and 'taboos' (*fady*) that guide royal action in Sakalava territory throughout western Madagascar. For example, strong prohibitions prevent a ruler from reconstructing, inhabiting, and even entering a predecessor's residence, for it is considered tainted by death and thus 'dirty' (*maloto*) or polluting to the royal body. Tsiaraso Victor III (Andriamanaitriarivo, r. 1966–1993),[3] the father of the current ruler, rebuilt the Palais Royal in 1989, yet he never stepped foot inside, preferring to rest in a simple and understated thatched *doany*, a dwelling that is smaller than many neighboring houses inhabited by local villagers. Nor during his reign did any other royalty ever attempt to sleep in the Palais Royal, fearful of the *lolo* or displaced spirits of the dead who might lurk within. Upon the instatement of this late king's son and successor, however, these fears appear to have been

---

Today only royal guardians and loyal Sakalava subjects live full-time at Ankify (Andoany). A third settlement of importance is the *mahabo* or royal tomb compound and its associated village. For the Bemazava, this is located on the smaller island of Nosy Faly.

[3] All deceased Sakalava rulers have at least two names. The first is the one they bear throughout their reigns. It is taboo (*fady*) to utter these names after rulers die (*mihilaña*, lit. 'turned their backs'). At this point rulers are assigned praise names (*fitahiaña*, from *mitaha*, 'to protect' [see Baré 1980: 290]) which make note of events or achievements that characterized their lives. As Feeley-Harnik notes, the Bemazava are 'proud of their liberal attitudes that relate not only to the birth and elaboration of royal lines, but also to the death of royalty' (1982: 36–7). For example, the Bemazava of the Sambirano apply these rules about naming very loosely, for they continue to utter living names of rulers after their deaths (albeit with lowered voices). Since praise names can be long and cumbersome for non-Malagasy speakers, I have chosen to follow contemporary custom, so that in most cases I use the living names of rulers. The one exception here is the founding ancestor, Andriantompoeniarivo, who is referred to solely by his praise name. The first time a ruler's name appears in the text it is cited as follows: living name (praise name; years reigned). The significance of some praise names will be made clear below. See chart following this article for a display of the Bemazava dynasty.

dispelled. Tsiaraso Rachidy IV and other royalty now hope to fur-
nish this Palace in grand style so that they may use it as their guest
quarters when they wish to vacation by the sea.

One is immediately inclined to interpret such unorthodox use of
royal space as evidence of the ongoing secularization of the sacred
in yet one more non-western society. As such, the developments
surrounding the Palais Royal mark the final demise of local culture;
or, if put in Sakalava terms, they sadly herald 'the loss of royal traditions' (*very ny fomba ny ampanjaka*) or the 'forgetting of customs' (*man-
adino ny fomba*). Such interpretations portray the Bemazava as victims,
their lives shattered by sudden changes wrought by foreign contact,
conquest, and colonization (cf. Apter 1993: 111). In short, their culture has been so undermined as to render it hollow and nearly obso-
lete. Here, at Ankify, the rules of sacred space have succumbed to
a material hunger, where local royalty apparently prefer pop culture
and the seaside vacationing style of the élite to those older privileges
that characterized a kingdom of bygone days.

Yet such a stance is deeply flawed, for it relies heavily on a romanticized—and even fetishized—notion of the 'traditional.' Such assumptions about 'tradition' are limiting, because they outrule any possibility
for addressing the resiliency of culture, or, more specifically, of religious belief and practice. At the very least, this romanticized approach
presupposes a static, rather than dynamic, nature of culture; at
a more profound level, it denies any possibility for deliberate, collective acts of innovation. As such, the old anthropological concept
of 'social change' allows only for the passivity of its victims, since
the impact of foreign culture(s) is assumed far too great to resist or
overcome.

Alternative understandings are possible only through a reformu-
lation of the meaning of social change. Thus, at issue here is the
question of interpretation. As Feeley-Harnik (1984) has argued elsewhere, historically Sakalava have resorted to ritually innovative approaches in response to French encroachment on royal domains. In
turn, recent concern in anthropology and related social sciences with
the concept of modernity offers a helpful paradigm, since it allows
us to re-evaluate cultural responses to external hegemonies (Comaroff and Comaroff, eds. 1993; Pred and Watts 1992). For one, change
may also mean innovation: such innovations spring from deliberate
reflections upon the past, which often assume surprising and creative
forms. How, for example, do societies (re)evaluate their sense of who

they are in a world dominated by a globalized market, and where instantaneous images make their way from satellites to village television sets? In what ways might ritual form generate seemingly unusual responses that, by the very nature of their unorthodoxy, ensure the continuation of a cohesive—rather than shattered—sense of collective identity? It is these sorts of ironies and contradictions of modern life that must be examined more carefully.

In response, the events surrounding the (re-)building of the Palais Royal require re-evaluation. As will be argued below, these are creative and astonishing responses to the social relations that characterize modernity. In Bemazava territory, they include the force of colonial political systems; the influx of foreign capital; and subsequent local developments, such as urbanization, wage labor, altered understandings of local identity, and responses to the impact of the globalization of mass media. Ironically, in the case of the Palais Royal, an analysis of the events surrounding its initial building by one and subsequent reconstruction by two other Bemazava rulers reveals that what may first be viewed as the demise of 'traditional culture' is in fact evidence of paradoxical innovations. Such innovations reformulate—and thus preserve—the multiplicity of meanings assigned to local identity in a contemporary African kingdom within a larger nation-state.

Thus, how might we begin to address the contradictions that characterize radical ritual innovation in colonial and post-independence settings? What, more specifically, are the contemporary understandings of Bemazava royal power and succession in the 1990s? As will be shown, within this kingdom deliberate attempts are being made to circumvent, alter, and embellish displays of royal power. Crucial actors in this ongoing process include not only living royalty but also the dead, each of whom reshapes, through the power of memory, localized understandings of royal history. In this Bemazava kingdom, the waning and waxing of royal power over time arises in response to larger political agendas.

Royal Difficulties

The honoring of royalty and their ancestors lies at the heart of the historical construction of Sakalava collective identity (Feeley-Harnik 1984; Kent 1979, 1968; Sharp 1993). Sakalava do not, for example, practice the *famadihana* or reburial characteristic of Merina culture

so often considered typical of Malagasy cultures more generally
(Bloch 1994 [1971]; Graeber 1995). Rather, Sakalava reserve elaborate
funerary practices for their royalty (*ampanjaka*) and, more particularly,
for rulers (*ampanjakabe*). Much of royal ritual involves the active participation of both living and dead royalty, the latter represented in
mediums (*saha*) who temporarily embody spirits of royal dead (*tromba*).
Even ceremonies which focus on commoners' lives—such as post-
partum practices and circumcisions—mandate that appeals be made
to the royal *tromba* spirits. These spirits also guide, advise, or dictate
the actions of living rulers whose well-being, in turn, affects the lives
of all members of a royal domain.

When Bemazava speak of 'sacred things' (*raha masina*), especially
royal practices, they typically couch their descriptions in such terms
as '*sarotra, sarotrabe ny fomba ny ampanjaka*': that is, 'royal customs are
difficult, very difficult.' Today, in the northern kingdom of the
Bemazava, this expression conveys two meanings. First, it reflects
local concern that many of the customs have been 'forgotten' (*nanadino*)
or 'lost' (*very*), a development arising in response to complex historical factors that will be outlined below. To follow royal customs
today, even as an adult, may very well mean studying or 'learning'
(*mianatra*) them with care, and, in so doing, potentially making numerous—and often grievous—errors.[4]

Such forgetting is common in Ambanja, a booming migrant town
which is also the royal center for the northern Bemazava (see Map 3).
Ambanja is the urban capital of the Sambirano Valley, a fertile plantation region which attracts Malagasy speakers from a wide variety
of backgrounds. Migrants who wish to be incorporated into local
Bemazava culture do, indeed, devote much time and attention to
understanding and learning local *fomba* and *fady* (Sharp 1993). Each
time I visit Ambanja, inevitably someone (who may or may not be
of Bemazava descent) will tell me in private that they do not follow
the *ampanjaka* because the associated customs are far too difficult to
understand or master, but they will then proceed to provide me with
detailed descriptions of the very customs of which they claim ignorance. As their concern and guilt make clear, a localized understanding of 'difficulty' is paired with the inevitable force of forgetting,
two concepts which together define a process seen to endanger the

---

[4] Even experts on royal custom accidentally break taboos. One close friend, who
is a member of the royal family, was fined heavily by tomb guardians when she
forgot to remove her shoes when we entered their village.

future of Bemazava society, culture, and the continued practice of associated ritual forms.

Second, this notion of 'difficulty' encompasses older meanings as well, for it stresses the complexity of royal ritual, whereby ritual observance is the outward manifestation of one's respect for and unwavering devotion to royalty. As Feeley-Harnik's comprehensive work from the Analalava region illustrates, royal ancestors themselves are described as 'difficult things' (*raha sarotra*) whose demanding nature is akin to enslavement (1991: 56ff., 74ff.; 1982). Baré likewise translates *raha sarotro* as objects and actions whose very 'difficulty' renders them 'precious,' 'dear,' 'dangerous,' and 'forbidden' (1980: 241, 289). The quintessential expression of 'love' (*fitiavaña*) and, thus, devotion and loyalty, is manifested through the actions of those 'who work for royalty' (*ampanompo*) or who perform 'royal service' (*fanompoaña*). This social category includes commoners, royal retainers, and servants or slaves (*Sambarivo*).

When viewed from the outside—by anthropologists as well as other Sakalava-speakers living elsewhere on the island—currrent developments among the northern Bemazava are often viewed as vulgar or bastardized versions of sacred ritual. Rumors (and false claims) drive discussions on the Bemazava of the Sambirano who are accused, for example, of 'having no relics' (*tsy misy dady*).[5] As a result, members of other neighboring royal houses at times question in private whether this is in fact a legitimate dynasty.[6]

---

[5] One informant used this phrase to make a pun: although the Bemazava may have ancestral *tromba* spirits (also called *dady*) at the *mahabo*, he asserted that the kingdom itself has no relics or remains collected from the bodies of founding and subsequent ancestors. (Other terms for relics include *razaña* or 'ancestors' and, according to Baré [1980: 240–1], *mitaha*, because they 'heal.') There are, in fact, relics that are guarded with care at both the Bemazava *zomba* and *mahabo*. These include the clothing and other personal possessions of former rulers, as well as the *Vy Lava*, or 'Long Knife' (lit. 'Long Iron') which embodies royal power. It is also my understanding (as noted below) that during recent mortuary ceremonies relics were made from portions of the late ruler's body and have been put away for safe keeping. In fact, not all Sakalava have relics, either because they lost them to enemy forces or because it is not their practice to take them from the corpses of dead rulers (see Baré 1986: 385–6; 1980: 242; Feeley-Harnik 1991: 95ff. and 372, who in turn cites Poirier 1939). More generally, opinions regarding the absence of relics may be due in part to the fact that the Bemazava of the Sambirano do not host a large-scale and public *fitampoha* or 'royal bath' for their relics, as does, for example, the much older southern kingdom of Menabe (see Nérine Botokeky 1983, Chazan-Gillig 1983). This event has become such an important marker for Sakalava identity that it is regularly advertised on national television.

[6] The Bemazava, on the other hand, view themselves as ritually flexible. For example, if I express surprise when a ritual has strayed from orthodox form, I am

In this light, a simplistic argument would be to view the construction of the Palais Royal as yet further evidence of the destructive effects of, in the words of some of Ambanja's more conservative educated élite, '*les forces modernes.*' These forces are described locally as including conquest, urbanization, the in-migration of non-Sakalava, and subsequent *métisization*, all of which are seen ultimately as undermining a cherished sense of 'traditionalism.' As this article will show, however, a more complex, dialectical process is in fact at work in the minds of royalty, in particular involving, on the one hand, the pairing of such concepts as 'difficulty' and 'forgetting,' with, on the other, newer cultural innovations, where 'learning' works in tandem with older definitions of 'love.'[7]

As I will show, Bemazava royalty play, in a very deliberate fashion, with local and nationalized meanings of the modern. Together these shape an ever evolving Bemazava identity in the face of disruptive forces that characterize modernity in the late twentieth century. For the Bemazava themselves, the re-building by Tsiaraso Victor III and his son Tsiaraso Rachidy IV of the Palais Royal upon the ruins of Tsiaraso I's *doany* is hardly evidence of the abandonment of sacred custom. Rather, it embodies a serious revival of or embellishment upon the past which ensures the continuance of 'traditions' (*fomba*) in the future. To understand the legitimacy of such developments and their inherent contradictions it is necessary, first, to gaze back upon local history.

---

often told that 'anything can happen,' especially where royal spirits are involved. Bemazava also speak of themselves as 'modern' (using the French term *modern[e]*); this is a concept I will return to later. One informant, who is an older member of the royal lineage of Ambanja, described the Bemazava as being more 'modern' or contemporary in their outlook because they tend to name their rulers in succession as do Europeans (such as Tsiaraso I, II, III, IV), whereas their royal neighbors of Nosy Be are wed to more archaic names such as Binao and Amada.

[7] This pairing of love and loyalty is a pervasive theme in the history of Sakalava royal power. Being Sakalava, for example, expresses the willingness to subvert oneself to the ruler, and such an idea lies at the root of the establishment of the earliest Sakalava (Maroserana) dynasty (Kent 1979, 1968; Mellis 1938; Valette 1958). Feeley-Harnik also stresses the theme of love (*fitiavaña*) contrasting it to enslavement, where Sakalava are those who 'choose to settle around royalty' (1991: 74–5). The identity of other ethnic groups is shaped in part by their refusal to submit to Sakalava rule: the Vezo, for example, temporarily fled their territory (Astuti 1995: 475–477), as did the Tsimihety, who refused to cut their hair in defiance of older Sakalava royal mortuary rituals (Wilson 1992).

II. *The Local History of Sacred Royal Space*

Dynastic Foundations, the Tumultuous Reign of Tsiaraso I, and its Aftermath

The newly constructed Palais Royal in the village of Ankify is a curious symbol of royal power for the northern Bemazava. This dynasty was founded in the 1820s by Andriantompoeniarivo (r. 1820–1821), who left his original homeland (*tanindrazaña* or 'ancestral land') and moved north following a dispute over royal succession. This new dynasty was established in a large expanse of territory, encompassing the upper and lower Sambirano Valley, which extends approximately 70 kilometers inland from the sea. Bemazava territory also includes Nosy Faly, an offshore island located farther north, where Andriantompoeniarivo and all subsequent Bemazava royalty are entombed.

Within seventy years of its founding (and six rulers later), however, the Bemazava dynasty was severely curtailed by the direct imposition of French colonial power in the region. Although the French had been active in the region since the 1820s, they were primarily based on Nosy Be, which was formally annexed by France in 1840 (Baré 1986: 383ff.; Dalmond 1840; Gueunier 1991–2; Paillard 1983–4). They rarely ventured into the Sambirano, fearful of Bemazava warriors. In 1895, under the direction of General Galliéni, French forces swept through the Sambirano, and within a year Madagascar was declared a colony of France.

At this time the *doany* or residence of the current ruler, Tsiaraso (referred to today as Tsiaraso I or Andriamandilatrarivo, r. 1887–1919), stood at the shore of Ankify. Tsiaraso I began his reign around the age of sixteen; he was approximately twenty-four years old when French soldiers seized control of his kingdom. What ensued was what Baré has aptly termed 'une atmosphère de violence assez inconcevable' (1980: 72), involving the conversion of meaning and rights to ancestral land (*tanindrazaña*) that, within a decade, reduced a royal kingdom to a patchwork of large agricultural concessions. Initially, French soldiers were given plots of land as rewards for military service; when they failed at farming, foreign planters from Réunion and elsewhere quickly moved in and bought their fields. They successfully cultivated pepper, manioc and sugar cane on plantations they gave such names as 'Mon Plaisir,' 'Horace,' 'Bemazava,' and 'Les

Palmes' (Service Topographique n.d.). In terms of securing French
control of the region, perhaps the most important professionals to
follow the army were the surveyors, who assisted other foreigners in
staking claims on local sacred territory. In the words of Paillard
(1983–4: 366), 'la vallée du Sambirano était la région la plus me-
nacée par l'intrusion de la colonisation agricole,' for it was the site
of the largest privatization scheme in northern Madagascar. From
1894 to 1904, over 600,000 hectares[8] of land were alienated from
the Bemazava (Koerner 1968: 168, as cited in Baré 1980: 72).

We can only imagine the thoughts of Tsiaraso I as he faced the
ambiguities and frustrations that must have characterized his reign.
From contemporary descriptions he appears circumspect and difficult to read. In 1897 General Galliéni described him as 'apathetic'
(Paillard 1993–4: 366), a term that conveys, on the one hand, the
frustrations of a colonizer and, on the other, the seemingly passive
yet firm resistance of a reticent ruler. Throughout the north, small
units of soldiers were stationed next to or overlooking royal compounds. Within a year, the Sambirano was in turmoil, as was much
of the island. Colonial records remark that Tsiaraso I assisted the
French by supplying their army with porters to penetrate more isolated areas of the kingdom, yet he was simultaneously suspected of
clandestine relations with rebel forces. The Bemazava raided military posts, and at least a dozen French guards and colonists were
killed in October and November, 1898. Tsiaraso I and other local
rulers quickly became immediate suspects in these insurrections. When
a neighboring ruler, Tsialana of the Antankaraña, was imprisoned
for fifteen days, Tsiaraso I refused to follow any orders issued to
him by the local French commander, who in response mounted
charges against him (Baré 1980: 73–4; Paillard 1983–4: 366–7).[9]

---

[8] A hectare is equal to 2.47 acres.

[9] Tsiaraso I also escaped the fate of another ruler, who was exiled to Ile Sainte-
Marie on the east coast. The Frenchman who mounted charges against him was
named Martin, a man whose story is further complicated by his obsession with a
young woman of Tsiaraso's lineage. Martin forced her to leave her husband, work
for him like a slave, and he beat her when she did not follow his orders. The
woman eventually fell ill; according to Paillard this affected Tsiaraso's involvement
in the revolt (1983–4: 359, 366). This story corresponds closely to another told to
me in the Sambirano in 1987: A Frenchman, stationed at Ankify, was well known
for his brutality towards his royal wife. When he was seen striking her about the
head (which is sacred), several of her kinsmen banded together and killed him. This
led to more intense policing of Ankify by the French.

Eventually additional military power was needed. Fresh troops were brought in under Lieutenant-Colonel Prud'homme, who policed the Bemazava and neighboring kingdoms, sought out the leaders of local insurrections, and arrested and imprisoned suspected rebels. French troops included warriors who had been conscripted from one region of Madagascar and used to put down rebellions in others. Galliéni relied on these warriors as a source of powerful propaganda, counting on them to communicate the strength of French military power to their own rulers back home. With the Bemazava in particular, experiences during battles with their enemy the Merina were especially significant, since the responses of awe and fear of the French smoothed the way for rapid occupation of the Sambirano. By early November, Sénégalese troops, under Captain Laverdur, were also brought to the Sambirano from Mahajanga. They landed at Ankify and were stationed at various posts throughout the kingdom (Paillard 1983–4). Today in the Sambirano bitter memories of the French military are often linked to the sadistic acts of the Sénégalese, for these soldiers were forced to do much of the dirty work of French *pacification*.[10]

In 1900, when the French felt they had a firm hold in the north, Tsiaraso I and two other neighboring rulers were taken to Antananarivo by Prud'homme to proclaim publicly their loyalty to France (Baré 1980: 73–4). This experience must have been both humiliating and frightening. Antananarivo was, after all, not only the seat of French power, but also the royal capital of the Merina, the hated enemy of the northern Sakalava. According to Paillard (1983–4: 339), this visit marked a significant turning point in relations between the French and Bemazava royalty. Broken under the yoke of conquest, Paillard ironically refers to northern rulers as being nothing more than *roitelets* or 'petty kings' to whom the French delegated only such mundane tasks as taxation and the forced recruitment of soldiers and laborers (1983–4: 344, 345).

It is at this point that Tsiaraso I (like so many other rulers throughout the island) was granted the honorary yet hollow title of Gouverneur

---

[10] Interestingly, Malagasy (especially prisoners and madmen) were transported to Sénégal by the French. Thus, just as the term *Sénégal* is a derogatory term in Madagascar, likewise, to call someone 'Malagasy' is a great insult in Sénégal (M. Mbodj, personal communication, 4/95). Such repressive actions were repeated when Sénégalese *tirailleurs* were employed during the 1947 insurrection (Mannoni 1990 [1950] 89–93).

under the French, which he maintained until 1915, a few years before his death (see Raison-Jourde 1983, Plate 4). He was thus among the first of a long line of royal, indigenous civil servants (*fonctionnaires indigènes*) of the colonial regime, a system initiated by Galliéni himself and which was designed both to rein in rulers and, ultimately, undermine local political hierarchies (Baré 1980: 70–3).[11] The location of Ankify must have assisted in isolating Tsiaraso I and rendering him powerless to control the subsequent capitalist initiatives of the French, for Ankify is separated from the center of the Sambirano by several kilometers of mangrove swamps that flood regularly at high tide.

Upon the death of Tsiaraso I in 1919, his palace was abandoned, as dictated by Bemazava custom. This response is characteristic of Sakalava custom elsewhere, as described in Feeley-Harnik's studies of royal ritual and work in Analalava. As she explains, '. . . the fact that "the earth is filthy" or "the earth is hot" because a ruler has died is the recurrent reason for moving the royal capital to a new location' (1991: 73; for specific examples see pp. 134–143). To defy such sacred rules is to incite the wrath (*tigny*) of royal spirits (Baré 1980: 289ff.). Thus, the palace ruins symbolized several things: first, this sudden and deliberate abandonment marked the end of Tsiaraso I's reign. Near this site other palaces were subsequently built by his sister and successor, Tsiresy II (Nenimoana, 1919–1935),[12] and, later, by her nephew, Rachidy (Andriamamefiarivo, r. 1935–1945), who succeeded her in turn. Its demise also marked a more profound eclipsing of royal power by the French. By the 1920s, Andoany at Ankify was little more than an isolated royal village, the base of French power being situated in the heart of the region's plantations on a site which later grew to be the town of Ambanja.

------

[11] As Baré (1980: 74–75) notes, the French did not even necessarily grant these honorary titles to the reigning *ampanjakabe*. On Nosy Be, for example, they overlooked the ruling queen, Binao, and instead granted titles to her husband, half-brother, and first advisor or *manatany*. She later abandoned her *doany* to her half-brother when she was forced to take up residence in the French town of Hellville. As Feeley-Harnik explains, 'from the French point of view, sovereign women were a contradiction in terms' (1991: 95).

[12] For a compelling description from an informant who helped to build this queen's *doany* see Baré (1980: 289). While digging the foundation this man found a large braid of hair that he assumed to be the remains of a fallen warrior or looter. Baré equates this experience with the dangers associated with royal bodies (*raha sarotro*) and how they instill fear in the living.

The 1940s marked the further decline of Bemazava royalty, an era that also defines a significant chapter in the development of Malagasy nationalism. Young men, who had served as laborers and soldiers in World War II, returned from Europe with the awakened consciousness of the politically oppressed (among these was the young ruler Rachidy). In response, the French stepped up their surveillance efforts in the Sambirano. The new ruler, Tsiaraso II (Andriamande-fitriarivo, 1945–1966), was forced to abandon the palace *doany* at Ankify and relocate to the residence or *zomba* in Ambanja, where he could be kept under the watchful eye of the colonial adminis-trator whose residence was perched just above on a small yet imposing hill.[13] This became particularly important in 1947, when insurrec-tions spread throughout the island.[14]

In the years which followed, even harsher restrictions were imposed on the daily lives of the Bemazava. Bemazava viewed this forced and permanent relocation of their ruler as a significant defeat, for it virtually destroyed what little independence remained. By this time, living rulers were so undermined that, in the minds of the Bemazava, royal power shifted from living rulers to the royal ancestors or *tromba* spirits at Nosy Faly (cf. Feeley-Harnik 1984). Subjects of the king often were more willing to follow the mandates of these spirits or of other more charismatic living royalty.[15] Their disappointment with

---

[13] My informants are uncertain as to the exact date when Bemazava royalty were forced to relocate to Ambanja. In 1907 the French established a new military post, along with a prison and cemetery for whites, at what is now the center of the town of Ambanja. Informants say that as late as 1912 Tsiaraso I was still living in Ankify and, at times, in Ankatafa (Ankazotelo). Baré, in a footnote to the informant's description of the building of Tsiresy's palace, describes Ankify as the location '. . . qui servait de résidence royale aux aristocrates Benazava [sic.] avant leur instal-lation définitive à Ambanja et Ankatafa' (1980: 289). My own informants are cer-tain that by 1945 (if not earlier) the *ampanjakabe* was living full time in Ambanja.

[14] The year 1947 defines a recent and significant chapter in the history of Malagasy nationalism; for more details see Rajoelina (1988), Randrianja (1983), Thompson and Adloff (1965), and Tronchon (1982).

[15] Among the more distinctive individuals of this period was Said Achimo, who had been a rival of Tsiaraso II at the time of his instatement—and virtual appoint-ment—by the French. Although Said was himself a powerful player in the colonial hierarchy (he, rather than the ruler, was granted the now more powerful position of Governeur, for example) he failed to gain the position of ruler that he so cov-eted. (Some Bemazava opposed his appointment, arguing he was royal by virtue of his mother rather than his father.) Nevertheless, Said invested much of his wealth in the *mahabo* at Nosy Faly. Upon his death, the *tromba* spirits declared that he was to be entombed with the founding ancestor Andriantompoeniarivo, honoring him for all the work and effort he put into this sacred village and the royal tombs.

Tsiaraso II is reflected in his *filahiaña* or 'praise name' Andriaman-defitriarivo, which means 'The Ruler who was Tolerated by Many.' This name stands in stark contrast to those of other royalty: for example, Tsiaraso I is Andriamandilatrarivo, or 'The Ruler who was Honored by Many.'

When Tsiaraso II died in 1966, his *zomba* in Ambanja was not abandoned; rather, his son and successor, Tsiaraso Victor III, took up residence there as well. Elsewhere in Sakalava territory, this dis-regard for the polluting nature of the residence itself would be viewed as a serious breach of custom, for it would be tainted by the death of Tsiaraso II and therefore endanger the life of its next inhabitant. As the town of Ambanja grew, so did the *zomba*, so that today it is a modest yet well-built one story concrete structure located at the heart of town and next to the central market. Always under the watchful eye of local civil officials, the hillside directly above that housed French administrators has since served as the residence for town mayors and presidents of the county seat. At Ankify, the official *doany* was and continues to be a small two-roomed thatched house typical of those inhabited by the poorest of commoners in Ambanja. On the few occasions when Tsiaraso Victor III chose to visit Andoany, he generally either stayed here or else borrowed the key to an impos-ing villa owned by one of the town's richest plantation directors. When I first visited Ankify in 1987, evidence of the old *doany* of Tsiaraso I was barely visible, marked only by the traces of a weath-ered foundation and crumbled walls. Here, people rarely congre-gated; rather, lazy dogs sunned themselves, and goats and chickens wandered freely beside tethered, grazing zebu cattle.[16] It is upon this same site that the new Palais Royal now stands.

Tsiaraso Victor III: A Reluctant King

To understand how and why the Palais Royal came to be rebuilt, we must turn to the reign of Tsiaraso Victor III. This king's life was rife with contradictions, and is one that in many ways embodied the effects of colonial rule. Born in the middle of this century, he was

---

[16] According to L. Gezon (personal communication, 9/95), throughout this cen-tury the Antankaraña to the north likewise have not built new royal residences (*doany* or *zomba*) following the deaths of former rulers. Only one did so at the turn of the century, but he was involved in a dispute over succession. The current ruler's two residences, however, were required to be purified before he could inhabit them.

among a select group of young royalty enrolled at the Catholic mission school established in 1908 specifically for Malagasy children. When he grew older, he traveled far from home, receiving additional specialized training that prepared him for a lifetime career as a civil servant. In the course of his education he became the first Bemazava ruler to convert to Catholicism, thus abandoning Islam, the faith that, in the Sambirano, serves as a marker for Bemazava royal status.[17]

A kind and shy man, Tsiaraso Victor III reluctantly became king following the death of his father, Tsiaraso II, in 1966, only six years after Madagascar had gained its independence. He ruled for nearly thirty years, working simultaneously as a tax collector at the local county seat. On a daily basis he expressed discomfort in assuming the role of king, and was often visibly repulsed and embarrassed by subjects who would insist on sitting at his feet when they came to see him at his office. In response, he would gently but firmly send them home, for he was unwilling to draw on royal privilege except in the evenings and weekends when he was at home at the *zomba*. In response, other Bemazava often described him as a 'simple' and 'timid' man.

Over the course of his life, Tsiaraso Victor III was successively married to three women (the first and third unions were officially and ritually sanctioned marriages, whereas the second involved a short-term concubine). In all he fathered fifteen living offspring. He was never wealthy, often struggling to feed his children, for although rulers are entitled to collect gifts and wealth from their subjects, they are also expected to care for them when in need. Although his directives would be quickly followed by many Bemazava respectful of royal custom, he rarely issued orders of any import. In general he

---

[17] Bemazava have little difficulty remaining faithful simultaneously to Sakalava religion and the world faiths of Islam or Catholicism. This is in part a result of the tolerance exhibited locally by Muslim and Catholic clerics, as well as the flexibility of Bemazava culture. Here, religious integration is not necessarily syncretic, but rather is marked by the ability to maintain Islam and *tromba* spirit possession, for example, in separate realms of understanding and experience. As I have described elsewhere (Sharp 1994), this is not true of Protestant faiths, whose officiants work aggressively to undermine local beliefs that contradict Christian doctrine. For this reason, very few Bemazava in Ambanja have converted to Protestantism. Although Tsiaraso Victor III was Catholic, other members of the royal dynasty have remained Muslim; one informant, a Catholic priest, described Tsiaraso III and other Bemazava royalty as 'sympathetic Muslims,' who embrace the first pillar (*shahadah* or the declaration of faith) but who otherwise are uninvolved with the daily practice of Islam.

was not one to initiate ritual events. Instead, he relied upon the counsel of official advisors as well as royal kin. More outspoken and active neighboring royalty to the west, at Nosy Be, and to the north, among the Antankaraña, would speak of him with puzzled dismay.[18] An important question that arises, then, is what factors led this timid king to break among the most serious of local customs and build an opulent palace upon the ruins of a famous predecessor? More importantly, how do his subjects, the Bemazava of the Sambirano, justify—and survive—such a serious breach of custom? Answers to these questions lie in the historical developments that overshadowed his reign.

Parallel Histories

Oddly, in the realm of civic duty, Tsiaraso Victor III was more influential than his neighbors—and rivals—realize. As noted earlier, Ambanja is the urban center for a fertile region of Madagascar. Today it is flanked on all sides by expansive fields of cocoa, coffee, and ylang-ylang, and it is among the more affluent areas of the island. The region experienced sudden and rapid economic development under the French, so that by the 1920s much of the Sambirano Valley had been converted into large-scale plantations run by foreign-born planters. The life of Tsiaraso Victor III was shaped by these and subsequent events, for it spanned four epochs of Madagascar's history. In other words, his own personal tale evolved alongside the development of Madagascar as a colony and an independent nation.

Born during the colonial era, the reign of Tsiaraso Victor III began under the newly elected independent President Philibert Tsiranana. In the period now referred to as the First Republic, Tsiranana maintained close ties with France; today many Malagasy look back on these early years of nationhood with great nostalgia, remembering it as a time of plenty (Razafimandimby 1995). A decade later, however, Madagascar's citizens felt the isolation of a new African country delegated Third World status. A growing political awareness among the nation's educated youth led eventually to their open opposition to neo-colonial institutions, making way for the Socialist

---

[18] A striking contrast to Tsiaraso Victor III is offered, for example, by Tsimiaro III, the current ruler of the Antankaraña to the north, who has revived and embellished a host of ceremonies. One, the *Tsangan-tsaina*, drew an estimated crowd of 7,000 subjects when I was there in 1987.

Revolution of the 1970s. This marked the beginning of the Second Republic, a time of great political revision that included massive land reform, the shift to state capitalism, and the pairing of isolationism with efforts at self-sufficiency under its architect, Didier Ratsiraka. President Ratsiraka was deposed in the early 1990s, a movement instigated by educated youth and the nation's peasantry. His successor, President Zafy Albert of the Third Republic,[19] has once again re-embraced capitalism, opening Madagascar to foreign investment. To many his style was reminiscent of former President Tsiranana, for he realigned Madagascar with western nations, including its former colonizer, France.

As a Bemazava ruler whose reign fell in the wake of Independence, Tsiaraso Victor III could have exercised much power locally, particularly under President Ratsiraka's socialist administration. An important component of Ratsiraka's political philosophy of the 1970s and 1980s (as outlined in his treatise, the *Boky Mena* or 'Red Book' [Ratsiraka 1975]), was *malagasization*, a bureaucratized form of nationalism which advocated the rejection of French-derived structures in favor of indigenous culture(s). At the local level, this approach often bolstered the power of local rulers. Ambanja certainly witnessed a revival of local customs, many of which had been outlawed during the colonial era or regarded as backward under President Tsiranana. For example, with Tsiaraso Victor III as the conduit, the royal *tromba* spirits of Nosy Faly became key players who generated innovative responses to economic development in the region (see Sharp in press [a]; 1993: 165ff., 222ff.; 1990).

---

[19] Many Malagasy have only one official name (that is, they lack a surname separate from a first name). Naming can further confuse non-Malagasy speakers since an individual's name may change over the course of his or her lifetime. Thus, the current Bemazava ruler, Tsiaraso Rachidy IV, was known as Parfait before he became ruler; he now carries the name of his father (Tsiaraso) and his great-grandfather (Rachidy). Also of note is the common practice of listing one's surname before the first name (*prenom* in French); thus, this ruler is referred to as Tsiaraso Rachidy IV rather than Rachidy Tsiaraso IV. Madagascar's three presidents have opted for various systems: whereas Tsiranana and Ratsiraka show a preference for placing their *prenoms* first, Ratsiraka's successor begins his name with his surname, Zafy. Out of respect for these individuals' choices I have written their names as they themselves do.

Since the initial publication of this article, President Zafy has been voted out of office and replaced yet again by Ratsiraka, who was sworn in as President of the Fourth Republic in February, 1997. It is too early to know what the effects of his newly declared '*République Humaniste et Ecologique*' (P. Hanson, personal communication 5/97) will be upon royal power and action in the Sambirano.

Tsiaraso Victor III played the pawn to Ratsiraka's desperate attempts to be re-elected in the late 1980s. The latter made several personal visits to Ambanja, an important stronghold for Ratsiraka's political party, AREMA, and he viewed Tsiaraso Victor III as someone who could influence Bemazava voting patterns. As a reward for Tsiaraso Victor III's support and assistance in spreading political propaganda, Ratsiraka promised to finance two large-scale projects: the reconstruction of the Palais Royal at Ankify, and, later, the installation of a powerful television satellite antenna for the town (making it one of approximately 80 promised nationwide). Ratsiraka failed to win the necessary votes nationwide needed to ensure re-election; nevertheless, he carried through with his local promises, providing the funds for supplies and masons. The Palais Royal was built in 1989. Today it stands as a proud and imposing structure at Ankify. In addition, Ambanja's many television viewers are no longer linked to the distant capital of Antananarivo, but with, for example, the international broadcasts of France 2 and RFO. Thus, ironically, an unpredicted consequence of Tsiaraso Victor III's assumed passivity is that people in Ambanja are now better informed in foreign affairs than, perhaps, even the cosmopolitan élite who inhabit this nation's metropole. More importantly, the legacy of colonial intimidation ironically has made it possible for a supposedly weak king to allow for— if not actively encourage—innovative responses to forces that would otherwise threaten the viability of his kingdom. As with the increased power of the *tromba* mediums at Nosy Faly and the building of the satellite antenna, likewise the Palais Royal stands as a puzzling yet impressive innovative response to the impending pressures of modern life.

A Sudden, Unexpected Death

Tsiaraso Victor III fell ill at home on Wednesday, December 8, 1993. Finding it increasingly difficult to breathe, by that evening he was taken to the town's private Catholic clinic. By 9:00 p.m. he was dead, diagnosed with myocardial infarction. He was only in his midfifties. Because of the suddenness of his death, he was later given the praise name Andriamanaitriarivo, or 'The Ruler who Surprised Many.' The events which followed had a profound effect on how the Bemazava currently conceive of themselves. Among the most significant events were the mortuary rituals which followed, the subsequent instatement of his successor, and the on-going construction of the Palais Royal.

It is difficult to judge how Tsiaraso Victor III would have reacted to the events which followed his death, since he often shied away from royal ritual. It seems fitting that he died under the care of Catholic missionaries, the successors of earlier Jesuits who had schooled him during his youth. As soon as the news had reached the Bemazava that Tsiaraso Victor III had died or 'turned his back' (mihilaña),[20] preparations were made to house his body far from his royal residence. After spending a night in the home of a kinsman in town, his corpse was moved with care during the next night to the village of Ambalavelona.[21] This village lies at a crossroads a few kilometers from Ambanja, where turnoffs lead to Ankify to the west and north-ward to the royal tombs at Nosy Faly.

This marked the beginning of the nearly month-long period of royal funeral service (fanompoaña). Housed in a temporary structure known as the zomba vita,[22] the ruler's corpse was cared for by the Sambarivo, a caste of royal servants or slaves. With meticulous attention to the fomba and fady that shape royal mortuary practices, the Sambarivo kept watch day and night, observing specific duties assigned since birth. Here the conception of the 'difficulty' of royal work is readily apparent. Even in the often intense tropical heat, the Sambarivo must work slowly and delicately. They are forbidden from perspiring, and they may only describe the king's putrefying remains as 'sweetly fragrant' (mañitry). The body is allowed to rot away, the

[20] A highly specialized vocabulary surrounds Sakalava royal ritual: many terms applied to the actions of commoners are not only deemed inappropriate but fady or taboo for royalty. Thus, rulers are never described as 'dead' (maty); rather, they 'turn their backs' (mihilaña), a verb which implies that they are still here (for example, they eventually assume the form of tromba spirits but have averted their gaze).

[21] A location deemed more appropriate was the village of Ankatafa, which lies along the road to Nosy Faly. Tsiaraso Victor III died, however, during the rainy season, and the road to Ankatafa was impassable.

[22] Other authors writing on related Sakalava dynasties refer to this and related structures as the zomba vinta as well as zomba mañitry (Baré 1980: 304; Feeley-Harnik 1991: 369; Lombard 1988: 25–6). The Bemazava version reflects local perceptions of the structure as being temporary or 'ready-made' (vita means 'ready' or 'finished'). This may perhaps be a linguistic variation of the word, or it may reflect the fact that my Bemazava informants have forgotten the original term and meaning. I've written it here as vita because four separate informants pronounced it in this way: one was a member of the royal family; two had spent a lifetime engaged in royal service; another had had a child by a man of royal descent, and her grandmother had worked for royalty (see also Jiel 1995).

effluvia collected with care in special earthenware pots (*sajoa*) and
discarded at night in a sacred location chosen for this purpose
(the *ala faly* or 'taboo forest'). Relics—including occiput bone and
patellae, teeth, hair, and nails—are retained for future ceremonial
occasions.

For three weeks the *Sambarivo* remained with the corpse in Ambalavelona, awaiting the auspicious time marked by a new moon. On
Monday, December 20, the king's remains were moved, once again,
at night. The royal entourage traveled by car through Ankatafa and
other villages on the way to Nosy Faly which lay fifty kilometers
away. December 24 marked the ending of the *fanompoaña*: late on
the evening (Jiel 1995: 11) of this Friday (the day of the week reserved
for royal rituals), the ruler's remains were placed within the confines
of the wall encircling the royal tombs (*mahabo*) and housed in yet
another temporary *zomba vita*, this one made of stone. Eventually a
permanent structure will be built, a process that may take years or
even decades to complete.[23]

Throughout the *fanompoaña*, the Bemazava experienced an intense
revival of their own sense of collective identity. Ironically, it was the
death of a relatively passive ruler which awoke the dormant loyalty
of many of his subjects. Throughout the *fanompoaña* Bemazava displayed publicly their steadfast devotion to their ruler in ways they
had not experienced since the death of Tsiaraso II thirty years before.
For nearly a month, commoners and royalty alike did not bathe,
change or wash their clothes; women were required to let down
their hair; and neither men nor women could comb their hair, wear
hats or head coverings, nor could they wear shoes. Both men and
women dressed in the body wraps characteristic of Sakalava dress.
As one informant explained, 'the death of the ruler is like a total
destruction of the world for us—nothing in daily life seems normal
or the same.'

---

[23] Because of space restrictions this must be a highly abbreviated description of
the funerary practices surrounding the death of Tsiaraso Victor III. Feeley-Harnik's
account of 'Tondroko's Burial' closely resembles the more recent events in the
Sambirano described here, with only a few relatively minor exceptions (1991: 368ff.;
see also Dandouau 1911; Decary 1954, 1962; Goedefroit 1991–2; and Raharijaona
and Valette 1959).

The Politics of Royal Succession: The Instatement of Tsiaraso Rachidy IV

Once a Bemazava ruler's remains have been placed within the tomb walls, formal public discussion may begin regarding the instatement of a successor. By December 24, nearly 2,000 Bemazava had arrived at Nosy Faly to honor their dead ruler. Royalty in particular had come prepared to put forth their candidates for succession. It was a moment of great tension and potentially heated debate: many felt it was the first time in this century when they finally held the power to determine directly the fate of their kingdom. The preceding four rulers were viewed as having been puppets of the French regime or of the subsequent local administration associated with this nation's First Republic. Even today many royalty I know remain angry and bitter over French interference in the royal succession of 1945, when the moderate Tsiaraso II became ruler, displacing several other candidates favored by the Bemazava.

In response, at the end of 1993 an unusual and surprising event squelched all possibility for debate and potential strife. On the morning of December 24, as the royal tomb guardians (*antimahabo*) were preparing to place the ruler's corpse within the confines of the tomb walls, the Bemazava dynasty's ancestral spirits (*dady* or *razambe*) held a conference. Their *saha*, or mediums, assembled in a separate house. Here the oldest *tromba* spirit, Andriantompoeniarivo, or *Dadilahy* ('Grandfather') as he is affectionately called, descended into the head of his personal medium. Other ancestors associated with his lineage soon followed. In the privacy of their spirit house, they conferred with one another, debating, in the presence of living tomb guardians, who should be the next ruler. A crucial issue was whether a child of Tsiaraso Victor III's first or third spouse should reign. Tsiaraso Victor III and many surviving kin had already expressed a strong preference for his present wife's youngest son;[24] yet another candidate was a classificatory sister of the deceased ruler. Surprising everyone, the spirits made a public declaration before the assembled crowd: the next ruler should be one of the two eldest sons of the first spouse. Since her oldest son had failed to attend the entombment of his

---

[24] Tsiaraso Victor III was a great fan of Black American vocalists, and so this child was affectionately named Harry Belefonte; as Tsiaraso Rachidy IV later told me, 'we also call him Otis, but I do not know why.' I suspect that perhaps little H.B. also carried a nickname designed to reflect his father's fondness for Otis Redding.

father's remains, the second, Andriatahery Parfait—stunned by and soon giddy from the announcement—suddenly found himself publicly declared the next Bemazava ruler. On the morning of Christmas Day he was officially placed (*nitsangana*, literally, 'stood up') before his people and declared the next ruler or *ampanjakabe*. When the mortuary rituals came to a close, the mood of the Bemazava shifted from intense grief to one of joy and celebration. As they made their way from Nosy Faly, Parfait was presented as the new ruler to the inhabitants of such villages as Ankatafa and Ambalavelona. He was soon renamed Tsiaraso Rachidy IV.[25]

Over the course of the next year, numerous rituals were held, marking the progression of this young man from an exiled son and private citizen to a ruler. Although he is the spitting image of his father, and he has recently begun to wear the same style of fedora that was his father's trademark, the life of Tsiaraso Rachidy IV contrasts significantly with that of his predecessor. As the son of his father's first wife, Tsiaraso Rachidy IV and his siblings were expelled from the kingdom at the breakup of their parents' marriage.[26] To prevent challenges to his father's rule, this prince was sent to Tulear in southern Madagascar (approximately 1800 km away by road), where he attended government schools and grew up among people unfamiliar with Bemazava customs. In 1993 he was only twenty-five years old. Thus, he belongs to the large cohort of Madagascar's youth schooled under President Ratsiraka's *malagasization* program, so that he conducted all studies in the newly developed language of official Malagasy. Whereas his father was fluent in French, Tsiaraso Rachidy IV neither excelled in nor completed high school (*lycée*). He is unable to follow even the simplest of sentences in the colonial tongue, and he still struggles to understand the bureaucratic nuances of official Malagasy. As a result, he is easy prey to the older advisors who now hope to control his actions.

In addition, Tsiaraso Rachidy IV knows little of his Bemazava heritage, and he is in many ways ill-equipped to rule his own kingdom. Raised during his country's isolationist socialist era of Ratsiraka's Second Republic, he lacks the worldliness of his father. Thus, he

---

[25] For comparative data on instating a new ruler see Baré (1980: 245ff.).

[26] In other areas of Sakalava territory royal children are separated from their parents at birth and raised by others (Feeley-Harnik 1991: 337–8). This has not been the case historically, however, in the Sambirano region.

also runs the risk of falling under the sway of bureaucrats stationed in his fertile kingdom as Madagascar was thrust toward a new economic 'openness' which stressed the need for the influx of foreign capital under the tutelage of such agencies as USAID and the World Bank. To be involved in the decisions that shape such developments (many of which quickly reached Ambanja), he must be able to speak French.

Tsiaraso Rachidy IV, however, is no fool; whether he will prove to be a Bemazava version of Henry V remains to be seen. One reason that his selection went undisputed is because he is viewed as savvy in national affairs, especially as they relate to goings on in the capital. Trained as a professional soldier, he has lived and worked in the company of strangers since he left school at age sixteen. When he was called back to his father's funeral, he had been in Antsirabe for seven years, a town located in the island's central high plateaux. Although this is in the Vakinankaratra, a region which lies outside Imerina proper, many Bemazava insist that he was living under their enemy the Merina, whom Bemazava perceive of as controlling the national army.[27] Such experiences, however, had their price: when Tsiaraso Rachidy IV assumed his position as ruler, his Bemazava retainers were not particularly concerned with the need to cleanse the *zomba* in Ambanja of the filth (*maloto*) or heat (*mafana*) associated with his father's death. Rather, of greater necessity was the need to cleanse the living body and mouth of this new king who, as a young soldier, had been tainted by death and had spoken the dialect of his enemies. Thus, when he formally replaced his father in 1994 and moved into the *zomba* in town, the building itself was deemed safe and 'clean' (*madio*), whereas he had to be purified so as not to pollute the sacred residence, rather than vice versa.

---

[27] Hostilities between the Merina and Sakalava are much older than this. In the early nineteenth century, the Merina ruler Radama I (r. 1810–1828) sought to expand his kingdom to include the entire island of Madagascar (a project continued by his successor, Queen Ranavalovana I, r. 1828–1861). Some communities of Sakalava are among those that were able to resist Merina encroachment. The elaborate tales of some royal spirits operate as a form of historical memory of these events, since several sacrificed their lives to save their kingdom. In Ambanja, the *rebiky*, a dance that depicts battles of succession, is interpreted by some as a reference to the Merina wars; for more on the Sakalava point of view on these wars see Baré (1980: 38ff.). These events had much to do with the decision among Sakalava royalty to convert to Islam as they sought allies against the Merina and, subsequently, the French (see Baré 1980: 38ff.; Guillain 1845: 107ff.; Mellis 1938; Noël 1843–4).

When I visited the Sambirano in mid-1995, I found that Tsiaraso
Rachidy IV had begun to settle in as the new ruler of the Bemazava,
showing signs of mastering—that is, of *learning*—the rules of Bemazava
custom. Nevertheless, his actions are also evidence of a young ruler
interested in breaking with the past through new displays of power.
As Feeley-Harnik explains, 'the first obligation of an ampanjaka[be]
to the royal ancestors was to carry out the funeral of his or her predecessor' (1991: 375). Interestingly, Tsiaraso Victor IV has instead
focused on the public display of power that characterized the very
end of his father's reign through activities at the Palais Royal. Within
a year of his father's death, the building had already begun to show
signs of disrepair, and when I visited there in July, 1994, I found
villagers using its concrete foundation as a place to dry massive piles
of sea cucumbers collected for export to Asia. Tsiaraso Rachidy IV,
however, has since made sure that it has received a fresh coat of
paint, and his frequent visits to Andoany are now announced by the
polyrhythmic beating of the sacred royal drums (*hazolahy*).[28] The Palais
Royal is, once again, being revived as a dance hall, and fears about
the *lolo* who may haunt the site seem to have been forgotten. As
one senior member of the royal lineage recently explained, 'as long
as no one lives there, it's fine . . . it doesn't matter if the *ampanjakabe* goes in or uses it *temporarily*.' For this reason it is now considered safe to develop it as a guest house for royalty who want to be
able to relax at the beach on weekends.

Recently, the Palais Royal was described to me as being like a
royal version of a 'Hôtel de Ville' or City Hall. This is a striking
comparison, since the Hôtel de Ville in Ambanja is a magnet for
public discourse on local identity. It is the town's bureaucratic center, and the site for public folkloric celebrations, as well as the occasional evening *bals* that are attended by the town's élite. It also houses
Ambanja's single public television, which can be viewed each night
by passersby from the main street and building's open courtyard.
Finally, the Hôtel de Ville houses the office of perhaps the most
powerful of this young king's advisors, a man who simultaneously
holds the coveted position as overseer of all construction and public events in town. Given this, one can not help but wonder if we
are viewing the secularization of royal space, or if this civic institu-

---

[28] Other larger drums can be viewed at the *mahabo*. For a brief discussion of
sacred instruments see Baré (1980: 308ff.).

tion has become paired with the *zomba* as a new power base for royal operations in town.

III. *Analysis: Royal Ironies*

As Pred and Watts (1992: 14) remind us, 'there is paradox and irony in [the] postmodern geography of late capitalism' (cf. J. and J. Comaroff, eds. 1993). In this light, what are we to make of the blatant contradictions that characterize the use of royal space in this particular kingdom? Should the Palais Royal be viewed as innovative, and these two recent kings as local visionaries? Or are their actions a form of reckless hubris, shadowed by the certain future danger from the curse (*tigny*) of angry and neglected ancestral spirits? It is insufficient to view the ongoing project of the Palais Royal as evidence of the destructive effects of '*les forces modernes*,' and thus simply the demise of royal power and Bemazava identity. Rather, local royalty are clearly playing deliberately with local and nationalized meanings of the modern. For the Bemazava themselves, the building of the Palais Royal is hardly evidence of the abandonment of sacred custom; rather, it embodies a serious revival of or embellishment upon the past, an action designed to ensure the continuation of 'traditions' (*fomba*) in the future, albeit in highly unorthodox forms. To understand this process, we must turn to a detailed analysis of the symbolic meanings embedded in the (re)construction of the Palais Royal.

Stone Houses and High Places

What exactly is the Palais Royal? Architecturally speaking, it is an anomaly whose symbolic references draw upon diverse and competing symbols, and whose contradictory elements define it as quintessentially post-modern in design. First, the Palais Royal is a 'stone house' or a *trano vato*, a label that connotes permanence, wealth, and power. A quick look about the beach offers helpful comparisons. Ankify is a favorite relaxation spot for Ambanja's inhabitants, facilitated recently by the establishment of a regular bus service. Malagasy families congregate here on weekends to swim and picnic, and the wealthiest plantation directors have built their own elegant *trano vato* tucked into a rocky cliff so that they may stay here in comfort. Today their impressive dwellings appear surprisingly modest, overshadowed by the grandeur of the new Palais Royal. This imposing structure is not only much taller, but it dominates the road entrance to Ankify, immediately declaring this as royal space.

Nevertheless, it is more akin to a villa than a Palace. The Palais Royal is similar in design to the grand commercial houses that line Ambanja's streets, where boutiques occupy the ground floors with private living quarters upstairs. These houses, too, speak of strength and permanence, unlike the many smaller dwellings of ravinala palm (*trano falafa*) or corrugated tin (*toly*), the older examples sagging to one side as their foundations give way over time. Display and opulence are the prerogatives of royalty; yet extravagance is also indicative of their insatiable appetites and greed (Feeley-Harnik 1991: 55–6; 1982). Embodied in the Palais Royal is a strange duplication of the wealth and status of local capitalists, rather than of a king tied to tradition.

Close comparison to the villas in town reveals other problems associated with understanding the symbolic intent of this Palace. Only the northern archway, with its inscription and moon-and-star emblem, alert the passerby that this building is ritually distinctive. Uninhabited, it is reminiscent of the airy structures that house government offices throughout northern Madagascar. It seems more akin to a warehouse, a police station, or a museum. Personally I always expect to see a canon housed inside as if it were guarding a harbor, as in the town of Hellville on Nosy Be. The northern face of the Palais Royal offers a particularly unusual feature: here three arched doorways look out into the open air, guarded only by metal gates, but no doors. From this side in particular the building resembles not a house but a tomb. As Feeley-Harnik has remarked, Sakalava tomb compounds or *mahabo* appear to have been modeled after royal residences or *doany* (1991: 106). The Palais Royal offers yet another inversion: as a contemporary *doany* it evokes the style of a *mahabo*.

If we combine these factors—size, opulence, and tomb-like presence—the significance of the Palais Royal begins to emerge. Goedefroit, in her discussion of Sakalava cemeteries, argues that royal tombs declare their sites as ancestral capitals (1991–2: 223). The very height of the Palais Royal-as-tomb attests to a contemporary embellishment upon this idea. Just as one keeps one's head lowered in the presence of elders, rulers, and possessed spirit mediums, so, too, the Palais Royal stands taller than all other neighboring structures.[29] As

---

[29] It is noteworthy that whereas the Palais Royal sits on flat ground, in contrast the *doany* at Analalava sits upon a hill (Feeley-Harnik 1982: 35). The symbolic

such, it bears resemblance in yet another way to a *mahabo*, a term which means, literally, 'that which elevates' (Baré 1980: 292). Interestingly, as such, the Palais Royal operates simultaneously to commemorate sacred space while obliterating any trace of a former ruler's grandeur.

The Color of Power

The inscription upon the archway exposes other contradictions. Written in red on white, it makes reference to the colors and heritage of royalty, for Sakalava dynasties are divided into two large subgroups: the *Zafin'i'mena* and *Zaf'i'fotsy*[30] ('Grandchildren of Gold/Red Metal' and 'Grandchildren of Silver/White Metal'). These colors, along with the moon and star, appear regularly in Sakalava royal rituals, from the cloths worn by spirit mediums and living rulers, to the regalia of the *ribiky* dance which celebrates royal history. Red and white operate as powerful symbolic references to Sakalava identity, distinguishing royal houses from one another. The ruling house of the Bemazava of Ambanja favors red, for it is *Zafin'i'mena*. In the words of Lombard, this designation operates as 'une idéologie spécifique' that includes a sense of territory and, ultimately, of belonging to a particular group with a shared history (1986: 143).

The color white conveys additional meanings. Although villas can be painted this color, in Ambanja yellow, green, and blue are more prevalent. For the Sakalava, white symbolizes coolness and thus vitality, life and health. Kaolin (*tany malandy* or 'white earth') is pervasive in healing rituals. For example, it is used to mark the skin of the *tromba* medium before she enters trance, protecting her from the injuries that mark the spirit's body. For royalty, 'coolness' is contrasted to the 'heat' of sickness and death. The land where a ruler has died, for example, is 'hot' (*mafana*) and must be cleansed of its impurity through the painstaking rituals of the *fanompoaña* described briefly above.[31] Thus, the color imagery of the Palais Royal, like its imposing size, communicates strength, vitality, and well-being.

---

significance of height makes the Frenchman's villa atop the cliff at Ankify a significant eyesore for the Bemazava. Its owner, however, is oblivious to the significance of its location, having chosen the site simply for the view.

[30] These are actually abbreviated forms of *Zafinbolamena* and *Zafinbolafotsy*; for more details see Mellis (1938).

[31] Coolness is also associated with health and well-being among commoners; this is most evident in the 'cooling' post-partum practices (*ranginalo*) adhered to by northern Bemazava women (Sharp 1993: 108–112, and in press [b]).

In a bold attempt to explore further the significance of the colors of the Palace we find a queer reference as well to bygone days, and thus to conquest, involving the subtle incorporation of the conqueror by the conquered. The palace is painted in blue, white, and red, the color scheme of the French flag. At the very least, this exposes ghosts that continue to haunt the collective unconscious of a subjugated people. A more direct reference to foreign power is embedded in the inscription itself, since the words are written not in Sakalava (or even official Malagasy) but in French. The Antankaraña kingdom to the north offers a compelling comparison, where the elaborate *Tsangan-tsaina* festival culminates in the mounting of a large pole on which Madagascar's flag is raised over that of the kingdom. This ceremony is a contemporary embellishment upon its performance during the colonial era, when it was the French flag that waved supreme. The difference here is that this Antankaraña festival communicates a subtle and intended irony: for the purposes of display, the Antankaraña ruler publicly acknowledges his inferior or subjugated status in reference to the nation-state, yet the estimated throng of 7,000 subjects who participated in 1987 demonstrated their steadfast loyalty first and foremost to their ruler. Similarly, the color scheme of the Palais Royal underscores the contradictions inherent to this struggle for a cohesive sense of collective—and particularly royal—identity in the post-colonial era. The irony here, however, lies not in the subtleties of displayed power, but the unintended results of rehabilitated symbols. It reveals the unresolved tensions between royal kingdom and colonial empire (cf. Campbell 1991–2; Paillard 1991–2).

Naming and the Power of Words Left Unspoken

The very name of the Palais Royal underscores its problematic status. Although it stands at the center of Andoany, it is not a *doany* itself. Surrounded by the houses of royal retainers, there is, nevertheless, little sense of this being a cohesive and active royal community or compound as is found, for example, in Analalava (Feeley-Harnik 1991: 320ff.). Thus, Ankify maintains an odd status in reference to royal power. After all, the ruler himself lives not here, at Andoany, but in town in a *zomba*, a structure which bears this name more in casual reference to the fact that the current *ampanjakabe* dwells there, rather than it being a fully ritually operating compound (*doany*). Its location dictated by the French, the sacred geography of the current *zomba* was undermined from the start. If we take a conservative stance, we could argue that each successive ruler sits imprisoned in the polluted space of his or her predecessor. Yet, oddly enough, this does not bother the Bemazava.

The status of the Palais Royal is ambiguous in other ways. This is illustrated, for example, in the manner in which it is currently used: here royalty hope to come to vacation, so that they, too, may inhabit a villa similar to those owned by rich merchants, plantation directors, and foreigners. As a dance hall rented out for discos, clearly it is not a royal seat in any normal sense. A *zomba* or *doany* is a site for celebration, but appropriate activities are the *rebiky* dances and elaborate praise songs (*antsa maventy* and *kolondoy*), all of which celebrate royal power (Feeley-Harnik 1991: 30, 92; 1988). Instead, today one is more likely to hear pop tunes of foreign origin, such as 'Tarzan Boy,' 'Life is Life,' 'All that she wants is another baby . . .,' and 'La Femme de Mon Patron,' alongside the tunes of such celebrated Malagasy singers as Jao Joby and Rossy, who sing of life's tribulations, their subjects ranging from unrequited love to HIV infection in the 1990s.

The confusion associated with these new symbolic meanings was brought to the fore during my most recent visit to Ankify in June, 1995. Tsiaraso Rachidy IV had come on a Sunday afternoon to inspect the Palace; for this occasion a sacred *hazolahy* drum was brought out into the open and leaned against the building's concrete foundation. Soon a villager, drunk from palm wine (*trembo*), approached and attempted in a pathetic fashion to beat out the appropriate polyrhythms; even more astonishing were his clumsy attempts to dance the normally slow-paced and graceful *rebiky*. Only a handful of giggling children paid him attention, and, more astonishingly, no one attempted to stop his antics, even when the *ampanjakabe* shot him a quizzical glance.

The Power of Forgetting

Ultimately, it is the recent death of a ruler that jarred local collective memory, for suddenly old and nearly forgotten customs such as the *fanompoaña* were revived and thus relived. As the mortuary rituals of the *fanompoaña* attest, the death of each Sakalava ruler throws the kingdom into disarray or chaos, and, thus, towards danger. The public display of mourning throughout Ambanja in December, 1993, was a powerful example of this. Individuals who had previously expressed guilt or dismay over not following and thus forgetting royal customs suddenly began to 'learn' (*mianatra*) them through the act of mourning. As they mourned, they also remembered, becoming, at least loosely, *ampanompo* or 'those who work for royalty.' Through mourning, the dead and the living were intrinsically linked. In turn, the sense of a unified rather than fragmented kingdom was reawakened.

This revival of older symbols was evident as well in the reactions to the odd coincidences surrounding the king's death. As the sole Catholic among Bemazava rulers, Tsiaraso Victor III died on the day of the Immaculate Conception, and he was entombed on Christmas Eve, events that local Bemazava found amusing. His successor, Tsiaraso Rachidy IV, guided by royal retainers, turned away from Catholicism, beginning his new life, instead, in step with the Sakalava ritual calendar. Although first presented in tentative fashion on Christmas day, his official instatement is viewed locally as beginning with the New Year. This is a time of remembrance for both the Sakalava and Antankaraña, when *tromba* mediums go to the sea (*rano masina* or 'sacred water') to bathe together, seeking the blessing of their ancestors and their living rulers. So, too, Tsiaraso Rachidy IV was bathed by retainers (in the water of the Sambirano River, which is only a brief walk from the *zomba* in Ambanja). As a manifestation of the process of learning, the new ruler was handled delicately during the ceremonies that marked his instatement: he walked slowly and carefully, and was guarded with care, as if he were an invalid. At particular moments an older man carried him in his arms as if he were an infant or small child. Similarly, he was forbidden from speaking of royal custom with outsiders (including anthropologists) prior to his official instatement ceremonies, for, again, he was like a child who 'lacked wisdom' (*tsy hendry izy*).

Rulers—especially young and exiled ones—must begin to learn or master their own customs when they assume their positions. They also face the difficult task of building their own base of power. They must strike a delicate balance as they obliterate evidence of a previous living ruler's presence while simultaneously honoring and working under the greater power and knowledge of deceased rulers who are now royal ancestors. The responses from Tsiaraso Rachidy IV, however, stand in stark contrast to the ceremonial behavior that surrounded his instatement. Oddly, though, subsequent actions which could easily undermine his royal stature have actually enhanced it.

As noted earlier, among the primary duties of a new ruler is to entomb his or her predecessor (again, see Feeley-Harnik 1991: 375). Interestingly, as Tsiaraso Rachidy IV has begun to assert his power, he has invested neither time nor funds in the building of his father's tomb. Rather than honoring his father as a new and great ancestor, Tsiaraso Rachidy IV has allowed his father's remains to lie in a temporary and modest stone *zomba vita* at Nosy Faly. Instead, this daring young king has focused his attention on a project initiated by his father, the Palais Royal, asserting his newly acquired power through a grand edifice that rests upon the old ruins of an even older predecessor's palace. In so doing, he proclaims himself as his father's successor among the living, ironically by embracing the symbols of *les forces modernes*.

Funerals, as liminal ritual moments, can expose hidden social conflicts and uncertainties (cf. Lambek and Breslar 1986). In this light, the celebrated mortuary rituals of the Merina offer interesting comparisons for elucidating the significance of recent events in this Bemazava kingdom. As Graeber (1995) has argued, a subtle yet tense battle is waged by living Merina elders and deceased ancestors for supremacy in the minds of the living: to be remembered is the ultimate source of greatness, yet such greatness can only be achieved in death. To become prominent ancestors, then, Merina elders must be able to restrain their own offspring, for 'the ultimate fame of a father almost necessarily [means] the eventual oblivion of his sons (and vice versa)' (1995: 265). Thus, just as Merina tombs serve as reminders of the past, they (and their inhabitants) always run the risk of being forgotten, as tombs fall into disrepair, and as the bodies of the dead are pulverized in the animated dances of the *famadihana*. Thus, the *famadihana* itself is not a form of remembering but of forgetting (again, see Graeber 1995).

To this we might add that *to forget is to remember*. As with the Merina, so, too, must Bemazava offspring be restrained, as illustrated by the exile of young princes from their father's kingdom. When such a child as Tsiaraso Rachidy IV later assumes power, he must struggle with the achieved stature of his predecessor whose body has now been reduced to relics and prepared for entombment in an imposing yet isolated tomb. The survival of Tsiaraso Victor III in the collective memory is assured once he appears as a *tromba* spirit

in a specialized medium of Nosy Faly, a process that generally takes
about two years. At that point, Tsiaraso Victor III will join the ranks
of the great ancestors or *razambe* of the Bemazava. No longer a mere
corpse lying in a cold tomb, he can address the living and serve as
a royal advisor to the rulers who succeed him.

The Dead and the Living

As Baré explains, the key to understanding Sakalava conceptions of
power lies in the opposition between the dead and the living (1980:
239). Similarly, Feeley-Harnik stresses the highly problematic nature
of this relationship: as she explains, 'to separate from the dead is to
live. To forget the dead is to die. But to recall them in ancestors is
to walk a most difficult path between the two, brushing against death
for life' (1991: 45–6; see also 1978: 405). Thus, although essential
to Sakalava identity, relationships with the dead are also dangerous.
The danger of such encounters in Bemazava territory are evident in
the odd inversions that stress the impermanence of both life and
death. As with Merina tombs, the Sakalava *mahabo* is a symbol of
permanence and serves as a constant reminder of the power associated with ancestors (cf. Graeber 1995: 262). But in the Sambirano—
and even more so in the town of Ambanja—the *mahabo* is seen today
as lying at a distant location, on the isolated, smaller island of Nosy
Faly. Only tomb guardians live full-time at the *mahabo*, and it is they
alone who lovingly care for the tombs and oversee the rituals that
occur there on a regular basis. In other words, the royal tombs and,
thus, the ancestors, remain far removed from the memories and
imaginations of the subjects who today inhabit this kingdom.

In the Sambirano, therefore, the inextricable link between the dead
and the living is exposed in unorthodox contexts. In addition to the
Palais Royal there is another secular building that commemorates
royalty, stressing yet again the permanence of royal power and the
need to remember the dead. This is the local high school. Completed in 1987, it bears the name of a familiar ruler: it is the 'Lycée
Tsiaraso I.' As with the Palais Royal, the construction of the local
high school defied several serious taboos, among which the most
significant involved using this ruler's name. As noted earlier, when
Sakalava rulers die, 'the name is buried with the person' (Feeley-
Harnik 1991: 39), and praise names replace the names they bore in
life. Surprisingly, the ancestors of Nosy Faly sanctioned this decision

(see Sharp 1993: 165–170). In turn, the *lycée* was treated not as a purely secular structure but also as a 'royal' one, for *rebiky* dances were performed at its dedication.

What, then, are we to make of such serious breaching of taboos? Kaspin offers helpful comparative data in her analysis of the *Nyau*, a dance that is a centerpiece of Chewa royal ritual in Malawi. She describes the *Nyau* 'not an artifact of cultural nostalgia, nor a discrete feature of Chewa society, but part of a repertoire of conceptual categories with which the modern world(s) is continually imagined and revised' (1993: 35). Within the context of the *Nyau*, contradictory yet thriving symbolic forms coexist (1993: 34). If we turn to the Palais Royal, we see that a dialectical process is set in motion: from the very actions which undermine older meanings spring newer forms. But whereas Kaspin interprets embellishments upon *Nyau* as undermining chiefly power, leaving it only ritually intact (1993: 36), I argue that the greatest irony of the Palais Royal and the *lycée* is that both further enhance and reconfirm royal power, albeit in new and strikingly unusual ways.

Together these two buildings have established Tsiaraso I as a local martyr of colonial violence. The high school stands upon land acquired from the oldest of plantations and, as *lycée* students explain, its name reminds them that this was the first in a line of kings named Tsiaraso who struggled with quandaries of the twentieth century. More generally, these young informants express an awakened awareness of royal history in response to the structure itself. And so Tsiaraso I stands in stark contrast to Tsiaraso II, who is remembered locally as a weak man who failed to stand up to the French, particularly at the height of Malagasy nationalism during the 1947 insurrection.

Graeber notes that 'no postindependence Malagasy government has, to my knowledge, ever erected a statue in the European sense—that is, one bearing some kind of likeness. Public monuments always take the form of standing stones' (1995: 277 fn. 23). Interestingly, Bemazava have erected large-scale *named* monuments of sorts, where massive 'houses of stone' (*trano vato*), such as the *lycée* and the Palais Royal, work to replace the more modest 'standing stones' (*tsanganbato*) found throughout the island. These two local buildings are even more remarkable since they bear names and rest upon the territory of a long deceased king victimized by a former foreign regime. Both are monuments to Bemazava resistance and to the man himself who now embodies such resistance, Tsiaraso I. But there is one more twist to this story: erecting such edifices is a French, not a Malagasy, practice. In the case of the Palais Royal, veneration occurs only by building over the former residence of an ancestor. It is as if a dead king were being brought back to life in a greater and grander style than was possible during his lifetime.

Concluding Remarks: Royal Conundrums and Paradoxes

Thus, in the end, what are we to make of broken taboos and misplaced customs? Of the merging of sacred red and white with the colors of the colonial flag? Of a seaside villa and the absence of a true royal residence? Of a dancing drunkard and disco nights? To view these as evidence of vulgarized custom in a community undermined by conquest begs these questions, for such an interpretation falls back on the far too simplistic explanations of victimization and hopelessness. Clearly, the innovations of the Palais Royal are new evidence of a dynamic cultural resiliency: such is the nature of modernity, where new forms of expression and reaction defy prediction. As this essay shows, anthropological inquiry must readdress the question of how contemporary cultures confront the influx of foreign capital in creative ways—for as foreign investment undermines a local economy, ironically it may offer radical symbolic embellishments that further understanding of that process. In this Bemazava kingdom, the interpretation of colonialism's destructive forces is exposed to constant scrutiny and re-evaluation. These are new symbolic hybrids— some innovative, others startling and even tragic. Ironically, in the end, it is the shy ruler Tsiaraso Victor III who emerges as the great innovator.

Thus, it is through the linked processes of revival and remembrance that a new sense of Bemazava identity has been instilled in the collective consciousness of this kingdom's residents. Such a process is embodied in the construction of the Palais Royal: for, in building this edifice upon its present site, it simultaneously commemorates an older *doany* while obliterating any traces of its former structure. Viewed historically, the Palais Royal defies old rules: as dynasties split over succession, new rulers venture out into unmarked territory. Andriantompoeniarivo, for example, moved northward into the Sambirano Valley; following his death he became the founding and thus oldest ancestor. Yet with such movement or separation there always remains a hunger for or attachment to the old. When the Bemazava call upon their founding ancestor, they still invoke other spirits of greater age and power entombed elsewhere. Such are the anxieties that underlie the difficulties and paradoxes of forgetting and remembering.

As Lombard reminds us, Sakalava royal history is the history of its foundation (1988: 145). Playing with this idea, what, then, of a building whose foundations rest upon history? The reconstruction of the Palais Royal upon sacred ground is indeed a form of hubris, for Sakalava rulers are prohibited from coming into contact with death in any form (cf. Feeley-Harnik 1991: 143–4). The dangers of this action are exemplified by the *lolo* spirits. If they can be forgotten, so, too, perhaps, can the dangers associated with this sacred space. Yet what if they do indeed still lurk about the Palace? Will the lively beat of a disco tune disturb these dangerous spirits? If there is a death on the highway, what, then, will be the responses of the ancestors or *razambe* of Nosy Faly? Ultimately, future events and their interpretation will affect the stability of the ruler and his kingdom.

The developments described in this article are driven by a question that haunts many of Ambanja's inhabitants concerning the nature of power. Many often ask, what exactly constitutes local government or the *fanjakana* in the Sambirano? This is perhaps the most perplexing of Bemazava royal difficulties. To answer this final question we must once more return to the concept of parallel histories. As Baré (1983: 156), explains, the term *fanjakana* itself designates those dangerous and difficult things (*raha sarotro*) which stand for the absolute power of the monarch or *ampanjakabe*; it also contrasts royalty with commoner, and the living with the dead. As the Antankaraña *Tsangantsaina* festival reveals, the meaning of *fanjakana* can be highly contested in ritual contexts. Other regimes have repeatedly recognized the power of royalty. The French, for example, attempted to label forced labor between the two World Wars as *fanompoaña* (Baré 1980: 166, Feeley-Harnik 1984); similarly, the government of the nation of Madagascar more recently has sought voluntary labor for roadwork by requesting the assistance of the *ampanjakabe*. As the actions of loyal Bemazava attest, however, one's true obligation of service is done out of love, and only for the ruler.

Ambanja is an arena where multiple hegemonies are at work, where power is dispersed among the state, the plantations, and the Bemazava royal house (Sharp, in press [a]; cf. Pred and Watts 1992).

In response to the quandary regarding the power of the 'government,' the *tromba* spirits of Nosy Faly themselves have chosen Tsiaraso Rachidy IV as the next ruler. This unmarried 'man-child' (*tsaiky lahy*) currently embodies the contradictions outlined throughout this article. Despite being the legitimate son of the former ruler, he is ignorant of royal custom. As a soldier, he has traveled and is considered familiar with bureaucratic forces that threaten royal stability, yet he lacks the ability to communicate in the re-emerging bureaucratic language of French. Nevertheless, the hope is that as a young man he will add new vitality to the kingdom, continuing those innovations that characterized the later years of his father's reign. Whether he will be a pawn of local or national forces is unknown; the kingdom is certain, however, to change under his rule. We have yet to see what forms of radical ritual innovation will arise from this young man, such forms steeped in localized interpretations of the meaning of the modern.

REFERENCES CITED

Apter, Andrew
   1993   'Atinga Revisited: Yoruba Witchcraft and the Cocoa Economy,
                   1950–1951.' In *Modernity and its Malcontents: Ritual and Power in
                   Postcolonial Africa.* J. and J. Comaroff, eds. pp. 111–128. Chicago:
                   University of Chicago Press.
Astuti, Rita
   1995   '"The Vezo are not a Kind of People": Identity, Difference,
                   and "Ethnicity" among a Fishing People of Western Madagascar.'
                   American Ethnologist 22:3: 464–482.
Baré, Jean-François
   1986   'L'organisation sociale Sakalava du nord: une récapitulation.' In
                   Madagascar: Society and History. C.P. Kottak, J.A. Rakotoarisoa,
                   A. Southall and P. Vérin, eds. pp. 353–392. Durham: Carolina
                   Academic Press for the Wenner-Gren Foundation for Anthro-
                   pological Research.
   1983   'Remarques sur le vocabulaire monarchique Sakalava du nord.'
                   In *Les Souverains de Madagascar; L'histoire royale et ses résurgences con-
                   temporaines.* pp. 153–173. F. Raison-Jourde, ed. Paris: Editions
                   Karthala.
   1980   *Sable Rouge. Une monarchie du nord-ouest malgache dans l'histoire.* Paris:
                   Editions L'Harmattan.
Bloch, Maurice
   1994 [1971]   *Placing the Dead. Tombs, Ancestral Villages, and Kinship Organization
                   in Madagascar.* Prospect Hts., IL: Waveland Press, Inc.
Campbell, Gwyn
   1991–2   'The History of Nineteenth Century Madagascar: "Le Royaume"
                   or "L'Empire"?' *Omaly sy Anio (Hier et Aujourd'hui)* No. 33–36:
                   331–379.

Chazan-Gillig, Suzanne
    1983 'Le fitampoha de 1968; ou l'efficacité symbolique du myth de la roy-
           auté Sakalava dans l'actualité politique et économique malgache.' In
           Les Souverains de Madagascar: L'histoire royale et ses résurgences contemporaines.
           pp. 452–476. F. Raison-Jourde, ed. Paris: Editions Karthala.

Comaroff, Jean and John Comaroff
    1993 Introduction. In *Modernity and its Malcontents: Ritual and Power in Postcolonial
           Africa.* J. and J. Comaroff, eds. pp. xi–xxxvii. Chicago: University of
           Chicago Press.

Dalmond, Pierre
    1840 Mission Saclave 1840. Manuscript in the Archives of the Institut
           Supérieur de Théologie et de Philosophie de Madagascar, Antsiranana.

Dandouau, André
    1911 'Coutumes funéraires dans le nord-ouest de Madagascar.' *Bulletin de
           l'Académie Malgache* 9: 157–172.

Decary, Raymond
    1962 *La mort et les coutumes funéraires.* Paris: Maisonneuve et Larose.
    1954 'Pays Sakalava.' *Encyclopédie Mensuelle d'Outre-mer*, pp. 279–282. Paris.

Feeley-Harnik, Gillian
    1991 *A Green Estate: Restoring Independence in Madagascar.* Washington, DC:
           Smithsonian Institution Press.
    1988 'Sakalava Dancing Battles: Representation of Conflict in Sakalava
           Royal Service.' *Anthropos* 83: 65–85.
    1984 'The Political Economy of Death: Communication and Change in
           Malagasy Colonial History.' *American Ethnologist* 11:1: 1–19.
    1982 'The King's Men in Madagascar. Slavery, Citizenship and Sakalava
           Monarchy.' *Africa* 52:2: 31–50.
    1978 'Divine Kingship and the Meaning of History among the Sakalava
           of Madagascar.' *Man* (N.S.) 13: 402–17.

Goedefroit, Sophie
    1991–2 'Analyse des coutumes d'ensevelissement des corps chez les Sakalava
            du Menabe: Manifestations d'ordre lignager et affirmation d'une hier-
            archie sociale.' *Omaly sy Anio (Hier et Aujourd'hui)* No. 33–36: 223–233.

Graeber, David
    1995 'Dancing with Corpses Reconsidered: An Interpretation of *Famadihana*
           (in Arivonimamo, Madagascar).' *American Ethnologist* 22:2: 258–278.

Gueunier, Noël J.
    1991–2 'Une copie de la lettre de Tsiomeko, reine des Sakalava à Louis-
            Philippe, roi des Français (1840).' *Omaly sy Anio (Hier et Aujourd'hui)*
            No. 33–36: 513–531.

Guillain, [Captain]
    1845 *Documents sur l'histoire, la géographie et le commerce de la côte ouest de
           Madagascar.* Paris: Extraits des Annales Maritimes et Coloniales.

Jiel
    1995 'Vie culturelle: Fanampoagna.' *Akony ny Sambirano* 13:11.

Kaspin, Deborah
    1993 'Chewa Visions and Revisions of Power: Transformations of the Nyau
           Dance in Central Malawi.' In *Modernity and its Malcontents: Ritual and
           Power in Postcolonial Africa.* J. and J. Comaroff, eds. pp. 34–57. Chicago:
           University of Chicago Press.

Kent, Raymond
    1979 'Religion and the State: A Comparison of Antanosy and Sakalava in
           the 1600s.' In *Madagascar in History: Essays from the 1970s.* pp. 80–101.
           Berkeley: The Foundation for Malagasy Studies.

1968   'Madagascar and Africa: Part II. the Sakalava, Maroserana, Dady and Tromba before 1700.' *Journal of African History* 9:4: 517–576.

Koerner, F.
1968   'La colonisation agricole du Nord-Ouest de Madagascar.' *Revue Economique de Madagascar*. Cujas-Université de Madagascar, pp. 165–193.

Lambek, Michael and Jon H. Breslar
1986   'Funerals and Social Change in Mayotte.' In *Madagascar: Society and History*. C.P. Kottak, J.-A. Rakotoarisoa, A. Southall and P. Vérin, eds. pp. 393–410. Durham: Carolina Academic Press for the Wenner-Gren Foundation for Anthropological Research.

Lombard, Jacaques
1988   *Le Royaume Sakalava du Menabe. Essai d'analyse d'un système politique à Madagascar. 17è-20è.* Paris: Editions de l'ORSTOM, Institut Français de Recherche Scientifique pour le Développement en Coopération. Collection Travaux et Documents No. 214.
1986   'Le temps et l'espace dans l'idéologie politique de la royauté Sakalava-Menabe.' In *Madagascar: Society and History*. C.P. Kottak, J.-A. Rakotoarisoa, A. Southall, and P. Vérin, eds. pp. 142–156. Durham: Carolina Academic Press for the Wenner-Gren Foundation for Anthropological Research.

Mannoni, Octave
1990 [1950]   *Prospero and Caliban: The Psychology of Colonization*: Ann Arbor: University of Michigan Press.

Mellis, J.V.
1938   *Volamena et Volafotsy. Nord et nord-ouest de Madagascar.* Tananarive: Imprimerie Moderne de l'Emyrne, Pitot de la Beaujardière.

Nérine Botokeky, Eléonore
1983   'Le Fitampoha en royaume de Menabe: Bain des reliques royales.' In *Les Souverains de Madagascar: L'histoire royale et ses résurgences contemporaines*. Pp. 211–219. F. Raison-Jourde, ed. Paris: Editions Karthala.

Noël, Vincent
1843–4   'Recherches sur les Sakalava.' *Bulletin de la Société de Géographie de Toulouse*. November 40–64 et 275–94, 285–366; Juin: 386–417.

Paillard, Yvan Georges
1991–2   'D'un protectorat fantôme au fantôme d'un protectorat: les metamophoses du pouvoir à Madagascar de 1885 à 1896.' *Omaly sy Anio (Hier et Aujourd'hui)*. 33–36: 559–583.
1983–4   'Les mpanjaka du nord-ouest de Madagascar et l'insurrection anticoloniale de 1898.' *Omaly sy Anio (Hier et Aujourd'hui)*. 17–20: 339–374.

Poirier, Charles
1939   'Notes d'ethnographie de l'histoire malgache: Les royaumes Sakalava Bemihisatra de la côte nord-ouest de Madagascar.' *Mémoires de l'Académie Malgache* 28: 13–18.

Pred, Allan and Michael J. Watts
1992   *Reworking Modernity: Capitalisms and Symbolic Discontent.* New Brunswick, NJ: Rutgers University Press.

Raharijaona, S. and Jean Valette
1959   'Les grandes fêtes rituelles des Sakalava du Menabe ou Fitampoha.' *Bulletin de Madagascar* 155: 281–314.

Raison-Jourde, Françoise, editor
   1983   *Les Souverains de Madagascar: L'histoire royale et ses résurgences contemporaines.* Paris: Editions Karthala.
Rajoelina, Patrick
   1988   *Quarante années de la vie politique de Madagascar, 1947–1987.* Paris: Editions L'Harmattan.
Randrianja, Fanomezantsoa Solofo Lalao
   1983   'La notion de royauté dans le mouvement d'émancipation malgache (1920–1940).' In *Les Souverains de Madagascar: L'histoire royale et ses résurgences contemporaines.* F. Raison-Jourde, ed. pp. 410–426. Paris: Editions Karthala.
Ratsiraka, Didier
   1975   *Charte de la révolution socialist malgache tous azimuts [Ny Boky Mena].* Antananarivo: Imprimerie d'Ouvrages Educatifs.
Razafimandimby, Noro
   1995   '35 ans d'indépendance . . . deux fois plus pauvre!' *Revue de l'Océan Indien Madagascar.* June, pp. 5–9.
Service Topographique
   n.d.   [Land tenure information for the Sambirano]. Volume I des titres 1 BP à 49 BP. Bureau des Domaines, Nosy Be, Madagascar.
Sharp, Lesley
   in press [a]   'Possession and Power in Madagascar: Contesting Colonial and National Hegemonies.' In *Spirit Possession, Modernity and Power.* H. Behrend and U. Luig, eds.
   in press [b]   'Royal Affairs and the Power of (Fictive) Kin: Mediumship, Maternity, and the Contemporary Politics of Bemazava Identity.' *Taloha* (Antananarivo).
   1994   'Exorcists, Psychiatrists, and the Problems of Possession in Northwest Madagascar.' *Social Science and Medicine* 38:4: 525–542.
   1993   *The Possessed and the Dispossessed. Spirits, Identity, and Power in a Madagascar Migrant Town.* Berkeley: University of California Press.
   1990   'Possessed and Dispossessed Youth. Spirit Possession of School Children in Northwest Madagascar.' *Culture, Medicine and Psychiatry* 14:3: 339–364.
Thompson, Virginia and Richard Adloff
   1965   *The Malagasy Republic: Madagascar Today.* Stanford: Stanford University Press.
Tronchon, Jacques
   1982   *L'insurrection malgache de 1947.* Fianarantsoa: Editions Ambozontany Fianarantsoa.
Valette, J.
   1958   '1700–1840—Histoire du Boina.' *Bulletin de Madagascar* 149: 851–858.
Wilson, Peter J.
   1992   *Freedom by a Hair's Breadth: Tsimihety in Madagascar.* Ann Arbor: The University of Michigan Press.

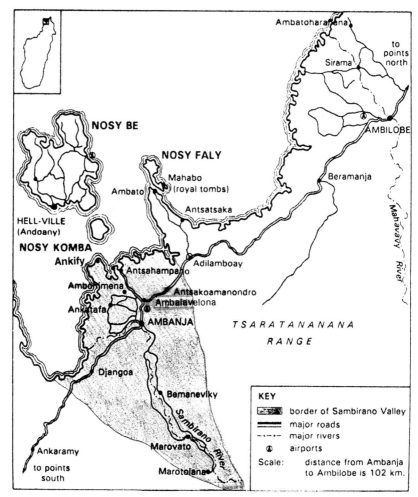

Map 3. Territory of Bemazava-Sakalava of Northwest Madagascar, including the Sambirano Valley. After Sharp (1993: 31).

SUCCESSION OF BEMAZAVA RULERS OF THE SAMBIRANO
IN NORTHWEST MADAGASCAR

NOTE: An asterisk (*) follows the names of rulers mentioned in this article; *italicized print* has been used to designate the three rulers who are central to the arguments presented in the text.

name during reign	praise name	years of reign
Boanamaka*	Andriantompoeniarivo*	approx. 1820-1821
Tsimandro	Andriamanotranarivo	1821-1832
Matandrabo [Malandiabo?]	Andriamandriambiniarivo II	1832-1837
Irana?	Andriamamelonarivo II	?
Tsiresy I	Andriamanomponarivo	1837(?)-1852
Monja	Andriamamahoñarivo	1852-1857
Tsiaraso I *	*Andriamandilatrarivo* *	*1887-1919*

- - - - - - - - - - - 1895-6: French conquest; Madagascar declared a colony of France - - - - - - - - - - -

Tsiresy II*	Nenimoana*	1919-1935
Rachidy*	Andriamamefiarivo*	1935-1945

- - - - - - - - - - - By 1940s, if not earlier, Bemazava rulers had relocated from the palace - - - - - - - - - (<u>doany</u>) at Ankify to the residence (<u>zomba</u>) in the town of Ambanja

Tsiaraso II*	Andriamandefitriarivo*	1945-1966
Tsiaraso Victor III *	*Andriamanaitriarivo* *	*1966-1993*
Tsiaraso Rachidy IV *	- -	*1993 - present*

Table 1. Succession of Bemazava rulers of the Sambirano in Northwest Madagascar

CHAPTER FIVE

THE IMAGINED COMMUNITY OF THE ANTANKARAÑA: IDENTITY, HISTORY, AND RITUAL IN NORTHERN MADAGASCAR[1]

MICHAEL LAMBEK AND ANDREW WALSH

The Antankaraña, occupants of the far northern portion of Madagascar, are generally described in the literature and by educated Malagasy as one of some 18 'tribes' or 'ethnies' into which the island is said to be divided. They were, in the 1970's, the second smallest 'tribe,' with a population of some 44,852 (e.g. Jenkins, 1987). In this paper we problematize this kind of hegemonic depiction of social groups as discrete, bounded, reified entities. We suggest that alongside it, and rooted more deeply in northwest Madagascar, is a logic of collective identity constituted less by categorization than performance and less by exclusion than by inclusion, though we recognize these are themselves relative emphases rather than discrete alternatives (cf. Lambek 1995). Ascertaining the specific boundaries between groups in northern Madagascar is problematic; groups overlap and flow into one another so that even the French have been taken by the Antankaraña into the very heart of their world (albeit in such a manner that their distinctiveness is not denied). The question then becomes how the meaningfulness of the core or centre is constituted.

In this paper we argue that Antankaraña identity is established less by a conceptual grid of ascriptive categories than by means of commitment to a certain historical narrative and its regular re-enactment

[1] Research for this paper has been supported by both a research grant (Lambek) and a doctoral fellowship (Walsh) from the Social Sciences and Humanities Research Council of Canada. We extend our thanks to Bob Dewar, Lisa Gezon, Rebecca Green, Janet and John Hough, Jean de Dieu Kalobotra, Bruno Ndriamahafahana, Jean-Aimé Rakotoarisoa, Elie Rajaonarison, Lesley Sharp, Jacqueline Solway, and Emmanuel Tehindrazanarivelo. We are indebted to the many people in Antsiranana, Ambilobe, and Ambatoharañana who spoke with us; especially to Prince Issa Alexandre Tsimanamboholahy (Tsimaro III) and to Said Abdourahimo Soultoany, as well as to the Ndrambavy Be, to Louis-Philippe d'Arvisenet, Abdo Solimana, and their families. An earlier draft of the paper was read at the University of Gent, Belgium. It also received a lengthy, incisive, and intelligent critique from Karen Middleton that has greatly improved it. Nevertheless we fall short of addressing all her criticisms; no one but ourselves is to be held responsible for any shortcomings.

in a ceremonial cycle. In discussing the cycle we pay particular attention to its spatio-temporal qualities and the sense of potent, yet controlled, rhythmical continuity it brings to Antankaraña social identity.
We show how ritual enactment instantiates the constitutional relationship between sovereign and subject. In the last section we turn
to the objectification of the ritual within present-day Madagascar.
Our central point is that the question—who are the Antankaraña?—
may be answered best by attending to the story they perform about
themselves and its fate in contemporary Madagascar.

In borrowing Anderson's (1991) term 'imagined community' we
deliberately refrain from casting the Antankaraña in the usual ana-
lytic terms for depicting collective identity. John Comaroff (1992)
has provided a lucid distinction between totemism and ethnicity as
ideal types, demonstrating the dialectical processes through which
ethnic groups form historically. As he recognizes, in practice it may
be difficult to distinguish 'totemic' from 'ethnic' groups; this is especially true in an environment of expanding chiefdoms and proto-
states with broad mercantile links such as characterized Madagascar
between the 17th and 19th Centuries, the time at which an Antankaraña identity was forming and to which the Antankaraña today
turn to explain who they are.[2] Following Comaroff, we can see the
gradual emergence of Antankaraña 'ethnicity,' but it exists alongside
a differently constituted model which still retains saliency in which
incorporating tendencies are at least as strong as demarcating ones.
Comaroff bases his argument on the assumption of a universal classificatory impulse, 'the marking of relations—of identities in opposition to one another' (1992: 51) without specifically distinguishing a
broad form from the distinctively modern rationalizing urge to impose
a uniform classificatory grid over social reality, tidying it up into
commensurable units (as in the picture of '18 tribes'). While we do
not question the role of classification in human thought, we wonder
whether classification by opposition has always provided the most
salient or critical basis for group or individual identities, especially
where bilateral principles assign people to multiple and overlapping
categories.

Hence in our analysis we privilege performance over classification
and centres over boundaries. Among Antankaraña, as among other

---

[2] Comaroff himself explicitly mentions Madagascar (1992: 57).

Malagasy (Bloch, 1989b), the attempt is to counteract dispersal; activities are directed more at reconstituting a centre than at setting up or patrolling external boundaries. Movements to and from the centre help to imagine Antankaraña-ness, irrespective of how Antankaraña may differ from others.[3] During the time invested in these 'meaningful practices' (Comaroff and Comaroff 1992: 37), an intensity (Durkheimian effervescence) is generated. Outside this social phase, which surely includes anticipation before the fact and recollection after, identity is somewhat more diffuse. In bringing out the importance of social context we are not speaking about 'situational ethnicity' so much as the significance of ritual and narrative practice in the imagination of identity. Indeed, our argument is the inverse of the situationalists since we focus primarily on moral order rather than instrumental strategy and since among ordinary Antankaraña it is precisely at the boundaries where categorical identity is *least* marked.

History

Most salient to the Antankaraña today is the story they tell about their survival in the face of pursuit and exploitation by the Merina (Hova, Borzan) in the 19th Century. We begin with a brief synopsis based on a standardized version recited to Lambek by the reigning Antankaraña monarch, Tsimiaro III in 1991. Many of the events mentioned here are elaborated in other stories.[4]

> Madagascar has 18 tribes. Each has its own king. But only one third still exist. Why? Because of battles within the family (*ady milongo*) [i.e., among the kings; note already, despite the King's appropriation of it, the insufficiency of the discrete tribal model in the face of an ideology which links all Malagasy rulers as members of a single 'family.'] The Merina king [Radama] wanted to be the only king, so he killed the others. The Antankaraña took refuge in the caves [in the karst massif which lies in their heartland and from which they draw their name, Antankaraña meaning literally 'People at the land of limestone rocks'] where they lived for over a year [probably in 1837]. A traitor

---

[3] While we draw from Anderson (1991) the notion of 'imagined communities', we emphasize that the relevant polity here is of a rather different order from the bureaucratic nation state; likewise, the journeys we speak about are a far cry from those of Anderson's peregrinating officials.

[4] The stories are taken up in greater detail in Walsh's forthcoming doctoral dissertation (University of Toronto).

disclosed their location to the Hova army. The king, Tsimiaro I, saw
they were in danger. He made a prayer, pledging that if the people
came out of the situation alive, safe and sound, their descendants would
be Muslims.

The Antankaraña managed to flee from the caves and sail to Nosy
Mitsio [a small island off the west coast]. The French were in Bourbon
[Réunion] at the time. Tsimiaro went to Bourbon to ask the French
to chase away the Hova. In return, in a treaty signed April 5, 1841,
Tsimiaro gave the French four islands off the coast (Nosy Be, Nosy
Mitsio, Nosy Komba, and Nosy Faly). By means of French support
the Hova were routed and the Antankaraña were able to return to
the mainland where they set up their capital at its present site of
Ambatoharañana, near the location of their capital at the time of the
Hova invasion. [In fact it took some 40 years before they were able
to return on a full-time basis.] Tsimiaro wished to be buried in the
caves with his ancestors, while his successor and subsequent monarchs
have been buried at the Islamic cemetery constructed adjacent to
Ambatoharañana.[5]

The king of France, Louis-Philippe, gave Tsimiaro a silver sabre.
This was stolen in November 1981 and caused the death of his [the
present ruler's] predecessor. Tsimiaro I was succeeded by his first son,
Tsialana II. The French gave him a golden sabre.[6]

The kingdom extends in the north to Diego Suarez and the Bobaomby;
in the east to the Bemarivo river; in the west to Nosy Mitsio; and in
the south to Tetezambato (which is by the road to Nosy Faly). The
kingdom occupies 2/3 of the province of Diego Suarez and [the king
continued in tourist brochure style], the biggest fête is the 'couronnement du mât royal, tous les 5 ans.'[7]

If we want to know who the contemporary Antankaraña are, it seems
to us clearest to describe them as those people who subscribe to this
narrative about themselves. They are people who not only accept
the referential aspects of the narrative, but who are committed to

---

[5] On another occasion the king told us 80% of the Antankaraña were Muslim;
in actual fact the number is much less and the Islamic practice of many local
Muslims is nominal.

[6] The sabre has jewels on its sheath and says *République Française* on one side and
Tsialana Roi on the other in an elaborate script. The silver/gold contrast is characteristic of Malagasy thought concerning royal dynasties. The connection between
the theft of the sabre and the death of the monarch suggests the potency of the
weapons.

[7] The king concluded by showing Lambek a French document indicating that
Tsialana (actually Tsialana II but referred to only as Tsialana in this document),
son and successor of Tsimiaro, was born in 1843 on Nosy Mitsio, and took the
throne in 1883. He helped the French military expeditions of 1883–85 and 1895
and sent his son Abdourahaman to fight in W.W.I. In return, the French gave
Tsialana the *Croix de Chevalier* of the *Légion d'Honneur*.

its regular active rehearsal, the enactment of its most salient portions on a cyclical basis, culminating in the fête just mentioned. This in turn means that they locate themselves within the chronotope (Bakhtin 1981), the particular time-space, that the narrative and its enactment establish. The Antankaraña live within their narrative and also on its behalf, just as it persists within and for them.

On a first reading the story seems to support conventional notions of ethnicity. Tsimiaro III makes use of the 18 tribes model, describes boundaries, and sets the Antankaraña off from the Merina. As we will argue later, there are good reasons why he does so, connected in large part to the contradictions of his agency and the politics of ethnicity within the contemporary national scene. Yet at the same time, the relationships to the French and to Islam are depicted as somewhat more complex. Moreover, the king develops his understanding of ethnic differentiation not according to a timeless logic of ascription but by means of a chronicle of specific historical events.

History is a major form of symbolic capital in northwest Madagascar, a treasured resource, and a subject of virtually universal interest. It is also intrinsically linked to power. The Antankaraña story is closely associated with the monarchy. As Feeley-Harnik (1978) points out for the Sakalava, it is only royalty who are fully entitled to ancestors and hence to history. However, these ancestors and this history exist on everyone's behalf. History is less object than ground. The king does not merely have the right to history because he is the king; rather he is the king because he is the object of history. We could say the king not only has history, but he *is* history. The history confers power upon him but it also binds him within its power. To a large degree the kingship is the symbol of the people and its story is their story.[8]

The links between the particular king, kingship, and history are subject to the changing fate of royal authority. In at least one sense the significance of the reigning king has increased over time: one of the structural changes has been the decreasing relevance of members

---

[8] The king is never fully autonomous and his position is vulnerable in a number of respects. One of the most interesting aspects of the political constitution is that as successor to the previous monarch, the reigning monarch cannot also inherit his parents' wealth; this goes to a sibling. Hence there is a separation of wealth from authority, material from symbolic capital, just as there is also a division of religious affiliation among royal siblings. This, in turn, contributes to the dependence of the monarch on his followers.

of the royal family who once functioned as regional representatives of the kingship in diverse parts of the kingdom and as potential competitors to the reigning monarch. It is here that the king's recognition in the national and transnational spheres has been critical. This has lead, doubtless, to a simplification, or purification, of the narrative and the decline of interest in alternate versions. Nevertheless, the king does not enjoy exclusive access to history; it is not he alone who gives voice to history or who can legitimate a particular version.[9] Moreover, although history may be a privilege that distinguishes royalty from commoners, this distinction is not absolute since access to membership in the royal group is by no means closed. In addition, the history is portrayed as one in which king and commoners acted collectively. It does not recount the exploits of individual heroes (with the significant exception of the *moasy*, potent diviners; in Antankaraña narrative these were women who neither married nor left offspring). Finally, in some ways entitlement to history is also a responsibility. The king is the person most bound by the implications of the narrative and the one on whose shoulders the burden of re-enacting it most heavily rests. Conversely, his legitimacy depends on the participation of the populace; if they failed to show up for the commemorative ceremonies his rule would be empty.

Identity

In this section we describe the broad context in which narration and performance of Antankaraña history takes place and out of which Antankaraña identity is constituted. Readers concerned exclusively with the interpretation of the ritual cycle may wish to skip to the next section.

People in northern Madagascar give you a variety of answers when you ask about their identity. One response is to give a 'clan' name (*karazaña*), although when we have asked people their *karazaña*

---

[9] Although most people appear to agree on the central elements of the collective story, there exist supplementary narratives that lend different shades of emphasis to, and digressions from, the main historical trajectory. However, those narratives that provide the scenarios for the ritual performances that are actually enacted are in turn authorized by them. They are the episodes within the repertoire to which the populace most clearly commits itself.

we often received answers such as 'Catholic' or 'Adzudzu' (Grande Comorian) rather than the traditional names (Zafimañahery, Anta-ñala, etc.) as listed in Vial (1954). It would seem that the significance of clans has dissipated somewhat since the precolonial period, giving way to religious, ethnic, and regional affiliations. However, this is partly an illusion, since what has happened is that 'religious' and 'ethnic' ascriptions have been subsumed into the local system of classification. Thus 'Makoa,' referring originally to non-Muslim East Africans, now share formalized pair relations (*lohateny*) with other clans. *Karazaña* means, in its most general sense, 'kind' (cf. Astuti 1995) and is based on a logic of inclusion. Clan affiliation is passed on bilaterally and is largely irrelevant in the selection of marriage partners. Hence the boundaries between clans are fluid and anyone can claim identity with more than one. Moreover, clans do not nec-essarily go back to an apical ancestor in a fixed moment of genealog-ical time but can be invoked at various levels of inclusion, levels which are not tidily nested in one another in any overarching seg-mentary model, and members do not necessarily view one another as kin. Thus, what we have clumsily translated as clans are not strictly commensurable with one another as equivalent units in a 'totemic system.' Some are conceptualized as focused on a particu-lar locality or territory whereas others have long been highly dis-persed. In general, and with a few significant exceptions linked most closely to the monarchy, clans are not now distinguished by exclu-sive rights, duties, or estates although these may have been critical in the past. From this it is clear that identifying one's *karazaña* as Adzudzu or Catholic is not at all anomalous. Rather than dividing up the contemporary landscape into mutually exclusive estates or indexing jural claims, they are firstly categories indicative of family origins. But aside from descent as a mode of inclusion,[10] *karazaña* are otherwise not derived according to a consistent set of principles.

In conjunction with the clans there exists a political system based on a hierarchical model, one that was explicitly rejected by the Tsimihety to the south and east. Pre-colonial political units were led by people of a noble dynasty, the Zafinifotsy, who claimed links to the Maroserana line that signifies royalty and sacredness over much of Madagascar. It is noteworthy that in the north the noble descent

---

[10] *Karazaña* affiliation through descent is expressed as '*valo añila, valo añila*, eight on each side,' cf. Feeley-Harnik (1991: 25) on Sakalava *valo razaña*.

group is not endogamous. This openness was such that even marriages with slaves on the part of both noble men and noble women were condoned and the offspring could be considered noble (though they could not succeed to the throne) (Vial 1954: 13). Hence nobility functions to a degree as simply one of a number of clans, if the most salient and prestigious one, in which large numbers of people can claim membership through either parent. Nobility can also be distinguished as a status group from commoners, *vahoaka, ankarabe*. And the noble clan is, or was, itself broken down into several lower-order segments stemming from various past rulers and their siblings.[11] The main point is that many ordinary people can find or imagine a consanguineal or affinal link with the nobles; conversely, the *andriana* and *ndrambavy*, as noble men and women respectively are called, can individually draw on identities with other clans, according to their respective genealogies. The nobles also stand out because it is through the re-enactment of their history specifically that the nodes around which other people attach themselves are constituted.

The word Antankaraña refers literally to people at the land of limestone rocks, the rocks in question today being a striking karst formation stretching several kilometres in a line parallel to the west coast and a few kilometres inland, north of the town of Ambilobe. The rocks now form an 18,000 ha. nature reserve over which the Départment de Eaux et Forêts, the World Wildlife Fund, and the Antankaraña maintain an uneasy collective authority. The name has been around since at least the time of Mayeur (1912) in the late 18th Century. Like many names and identities in Madagascar it is grounded in a particular locality, yet it has come to take on something of a broader function; people as far away as Antananarivo with roots in this area may refer to themselves as Antankaraña.

Although the term functions here as something like a highest order 'clan'-like grouping, it can also be understood to refer to a polity and its subjects.[12] Viewed in this sense, the Antankaraña are members of a territorially identified political unit; within the domain subjects are required to demonstrate a degree of loyalty to the collective customs and, in particular, to the authority of the reigning monarch. The political and territorial boundaries are not coterminous. Not all

---

[11] See Vial (1954) for a list.

[12] We use the word 'polity' to evade typological specificity. Here we follow Susan Drucker-Brown on the Mamprussi of northern Ghana (personal communication).

local residents identify themselves as Antankaraña or show the same degree of obedience to the monarch. Conversely, people living outside the salient territory may also assert loyalty to the king. Nevertheless, the territory itself is potent; even non-Antankaraña living in the heartland of the territory must obey certain local customs and taboos, that is, act to a degree like Antankaraña, and the more they do so, the more they become Antankaraña.[13] Conversely, it is when they don't that the Antankaraña identity of the offended becomes most significant. The longer they stay, the more Antankaraña they become, although such identification is partly pragmatic and does not necessarily replace the identifications they bring with them.[14] Likewise, Antankaraña living outside the territory feel less compulsion to obey its rules.

The main exception to such easy incorporation are people identified as Merina (*Borzan*), for reasons identified in the king's narrative. Their exclusion illustrates that a historical dimension is intrinsically linked to the geographical in the formulation of Antankaraña identity and the composition of the polity. Ethnic relations are produced out of the meanings assigned historical processes and events.[15] It is also important to recognize that despite the ostensible continuity of the Antankaraña polity since at least the accession of Lamboeny Be, said to be in 1710 but probably some 50 years later (Vial 1954, Vérin 1986), and the explicit attention given to commemoration of the past, in fact its constitution has changed dramatically over the intervening years.

Although the notion of the polity presupposes a degree of centralized authority, and coercion undoubtedly played a central role in the past, especially with regard to labour, at the present time commoners have little material need to work for royalty. The north is a well-watered area characterized by sufficient arable and grazing land. The economy is mixed; in the contemporary Antankaraña

---

[13] Compare the process of becoming Sakalava in Ambanja described by Sharp (1993) as well as Astuti's lucid argument for activity rather than ascription as the basis of being Vezo (1995). On the significance of taboos to legitimate identity see Lambek (1992). Graeber (1996: 2) makes the important point that authority in Madagascar is often 'negative,' i.e. 'rooted in the power to stop others from acting, rather than the power to initiate or direct the action of others.'

[14] More recently, some migrant groups appear to have the power and economic base to resist incorporation.

[15] It is worth noting that it is precisely vis-à-vis the Merina that the Antankaraña best fit the model of ethnic consciousness set out by Comaroff.

heartland it is comprised of a combination of rice, cattle, fishing, and cash crops such as sugar cane. Shrimp fishing is highly lucrative and open to anyone. Many Antankaraña families include members who operate directly in the wage sector. This is especially true of the nobles who are likely to have family members with positions in the civil administration, education, the trades and professions. Wage labour is to be found in the towns of the region or elsewhere in Madagascar, but links are retained with those kin who remain on the land. The Antankaraña are not particularly poor; what they primarily lack is access to adequate health services and education.[16] These may have been more accessible to members of the royal family, but the king has not been able to dispense these scarce and valued services to the population. One consequence of all this is that the ritual centre tends to be rather under-populated; the king himself, like many members of his descent group, lives in the nearby market town and administrative centre of Ambilobe.

Relatively few Antankaraña have worked as proletarian labour on the enormous sugar estate and factory that lies within their territory in the delta of the Mahavavy. This estate was once French-owned but has long since been a state corporation. The relationship between SIRAMA and the Antankaraña is a complex and interesting one that cannot be the subject here, except to say that cession of the land is one of the notable lapses in the Antankaraña master narrative. (Vial mentions that it did not occur without resistance whereas the current monarch has explained to us that SIRAMA's domain was a gift from one of his predecessors.) At the beginning of the annual cane harvest an Antankaraña official (the *manantany* Dzaobe) is called in to perform a blessing (*joro*) by the cutting machine at the factory; in 1991 3 oxen were killed. SIRAMA likewise contributes material aid to the royal ceremonies. The main point here is that most Antankaraña have been well enough off that they have not had to work for SIRAMA. By contrast, for people from many other parts of Madagascar, employment in the fields or factory has been an opportunity much sought after. That is also why today the Antankaraña are not in a majority in the lower valley of the Mahavavy but only in the more isolated parts of their country and especially in the coastal plain stretching north and that encompasses the centre of their sacred landscape. The presence of the large polyethnic

---

[16] We thank Emmanuel Tehindrazanarivelo for clarifying the point.

community at SIRAMA may be a factor in heightening a new form of Antankaraña ethnic consciousness different from the one we describe in this paper, as exemplified by participation in ethnically based associations and clubs.

The political model of identity suffers from the same handicap as the ethnic model, namely its implicit assumption of discrete entities, that is, its concern with boundaries and their contents set in a field of opposed, similarly bounded, but discrete units characterized by exclusive memberships. It is possible that in the precolonial period the boundaries between indigenous political units were sharper than they are now, but political affiliation was based not only on territory but also on loyalty to particular members of the noble descent group who, moving across the landscape, were able to establish their rule at certain places within it. The power relations among noble kin, and hence between the territories and people over whom they exercised authority, were often fluctuating and ambiguous. Thus there is a noble branch on the southern flank of the kingdom that was not readily controlled by the reigning monarch and that even today needs to supply its blessing to a new king if the rite of succession is to be accomplished. Despite the imposition of rigid boundaries comprising the administrative units of the colonial and post-colonial state, it makes more sense to speak of centres and relative connection to, and distance from, them.

Between centres there has been a good deal of overlap. Thus the relationship of the Antankaraña to the Sakalava is not that of one 'tribe' or 'ethnic group' to another, nor of distinct neighbouring polities. Instead it seems that the Antankaraña were formed on a model similar (but not identical) to that underlying the Sakalava polities and were products of a common set of social forces. Additionally, there were times when the Antankaraña polity was subordinate to the Sakalava of Boina and paid them tribute, a time even when a Sakalava king sat in the Antankaraña capital. Hence the autonomy of the Antankaraña has been based on their ability to establish a legitimate centre of their own, to maintain its integrity, to impose their custom on its inhabitants, and to draw on distinctive local custom. Such autonomy must needs be relative and such identity non-exclusive. The role of the king in negotiating with the greater powers that have surrounded them has also been critical.

The fuzziness of the contemporary boundaries may be illustrated by the fact that Folo, the man who performs today as ritual purifier of the Antankaraña king, comes from a Sakalava clan of purifiers, the Jingô, and was born and raised near Analalava, capital of the southern Bemihisatra Sakalava. 'Looked after' (*nitarimy*) there by the *tromba* spirit Ndramarofaly, Folo came to Ambatoharañana, the capital of the Antankaraña, at the request of another *tromba*, Dady ny Kôto (interview with Folo, 1992).[17] It is relevant to understanding this particular account that Ndramarofaly is remembered for being the product of the union of Zafinifotsy and Zafinimena parents, branches of Malagasy royalty identified, respectively, with Antankaraña and Sakalava rule. Dady ny Kôto is Zafinifotsy.

This transfer can be viewed as part of the continuing attempt to reproduce complete royal centres on the authority of a dominant Sakalava model (and illustrates the role of spirits and mediums in the process). However, the Antankaraña do not conform entirely to this model; part of what makes them autonomous is the distinctive ceremonial form by which they reproduce their centre.

The closer to the centre, the more Antankaraña, and the more distant, in several senses, not only a spatial one, the less Antankaraña. The clearest index of this is that the closer to the centre one lives, the more one has to follow specifically Antankaraña taboos. For example, people identifying themselves as Antankaraña in Antananarivo follow fewer taboos there than they do when visiting family in the North. Identification is not merely through ascription but is embodied in daily practice, a practice that shifts with locality, social position, and context (Lambek 1992).[18]

Tsy tany mandeha, fô olon belo ('it is not land that moves, but people'), one of the most cited of proverbs, means, in part, that, unlike the constancy of land, people do not remain the same when they move. They do not give up those aspects of their identities constituted by the movements, in turn, of their ancestors, but they also accede to the customs of the new place. Continuity is anchored in the land and the marks that the ancestors leave on it; history is made by movement across it. Moreover, movement generates and is generated by marriage. Bilateral descent provides multiple identities and choice of affiliation; movement introduces diversity and accre-

---

[17] *Tromba* spirits are the contemporary manifestations in the bodies of mediums of deceased members of the ruling family.

[18] The point is somewhat similar to Ramanujan's (n.d.) on the contextualizing qualities of South Asian identities. Cf. Astuti (1995) on the Vezo.

tion to personal practice (cf. Bloch 1971, 1996). History is recouped by retraversal.

In sum, the logic of social identity in northern Madagascar is very different from its explicit cast in the West, though perhaps not quite so different from the more tacit forms of Western practice. It proceeds by a logic of relatively open boundaries, multiple and overlapping affiliations, and mutual incorporation. This incorporative tendency is evident in the name of the reigning monarch as represented on his recent visiting card given Lambek in 1991:

> ISSA Tsimanamboholahy Alexandre
> TSIMIARO III—Le Prince Antakarana
> Chevalier de l'Ordre National Malagasy
> President d'Honneur des Associations:
>   W.W.F.
>   Alliance Française d'Ambilobe

Note that the king's name is composed of Arabic, Malagasy, and French segments, indexing respectively Islamic, 'ancestral' Malagasy, and Christian components of his identity. Similarly, the titles of past kings are referred to by the Malagasy royal name plus the emphatic French numeral (Tsialana *Deux*, etc.) rather than exclusively by purely Malagasy posthumous praise names as among the Sakalava of Boina.[19] In addition the king is ready to draw on various externally derived sources of authority and prestige to bolster his identity. It is interesting, however, that his card did not include his position as local state functionary in the ministry of sports and leisure.

Religious affiliation is a critical avenue of incorporation and mixing. When we collected the names of the present king's children and were satisfied with a single name for each, they showed the same diversity evident in the components of their father's name, some being called by Muslim names, some by French, and some by Malagasy. And while the king identifies himself as Muslim, his wife is Catholic. Her mother, in turn, is Muslim. All the king's offspring are Muslim except for one daughter, a Catholic. One explanation for why the present king's father's brother did not succeed to the throne was that his father had designated him a Catholic; the father, monarch two reigns ago, placed each of his sons in a different denomination.

---

[19] Many Antankaraña do make use of the posthumous praise names in informal speech.

Such intermixing of religious affiliation, including various Protestant denominations and those who state simply that they belong to none of these institutionalized religions (*tsy mivavaka*) is characteristic of family and community life in the region. Rather than lead to sectarian strife, it provides a dense network of cross-cutting affiliations.

The incorporative quality of northwestern Malagasy social organization means that people have also embraced a model that is inconsistent with its basic premises. Indeed, they have had little choice. The model of ascriptive, discrete, equivalent, juxtaposed ethnic groups is superimposed upon the incorporative, performative one. If the one model makes sense in local and regional arenas, the other plays a role on the national scene. Indeed, the division into 18 *ethnies* is a central means by which the nation is imagined as such. And to the degree that Antankaraña power, and especially the power and authority of the monarch, depend on national authorization and material support, this model gains precedence. Hence, seeing the world in 'tribal' or 'ethnic' terms provides a new source of legitimation for the monarch, enabling him to stand on the national scene as the representative of 'the Antankaraña.'[20] Here the emphasis has shifted toward the sort of 'ethnic' consciousness delineated by Comaroff from the local model we try to portray in the paper. We turn now to the kind of Antankaraña-ness that is constructed and made manifest in the ritual cycle.

Ritual

The Antankaraña historical narrative is enacted in a ceremonial cycle that constitutes and reconstitutes the polity, climaxing in a mast-raising (*tsangantsaiñy*) which takes place every 5 or 6 years in the capital Ambatoharañana. This has occurred most recently in 1993.[21] The ceremonial cycle reproduces the chronotope, at once a sacred geography and a sacred history. In the year prior to the mast-raising the king must retrace the travels of his ancestors/predecessors and visit their tombs in order to inform them of the upcoming event and ask for their blessing. This reconstitutes both the Antankaraña domain as well as the living monarch's legitimacy and also acknowl-

---

[20] We thank Jacqueline Solway for this observation.
[21] Walsh attended the event in 1993. The two previous mast-raisings occurred in 1981 and 1987.

edges the continuous presence of the royal ancestors. In 1992, accompanied by a large number of ritual assistants, nobles, and members of the general public, the king first traveled to the island of Nosy Mitsio to the west of the capital to visit the site of exile and the tombs of deceased relatives (none of whom were reigning monarchs). He then returned to the capital and later went to the tombs of his ancestors in the caverns to the east of the capital. The king's movements recreate those of the Antankaraña of the 1830's who were holed up in the caverns and then fled and remained for several decades on Nosy Mitsio, Tsimiaro I returning to the mainland only after his death on Nosy Mitsio for burial in one of the caverns. In traversing the landscape the reigning king traverses ancestral history.

Held a year later, the mast-raising (*tsangantsaiñy*) itself takes some 15 days from the selection and cutting of the two trees in the forest and their conjoining to the planting of the mast. It is significant that the trees must be selected from a forest south of the Mahavavy River and then carried (horizontally) virtually straight northward to the capital. The mast is accompanied by large numbers of people who are met at the capital by the portion of the population arriving from the north. The northward journey represents the origins of the Antankaraña monarchy in the south. The north/south division is repeated in the structure of the capital itself in which the northern portion is inhabited by nobles and the southern portion by commoners. The king's residence, the *zomba*, lies at the southern limit of the northern portion, thus at the centre of the village. The mast is planted in the large plaza immediately north of the *zomba*.[22] Adjacent to the mast, on the west side, is the *toñy*, the northern village altar, composed of two permanently placed vertical polyhedral stones brought from Nosy Mitsio. In sum, the ritual entails a series of movements from and to the centre, reconstructing and reaffirming that centre through the movements and the erection of the pole.

The integral unity of space and time in this reconstruction of the Antankaraña universe is demonstrated by recent innovations on the part of the king.[23] He has lengthened the cycle by a year, adding a

---

[22] North of the plaza is another *zomba* built when Lamboeny II became king and inhabited until his death by his son, the most highly regarded elder, Said Abdourahimo Soultoany.

[23] The process of innovation is not new. If the ceremony itself predates 1840, which it well might, then it has absorbed significant events into its commemorative chronology over the course of its own history.

pilgrimage to the tomb of an earlier ancestor the year prior to the
visit to the caves. This ancestor, Kozo Be, the early 17th century
founder of the Zafinifotsy dynasty in which current Antankaraña royalty include themselves, is buried further to the south, near Ambanja.
In 1993 he added yet another trip, this time to tombs at Bemarivo
in the east. The visit to these ancestors remembers a conflict with
the Sakalava in the late 17th Century during which some family
members stayed behind after a period of refuge in Maroansetra.
Hence the expansion in time is matched by an expansion in space;
in both cases a step backwards, but one that enlarges the Antankaraña
world. This world has an axis that is simultaneously temporal as well
as spatial.

The mast-raising ceremony, which forms the climax of the cycle,
affirms the re-placement of the capital in the Ambatoharañana region
despite predations by the Merina. This is today the salient centre of
the chronotope. As such it is not merely commemorative of a single event of Antankaraña history. Just as it pulls together the spatial elements of the kingdom, so it pulls together time; events before
and since the return from exile are brought together into a single,
multi-layered whole. Thus the *tromba* spirits who rise display simultaneously kings who reigned consecutively (cf. Lambek n.d.). *Trombas*
from a much earlier date are invoked during the commemoration
of the concealment and exile that happened well after the time when
they were alive. The diachronic march of history is thereby partly
synchronized, much as the space of the kingdom is drawn together
and concentrated in the capital.

The mast-raising is repeated every few years and events from
various periods, including present-day national/regional politics are
interpreted by means of the model it establishes. However it would
not be correct to say that the Antankaraña sense of time is entirely
cyclical or that historical events are treated as entirely 'external' to
the structure (cf. Bloch 1996, Lambek 1996). The Antankaraña do
recognize events prior to those commemorated in the mast-raising
(including the fact that the capital was located at several other sites
before they took refuge in the caves). Moreover, while focused on a
central and repeated moment, the sense of time constituted by the
ceremonies is not exclusively cyclical but has unidirectionality as well.
At each successive ceremony the mast should be a few centimetres
higher than the previous one. Similarly, once the throne changes
patriline, as it has at least once, the succession is irreversible (at least,

so say the members of the present reigning line) and cannot go back to the source. In other words, succession is never from son to father (i.e. to father's brother) and once it has passed to sister's children it should not revert to the former patriline but begins a new one.[24]

The mast or the flag?

If the *tsangantsaiñy* (mast-raising) serves as a vehicle of historical reproduction there is some recognition that it too has a history. Indeed the mast-raising itself may be of some antiquity, preceding the historical events it now serves to commemorate. Tsimiaro III has told us it dates back to 1700, i.e., well before the altercation with the Merina, while the leading elder, Said Abdourahimo Soultoany has placed its origins with the treaty with the French.[25] Others (Vérin 1986, Vavihely 1963, Fulgence Fanony and Lisa Gezon personal communications) have suggested an origin tied to the influence (if not behest) of a late 18th century emissary of French interests (Benyowsky) on the island. Whether rooted in indigenous (i.e. pre-mercantile) or foreign (i.e. European) systems of power symbolization, there is no denying the syncretic nature of the event today. One need only look to early descriptions of indigenous and colonial 'mast-raisings'[26] to note the interesting mixture of 'outside' and 'inside' meanings which the contemporary performance of the *tsangantsaiñy* seems to incorporate.

The chief point, which Walsh is addressing in his research, is that the performance and meaning of the ritual has shifted over time. *Saiñy* is a wonderfully polyvalent word. It might refer most directly to the pole. Since *tsangan* means to raise to a standing position, *saiñy* appears to refer to the mast. Moreover it is the mast that is subject to the most attention and vertical posts (*hazomanga*) are found in the

---

[24] Succession is somewhat more complicated than this but cannot be elaborated here.

[25] In another context (Tsitindry 1987) Said Abdourahimo Soultoany has given a 17th century origin of the rite as well. Rather than consider these two sources as simply conflicting we suggest that they indicate something important about the nature of the history of the *tsangantsaiñy*. While it may have originated in the 17th century, as Tsitindry's transcribed interview suggests, it may also have undergone a transformation following the treaty with the French.

[26] We refer specifically to accounts recorded in Benyowsky (1904) and Decary (1960).

rituals of numerous other parts of Madagascar. Yet today people often translate *saiñy* as flag (although Said Abdourahimo Soultoany refers to the flags as the *raving ny saiñy*, the leaves of the mast) and the culmination comes when a man climbs the mast to position the rope used to hoist the flags in place. In recent events the flags raised have been those of the Antankaraña (a red lunar crescent and star on a white background) and the Malagasy Republic. In other years the French *tricolore* has flown along with the Antankaraña flag. The King sometimes refers to the *tsangantsaiñy*, in translation, as the '*couronnement du mât*.' Indeed, the mast itself may be, or have been reimagined as, a flagpole on the French military model. (In earlier times the French themselves may have placed as much weight on the pole as on the flag; Mayeur writes of raising the *mât du pavillon* at his trading posts.)[27]

Sovereign and mast are identified with one another and at times the mast is referred to specifically as *Ampanjaka*, i.e. 'king.' It is made of wood known as *hazoambo*. This wood cannot be used for anything else that rests on ground. Thus it can be used for building a roof but not a floor. As a species, it is referred to as 'the king's tree and the king of trees, *kakazo ny ampanzakan ndraiky ampanzakan ny kakazo*.' Until it is firmly planted, the king and the mast stand in an avoidance relationship or one of 'rivalry' (*mirafy*). Once the mast starts its journey to the capital the king must remain concealed until it is upright. In effect, the king is symbolically dead until reborn via the erection of the mast.

The political meaning of the *saiñy* is grasped by comparison with the anti-monarchical Tsimihety who have a government referred to as *manzaka maro saiñy* which may be translated as 'the rule of many minds' (E. Tehindrazanarivelo: personal communication). Hence the Antankaraña single pole, its displacement across the landscape born by large crowds, signifies the 'single mind,' i.e., the political unity of the kingdom, the general will summed up in the person of the king and indexically re-established each time the populace replaces the mast at his behest. The mast-raising is at once indexical of the king's support (i.e. the will of the people), iconic of the potency of the king-

---

[27] While the mast remains standing until it falls, the flags are lowered on the afternoon of the ceremony, to be raised again on special occasions. Thus Walsh was told that a visit by President Zafy Albert would have warranted a raising of the flags.

ship, and symbolic of the unity of the Antankaraña polity and its renewal. At the same time, the dual flags signify the inextricable linkage of the Antankaraña with other powers.

The mast, some 11 metres tall, signifies the force of the kingdom. The phallic properties are obvious and reinforced by the fact that mass circumcisions take place the very night the mast is raised. However, the mast is not merely phallic but generative in a sexually more complementary sense, the product of the union of male and female.[28] It is composed of two pieces joined together to form a single whole and referred to as the male and female parts. In addition, at each circumcision ceremony a single smaller vertical post and another 'y' shaped one, representing male and female elements respectively, are planted in the plaza adjacent to the main post to the south of it. These tend to remain vertical much longer than the mast so that there are always several of them standing whereas there is at most only one standing mast. They may symbolize the products of fertility, namely the desired male and female offspring of boys to be circumcised the night of the *tsangantsaiñy*, or the populace vis-à-vis the king. Sexual vitality is also emphasized in descriptions of the night prior to the mast-raising which is said to be a time in which ordinary sexual taboos are lifted and partners can freely select each other. In fact, it is not that taboos are lifted so much as that offenses committed at this time go unpunished, a significant distinction which emphasizes the temporary absence of rule in the liminal period just prior to the restoration of the monarchy with the raising of the pole. This sexual activity is more a topic of conversation than fact; the mast-raising does not appear to be the scene of any more or less promiscuity than accompanies any large gathering.[29]

One of the interesting features of the mast-raising is that while the mast is in some sense the representation of the king and vice versa, the cycling of monarchs and masts are not synchronous. Indeed, the attention paid to the mast in some sense offsets the need for

---

[28] Among the Antankaraña, unlike the Sakalava, only men can become king (*Ampanjaka*). However, there is a complementary position for women (not found among the Sakalava), that of the *Ndrambavy Be* ('First Lady'). She is not the king's wife and usually not his mother, but is chosen from among the closely related noble women. The kingdom is understood to be the product of the unity of male and female.

[29] As Middleton points out, the 'night of freedom' is not uncommon in other Malagasy societies.

elaborate ceremonies of royal succession and burial.[30] One might
well ask why the ritual recurs with such frequency. The immediate
answer is that the mast falls after two or three years and must then
be replaced, but inquiry demonstrates that in the past the mast
remained standing for much longer and hence ceremonies were far
less frequent. Indeed, an entire reign went by (that of Lamboeny II,
1925–38) in which no *tsangantsaiñy* occurred.[31]

While other Malagasy groups emphasize the hardness of wood in
signifying the enduring qualities of descent (e.g. Bloch on the Zafimaniry), the Antankaraña have deliberately replaced the hardwood (*teza
lintañono*) masts of the past with softer ones (*hazoambo*) in order to
hold the ceremony more frequently. When in the 1960's President
Tsiranana offered to provide a metal pole embedded in concrete to
save the trouble of continual replacements, the gift was turned down
with alacrity. The mast *has to* fall and be replaced. It provides a ritual of renewal. But the point may also be that the mast symbolizes
not only the kingdom and the kingship but the authority of the king
himself. The king is not all powerful. He owes his position to the
will of people, a point of which he is vividly reminded at each mast-
raising, when he is, in a sense, removed and installed anew. Indeed,
in the temporary disappearance of the king the ritual bears striking
similarity to rites of installation elsewhere in Africa (Turner 1969).

The mast-raising indicates very clearly that no single monarch is
indispensable and that the kingdom cannot persist without the collective efforts of the populace.[32] The rise and fall of individual masts
suggests the people's ability to raise up—and to depose—any given
king.[33] Replacement rather than permanence is the form of conti-

---

[30] According to an informant, 'Once the mast starts to lean it is cut down. It
makes people sad. They untie their hair for a week; men don't wear hats. It's like
a funeral. No hats, shoes, or pants are permitted.' This mourning lasts a week. We
cannot here explore the parallels between the disposal of fallen masts and 'ancestral' (non-Muslim) royal burials. It is interesting in this regard that the very shift
from 'ancestral' to Muslim burial practices forms part of the narrative commemorated by the ritual cycle.

[31] The mast raised in the autumn of 1987 fell in December 1990. That of October
1993 fell in the autumn of 1995 (Lisa Gezon, personal communication).

[32] A point we cannot address here is that the populace is not undifferentiated
but divided by *karazaña* according to specific responsibilities in the preparation and
transportation of the mast. It is of interest also that the 'y' shaped post that holds
the mast (referred to as *ampanjaka*, king) in position just before it is planted is referred
to as *rangahy*, that is, councilor.

[33] The king himself is not an autocrat. Although we don't know of any king who

nuity here and it occurs through the will and efforts of the populace. The polity is understood not as an essentialized entity but the product of continuous human investment in it. The commoner who told us the story of President Tsiranana's offer emphasized very strongly that participation at a mast-raising is not obligatory. He said, 'It is the *volonté* of the people to provide the mast and the oxen,' and he emphasized there is even competition over the size of contributions.[34] From this perspective the *sañy* appears less far from the Tsimihety political model. In a sense, the ritual is the re-enactment of the Antankaraña 'constitution.' However this is not a mere representation of something existing outside the performance. The performance of the *tsangantsañy* is itself the real thing, as people re-establish their rights, obligations, and powers, as well as reaffirm their continued commitment to them.

The State

An additional reason for the shortening of the cycle is that the ritual has become the very life of the monarchy as the latter has become embedded in and subordinated to the Malagasy state. In effect, the king has little power or autonomy and the Antankaraña little national visibility other than through the management and enactment of the ceremonial cycle. Without the cycle, Antankaraña identity would today lose a good deal of its saliency (perhaps becoming analogous to reference to a 'clan' like the Anjoaty, whose identity is

---

was deposed (though perhaps Boanahadj was), there is a sense that he rules at the pleasure of his people and on their behalf. Middleton points out that the idea that the king cannot exist without the people is found throughout Madagascar (e.g. Feeley-Harnik 1991). Today the position of the Antankaraña monarch is a somewhat precarious one since he must not only contend with the faction who lost the succession battle but must attempt to mediate between hotly debated positions in national politics. It is a matter of common knowledge in the north that he has not always been able to keep to the neutrality he advocates; moreover his position on national issues has not always corresponded to that advocated by the majority of his people. This has brought him into no little difficulty and necessitated rituals in which he was purified of the insults caused to his person.

[34] The popular contributions, over 100 oxen slaughtered in 1987, are also simultaneously religious in nature; the Antankaraña are giving to the ancestors and asking for blessings in return. Whether submission to the ritual language and practice itself creates the sense of desirability of giving to royalty is a significant general question raised by means of Merina ethnography in the work of Maurice Bloch (e.g. 1989a).

constituted by allusions to potent practices that have probably long since disappeared). Thus one could almost say that while the Antankaraña hold the ceremony because they are Antankaraña, the identity 'Antankaraña' exists largely because they hold the ceremony. In sum, the mast-raising is not simply a memorial to a past identity, but a condition for the present and future one.

In their near conquest by the Merina, the Antankaraña suffered a collective trauma in which their identity virtually disappeared. But their identity since has been predicated on the event of the trauma and on the relations with significant others that it established: as Muslims, as allies of the French, in avoidance relations with the Merina. The explicit subject of the memory is less some 'pristine' or 'primordial' state of Antankaraña-ness that existed prior to the trauma, was threatened by it or was what they tried to preserve during it, than the new set of relations that the trauma and its overcoming set into motion. What they remember most vividly since the original trauma are the acts of remembering, *the passage of previous mast-raisings*. Indeed, Antankaraña identity is an identity as rememberers. This is not a situation of becoming stuck in the past, of a society so focused on a traumatic loss and its commemoration that it cannot move forward,[35] but rather of harnessing the traumatic experience to express a collective mode of historical practice. In contemporary Madagascar, moreover, remembering has proved to be an adaptive position and one upon which the Antankaraña capitalize. As one of the last 'traditional' polities to retain a regular ritual cycle, they have moved from the position of a relatively insignificant and marginal people to becoming exemplars of Malagasy tradition. Their capital was described in a village meeting as 'the most famous village in Madagascar.'

The 1981 *tsangantsaiñy* was filmed by Malagasy ethnographers. The film was shown in Ambatoharañana (the ritual capital) and in Ambilobe (the administrative centre) and then, on the occasion of the international historical congress, in the city of Antsiranana [Diego Suarez] in 1987. Two showings at the large cinema of that northern city were packed and a third showing, arranged on the city square, attracted over a thousand people. Although the majority of the citizens of Antsiranana are not specifically Antankaraña, as north-

---

[35] The analogy here is to the individual patient suffering some form of hysteria or other painful and unresolved response to trauma (cf. Antze and Lambek 1996).

ern Malagasy many identify to one degree or another with the Antankaraña and are proud of the ceremony. The *tsangantsaiñy* of 1987 was filmed for Malagasy television. The king has a copy of the video, of which he is especially proud since it was the first mast raising since he took office. However he was very eager to have an international film crew at the next ceremony and urged us to return with one.[36] He argues that the ceremony is significant in raising Antankaraña consciousness (perhaps another translation for *saiñy* . . .) of themselves and also in raising their profile within the Malagasy Republic, and beyond. The king is proud, in his words, that he is the only king with a mast. What he means, in part, is that the Antankaraña are nationally recognized as one of the few local polities to continue to publicly reproduce themselves through 'traditional' ritual and thus to maintain the kind of power which that entails.[37]

The national interest in the ceremony has a paradoxical dimension since what has come to give the Antankaraña value on the national scene is precisely a statement of resistance to the national model. For the nation as a whole, and for its intellectuals, the Antankaraña ceremony has become a metonym for ancestral culture and religion. Although most Malagasy who work in the urban and public sectors have long been converted to Christianity, they still see the ancestors as a source of value and some find meaning in the continuity that appears to characterize the Antankaraña. But while the citizens of Antananarivo and the audience of Malagasy television may view the ceremony as a part of the national heritage, for the Antankaraña themselves the ceremony commemorates and keeps alive the political scenario of the 19th Century in which the Merina, the largest group and today still associated in the provinces with the state, were the enemy and the French, the subsequent colonial power, were their allies and even their fictive kin. A ritual that signifies equivalence on the national scene ['each tribe has its customs; every Malagasy group respects the ancestors'] signifies for the Antankaraña themselves their distinctiveness and relative autonomy.

---

[36] The 1993 event was filmed, though not by us, and the resulting documentary was subsequently shown on French television. A video record was also made by Rebecca Green.

[37] Moreover, as we stated earlier, the identification of the king with the mast is a profound one. The mast represents the kingdom, the kingship, the royal ancestors, the people, and the king, and at the same time, the king is, as he put it, the living mast.

The Antankaraña celebrate survival in the face of encroachment from Antananarivo.[38] They reject that encroachment and turn instead to their alliance with the French. For them the alliance continues.[39] The French diplomatic community are regularly invited to the ceremonies as most honoured guests—and are also invited to contribute to the development of the kingdom, renovation of the palace, the roads, etc. The Antankaraña portray themselves as the only group in Madagascar to have such an autonomous alliance with the French. They exhibit the French flag and the sabres that were the gifts of King Louis Philippe (Rafilipo) and his successors. At the mast-raising the king appears in his 19th Century French military uniform complete with *bicorne*.

As the Antankaraña elder, Said Abdourahimo Soultoany, put it: 'It was the treaty between the Zafinifotsy [the royal dynasty] and the French that was the origin of the *tsangantsaiñy*. None of the other kings have one. Only the Antankaraña practice the mast-raising. It was the treaty with Rafilipo. The meaning of the mast-raising is that the French and the Antankaraña are kin. When there is a mast-raising, the President of the French Republic comes here; Giscard d'Estaing came here. General De Gaulle himself came here for the mast-raising at Ambatoharañana.[40] Mitterand has not come, but the Consul and the French Ambassador have come.' On another occasion we heard, 'The *tsangantsaiñy* was started after the French came, to celebrate the fact that the Merina were gone. The people were happy the French came and delivered them. We do the fête as a souvenir.'

Today other whites have been assimilated to the French allies. The ceremony has been attended by members of the anthropological and high cultural establishment as well as by the French diplo-

---

[38] The present king says he tries to stay out of politics and to get along with whomever is in power nationally. Some of his subjects are pro-government, some are in opposition. So, he says, if he were political himself it would increase divisiveness among his people and would run counter to his role. In general his politics is one of pro-Antankaraña, anti-Merina sentiment. He attributes contemporary events in Antananarivo, as well as past history, in terms of Merina versus coastal people (*côtiers*), thereby deploying an oppositional notion of ethnicity.

[39] There is a certain parallel with the treaties some First Nations in Canada would retain with Great Britain rather than the federal government. Our thanks to Ronald Wright for this point.

[40] Bruno Ndriamahafahana suggested that perhaps this occurred when De Gaulle was French representative here during the colonial period. We have not verified it.

matic community, and the king would like to use it as a tourist attraction. This kind of objectification of culture of course changes its nature. But we should be wary of saying it is no longer 'authentic.' It is rather the terms by which authenticity is legitimated that have changed.

We close by mentioning perhaps the most striking and, in a sense, poignant omissions from the public cycle. The Antankaraña story is one of conflict with, yet freedom from, the Merina and alliance with the French.[41] As regards the first, the Antankaraña commemoration omits the times their kings were subordinated to the Merina or possibly even in alliance with them. Tsimiaro's father was forced to accept vassalage. It was only when Tsimiaro began to harry the Merina that the latter turned on the kingdom a second time and people were forced to flee into the caves. As regards the second, the commemoration omits two critical points: what the French thought of the Antankaraña and the nature of their treaty; and the actual difficulties the Antankaraña monarchs had with the French subsequent to its signing.

The trauma of Merina aggression is emphasized; the trauma of French colonialism overlooked. Nevertheless, it too was a significant historical experience. Tsimiaro's difficulties during the protectorate are evident, if unintentionally, in the account by Boudou (1911). And although the Sakalava and Antankaraña helped the French in their campaign against the Hova in 1883–85, in the subsequent treaty France gave the Hova (Merina) control over them in return for rights to the port of Diego Suarez. The French envoy wrote to the Ministère des Affaires Etrangères, 17 juin 1886, 'Les Sakalaves et les Antankares [in contrast to the Merina] . . . ne sont que des nègres de race inférieure' (cited in Berisika 1983: 10, our addition). The Antankaraña were subject to the same colonial policies that subsequently incited resistance and revolt throughout Madagascar, including sections of the north. Yet none of this is included in their master narrative.

Any collective identity is imaginatively constructed in part by selective omission and the historian plays a role, whether by helping the chosen nation develop a suitable narrative or by critically taking the received truth apart (Anderson 1991, Hobsbawm 1992). The dilemma

---

[41] The Muslim connection is put to one side at the present time though it is ready for use and affirmed in the annual *ziara*, the visit to the Muslim tombs, and in the Muslim emblems on the Antankaraña flag.

is no less great for anthropologists, especially when we work in a
society that is neither our own nor very powerful in the larger scale
of things. Perusal of the documents leaves us in an ethical quandary.
Do we draw attention to the contemptuous racist and paternalistic
remarks of the French officials? Do we demonstrate how they sought
to and sometimes succeeded in exploiting Antankaraña? But this
raises a series of more significant questions: To what degree is
Antankaraña silence on these subjects a deliberate political and rhetor-
ical strategy? To what degree is it due to the inconceivability of
fictive kin (*fatidra*), as the tie with the French was constituted by the
Antankaraña, acting in such a manner toward their 'blood brothers'? Perhaps it is neither naive ignorance nor cynical strategy but
a product of the collective will to transcend such sentiments and
events and, by putting their past choices in the best light, to transform through their artistry the present into the future.

REFERENCES CITED

Anderson, Benedict
    1991   *Imagined Communities*. London: Verso.
Antze, Paul and Michael Lambek
    1996   *Tense Past: Cultural Essays on Trauma and Memory*. New York: Routledge.
Astuti, Rita
    1995   *People of the Sea: Identity and Descent among the Vezo of Madagascar*. Cambridge:
        Cambridge University Press.
Bakhtin, Mikhail
    1981   *The Dialogical Imagination*. Michael Holquist, ed. C. Emerson and M. Hol-
        quist, trans. Austin: University of Texas Press.
Benyowsky, Maurice Auguste Count de
    1904   *Memoirs and Travels*. London: Kegan, Paul, Trench, Trübner and Co.
Berisika, Omer
    1983   *Diego-Suarez: De l'occupation d'une baie à la création d'une ville 1885–1905*.
        Mémoire de maîtrise, Paris VII.
Bloch, Maurice
    1971   *Placing the Dead*. New York: Seminar Press.
    1989a   'Symbols, Song and Dance and Features of Articulation: Is Religion
        an Extreme Form of Traditional Authority?' in: *Ritual, History and Power*.
        London: Athlone, pp. 19–45.
    1989b   'The Symbolism of Money in Imerina.' In J. Parry and M. Bloch, eds.
        Money and the Morality of Exchange. Cambridge: CUP, pp. 165–190.
    1996   'Internal and External Memory: Different Ways of Being in History.'
        In Paul Antze and Michael Lambek, eds. *Tense Past: Cultural Essays in
        Trauma and Memory*. New York: Routledge.
Boudou, R.F.A.
    1911   'Querelles de roitelets Antankaraña et Sakalava 1865–75.' *Bulletin de
        l'Académie Malgache*, tome XXIV, p. 171.

Comaroff, John
   1992   'Of Totemism and Ethnicity.' In Comaroff and Comaroff, *Ethnography and the Historical Imagination*. Boulder: Westview, pp. 49–67.

Comaroff, John and Jean Comaroff
   1992   *Ethnography and the Historical Imagination*. Boulder: Westview.

Decary, R.
   1960   *L'île de Nosy Be de Madagascar: Histoire d'une Colonisation*. Paris: Editions Maritime et d'Outre Mer.

Feeley-Harnik, Gillian
   1978   'Divine Kingship and the Meaning of History Among the Sakalava of Madagascar.' *Man* 13: 402–17.
   1991   *A Green Estate*. Washington: Smithsonian Institution Press.

Graeber, David
   1996   'Love Magic and Colonial Labor Policy in Central Madagascar.' *Gender and History*, 8.

Hobsbawm, Eric
   1992   'The Opiate Ethnicity.' *Alphabet City* 2: 8–11.

Jenkins, M.D., ed.
   1987   *Madagascar: An Environmental Profile. Int. Union for Conservation of Nature and Natural Resources*, IUCN: Cambridge UK.

Lambek, Michael
   1992   'Taboo as Cultural Practice among Malagasy Speakers.' *Man* 27(2): 245–66.
   1995   'Choking on the Quran: and Other Consuming Parables from the Western Indian Ocean Front.' In: *The Pursuit of Certainty*, ed. Wendy James, London: Routledge, pp. 258–281.
   1996   'The Past Imperfect: Remembering as Moral Practice.' In Paul Antze and Michael Lambek, eds. *Tense Past: Cultural Essays in Trauma and Memory*. New York: Routledge.
   n.d.   'The Poiesis of Sakalava History.' Paper presented to the 1995 Satterthwaite Colloquium.

Mayeur,
   1912   'Voyage dans le Nord de Madagascar.' *Bulletin de l'Académie Malgache*, v. 10.

Ramanujan, A.K.
   n.d. (1981)   'Is There an Indian Way of Thinking?,' circulated draft.

Sharp, Lesley
   1993   *The Possessed and Dispossessed: Spirits, Identity and Power in a Madagascar Migrant Town*. Berkeley: University of California Press.

Tsitindry, Jeanne-Baptistine
   1987   '*Navian'ny Tsangan-tsainy*.' *Omaly sy Anio*, 25–26, pp. 31–40.

Turner, Victor
   1969   *The Ritual Process*. Chicago: Aldine.

Vavihely, Alphonse
   1963   'Note sur la généalogie des Rois Antakara.' *Bulletin de l'Académie Malgache*, v. XLI, pp. 67–68.

Vérin, Pierre
   1986   *The History of Civilisation in North Madagascar*. Boston: A.A. Balkema.

Vial, Maurice
   1954   'La Royauté Antankaraña.' *Bulletin Malgache*, no. 92, pp. 3–26.

Plate 4. Raising the mast over the Antankaraña royal capital at the *tsangantsaiñy* ceremony of 1993. Photograph: Andrew Walsh.

Plate 5. The Antankaraña king, dressed in 19th century French military uniform complete with *bicorne*, welcomes the French consul at Diego-Suarez and Rear-Admiral Collondre at the *tsangantsaiñy* ceremony of 1968. The Antankaraña portray themselves as the only people in Madagascar to have had an autonomous alliance with the French. Photograph: Rouméguère.

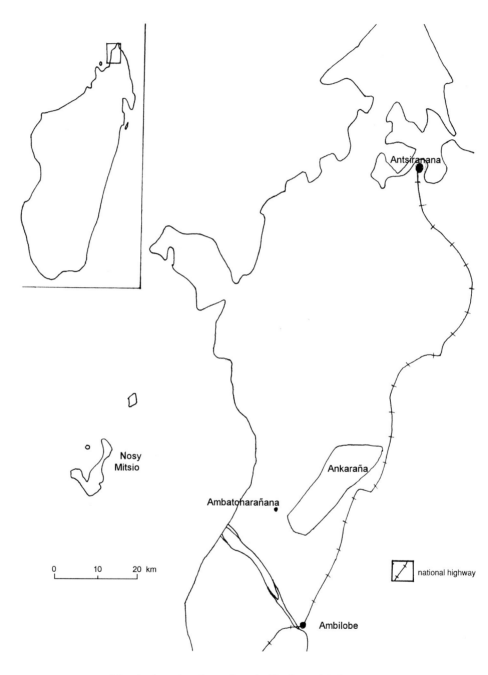

Map 4. Antankaraña territory in Northwest Madagascar

CHAPTER SIX

'EATING' YOUNG MEN AMONG
THE ZAFIMANIRY

MAURICE BLOCH

This chapter explores the involvement of young Zafimaniry men in violence. The violence I shall be discussing is not of the kind that characterises the functioning of certain Amerindian[1] or Melanesian[2] societies, where its expression has been made a fundamental cultural value. Neither is it the type of violence that has been the focus of most anthropological discussions, namely, the violence which erupts in the very middle of everyday life, tearing the social order apart. Nor is it exactly like the highly ritualised violence that one finds, for example, in sacrificial ceremony. The manifestations I shall describe are less spectacular and therefore more difficult to grasp. They concern what I shall term a *semi-institutionalised* kind of violence, in a society which in other respects would not seem to be particularly violent in the usual sense of this term in anthropology.[3] We could compare them with the violence that regularly accompanies football matches in our own cultures, particularly when it becomes almost impossible to distinguish the theatrical aspect from the element of true aggression, or, to take a rather different example, the violence of military marches, if, setting aside their connection with war, we were to consider them simply as exhibitions in brightly coloured costumes. In all these cases, we are dealing with phenomena which are situated halfway between ritual and non-ritual, between spectacle and war, between feigned and real aggression.

---

[1] P. Descola, 'Les affinités sélectives. Alliances, guerre et prédation dans l'ensemble Jivaro', *L'Homme*, 126–128, 1993, pp. 171–190.
[2] P. Lemonnier, *Guerre et festins: paix, échanges et compétition dans les Highlands de Nouvelle-Guinée*, Paris, Éditions de la Maison des Sciences de l'Homme, 1990.
[3] D. Riches (ed.), *The Anthropology of Violence*, Oxford, Blackwell, 1986.

Violence in Malagasy Rituals

The starting-point for this reflection on semi-institutionalised violence among the Zafimaniry was the earlier study I made of circumcision ritual among the Merina, another Malagasy group.[4] Admittedly this earlier analysis concerned a ritual involving highly institutionalised elements of violence. However, there are two reasons why it can serve as an introduction to the Zafimaniry case. To begin with, the Zafimaniry and the Merina are culturally very similar, and their circumcision rituals are almost identical. Moreover, the underlying structure of the Merina ritual, and the use it makes of violence, have, as I have suggested elsewhere,[5] some near universal characteristics.

Merina circumcision ritual is built upon a paradox. The explicit purpose of the ceremony is to *bless* not only the child who is to be circumcised but also the whole community, particularly the young. What the Merina mean by *tsodrano*, the term I translate as 'blessing', is the 'gift of vitality' which comes from the ancestors and from God, and which is transmitted by the intermediary of the elders. This 'vitality' is clearly defined in the course of the ritual: it encompasses fertility—that is to say, the power to produce in abundance children, cattle, and rice—, strength, health, wealth and good fortune. The paradox is that this gift of vitality, which comes from the ancestors and the elders and is bestowed upon the young, is the gift of qualities that, for the Merina, the young already possess, but which the elders, and *a fortiori* the ancestors, plainly no longer have.

The ritual resolves this paradox symbolically by a double violence: first, by stripping the young men of their potential strength, and then, in a second stage, by restoring it to them in a changed form.

In the first phase of the ritual, the vitality of the young boys is represented as essentially powerful, aggressive, and antisocial. This representation is elaborated partly in the course of the ritual itself, when a correspondence is established between the young men and certain plants and animals, in particular, cattle which for the Merina evoke strength, virility and aggressiveness. However, it is also anticipated in a kind of bull-fight that precedes almost all Merina and

---

[4] M. Bloch, *From Blessing to Violence: History and Ideology in the Circumcision Ritual of the Merina of Madagascar*, Cambridge, Cambridge University Press, 1986.

[5] M. Bloch, *Prey into Hunter: the Politics of Religious Experience*, Cambridge, New York, Port-Chester, Cambridge University Press, 1992.

Zafimaniry rituals, during which the young men chase the cattle that will be killed during the ceremony.

This bull-fight is extremely aggressive. Domestic livestock is chased as though it were wild animals and young men behave as though they were hunters. The animals are beaten, tortured, mutilated with axes. Blood flows freely. One might see, for example, a young boy hold the tail of an animal while another severs it. The behaviour demonstrates the force and the brutality attributed to young men, but since, as I noted, the young men are symbolically assimilated to the cattle, they are also its victims. They are simultaneously both prey and hunter, both subject and object of the violence. But they are also the medium by which a generalised violence is directed against the community, the village, and the houses. Driven wild by their injuries, the cattle attack everything that stands in their way. Consequently, everybody tries to avoid them, without, however, moving too far away for they want to miss nothing of the spectacle. All want to join in the intense excitement—the strength, the vitality, and the violence—that emanates from the animals and those in pursuit.

Moments of violence are also an essential part of the ritual itself. This is most notable during the staging of the 'conquest' of the innate vitality of the young men, when violence intervenes in two ways. First, when the young men imitate the cattle and are symbolically 'killed', in the fashion of the animals that in the course of the ritual will actually be put to death. Subsequently, in the very act of circumcision which, with one cut of the knife, not only 'removes' their vitality but, at the same instant, associates them with the ancestors.[6]

Another type of essential violence occurs subsequently when a new vitality, this time controlled by the ancestors, is given back to the circumcised boys. This restores strength to the young men as well as to the whole community, and participants mark the return by eating the meat of the slaughtered cattle and by behaving aggressively.

The symbolic logic underlying the succession of different stages of violence in the course of the ritual can be summarised in the following way. The young boys must be 'killed' because they are powerful and violent like wild animals. Their strength, transformed by the authority of the elders and the ancestors, can then be transmitted to the whole community, just like the strength that comes

---

[6] Anticipating the violence of circumcision, the symbolic 'conquest' of the young men is played and replayed in the course of the ritual.

from eating the meat. But, since the ritual makes the young boys into members of the community, they too share in and in a sense are the primary beneficiaries of this vitality, which has not been lost but simply brought under control, and now makes everyone, but especially them, strong and aggressive.[7]

My analysis of Merina circumcision focused primarily on this sequence in the ritual. Yet, as I noted, this sequence proceeds from the prior construction of the young boys as violent and antisocial beings, not only in earlier phases of the ritual, but also during the preceding bull-fight. This preritual in turn depends upon an earlier construction which takes place in contexts that have little, if anything, to do with ritual.

The Zafimaniry

The Zafimaniry are a small group of around some twenty thousand people who live in the high montane forests of east Madagascar.[8] They are primarily swidden cultivators, although this is increasingly giving way to irrigated rice cultivation.

From the political perspective, the Zafimaniry are a strikingly non-violent people, and this is how they represent themselves. They live in an environment which most Malagasy, and they in particular, consider hostile on account of its chilly climate and its very hilly terrain. This has enabled them over a long period to avoid the power and aggression, first of neighbouring states in the pre-colonial era, and then of the centralized modern State.

Non-violence is an explicit value for them which seems to be observed faithfully enough in practice and in speech. In fact, everything appears to be done to avoid public confrontations. Courtesy is the order of the day, children are almost never hit, and everyone

---

[7] Jennifer Cole in the following chapter in this book makes a similar point about the ambiguity of cattle killing among the Betsimisaraka.

[8] D. Coulaud, *Les Zafimaniry: Un groupe ethnique de Madagascar à la poursuite de la forêt*, Tananarive, FBM, 1973. M. Bloch, 'What Goes Without Saying: The Conceptualisation of Zafimaniry Society', in A. Kuper (ed.) *Conceptualising Societies*, London, New York, Routledge, 1992, pp. 127–146; 'The Resurrection of the House Amongst the Zafimaniry of Madagascar', in J. Carsten and S. Hugh-Jones (eds.) *About the House: Lévi-Strauss and Beyond*, Cambridge, New York, Cambridge University Press, 1995, pp. 69–83. P. Vérin, 'Les Zafimaniry et leur art. Un groupe continuateur d'une tradition esthétique malgache méconnue', *Revue de Madagascar*, 27, 1964, p. 176.

speaks readily, and in a manner that Europeans find somewhat sentimental, of the importance of mutual love, unity and peace between members of one family or of one village.[9]

There are, however, some exceptions to this rule: not only the ritual and preritual violence that I have just evoked, but also a seemingly semi-institutionalised kind of violence which regularly disturbs the gentle calm of everyday village life. Associated most obviously with the young men, this violence occurs most frequently in the context of public bouts of drunkenness.

Gender and Age among the Zafimaniry

The behaviour of the young men, and the way in which it is perceived, can only be understood in the context of Zafimaniry ideas about gender and age, and the relationship between the two.

Let us begin by exploring what being adult means for the Zafimaniry. To be an adult, that is, to participate fully in the political life of a village, means first of all being part of a married couple who have successfully produced descendants. In other words, it is necessary to be a parent, to be what the Malagasy term *raiamandreny*. Strictly speaking, this word translates as 'father and mother', but it also designates the status conventionally translated as 'elder' in the anthropological literature on Madagascar.[10] Thus, a head of a Zafimaniry community is, above all, someone who has *truly succeeded* as a parent, that is to say, who not only has had many children but has raised them, and nurtured them, and kept them in the village in such a way that most, if not all, members of the community think of themselves as their children or their grand-children or their great grand-children.

Many other traits distinguish adults from children, although none are as important as their status as parents: adult bodies, in contrast to those of children, are dry, bony, and straight; their minds are

---

[9] Extremely violent incidents do happen, although they are very rare. For example, after several warnings, a man, who had raped a number of women and who was almost certainly mentally disturbed, had finally been killed by all the men of the village. By contrast, I was very struck to see how quickly a man, who had committed some heinous offences against a village elder, was reintegrated into the communal activities of the village.

[10] Whenever the word 'elder' is used in this chapter, it is the translation of *raiamandreny*.

wise and calm; their speech, when they speak as *raiamandreny*, is
fine and clear, embellished with proverbs and allusions to the ancestors; their behaviour is dignified and gentle for it is they who make
the peace; they are tied closely to the ancestors, whom they will
soon join.

Adults are also characterised by a relative lack of individuality,
partly because as parents they have transcended the dichotomy based
on gender. They are simultaneously 'fathers and mothers', that is to
say, a single entity, and represent a productive unit which conjoins
the masculine and the feminine, and transcends the different generations, by encompassing all those it has engendered together with
their descendants. Moreover, through marriage, adults begin a process
which progressively assimilates them to objects. For the Zafimaniry,
the union which transforms spouses into *raiamandreny* and the house
in which they live are, in effect, two indissociable aspects of the same
process. Marriage essentially begins when a boy starts to build a
house near to that of his father, setting up its central post, to which
a woman then adds artefacts associated with the hearth (a cooking-
pot, a big ladle, and a wooden plate). The house, that is to say the
conjunction of hearth and post, is the most important symbol for
the Zafimaniry. What most interests them is its potential to grow
and become beautiful.

In effect, if the social success of parents is measured, first, by the
number of children they can raise, nurture, and keep alive, and subsequently by the number of their descendants, it is also demonstrated
in the transformation of the house. The house 'hardens' as the children gradually replace the walls of woven bamboo with heavy hardwood planks, which in turn are decorated with carvings over the
years. The transformation of the house is tangible proof of the 'hardness' of the marriage and of the couple's successful reproductive
activity in time and in space. In the course of time, the original
house is surrounded by houses belonging to the couple's sons; it
becomes the heart of a village, the focal point of the family's economic activity. For the children, the grand-children, and the great
grand-children, it becomes the holy place where they gather to receive
their parents' blessing. The identity of the house as a living social
organism becomes particularly clear after the parents' death because
the young then address the central post and the hearth as though
they were the founding couple and were able to bless them.

Zafimaniry Youth

The Zafimaniry represent youth as fundamentally different than the status of *raiamandreny*, even though a person slips imperceptibly from the one condition to the other and even though being young, like being *raiamandreny*, is a process of continual transformation.

Like all Malagasy, the Zafimaniry consider that the body of the child is still soft and wet. The young inevitably lack wisdom; they are impulsive in their behaviour and speech. But above all, in contrast to adults, they are completely distinct individuals. And because their individuality is so pronounced, their gender identity is strongly marked. The typical characteristic of their sexual encounters and love affairs is that they are brief and resemble games in which the partners change very rapidly. These encounters, which are not allowed in proper houses, generally take place in huts near to the swiddens. But what most sharply differentiates the sexual activity of the young from that of the *raiamandreny* is the fact that the former produces no recognised issue. If a girl bears a child, it is considered to be the child of her parents, that is, it counts as her brother or sister.

The contrast between the young and the *raiamandreny* is particularly marked in the economic division of labour. The young are primarily associated with hunting and gathering, thus with the uncultivated forest. Little girls are encouraged from a very young age to go to look for berries and fruits in the forest, a food which, despite its nutritional value, is not considered to be 'life-sustaining'. Likewise, the young boys begin at a very early age to hunt insects, birds and small mammals, but there again these are animals which are seldom eaten by adults. In this way, the distinction between the generations encompasses an opposition between the adults as a group of cultivators who produce the food which sustains 'life' and the family and the young group of hunter-gatherers who collect products said to be of 'no importance'.

Finally, adults work in teams combining men and women, parents and children, while the young gather in separate groups divided only by sex and age, regardless of their kinship bonds.[11]

The separation between the activities of the young and those of

---

[11] In general, the young people are related to one another, but it is not this which unites them.

the parents is primarily affirmed in the rhetoric concerned with work. In practice, the boundary is less marked. First of all, this is because the passage from one status to another happens very gradually. Secondly, because the young are also expected to help their parents in their tasks and therefore temporarily become cultivators, members of the encompassed household. In fact, the young men tend to do this type of work very reluctantly, and it is mainly the girls who carry it out, thereby imperceptibly passing into the adult world more rapidly than the boys. Finally, even parents and elders can behave like children in certain contexts. This is particularly true of the men when, with obvious pleasure, they find themselves deep in the forest with others of the same sex and age. On these occasions, the most venerable of *raiamandreny* may again, in play, become an aggressive hunter surrounded by his 'band'.

The Violence and Vitality of Young Men

Zafimaniry girls marry at a much younger age than Zafimaniry boys and therefore become parents, that is to say, adults, far sooner. For boys only, between the ages of fifteen and twenty-three years, youth therefore extends into a 'late youth'. In this period, they keep all the characteristics of youth—extreme mobility, marked individuality, and highly differentiated sexual identity—but their role as hunters, while staying basically the same, takes on another dimension. The young men—or 'old boys' rather—are typically hunters, but hunters who venture far in the forest in search of bigger game, particularly wild boar. It is they who supply the community with meat, in both a real and symbolic sense (as we have seen, it is also they who 'hunt' the cattle and other domestic animals in the preritual bull-fight).

The imagery of the adventurous, young hunter is associated with other activities that are typical of young men. For example, hawking and peddling which involve hazardous journeys through the forest but above all the seasonal wage work they undertake for several months each year in other parts of the island and which basically involves looking for and cutting down valuable timber in distant forests for various employers. Such wage work means making long and dangerous journeys deep into the forest, during which time the young workers live together in small groups, for periods lasting several weeks. This style of life is reminiscent of that of the hunt, as much on account of its location in the uncultivated forest as in the organisation it requires. Moreover, the young men emphasise this association by singing the same kinds of songs and by behaving a little in the same manner as in the hunt.

The strong identification of young men with the wild domain of the hunt and the forest has another aspect, less explicit, but particularly important here. This is the correspondence that is established between youth and the prey they hunt. Like it, they are wild, dangerous, and strong; and their typical habitat is also the forest. *Biby ny tovo lahy*, 'young men are wild animals', people often say, in an admiring way.[12]

Above all, the young men are associated with the wild boar which, for the Zafimaniry, personify force and health. These undomesticated animals are antagonists of everything the house stands for, devastating the crops of peaceful, united couples. The image of strength and health which wild boars evoke explains why the Zafimaniry blessing, uttered during every blessing by elders for the benefit of the young, begins with the phrase *Lambo lambo*, 'Be wild boars'.

'Constructing' Young Men

This last point leads me to clarify what I mean by the 'construction' of young men. The activities that are typical of young Zafimaniry men cannot be considered simply from their economic or technical character. An emphatic theatrical element is also always highly evident. The young men indulge in 'artistic' excesses that very obviously have little to do with practical necessity but rather are primarily intended to demonstrate their vigour and their strength. This is particularly evident in the (at times rather wild) manner in which they handle their axes when cutting down trees, and in the brutality they show towards their animal prey.

Behaviour of this kind is encouraged in young boys at a very early age by family members. Even before they know how to speak or

---

[12] I heard this expression for the first time when, in a driving rain, young men were carrying a corpse, with the violence and lack of respect that custom requires, in order to place it in a tomb which was hidden far away in the forest, like all Zafimaniry tombs. At the time I did not fully understand the expression and interpreted it in an entirely negative way, only to be quickly corrected in a way which shows the ambiguity of the violence of young men.

walk properly, little boys are enjoined by their seniors and the elders to participate in mock hunts. Whenever domestic livestock, especially pigs, is slaughtered in the village, a chase, modelled on the preritual bull-fight, takes place. They chase and torment the animal before handing it over to adults for the *coup de grâce*. Even the smallest boys are pushed forward to watch when a pig is slaughtered, to kick it as its blood is let, to collect the blood, and then to remain present while the carcase is cut up. Furthermore, they are often given the pig's severed ears or feet to play with. Some little boys seem afraid when the animal squeals under the blows, but they are strongly encouraged to take part. On the other hand, little girls are normally kept out of the way.

It is clear that, once the initial shock is past, this aesthetic of violent strength gives much pleasure to the young boys, as, indeed, it does to the entire community which appears to be delighted by the aggressiveness. And although these displays of violence are conventional and staged, the powerful emotions they stimulate imbue them with a vitality and a naturalness that the word 'construction' might obscure.

The Antisocial Force of Young Men

The construction of young men as vigorous, strong, healthy and violent beings also has negative aspects for the community. This becomes clear in the light of the incidence of drunkenness among the young, which periodically spills over into unfeigned violence.

The Zafimaniry drink heavily, too heavily in fact. They themselves are the first to acknowledge this and to denounce its negative effects. However, their opinion on the subject differs radically according to whether it concerns adults or young men. The Zafimaniry think that it is good that parents and the old should drink heavily. For them drunkenness facilitates peaceful conviviality during feasts between kin; it helps the elders communicate with the ancestors, and thus promotes the flow of blessing. In other words, when the *raiamandreny* drink, the fundamental values of community life are held to be reinforced.

On the other hand, the Zafimaniry disapprove of excess drinking on the part of the young because, they rightly say, it is frequently the cause of quarrels which, notably on market days, often degenerate into serious brawls. On occasions, these fights spread, and bands of young men become involved in what are effectively pitched battles.

This is what happened during one of my stays in a Zafimaniry village in 1992, when all the youths, all highly inebriated, set off on an expedition against those of another closely related village and a enormous, bloody brawl ensued.

A fight like this obviously runs counter to Zafimaniry norms. More to the point, it constitutes a sacrilege against the holy house of the ancestors common to both villages, ancestors who, like all ancestors, demand that their descendants should live in harmony.

The element of sacrilege becomes even more pronounced when young men, under the influence of alcohol, directly attack the holy houses. It is said that one evening a young boy, drunk on rum, threw a stone against a shutter of the holy house of the village, breaking it. Another, equally inebriated, attacked the central post of this house with a plastic bottle. Both these acts were highly reprehensible. The holy house is the very source of life for the village, and its central post personifies the man of the original couple. Nonetheless, despite the horror it arouses, such behaviour is also considered as constituent of youth. In an apparently contradictory fashion, the Zafimaniry celebrate the strength and savagery of youth while condemning its effects. One might think that this was only a question of an excess in relation to a behaviour which, if practiced with moderation, would be good in itself. In fact, it is not so simple.

It is very clear that it is the very same adults or elders, who, in general terms, complain strongly against the violence of the drunken youth and their impious conduct, who are often those who encourage them to drink to the point that they lose all self-control and commit very serious sacrilegious acts, such as the attack upon the holy house.

This element of egging on was quite explicit during the brawl I witnessed. All the inhabitants of our village, including the women and the old, were perched on the surrounding wall in a state of great excitement, from where they noisily followed the progress of the band of youths across the valley separating the two villages, encouraging them with songs and shouts to go to fight against their close kin. The same jubilation marked their subsequent commentary on the fracas which followed their arrival, and which resulted in at least one fracture and many bloody noses.

To understand this paradoxical behaviour of the elders, we need to take a number of factors into account.

First of all, the Zafimaniry always interpret the violence of the young men, even negative, as an expression of the strength and future vitality of the village and of the families who compose it. To encourage this strength is to celebrate the element of potential vitality of the village, the element which, to a certain extent, is masked by the ideal of peace and the well-ordered reproduction of the house which dominates the speeches of the elders. Everyone, young and old, women and men, takes a visible pleasure in participating in these external expressions of this vitality.

Next, it is necessary to bear in mind the emotions that these events arouse among the *raiamandreny* men. In effect, it is they who most openly encourage the antisocial violence of young men. In a sense, the outbursts of aggression to which the young are prone are the negation of all that the elders represent, the house, peace, the unity of the family and of the village. It should not be forgotten, however, that, unlike the ancestors, the elders not immutably fixed in their roles; from time to time, in certain contexts, such as deep in the forest, they too can become young men again, in their behaviour at least. This too helps explain some of the pleasure that they take in encouraging 'delinquency' among the young.

Finally, the *raiamandreny* know far better than the young men what will be the ultimate consequence of their sacrilegious acts.

'Eating' Young Men

The day following the famous raid against the neighbouring village, the *raiamandreny* of both villages met together and initiated a series of 'conclaves' during which they deliberated at great length the manner in which they should punish the young men of both villages for having fought with kin. The punishment they finally decreed was a fine of around fifty litres of rum and thirty litres of honey.

In the rather more serious case of the young man who had struck the central post of the holy house with a plastic bottle, the discussions took much longer and a far heavier fine was imposed. It was decided that the young man should be made to offer two head of cattle in a sacrifice to the village and the ancestors. The elders took a long time to arrive at this verdict. Discussions had been resumed on a number of occasions, always with the same ceremony, in the holy house around the central post, where a meal was cooking for the elders upon the hearth. The elders had spoken at great length, one after the other, with no obvious discord. The accused was always present, his head bowed, most of the time covered by a cloth. Not permitted to say a single word, he seemed to have become invisible in the order of the house.

All the elders partipating in the deliberations knew well the consequences of imposing such a high fine. It is quite impossible for a young man to accumulate the required sum in the village. In order to save the money to buy the cattle for the sacrifice, he had no other option than to leave the village and to work for wages as a wood-cutter for some months. On his return, it would then be possible for everyone, ancestors and living, to participate in an important ritual to remove the sin committed against the post of the holy house.

One explanation of the pleasure shown by the elders in the anti-social violence of young men, and their more or less explicit encouragement of it, is thus that they know what will be the outcome of such excess. As a result of the punishment they will administer, they will be able to appropriate the product of the strength and labour of young men. They will be able to consume its product and share it with guests during the sacrifice. On such occasions, they will drink the great quantities of rum that such a celebration demands, they will weave the links of solidarity that alcohol fosters, and above all they will supplement their basic diet, derived mainly from starch crops grown by the conjugal unit, with meat from the animals whose sacrifice they have required (meat from cattle is not eaten other than on such occasions).

However, there is much more to it than this. The assimilation of young men to their prey, discussed above, (here false 'prey' in the shape of the cattle slaughtered during the ceremony), means that, in a sense, it is not only the *product* of the strength of the young men that is eaten but they themselves. The strength of the young men is thus consumed in order to revitalise the entire village, as the meat that one eats on such occasions gives strength to the whole community.[13]

From the Construction of Young Men to Ritual

Here again we find the schema, discussed at the beginning of this chapter, which underlies all Zafimaniry and Merina rituals. The chief

---

[13] This representation recurs in the architecture of the house. The house is the symbol of the married couple conjoined in a fruitful and peaceful union, sustained by agriculture. However, the name of one house-part evokes another symbolism:

purpose of these rituals is to transmit the blessing of the ancestors and of the elders to their descendants. However, vitality must also be added to this blessing, a vitality that young boys possess in abundance in a raw, wild form, amoral and antisocial, but which the ancestors lack. If order as well as strength are to reign in the village, two antagonistic elements must therefore be combined. The rituals effect this beneficial combination of the qualities of the young with those of the ancestors by first capturing the uncontrollable, animal vitality of boys and animals, then transforming it into an element which, once consumed, vitalizes the whole community. A constitutive and essential part of the ritual is therefore the representation and even magnification of the uncontrolled strength of the young and of animals who will then be conquered in the course of the ceremony. This is the starting-point of the symbolic operation. What I have sought to demonstrate here is that this theatrical preliminary to ritual begins well in advance of the ritual itself. It begins with the bull-fight, but also with the construction of the representation of youth, and more especially of young men, in a more day to day context.

This conclusion needs to be qualified in two ways, however. First of all, it would be mistaken to suppose that the construction of the violence of young men is *nothing other than a preliminary* to ritual. In fact, this construction so completely pervades the Zafimaniry way of life that to explain it solely in terms of its relationship to ritual would be wrong. We can only say that this representation of masculine youth articulates perfectly with the rituals without being necessarily their cause or their effect.

Secondly, we must take care not to think that, just because the representation of masculine youth is *constructed*, it is not for all that underpinned by extra-cultural impulses and drives. Many aspects of this representation are familiar to us from our own and other cultures, and it is very unlikely that this is by chance. Here it seems to me important to remember that to insist upon cultural specificity in no way precludes the possibility that it is constructed upon an universal basis.

---

this is the corner under the ridge-pole to the front of the roof which is called 'the boar's head', the animal which is associated with the forest, the destruction of crops, and the healthy and violent strength of young men. In this instance, though, the savage force is brought under control, just as the force of the young men is controlled by the elders. The corner is literally 'framed'. It was explained to me that, by lending its force to the house, the boar's head 'brings it forward'.

Plate 6. Two young Zafimaniry boys torment a pig. Photograph: Maurice Bloch.

Plate 7. Zafimaniry men, armed with sticks, rope, and knives, chase a bullock prior to a sacrifice. Whenever domestic livestock is slaughtered in the village, a chase modelled on the preritual bullfight takes place. Photograph: Maurice Bloch.

CHAPTER SEVEN

SACRIFICE, NARRATIVES AND EXPERIENCE IN EAST MADAGASCAR*

JENNIFER COLE

This essay examines the role of sacrifice in mediating individual and collective experience through an analysis of sacrifice as it is practiced among rural Southern Betsimisaraka of east Madagascar.[1] The practice of cattle sacrifice is central to the constitution of Southern Betsimisaraka identity, both mediating and transforming people's experience of, and relationship to, their ancestral homeland and the outside world.[2] Again and again throughout their lives, villagers find themselves thwarted by more powerful beings, either caught between ancestral demands and the need to fulfill their personal desires and ambitions, or faced by the need to negotiate the economic and political forces of post-colonial Madagascar, forces they are keenly aware operate differently from, and are more powerful than, their own. I will focus specifically on sacrificial narratives, produced in the long speech, or *kabary*, performed just prior to the slaughter of the animal.[3] Sacrifices are held when people do things that displease the ancestors, thereby provoking their illness-inducing and potentially murderous wrath. Narratives produced in sacrifice are thus about

* *Acknowledgements*: Doctoral dissertation research was conducted in east Madagascar from July 1992–December 1993. Funding was generously provided by Fullbright IIE, The Wenner-Gren Foundation for Anthropological Research and the Rocca African Studies Fellowship. Writing up has been supported by the National Endowment for the Humanities. I would like to thank Karen Middleton for her careful reading of an earlier draft of this essay. David Graeber and Maurice Bloch have both provided important advice and encouragement along the way.
[1] The research for this paper was conducted in the village of Ambodiharina, located on the Mangoro river, and surrounding areas. During my fieldwork I attended and tape-recorded over twenty-seven different ceremonies.

[2] The ancestral homeland, or *tanindrazana*, is an important component of identity throughout Madagascar, and refers to the location of one's ancestral tomb. For a classic formulation of the socio-symbolic importance of the *tanindrazana* see Bloch 1971.

[3] *Kabary* refers to a particular kind of authoritative, formal oratory performed in ritual and political contexts throughout Madagascar. For a sociolinguistic analysis of *kabary* see Keenan (1974).

the stories and dramas produced as villagers go about the intensely absorbing business of 'making themselves living,' and how their quests for life, love and fortune inevitably bring them into conflict with forces more powerful than themselves. Such narratives inform the experience of village life, providing an array of possible interpretations of the human predicament, as people try and shape a refractory world to the measure of their own intentions. Further, narratives produced in sacrifice extend well beyond the ritual context, as people who attend the sacrifice return to their homes and continue to discuss and reflect on the negotiations that took place.

In his theory of symbolic action, Godfrey Lienhardt provides a powerful tool for understanding how the practice of sacrifice works to mediate people's experience.[4] He argued that in sacrifice Dinka dramatize situations they seek to control. For example in a sacrifice which marks the end of a feud between two parties, the sacrificial cow is divided in two across the belly, the division of the beast being intended to stand for the termination of the feuding relationship (1960: 288). Through this symbolic act, Dinka are able to control 'primarily a set of mental and moral dispositions' which 'if they do not change actual historical or physical events . . . do change and regulate the Dinka's experience of those events' (*ibid.*, 291). Lienhardt's approach represents a significant advance over earlier theories, many of which, following the sacrificial schema proposed by Hubert and Mauss (1964), focused on how sacrifice, by putting people in contact with the divine, enables the transformation of social status.[5] What Lienhardt's theory failed to take into account, however, is the particular social processes through which the attitudes and beliefs reflected

---

[4] Typically, sacrifice is thought of as the act of offering something precious to the deity. The word evokes notions of exchange, the surrender of one thing for the sake of something else, ideas that, enshrined in the Nuer dictum that 'cattle substitute for the lives of men' (Evans-Pritchard, 1956), have been central to the anthropological analysis of the topic. Early analyses explained sacrifice as a gift to the gods (Tylor 1889), a communion with gods created through a shared meal (Robertson-Smith, 1894) and a form of mediation, enabling contact between the sacred and the profane (Hubert and Mauss, 1964).

[5] According to their interests, scholars have focused on either the religious aspect (man's relation to god) or the socio-political one. We know that human relationships are mapped onto the body of the sacrificial cow, and that important relationships between members of different groups are expressed through cattle (Lienhardt 1960), that sacrifice mediates the individual's relation to god and absolve humans of their sins (Evans-Pritchard 1956); and that sacrifice is central to the negotiation of lineage authority (Middleton, 1960).

in sacrifice become internalized, a part of people's understanding about how the world works, thus constituting a particular kind of subjectivity or orientation.

In analyzing the Betsimisaraka practice of sacrifice I wish to extend Lienhardt's insights into how sacrifice works as symbolic action by examining the role of sacrificial narratives, and the way they inform and shape people's experience. We know that the histories of other people's experience saturate the various worlds in which we live, just as experience is produced in tension with the tropes and conventions, the borrowed plots and moods of other people's stories (Steedly, 1993). Moreover, narratives simultaneously produce dual landscapes of action and consciousness (Bruner, 1986), help form a sense of self and identity (Schafer, 1992), and are central to the constitution of meaningful subjects (Borneman, 1992). Finally, as Peel has brilliantly argued, 'narrative empowers because it enables its possessor to integrate his memories, experiences and aspirations in a schema of long-term action' (1995: 587). For Betsimisaraka, narratives produced in sacrifice play a crucial role in the connection between the public act of sacrifice and private experience. Stories produced both within and beyond the practice of sacrifice are pivotal in shaping human action, as they form the critical link between the actions of the past and intentions of the future.

There are two dimensions of narrative implicit in Betsimisaraka sacrifice. First, the ritual of sacrifice itself provides a dramatic narrative of ancestry, community and connection as people come to share the flesh of a cow, one that symbolizes their link to the ancestors and to one another. Second, and more importantly, the stories that people tell about sacrifice—why ones does it, whether it works, and what happened at the event—are a part of how people narrate their daily experience, how they derive a sense of themselves and their place in the world. Through the narratives created in and around the activity of sacrifice, Betsimisaraka create the sacrificial cow as a third object, one through which the imagined community of the village and beyond is constructed and reconstructed. Talk about cows is always talk about social relations, whether proper or improper, and practices associated with sacrifice are how the imagined community gets played out and manipulated in the process of daily life. At the same time, the talk that occurs in the context of cattle sacrifice is always about ancestors and hence about the past. Discourse associated with the practice of cattle sacrifice reflects

Betsimisaraka notions of history; it is also the primary domain of ritual and political action as locally construed. The activities surrounding sacrifice reflect how the past operates to constrain and empower people in their endeavors and how people in turn try to affect and reinterpret the past through the practices surrounding cattle. Ultimately, the stories people tell about sacrifice are central to the constitution of subjectivity, providing people with a sense of themselves in relation to the past, and hence the present and future. To understand how all this comes about, it is necessary to locate the practice of sacrifice in its social and discursive context. In order to do this, I will consider the significance of cattle, the nature of the dead and their relationship to the living, local conceptions of history and the predicaments of the living, and how, through the narratives produced in the context of cattle sacrifice, they constitute the Betsimisaraka social imaginary.

Betsimisaraka Identity

The Betsimisaraka, third largest of the twenty 'ethnies' of Madagascar, inhabit the east coast of the island, from Vohemar in the north till Mananjary in the south.[6] This is a rainy, and in parts, densely forested region. Travel, difficult in most parts of Madagascar due to the poor condition of the roads, is especially treacherous here. The coast is frequently transected by rivers that empty into the Indian Ocean, and those seeking to make their way either north or south are constantly confronted with river crossings. Slow ferries designed to transport cars or cargo can be found at most crossings, but they are usually out of gas, or out of order. Instead, most people rely on small dug-out canoes to get from place to place.

The geographical division and compartmentalization of Betsimisaraka country is reflected in a political history that is equally fragmented, which is why the name, Betsimisaraka, which means 'the many who will not be sundered,' is such a misnomer. Unlike other Malagasy peoples widely known within Anglophone anthropology through the

---

[6] According to the official census, there are 19 different ethnic groups in Madagascar. However, as numerous commentators have observed, the idea of discrete, bounded ethnic groups is in fact a result of colonial attempts to identify, categorize and govern the local populace. In reality, the production of identity in relation to ethnicity appears to be much more fluid.

writings of Bloch (1974; 1986), Feeley-Harnik (1992), and Kottak (1980), among others, the Betsimisaraka never had a centralized kingdom. In fact, the 'many who won't be sundered,' was initially more of a political slogan than anything else, a name acquired to refer to a federation of northern ancestries that united in order to achieve certain political and economic ends in the eighteenth century. The federation lasted only forty years, scarcely more than a generation. Moreover it only operated in the northern third of what is now referred to as Betsimisaraka country. Although the region where I worked is in many ways culturally similar, it seems unlikely that the ancestors of the people I knew ever belonged to the Betsimisaraka federation. I do not know when the name Betsimisaraka was extended to refer to the inhabitants of the southern part of the region, but I suspect it occurred following the conquest of the area by the Merina in the nineteenth century, and was further reified and codified under the French.[7]

For contemporary Southern Betsimisaraka, identity is based not on the historical link to the nineteenth century political federation, but rather on a rejection of any centralized authority whatever.[8] As my friend Jonah was fond of saying, 'We Betsimisaraka never had a king. We're too feisty!'[9] Jonah's statement, however, must be read against the reality of double colonization, by the Merina, from 1823–1895, and then the French from 1895–1960. Despite their rejection of centralized authority, Betsimisaraka have been subject to more powerful outsiders for quite some time. This history of double colonization is an important aspect of current Betsimisaraka identity, as villagers conceived of themselves as powerless little people, flotsam and jetsam tossed about by a larger historical sea. This rejection of outside power, and the awareness that they have, nevertheless, been forced to endure it, is matched by a strong sense of identity derived from local ancestors. In contrast to a common identity as members of a kingdom, or as subjects equally dominated by

---

[7] Previously this group of people, referred to as the Betanimena, had been the historic enemies of the northern Betsimisaraka.

[8] I have specified that I am talking only about Southern Betsimisaraka here. For the rest of the paper, however, I will refer to them as Betsimisaraka which is less cumbersome.

[9] French officials too, tended to characterize Betsimisaraka as 'apathetic' and 'placid' a view that was proved wrong during the anti-colonial insurrection of 1947. See Cole, 1996.

a colonial power, however, local notions of identity highlight the importance of differentiation: attachment to particular ancestors, knowledge of their deeds, following their taboos, and inhabiting their land, are crucial practices through which identity is forged. The tension between these two poles—the importance of local ancestral power and the reality of demands imposed by the outside world— are a central aspect of Betsimisaraka experience negotiated through sacrifice.

The Significance of Cattle[10]

Southern Betsimisaraka are not a pastoral people. They are above all rice farmers, and only a handful of people in the village have cattle at any given moment. Cattle are not an important part of the daily diet and one does not need to actually own them to be able to use them for trampling fields twice a year.[11] Yet, despite their limited material use, cows are central to Betsimisaraka life. Betsimisaraka, like the Nuer, say that cows substitute for the sins of humans, and this is one clue to their importance. But cows are also the link between people. They are 'the big ax for cutting knots off a tree' where the community of the living is essentially compared to a tree and the sacrificial cow the ax with which flaws are removed. Most importantly, cows, through the practice of cattle sacrifice, provide the indispensable link between the living and the dead. Because they link the living and dead, who are considered the ultimate source of power and authority, fortune and failure, sacrificial cows are, in a more general sense, directly implicated in the achievement of a materially, spiritually and morally successful life.

Cows are expensive. At the time I was conducting fieldwork, a cow cost about 250,000 fmg., which is considerably more than most families make in a year. As a result, few people have cows, yet at certain times, everybody needs them, because of the ritual-political

---

[10] Throughout this essay I will refer to all cattle used in sacrifice as 'cows' because I believe this best translates the Malagasy word *aomby* which is gender neutral. At times there are certain specifications for which kind of cattle are to be sacrificed. For example for a circumcision ceremony, a bull is required. Most of the time, however, it is the color of the beast, and not the sex, that matters.

[11] By working out trade/loan agreements between neighbors and kin, people who didn't own cows could easily borrow cows to trample their fields, thus preparing them for sowing and transplanting rice.

negotiations for which they are essential. What this means is that a crucial—and paradoxical—imbalance occurs. On the one hand, cows link the living and the dead, and a cow sacrificed by a given family is ideally supposed to connect all of its members to the ancestors equally. This ideal of solidarity is expressed in the aphorism that 'where the ancestors are concerned all must eat' and 'with talk of ancestors one doesn't need differentiation.' This includes not only the living where every last bit of cow is divided among the witnesses and each is scrupulously given his lot or portion (*anjara*), but the dead as well. Failure to call the name of an ancestor—whether related through blood or marriage—is a grave offense and can even lead to divorce. On the other hand, however, some people have more control over the cow—through their material wealth—than others. What this means is that some people have more access to the kind of social-symbolic manipulations made available through cows than others. As a result, sacrifice is one of the major contexts for the simultaneous expression and production of inequities among villagers. Those with money—in this case the handful of people who had either taught and thus received a salary from the state, or those who had been in the army and were now retired and received a pension—will use their money to buy cattle. In short, power derived from involvement in the outside world quickly becomes translated into wealth in village terms and a more secure position in relation to the ancestors.

This uneasy tension is further exacerbated by the fact that while a particular person may sponsor the sacrifice, sacrifices are never an individual affair: rather, they involve all the members of a family, and any person related to the sponsor may use the opportunity of a sacrifice to achieve some ritual end. While the organization of a sacrifice requires the combined wealth of a given ancestry, it is inevitable that some people feel they have contributed more than others. As a result, fights over cows at a sacrifice frequently ensue, sometimes resulting in the argument being brought out again and resolved in a future sacrifice. While equality is the ideal, in reality people are aware of differentiation. This disjuncture creates tension, but it is precisely this constant play between the ideal of equality and the reality of differentiation that make cows and the complex of ideas and practices surrounding them a key site for the production of social discourse.

Tensions among the living at a sacrifice are further exacerbated by the dangerous presence of the dead. Sacrifices are held when people do things that displease the ancestors, thereby provoking their misfortune-inducing and potentially murderous wrath; they are in fact an elaborate attempt to cure ancestrally inflicted illness. And yet, according to official explanations, sacrifice is a joyous occasion on which people join together to beg blessing from the ancestors. This paradox—the tension between blessing and killing (cf. Bloch, 1992)—is echoed on other levels as well: in many ways sacrifice is an event which simultaneously empowers and weakens the ancestry who sponsors the ceremony. The most direct explanation of what occurs in sacrifice is that the ancestors are called to eat directly of the flesh of the cow. Sacrifice is thus assumed to empower the group who arranges the ceremony because it pleases the ancestors by honoring them with food, and the ancestors are then willing to bless their descendants. Yet it may also be said to weaken the family by exciting the greed of the ancestors whom they call to eat: people worry that the insatiable ancestors will never be satisfied with just one cow as a victim but may be tempted to take more.[12] As my friend Antoine observed, one evening as we picked our way gingerly over the dikes of rice on our way home, 'A cow substitutes for the life of people, but what if it's not enough? What if they're [the ancestors] still hungry?' Again, the disjuncture between the ideal of sacrifice as a ceremony in which descendants gather to thank and honor their ancestors and the ancestors in return bestow blessing, and the underlying fear that ancestors are in fact unspeakably greedy ghosts who feed parasitically off the living, means that sacrifice is in fact a highly ambivalent undertaking. Peoples' delight in the ceremony is always laced with an undercurrent of fear. And yet it is the productive tension between these two extremes that makes sacrifice such a powerful vehicle for reflecting on people's experience in the world.

How the Dead Live

The tremendous ambivalence implicit in sacrifice—the desire to honor ancestors and the wish to avoid them—is rooted in people's complex relation to the dead. For Southern Betsimisaraka, the political, ritual and moral order is predicated on the fundamental connection

---

[12] See Gibson (1986) for a similar argument about Buid links to pig eating spirits.

between the living and the dead.[13] Following God in the cosmic hierarchy, the world might be said to contain two categories of people,
living people and dead people. The word for people, *olona*, is modified
with the word *velona* or living. This is opposed to *olomaty* which means
dead people who are also referred to as *razana*, the root of which is
also used to form the words *karazana* which one might gloss as *firazana*
or kinds and which I shall refer to as ancestry.[14] Villagers conceive
of the world as inhabited by the living and the dead. Living people
talk about dead people as if they were alive and engaged in much
the same kinds of activities as the living. More precisely, the village
and the rice fields are all peopled with the dead and the living move
among them. Seeking to convey the idea that ancestors are present
yet invisible, one man said they were covered by a thin fog—you
can't see them, but they are there nonetheless. Ancestors are thus
immanent in daily life, moving in and around the living, watching
their descendants and guiding them in their decisions.

Not only do the dead move among the living, but the dead are
in fact organized into groups which reflect an idealized image of
the world of the living. Briefly put, the living are conceived of as
organized into exogamous ancestries, which are people who share
the same name, taboos and history.[15] Membership in ancestries is
traced bilaterally, so that people belong to a number of ancestries,
usually traced out to eight lines of descent (*valo ila*), on both the
father and mother's side. This means that people have a range of
affiliations to choose from, although the emphasis on links reckoned
through men means that most people keep closer ties to their father's
kin. Within a given ancestry, the members are ordered hierarchi-
cally according to age and gender. Descendants of senior lines take

---

[13] The complex links between the living and the dead are a recurrent theme in
the ethnography for Madagascar. For other parts of the island see Astuti (1995),
Bloch (1971), Feeley-Harnik (1992), Graeber (1995), and Sharp (1993).

[14] Feeley-Harnik (1976: 173) has a similar discussion. However she adds *lolo* the
third category of beings that have not achieved ancestor status. Among the Betsimisaraka with whom I worked there was no such category and *lolo* were rather ill-
defined spirits that might also be referred to as *biby* or creatures.

[15] I am using the term 'ancestry' to refer to what Lambek and Walsh (this volume)
have termed 'clans.' In many ways Betsimisaraka clans contrast in interesting
ways with their description of 'clans' among the Antakarana: to wit, while there is
a great deal of fluidity, people nevertheless do tend to identify themselves more
with one 'clan' than another, although how this identification comes about includes
not only descent but residency and involvement in ritual activities as well (cf. Bloch,
1974).

precedence over the descendants of junior lines while descendants of men (*zanin'lahy*) take precedence over descendants of women (*zanin'vavy*). Further, the members of each ancestry are divided into separate 'great houses' (*trano be*) the house inhabited by the *tangalamena*, the ritual specialist in charge of mediating between the living and the dead. It is the great house/*tangalamena* pair that is the relevant political and ritual unit: members of a common great house come together to care for ancestors, be it arranging a sacrifice or contributing money and labor for the building of a new tomb.

So too the dead. As one woman put it, the dead are ordered into houses, each with its own *tangalamena*, all inhabiting the same courtyard. It is like a town for the dead, she explained. The difference is that tombs, which are simple wooden structures roughly resembling a canoe, are referred to as 'ancestors' houses' (*tranorazana*) so that the word house is modified to specify that it is a house for the dead and not the living. Not only does the social organization of the dead reflect that of the living, but the dead are assumed to have many of the needs, preferences and peculiarities as when they were alive. Once dead, ancestors continue to enjoy food, drink and music they liked while still alive, and so the living are likely to bring chewing tobacco, coffee or a favorite brand of rum to give to a particular ancestor. The dead are also buried with the spoons, cups and plates they used when they were alive. People claim that a dead person who is buried without these things will be chased out by the other ancestors, who have arrived previously, and told to go and get what is his due from the living.

Parents and Children, Ancestors and Descendants

Ancestors, then, are conceived of, remembered and treated much like living people. In order to understand the particularities of how the ancestor-descendant relationship is imagined, however, it is necessary to consider the relationship of parent to child, as this is the core relationship on which all other hierarchical relationships are modeled.

The relationship between parents and children is supposed to be one of mutual respect and reciprocity. Ideally, children are supposed to love and care for their parents, where love is equated with ritual respect and the willingness to give of labor and material goods, to constantly remember the roots of one's existence. The reciprocal links that bind children to parents are often expressed as 'having horns.' One man explained it thus:

> Whatever you want to do, you lean on your children. Your children are your protectors so you say you have horns. When they're still small you carry them on your back and later they become your horns.

Or, as another woman expressed it, 'parents are like your private god, and you must always remember and honor those who bore you.' In return, parents are supposed to love and care for their children, to bless them and make them prosper. Just as children need parents, so too parents need children. Children are those who 'removed your lice.' To be without children, one woman explained, is 'total poverty, they are your wealth and your comfort and those you raise will always remember you.'

Such is the ideal. In practice, of course, it is a fragile and contextual kind of exchange that obtains. Indeed, if a soap opera were written for Ambodiharina, the dramas of parents and children would take center stage, while the stories of husbands, wives and lovers would be relegated to a minor subplot. Parents can be grasping and cruel, or favor one child over another, while children are at times notoriously self-involved, heedlessly feeding off their parents' wealth. The twists and turns of the relationships between parents and their children are a staple of village gossip. People love to meditate on, say, how horrible Poratsara's father was as a parent as he had banished his son for minor pilfering or how thoughtlessly Monsieur Gaston behaved towards his mother when he went travelling upcountry with magicians while his mother was ill. Moreover, while parents are theoretically more powerful because they have the ability to impose a curse if the child misbehaves, children can, if parents neglect their responsibilities, refuse to honor their ritual obligations, thus depriving the parent of their authority, or at least signaling to them that their behavior is wrong. Normative statements aside, relationships between parents and children are constantly negotiated: the fact that parents hold ultimate sanctions of cursing does not determine how actual struggles over power and authority are resolved, at least not all of the time. Which is of course why village gossip about grasping parents and heedless children is always such a fascinating topic of conversation: you never know ahead of time how any given drama is going to play itself out.

Like the parent-child relationship on which it is modeled, the relationship between ancestors and descendants is supposed to be one of mutual respect and reciprocity. In theory ancestors bless the living with prosperity—any success you might have is perceived as a result of the ancestors' intervention. As Jonah emphasized, and as I was told repeatedly throughout my stay in Ambodiharina, 'You look for wealth, your rice prospers, you find cows or money, all of this is blessing bestowed by ancestors.' The paradox, of course, is that ancestors are not only the cause of prosperity and success, but are also a possible cause of suffering, disease, even death. Wealth, children, good health, nothing is bestowed freely, but must be reciprocated through propitiation. Because ancestors bless their descendants they also seek a response. Their demands for propitiation are sanctioned and endowed with power by God: 'go to your children, says God to the ancestors, for you suffer!' And so, people explained, the ancestors come and make their descendants sick. In contrast to Imerina where ancestors have been conventionally portrayed as the moral guardians of the community, bestowing prosperity on their descendants (Bloch 1971), and where even those who suggest the possibilities of ancestral violence (Graeber 1995) note that most elders are extremely uncomfortable with the topic, villagers in Ambodiharina complain constantly about just how *masiaka* (cruel, savage, brutal) their ancestors are.

Death confers power, a power on which the social order is based (cf. Feeley-Harnik, 1978). While parents and children are still alive, the relationship is subject to twists, turns and negotiations like any other. Once parents die and become ancestors, however, the mutual demands which were once subject to challenge are, through death, made to transcend the vagaries characteristic of relations among the living.[16] And yet it is precisely ancestral caprice and power that draws the opprobrium and perpetual astonishment of the living: no matter how many times descendants fall sick and are forced to sacrifice cattle in propitiation, they never cease to speak with amazement of how insufferably greedy and demanding the dead are.

[16] While the Betsimisaraka focus on parents and children as a model for the ancestor-descendant relationship is reminiscent of West African models of ancestor worship, best articulated in the writing of Fortes (1957; 1987), there are important differences. Namely, while Tallensi ancestors are portrayed on the model of a fierce yet just father, Betsimisaraka portray their ancestors as infinitely more unreasonable and capricious, a meta-commentary on the nature of power rather than a powerful mechanism for reinforcing the social structure.

Hasina *and the Burden of the Past*

It is through history as it is locally imagined that the tensions of ancestral power and constraint manifest themselves in their descendants' lives. For Southern Betsimisaraka, the quintessence of the past, of history, is the choices and actions of one's ancestors as they have become reified and embodied in material sites like houses, land and tombs and the bodily practice of taboo. Villagers maintain that the houses, land, fields and water around the village are powerfully efficacious (*masina*) because of the ancestors who inhabited and worked that land and now lie buried therein. The operative principle here seems to be the idea that individual ambition becomes externalized through work and care: the act of tending and caring for something, be it a house, tomb or particular rice paddy is always partly the act of imbuing that place with one's personal desires and ambitions. Once achieved, the goals and intentions of the actors become a more permanent part of the landscape, thus acting to constrain and empower the lives of future descendants.

The sacred efficacy (*hasina*) inherent in such sites, the force which enables 'ancestors' children' to prosper in their endeavors must be maintained in daily practice, which villagers call remembrance. The state of prosperity and fruitfulness, which most villagers cite as evidence of ancestral blessing, in fact requires the successful alignment of one's own desires and motives with those of one's ancestors who came before. It is as if all the actions and desires of previous generations were fixed by virtue of their death. Your own happiness and well-being hinge on the successful negotiation of your ancestors' prior choices, which impinge on your ability to 'seek' and 'make yourself living.' What this means is that villagers must reconcile their own desires with those of the dead, and struggle constantly to both placate ancestors and profit from them at the same time. This connection between remembrance and efficacy acts to impose a powerful system of moral constraint on the lives of those who, in the hopes that they will benefit from the power of the past, are forced to 'remember.'

The tension between ancestral power and constraint, the need to remember and the desire to forget, is constant and exists on almost every level of Betsimisaraka practice, pervading people's relationship to houses, the land, tombs, even bodily practice such as healing and taboo: whatever the context, descendants are expected to honor, even extend their ancestors, particularly their parents', projects and ambitions. Ideally one should inhabit one's ancestral land and continue to farm the same rice fields that were farmed by one's ancestors. One should also respect ancestral wishes as to where to be buried and maintain their tombs. So too, one must follow ancestral taboos (*fady, sandrana*), the ancestral injunctions not to engage in certain kinds of behavior or eat particular kinds of food, which, because of the power conferred through death, are a further example of how ancestral power comes to shape descendants' lives. In return for these diverse forms of obedience, or as villagers would put it 'remembrance,' ancestors are supposed to bless their descendants and make them have good harvests, good health, wealth and numerous children. In contrast, to sell one's ancestral land or violate taboos is to 'forget' and 'obliterate' the memory of ancestors, or as one man put it, it is to leave your parents with 'no standing stone' a reference to one of the more enduring memorial objects in the village. It is also to leave oneself vulnerable to ancestral wrath. It is to choose sickness, death and obliteration over health, life and posterity. The existential dilemma people face is the need to negotiate between the constraints of the past and the opportunities and contingencies of the present: the trick is to mediate between the danger implicit in pursuing one's own choices and desires and the relative safety of remaining within the parameters defined by prior ancestral choice.

Sacrificial Narratives

The delicate balance people seek to maintain, between satisfying ancestors and pursuing their own ambitions, is impossible to achieve all the time. More often than not, people—through avarice, thoughtlessness, desire—find they have done something that angered a particular ancestor, and are forced to sacrifice a cow.[17] What I wish to focus on here is the long speech (*kabary*) that precedes the actual slaughter of the cow, during which the private suffering that has

---

[17] The sequence of events leading up to a sacrifice are similar to what has been described for the African continent (Lienhardt 1961; Middleton, 1960), where a person falls sick and then goes to a diviner who, via divination, figures out which ancestor is causing the illness and what actions are necessary to remove the sickness. For Betsimisaraka, ancestors are not the only cause of illness which may also include having offended a certain nature spirit or possibly medicines planted by someone else. There are some kinds of sacrifice where the cow is demanded by a land spirit. For a more detailed account, see Cole (1996).

resulted in sacrifice is publicly announced and explained to the community. It is the particularities of these sacrificial narratives that constitute local commentary on the predicaments of living people, and inform people's understandings as they attempt to forge their lives within the parameters set by ancestral constraint. At the same time, the fact that it is above all through *speech*, that people's relationships to their ancestors are mediated, is significant: speech is considered a powerful kind of action in the world. Just as it is through speech that ancestors may seek to control their descendants in the form of a curse, so too it is this same power of speech that descendants use when they, in turn, seek to reconstitute their relationship to ancestors. What follows is a speech taken from a sacrifice in August of 1993, a 'flourishing' (*fahavanonana*) ceremony thrown by Gabe and Marie in a town called Salehy, which I have chosen because it conveys a wide range of the different dilemmas people face and the ways these are creatively narrated and reworked in the context of sacrifice.

The Speech

Speech maker: Pardon, but we have a child who lives across the water, according to her horn's name (*anaran tandroka*), Marie. She has deep roots here in Salehy. Her father is Rakala over there and her mother is Marovavy, that is where Marie comes from. If she lived across the river then time passed and she grew into womanhood and she was taken by Gabe and they live in their house in Ambodiharina. And since they've lived there they have given birth to many children, and as they had many children they thought of little else than raising and caring for those children and earning their livelihood. Yet they were forced to give a cow for Gabe's mother; when she asked them for a cow they didn't refuse or forget about it but did everything to make the ceremony possible. They worked very hard, Gabe and his wife, to fulfill the work demanded by the mother of Gabe and so they sacrificed the cow and completed the work and when that was finished they turned to their livelihood once again. They continued to work and care for their children.

Yet just recently Marie fell sick. They took her to the doctor but he couldn't cure her, they bought European medicine but she didn't get better. 'Ahh' said the husband. 'My wife, you've been sick for too long let us go to the diviner.' So they went to the diviner and spread out the many red [*maro mena*—a reference to the color of the seeds] and when they did this, the seeds spoke, 'All things must compete— you've given a cow to the mother of the man and it is finished and so too you have prospered but have not given here, and so we [here] are insulted. That is the origin of this work. So they discussed the matter with their children. 'Ahh children you have grown, so I've gone to the diviner and saw in the seeds that we have prospered and that is why Marie has fallen sick.'

And the children replied, 'We have heard your decision—long illness is not a friend to life. If that causes her suffering, then we'll take care of the matter.' At that time they didn't merely sit, but worked, especially the children, to complete the sacrifice. When they saved up they purchased the cow and so their ancestor's desire for wealth has been realized. The reason then we sacrifice the huge cow is that Gabe and Marie have prospered and so we must announce it to you the assembly.

The second reason [we are sacrificing the cow] is that there was a circumcision ceremony here, done by Father of Flavy and so he called together those of one stomach. 'Ah,' he said, 'there is work I must do, a circumcision, and I must tell you all.' 'Yes,' said Father of Namo, 'we have heard, and let the ceremony progress as we are here [and ready to assist].' But when the ceremony progressed the bull was brought out and tied down to the stake and later when it came time to cut up the cow Jerome spoke, 'You Father of Namo, you are not the master of this sacrifice.' Well, at that time we all shook with fear, even his younger brother married to the north, we were all here. They carried on with the customs and the next morning it was time for the presentation of cooked meat to Zanahary and so they went to call Father of Namo. Three times they went, but he refused to come, none of us could attend, not even our descendants, because of those scornful words, 'you're not master of this ceremony Father of Namo.' We were shamed and lost honor at that time. So the reason we kill the bull today is to remove the slight! For truly we have children and descendants if we have produced a ceremony such as this, we have a son-in-law too, Gabe. Those are the reasons we kill the cow and we must present them to you [the assembled group].

So too, we have a child, Jean, son of Rakala and he ate *sokina* [a kind of tiny hedgehog], but *sokina* is not eaten by the ancestors—a tabooed food. Yet he ate it—and his mouth broke out in sores and he told his father, 'Ahh, father, I've eaten a tabooed animal, a *sokina*.' When we discussed the sacrifice we decided to remove his broken taboo. And so we asked the diviner what he thought and he said, 'yes, that is the custom'. So that is the reason we kill the bull and we must present it to you the assembled group.

Also, 'words' were spoken by the ancestors of those who live across the river [i.e. the maternal ancestors to the parties involved who came from Ambodiharina], 'If our child wants to go north, even to join the army, there is no road for him to take. The descendants were forbidden from going north, for people in the old days couldn't bear to separate from their children and so they spoke those words. But Jacques brings cows to the north in order earn his livelihood. For wealth he goes north, west, south and east and he brings cows all the way to Brickaville. Twice when Jacques got to Vatomandry he could go no farther but when that happened he came home and told his parents about it, 'I fell sick and could go no further than Vatomandry and my friend went on to Brickaville that's why our voyage took so long.' 'Ahh' said the parents, there were last words (*farabolana*) made by the ancestors, and so now we sacrifice a cow to remove all that—Let them [descendants] prosper. The reason we kill the bull is to cleanse that.

I too have a reason [for killing the cow]. My mother's brother's (*zama*) coffee forest was taken by the school. I intended to build a house there but when I went to build the house they came and built the school and so I stopped my project. But at that time a few days went by and I fell off the bridge and was wounded with a hole in my thigh—I wasn't drunk or anything. Everyone in the town gathered. It turned out my ancestors were after me as I was leaving the land on which my ancestor's journey ended (*nahavery dia*) and where they lived. At that time I cried, my tears fell because of what had befallen me— and I thought, 'If I live well and close to my friend [wife] I'll rejoice.' I have a son who lived across the water [in Ambodiharina] and he fell sick and when we went to see him the diviner spoke, 'Something harmed you and you cried hard' and that is why your child has fallen ill. So we invoked the ancestors and begged them but it didn't help. God does what he will and the child died. So now [I've decided] I'll live here in the place of my ancestors and my father. May it bless me! That is what I have to tell the assembled group.

Analysis

For Southern Betsimisaraka, the realm of sacrifice and the practices associated with it combines symbolic and political levels of action. Predicated on the dangerously powerful capacity to directly link the living and dead, the source of power on which the social order is based, the practice of sacrifice has the ability to integrate and trans- form different levels of Betsimisaraka experience. While the institu- tion of sacrifice appears to be of considerable historical duration, and examples of sacrifice are cited by travelers to the east coast as early as the eighteenth century (see Grandidier and Decary, 1958), the content of sacrifice, the kinds of problems and issues it seeks to address, are historically contingent. Significantly, sacrifice mediates the two axes along which Betsimisaraka identity is constructed, as it enables both the manipulation of ties between ancestors and descend- ants and among the living, as well as villagers' relationships to the outside world. The experience narrated through sacrifice, and how these stories create and inform the context of villager's daily lives will become clearer as I examine each particular practice in turn. In so doing, I shall follow the order provided by the speechmaker in the speech at Salehy cited above.

Responding to Care

At its most basic level, the sacrifice performed at Salehy was a flourishing sacrifice (*fahavanonana*).[18] The official explanation of the flourishing sacrifice holds that ancestors bless their descendants and make them prosper, and that once descendants have reached a certain level of success—reproductive and material, the fulfillment of their personal ambitions whatever those might be—the ancestor in question begs for a cow: 'We have made you prosper, so now give [that which is due] to us!' So it was explained to me again and again. It is considered a fair and moral exchange. And yet in order to get their cow the ancestors are willing to inflict illness, suffering, even death on their own descendants. Prosperity, longed for by all, is nevertheless a vulnerable and fleeting condition once attained—vulnerable to the evil intentions of other people and the greed of one's own ancestors as well. Prosperity, which one might describe as the manifestation or state of ancestral blessing (*tsodrano*), is in fact a delicate negotiation between the intentions of ancestors and the needs of living people. Blessing is received in exchange for following ancestral ways, which are in fact a crystallization of the ancestors' particular historical experience. The flourishing ceremony marked the successful negotiation of this delicate balance; ultimately, however, it also signaled descendants' capitulation to ancestral power.

The logic of the flourishing sacrifice is a further reflection on the relationship of blessing and killing, generosity and avarice, sincerity and deception, caring and abandonment, that characterizes the relationship between parents and children, and which is ultimately the model upon which all other hierarchical relationships are predicated.

---

[18] I have chosen the word 'flourish' to translate what is locally called a '*fahavanonana*,' the nominative form of '*vanona*' which means to 'come to perfection,' or, with the prefix '*maha*,' to 'bring to perfection, to complete, to conduce to growth.' The idea is one of general prosperity, but flourishing better conveys the notion that people, like plants and trees to which they are so frequently compared, might grow and thrive.

While morally (and materially) the most important relationship, the link between parents and children is nevertheless characterized by instability and conflict. Like everything conceived of as 'powerfully efficacious' (*masina*), this relationship too has the power to 'turn': there is always the potential for betrayal. The imagined ghosts feeding off the body of the cow, the cow that participants are keenly aware substitutes for the lives of humans, made each flourishing ceremony less about the particular relation between a certain mother or father and their children and more an abstract commentary on power, reciprocity and ancestral ability to shape human action in the world.

In the case of Gabe and Marie's flourishing there was another element at play as well, that of equality of spouses. Prosperous, successful people signaled powerful ancestors. To give a cow to Gabe's ancestors was to imply that Gabe and Marie's combined fruitfulness was somehow due more to his ancestors' intervention than to hers. Moreover, to suggest such a thing was a grave insult to Marie's ancestors—after all, weren't they efficacious as well? Hadn't their blessing enabled Marie and Gabe to grow wealthy and raise numerous children to adulthood? If Gabe and Marie had married that meant they were equal; and if they were equal then so too were the ancestors from whence they came. To give to his ancestors instead of hers was to make Marie a slave, as slaves were, by definition, people who depended on the ancestors of others. And if Marie was a slave then, of course, her ancestors were slaves too! So ran the local logic. Thus to have given a flourishing ceremony for one and not the other was to suggest that one member of the couple was more important and powerful than the other. That one member of a couple is indeed more powerful than the other, in terms of personality or family connections, is not surprising; equality is an ideal that is only rarely achieved. Yet to sacrifice to first one and then the other set of ancestors ensures that inequality in this life (struggles for control between a husband and wife) is not carried over into the unequal worship of the dead, the defining characteristic of slavery.

The Big Knife that Removes Knots and the World of Living People

During the speech at Salehy, a fight was brought out and 'cleansed' (*sasana*) or 'gotten' (*mangala*) over the body of the cow, reflecting the way the practice of sacrifice was also often compared to the 'big

knife that removes knots,' creating and dissolving relationships, smooth-
ing over and repairing flaws in the community as a knife removes
knots from a tree. The first involved a circumcision thrown by the
tangalamena, Father of Jerome, during which his son, Jerome, insulted
his uncle, Father of Namo, by saying, 'you are not master of this
sacrifice'; the insult served as a pretext to publicly avoid participation in the rest of the ceremony that continued the next morning.

In order to understand the kind of struggle revealed here it is
necessary to point out that while all the parties involved were of one
ancestry, Father of Jerome was connected to the ancestry as 'child
of women' (*zanin'vavy*) while Father of Namo was 'child of men' (*zanin'lahy*).[19] In the usual hierarchy 'children of men' are believed to
have closer ties to ancestors and are responsible for 'carrying' the
ancestors and working as *tangalamena*. Here, however, the normal
hierarchy had been reversed by the cross-cutting hierarchy of younger
and elder sibling: Father of Jerome was 'child of women' but he was
also much older than Father of Namo, and so the power to carry
the ancestors passed to him, at least temporarily. The assumption
was that once Father of Namo was old enough then Father of Jerome
would hand over to him the stick used for invoking the ancestors
which stood for the position of *tangalamena*. But Father of Jerome
and the 'children of women' faction were loath to part with their
position of power. Tension had probably been building for some
time when the fight actually took place over the body of the cow
and the consequences were permanent. To refuse to participate in
customs is one common way of publicly announcing a break with
the parties involved; Father of Namo was deeply insulted and used
the incident as a pretext to break off and start his own great house.
From the point of view of the speech presented here, however, the
conflict described is now well over and the division has already
occurred. Yet part of the danger of any dispute and subsequent division is the ancestral blame and anger (*tsiny*), that may be incurred:
it is this potential guilt and the shame provoked by the prior fight

---

[19] All people belong to their mother's ancestry as 'children of women' and their
father's ancestry as 'children of men.' However, at times—perhaps because the child
never lived with his father's family—people become integrated mainly into their
mother's ancestry, albeit in a slightly less powerful position. In the case of the
conflict described here, it is quite likely that eventually Father of Jerome would split
off from his mother's house to avoid his position as 'child of women' and start his
own great house.

that Father of Namo, now firmly in possession of the *tangala* (sacrificial stick) as rightful 'child of men,' wishes to deflect.

Will of the Living, Voices of the Dead

For Southern Betsimisaraka, parents have the ability to powerfully constrain their descendants' actions through the use of words in the form of a curse (cf. Graeber, 1996). If verbalized, momentary anger or grief could thus have permanent effects, ones that lingered on in the world: strong emotion lent efficacy to speech. Descendants were left to suffer the consequences or deal with them as best they could. One means of doing so was to 'remove the words' or 'return the words' over the body of the cow.

People often found themselves confronted with 'last words,' usually words that ancestors had uttered prior to death concerning the specific things descendants are not supposed to do, like burying a particular person in the tomb, or engaging in a particular action. Often, these become the taboos (*sandrana/fady*) of a group, thus preventing people from farming certain plants or eating certain foods (cf. Lambek, 1992; Ruud, 1960). Fixed at death, last words are supposed to be beyond the means of human action. In practice, however, the array of prohibitions to which different actors are subject is constantly changing. Sacrifice is the arena in which 'ancestral words' are removed and manipulated so that the late-come children (*zaza-fara*) might lighten the ancestral weight of the past. The business of removing taboos, however, is always a dangerous one, as the potency of the last words varies depending on how long the person had been dead and whether the occasion for the curse is remembered: the more distant and half-forgotten the curse is the more hesitant people are to remove it. *Fady*, mere prohibitions that might have been imposed by a diviner who subsequently died and forgot to remove them, are distinguished from *sandrana* which are ancestral prohibitions carried for generations.

Prohibitions and last words reflect the desires and predicaments, the historical experience, of those who came before, and they are inherited, for better or for worse by those who came after. The problem for descendants is that circumstances and opportunities inevitably change, and so they find themselves forced to negotiate between the two. In the example from Gabe and Marie's speech, one child sought to make his living as a butcher, carrying cows from the south up to Tamatave in the north where he could sell them for a profit. He was foiled in his attempts at what should have been a lucrative business by an ancestor who had declared that 'no descendant of mine shall find a road to the north, not even to join the army.' The capricious nature of the prohibition, for which no one could remember the initial impetus, was nevertheless confronted: Jacques begged permission to disregard the taboo. If on his next trip to Tamatave he prospered, people explained, then he had got his 'blessing.' If not, he would just 'take what he'd got' (*mitondra ny azo*). After all, the logic ran, you 'begged' but only knew your request had been 'heard' by seeing what actually happened.

So far I have concentrated on strategies, such as the removal of ancestral prohibitions and words, that people use when particularly inconvenient manifestations of ancestral power impinge on their lives. The problems presented and the solutions tried, however, are not always so clear-cut. It is much more likely that an individual's momentary yielding to private desire, intense emotion, the heedless act of a child or submission to the more powerful force of the national government, is later rectified through sacrifice: people give in to or partake of the non-ancestral only to reassert an ancestrally defined identity later on. In these narratives, participants explicitly acknowledge that ancestral ways, particularly the food prohibitions which came to stand synechdocally for a particular kind of power and moral order, a way of being in the world, are impossible to follow all the time. And yet respect for 'tabooed things' (*raha sandrana*) is the explicit ideal: because a given ancestor decided not to eat, say striped eel or wood pigeon, a certain kind of lemur or crocodile, his descendants can't either.[20]

---

[20] Here it is important to note that there is nothing intrinsically dirty about any of these animals, nor do they present anomalies in any classificatory system: the notion that they are 'matter out of place' doesn't apply (see Douglas, 1966). Rather, 'tabooed things' came to be considered dirty by ancestral fiat: a particular ancestor decided to forbid a certain food for whatever reason and so the animal was defined as 'dirty,' something 'not eaten by the ancestors.' If that not eaten by ancestors was dirty, then conversely, ancestors were defined as 'clean.' This focus on cleanliness or pureness as someone who has never transgressed, which in this case means to have eaten a tabooed food, is particularly emphasized with reference to the family tomb and is also important for any contact with ancestors such as that initiated by the *tangalamena*.

One kind of narrative frequently heard in sacrifice is that of someone who had, wittingly or not, eaten a forbidden food. When this
occurs by accident, diagnosis is performed through divination, and
testifies yet again to the subtle yet constant conflict between ancestral dictate and the realities of living people. The speech from
Salehy quoted above tells only of a certain Jean, who ate *sokina*, a
tiny hedgehog-like creature. But a single broken taboo brought forth
in any given sacrifice is the exception—most speeches revealed numerous transgressed prohibitions and their subsequent negotiation. It is
inevitably teenage boys and young men who knowingly broke taboos,
for revenge, as in a young boy who ate the crocodile that killed his
brother, or out of curiosity or mere desire. As a speechmaker in one
village observed, 'if there is that which is fat and tasty it is *tsaky* (the
fatty, salty meat one eats when drinking rum). I told old Jean-Paul
but he wouldn't listen and ate *tono* (a kind of eel); but *tono* is not
eaten by the ancestors! And yet it is so fatty.' One can almost hear
the wistful craving in the speaker's voice. Adolescents and men know,
of course, what their taboos are; everybody except very small children do. But they are more likely than women or elders to challenge ancestral authority embodied in prohibitions. Men are said to
have a closer relationship to ancestors, but if it is close it might also
be described as more agonistic. Moreover, because they tend to travel
more, including beyond the confines of the ancestral land, men are
more likely than women to be exposed to things 'not eaten, not
done' by the ancestors.

Creating Boundaries

A crucial aspect of sacrificial narratives is the way they mediate people's experience to the outside world. There were two paradigmatic
reasons that villagers left home that signaled interaction, willing or
not, with forces that came to stand for all that was quintessentially
unancestral: the French colonial, and later the Malagasy national,
government. Typically, this interaction with outside power took two
forms, the army or prison. Until independence, both prison and military service shared the common feature that both required, indeed
forced, men to leave their ancestral homeland and participate in a
social order with different codes of behavior and premised on a
different kind of moral order.

Men who return from the army are required to reassume their ancestral taboos publicly in sacrifice. The notion that recruits to the army or prisoners are forced to participate in a system that is antithetical to ancestral power is rooted in a wider cultural logic and embodied in the proverb, 'the colors of the land are taken by the potato' (*soron'tany arin'ny ovy*). Just as the potato sinks its roots into the land and becomes colored by the nutrients it takes in, so people take on the customs and ways of the land in which they live. Land's customs have an intrinsic and persuasive power (see also Astuti, 1995). Ancestral power embodied in prohibitions is only efficacious within the context of the ancestral land: in other words, ancestral anger and retribution only occur if taboos are transgressed within the bounds of the *tanindrazana* (the ancestral homeland). In turn, people expect that an army recruit will follow the 'laws of government' while away: the historical experience of one's ancestors, in the sense described earlier, is only relevant within the confines of one's ancestral homeland. Beyond the ancestral land, other forms of power are thought to obtain. What happens in sacrifice is the negotiation of socially constructed boundaries, as the traveler is 'washed' of his experiences with the outside world and remembers his place in an ancestrally conceived and constituted order.

Through stories constructed in sacrifice, people transform nonancestral experience and make it ancestral, thus allowing them to negotiate between otherwise contending models of how the world works. What this means is that the content of 'tradition,' in other words what counts as 'ancestral,' is constantly changing: it is through sacrifice that change is effected. What villagers view as the inherent persuasiveness of practice means that the resumption of taboos in sacrifice, or the announcement of someone's arrival, effectively signals a person's return to the ancestrally constituted cultural order. To return home is to enter once more into the flow of village life, the give and take between the living and the dead, the multiple layers of witnesses to different kinds of prosperity, legitimate and stolen and the many half-secret kinds that exist in between. It is to make oneself vulnerable once more to the local bonds of reciprocity and constraint, and it means one's choices are always a strategic mediation of ancestral fiat and personal ambition.

Conclusion

Sacrifice is about the attempt to escape death by imposing one's own will on those ancestors who are perceived, in conjunction with God (*Zanahary*), as the source of life and death. While Lienhardt's approach to sacrifice pointed to the significance of symbolic action as a way for people to try and control an uncertain world, and even mentioned that sacrificial speeches among the Dinka were made, he failed to explore the mechanisms through which the modulation of experience came about. For Southern Betsimisaraka, the cohabitation of the living and the dead enabled by sacrifice allows for what Steedly has called 'a momentary bridging of borders between past and present, between experience and imagination' (1993: 10). Sacrificial narratives performed in the context of sacrifice provide the crucial link as they mediate between the ritual context and everyday life, providing people with a powerful means for reflecting on the possibilities and limitations placed on human action in the world. Moreover, as Peel (1995) has shown, life is shaped by narratives, just as narratives are shaped by life. For Southern Betsimisaraka, sacrificial narratives, because of their link to the ancestors, become the authoritative versions of events that occur, albeit always subject to negotiation.[21] These narratives are above all about the uncertainty of the human condition, the struggles and ambiguities of human relations and the way individual desires and intentions are thwarted by the desires of predecessors rendered powerful by virtue of their death. Yet these stories produced in sacrifice are also a means for villagers to talk about the position of local practice in relation to the outside world, a world which villagers are keenly aware is more powerful than their own, even as people attempt to harness the power inherent in sacrifice as a means to mediate between the two. Ultimately, of course, the negotiations attempted in sacrifice—the attempt to reconfigure one's relationship to the more powerful past, or more powerful outsiders, and thus tie a now-mastered past to a hopefully brighter future—may fail. No one ever knows whether a particular negotiation will work. It might, but then again it might not. The possibility of change, however, means that people have every reason to try.

---

[21] For example, if people tried a particular negotiation through sacrifice and the sacrifice didn't work, people will usually re-interpret the cause of the illness.

BIBLIOGRAPHY

Aly, J.M.
  1984   *Le discours rituel chez les Betsimisaraka de la cote-est de Madagascar.* Presence Africaine, 54–61.
Astuti, Rita
  1995   *People of the Sea.* Cambridge: Cambridge University Press.
Aujas, L.
  1927   *Les Rites du Sacrifice a Madagascar. Memoires de l'Academie Malgache 2.*
Bloch, Maurice
  1971   *Placing the Dead.* New York: Seminar Press.
  1986   *From Blessing to Violence.* Cambridge: Cambridge University Press.
  1992   *Prey into Hunter: the politics of religious experience.* New York: Cambridge University Press.
Borneman, J.
  1992   *Belonging in Two Berlins.* Cambridge: Cambridge University Press.
Bruner, Jerome
  1986   *Actual Minds, Possible Worlds.* Cambridge, MA: Harvard University Press.
Cole, Jennifer
  1996   *The Necessity of Forgetting: Ancestral and Colonial Memories in East Madagascar.* Ph.D. Thesis, Dept. of Anthropology, UC Berkeley.
  1997   Quand le mémoire resurgit: la rebellion de 1947 et la representation de l'état contemporain à Madagascar. *Terrain,* Numero "Miroirs du Colonialisme," Mars.
de Heusch, L.
  1985   *Sacrifice in Africa.* Bloomington: Indiana University Press.
Detienne, M.
  1989   'Culinary Practices and the Spirit of Sacrifice.' In *The Cuisine of Sacrifice Among the Greeks* (eds.) M. Detienne and J.P. Vernant. Chicago: Chicago University Press.
Douglas, Mary
  1966   *Purity and Danger.* USA: Routledge and Kegan Paul.
Evans-Pritchard, E.E.
  1956   *Nuer Religion.* Oxford: The Clarendon Press.
Feeley-Harnik, G.
  1992   *A Green Estate: Restoring Independence in Madagascar.* Washington, D.C.: Smithsonian Institution Press.
Fortes, M.
  1957   *The Web of Kinship Among the Tallensi.* London: Oxford University Press.
  1987   *Ancestors in Africa. In Religion, Morality and the Person.* J.R. Goody (ed.) Cambridge: Cambridge University Press.
Gibson, T.
  1986   *Sacrifice and Sharing in the Phillippine Highlands.* London: The Athlone Press.
Graeber, D.
  1996   *The Disasterous Ordeal of 1987: Magic and History in Rural Madagascar* (Ph.D. thesis) Department of Anthropology, University of Chicago.
Grandidier, G. & Decary, R.
  1958   *Histoire Physique, Naturelle et Politique de Madagascar.* Livre III. Histoire des Tribus autres que les Merina.

Hubert, H. & Mauss, Marcel
    1964 [1899]   *Sacrifice: Its Nature and Function*: London: University of Chicago
        Press.
Keenan, Elenor Ochs
    1974   *Conversation and Oratory in Vakinakaratra, Madagascar* (Ph.D. thesis),
        Department of Anthropology, University of Pennsylvania.
Kottak, Conrad P.
    1980   *The Past in the Present: History, Ecology and Cultural Variation in
        Highland Madagascar.* Ann Arbor: University of Michigan Press.
Lambek, M.
    1992   *Taboo as Cultural Practice Among Malagasy Speakers.* MAN (27):
        254–266.
Lienhardt, Godfrey
    1961   *Divinity and Experience.* Oxford: The Clarendon Press.
Middleton, John
    1960   *Lugbara Religion: Ritual and Authority Among an East African People.*
        London: Oxford University Press.
Peel, J.D.Y.
    1995   'For Who Hath Depised the Day of Small Things? Missionary
        Narratives and Historical Anthropology' *Comparative Studies in
        Society and History* (37) 3: 581–607.
Rudd, J.
    1960   *Taboo.* Oslo: Oslo University Press.
Schafer, Roy
    1992   *Retelling a Life: Narrative and Dialogue in Psychoanalysis.* New York:
        Basic Books.
Sharp, Lesley A.
    1993   *The Possessed and the Dispossessed.* Berkeley: University of California
        Press.
Smith, W.R.
    1894   *The Religion of the Semites.* London: A.&C. Black.
Steedly, Mary Margaret
    1993   *Hanging without a Rope: Narrative Experience in Colonial and Post-
        Colonial Karoland.* Princeton: Princeton University Press.
Turner, V. & E. Bruner
    1986   *The Anthropology of Experience.* Chicago: University of Illinois Press.
Tylor, E.B.
    1889   *Primitive Culture 2.* New York, Holt.
Vig, L.
    1977   'L'idee de substitution dans la religion malgaches' in *Croyances et
        Moeurs des Malgaches.*

Plate 8. The cow is purified and marked with white clay (*tany mavo*) prior to a Betsimisaraka sacrifice. Photograph: Jennifer Cole.

Plate 9. The *tangalamena* grasps the tail of the bull to ensure that his voice will be heard by God and the ancestors, and bids the ancestors eat the flesh of the bull. The speechmaker stands to his right. Photograph: Jennifer Cole.

CHAPTER EIGHT

CIRCUMCISION, DEATH, AND STRANGERS*

KAREN MIDDLETON

In his book *How Societies Remember*, Connerton (1989) shows the importance of bodily performance and commemorative ceremonies in the conscious evocation of the past. 'For images of the past and recollected knowledge of the past,' he argues, 'are conveyed and sustained by (more or less ritual) performances' (p. 4). The Jewish practice of circumcision provides a very good example of what Connerton means by the 'theology of memory,' for through the re-enactment of the prototypical event in the making of God's people, the circumcision of each boy, and then the circumcised body itself, come to serve as a powerful mnemonic of Jewishness. In this essay, I draw upon Connerton's argument to move in a contrary if complementary direction by looking at a people who once practised circumcision but now no longer do. I shall show how the *un*circumcised body, in evoking the memory of a ritual they no longer perform, can equally be a form of commemoration, a kind of bodily memory, of a people's history, culture, and identity.

Let me begin at the beginning, however, with the issue as I first encountered it. I was working among the Karembola of southern Madagascar, and I had gone to a funeral at Marokipa with Iavimasy and Dany. There we had spent the day watching the ceremonial boasting of rival clans as they made gifts of cattle and money to our hosts. We had also enjoyed the dancing, the singing, the wrestling, and the cattle stampedes that bid the deceased farewell. Now in the late afternoon, the time had come to bury the corpse. With the

* *Acknowledgements*: Fieldwork was carried out among the Karembola of southern Madagascar from November 1981 to October 1983 and from March to August 1991, with financial support from the Economic and Social Research Council (UK) and The Leverhulme Trust (UK). For making the research possible, I record my gratitude to MM. Manassé Esoavelomandroso, Fulgence Fanony, and Eugène Mangalaza of the then Centre Universitaire Régionale at Toliary, Madagascar. I should like to thank Jennifer Cole, Adrian Hastings, and Michael Lambek for their careful comments on earlier drafts of this essay.

coffin perched precariously over the newly dug grave, a man took a knife and scored a deep notch in the wood. 'The deceased was uncircumcised,' Iavimasy commented, 'ancestral custom had not been observed.' 'You see,' he continued by way of explanation, 'we Karembola have forgotten our ancestral customs. We lost them all when the strangers came.' 'We're a people broken in by foreigners,' Dany added, 'like oxen put to yoke. The path today is held by strangers, and we just follow where they lead.'[1]

At one time, the kind of explanations Iavimasy and Dany offered for the decline of circumcision ritual would apparently have posed no difficulty for anthropological interpretation. For the decline of 'traditional' ritual, as of 'traditional' authority or 'traditional' values, was taken as the natural corollary of the imposition of colonial rule. Over the last twenty years, however, many anthropologists and historians (e.g., Cohn, 1987; Comaroff, 1985; Comaroff & Comaroff, 1991, 1993; Dirks, 1992; Feeley-Harnik, 1984; Guha & Spivak, 1988; Ranger & Kimambo, 1972; Sahlins, 1985; Stoler, 1989) have been concerned to challenge this kind of over-simple model of the 'colonizer' and the 'colonized,' by exploring the ways in which individuals and societies have responded actively and creatively to experiences of political domination, economic exploitation, and administrative control. As a result, the 'colonial encounter' has been shown to be a far more complex and diverse process of engagement between 'colonizing' forces, on the one hand, and indigenous socio-cultural systems, on the other, than earlier models of 'acculturation' assumed. Indeed, given the gap that often existed between administrative discourse and practice, it has become clear enough that colonial regimes were seldom as monolithic or as potent as they have been sometimes made to appear (Cohn, 1987; Cooper, 1994; Denning, 1988; Stoler & Cooper, 1989; Vaughan, 1991; but see Mitchell, 1988).

Perhaps it is because recent scholarship has thus been framed as a critique of earlier assumptions of indigenous passivity and impotence that few studies today focus on the *decline* of ritual *qua* decline. Indeed, writers appear rather too inclined to pass over this kind of development, preferring to look at either the growth of new, often syncretic, forms of ritual expression or the resurgence of 'traditional' ritual in the post-colonial era. While such studies have underscored

---

[1] *Folake vazaha. Le mitarike lalañe i vazaha'ay henanike, le mañorike avao zahay.*

the complexity of the 'colonial encounter,' they have still left certain things unexplained. Jean Comaroff's (1985) account of historical transformation among the Tshidi of southern Africa, for example, is concerned to explore 'the role of the Tshidi as determined, yet determining, in their own history' (p. 1). To this end, it counterposes a detailed analysis of the poetics and politics of traditional Tshidi circumcision ritual, as the key to the pre-colonial socio-cultural order, to a close examination of Zionist practice, as one of the ways in which Tshidi have sought to 'acquiesce yet protest, reproduce yet seek to transform their predicament' (*ibid.*). The monograph, however, says very little directly about the decline of collective circumcision ritual or what its decline means to Tshidi today. Having stood for the pre-colonial socio-cultural order, this practice more or less disappears without trace. Comaroff's silence here is especially curious in so far as her analyses place a particular emphasis upon *bodily* reform as historical practice (also 1992). The end of circumcision ritual must surely count as among the more significant reforms of Tshidi body practice. What kind of traces, then—of powerlessness or of resistance—has it left upon Tshidi historical consciousness?

In this essay, I have chosen to look at Karembola narratives around the *decline* of a ritual in the early colonial period because they would seem to present particular problems of interpretation given recent models of ritual change. I shall, however, be looking at the decline of circumcision ritual, not simply as a *negative*, but as a ritual performance in and of itself. Lambek (1992) points to the important role negatives play in the form of taboos in defining identity in Madagascar (see also Ruud, 1960), and certainly as we listen to Karembola describing themselves as a 'people who once practised circumcision but no longer do' (*ondate nisavatse taolo feïe tsy henane*), it is difficult to avoid concluding that a negative here bears dense, profound meaning about who Karembola were and what they have become. My premiss, then, is that, as a body practice articulated to both past and present, *not* being circumcised is significant, and that in it and by it, Karembola make a kind of remembrance: they tell the story of the making of their contemporary selves.[2]

---

[2] As in many parts of Africa, the decline of Tshidi circumcision ritual seems to have been linked to changes in politico-military organisation. In this paper, I am not concerned to argue against this kind of interpretation but rather to focus on a neglected dimension, namely, the capacity of the *decline* of ritual to constitute

As I noted, however, Karembola narratives around the decline of circumcision ritual present the uncircumcised body as a metaphor for their sense of political impotence and cultural decline in a 'modern' age shaped predominantly by foreigners. Taking my cue from the 'gap' in Jean Comaroff's study of Tshidi ritual transformation, the question I want to ask is this. Are Karembola essentially right when they present the decline of circumcision ritual as indicative of their political and cultural impotence? Or can this particular 'body reform' also be understood to constitute a kind of resistance on their part? Actually, as I shall show, the data are more than equivocal. For if in the immediate sense the historical circumstances I shall describe make it difficult to see the decline of circumcision ritual as any other than a 'reaction to conquest,' it did also constitute part of a wider performative in which Karembola both remained rooted in their own culture and reclaimed their autonomy.

I begin by describing some of the values Karembola attach to circumcision, before exploring the explanations they give for its decline.

Stepping over Corpses

The Karembola live in the southernmost tip of Madagascar, on the limestone plateau that runs south from the little administrative and market town of Beloha to the sea. Here in an arid land, celebrated for its highly specialized xerophilous flora, they struggle to grow their crops of manioc, maize and sweet potatoes and to raise their herds of zebu cattle and goats against the ever constant threat of drought. In culture, dialect, and socio-political organization, the Karembola have much in common with their better-known neighbours, the 'Mahafale' to the west and the 'Tandroy' to the north and east. Similarities include pronounced agnatic ideologies, combined with a strong sense of being 'kinded,' that is, of belonging in named clans and lineages (Esoavelomandroso, 1984; Heurtebize, 1986). In defining themselves as the 'in-between people' (ondate añivo), however, Karembola like to stress the differences too.[3]

---

a ritual performance in and of itself, and of the uncircumcised body—a seeming negative—to carry memory.

[3] For a discussion of Karembola identity, see Middleton, 'Lords of the Karembola: ethnogenesis and state building in precolonial Southern Madagascar,' *Ethnohistory*, forthcoming.

Among Karembola, as among most peoples of Madagascar (e.g. Bloch, 1986; Grandidier & Grandidier, 1928; Ruud, 1960), circumcision is held to be 'an ancestral command' (*lilin-drazañe*). To be circumcised, Karembola say, is about obtaining ancestral blessing: it is to be in possession of *asy*, a kind of spiritual essence, a sacred efficacy, to be in a state of grace. The boys, Iavimasy explained, cast off what is dirty and polluted in order to become 'clean' (*malio*) and 'good' (*soa*); they sought 'to make themselves live' (*mahaveloñe anteña*). Not every man was circumcised, however, and in the intensely hierarchical milieu of southern Madagascar the ritual served to make political statements about 'kinds of people' and their worth. Decary (1933: 91), I suspect, records the prevailing cultural ethos when, noting that certain Tandroy were uncircumcised, he finds the reason most likely to lie in their origin, viz, that they belong to a clan which had lost or never had the right to a *hazomanga*[4] (the ritual cult that is a key marker of descent identity ('ancestry') in the deep south); this, he adds, would have been the case for former slaves and families rejected by their clan of origin. This is certainly the view Karembola take of the matter: for them to be uncircumcised is to be without *hazomanga*, to be without ancestry, to be without history, to be akin to a slave. The very opposite of 'worthy people' (*kieñe ondate*), uncircumcised men are 'dead' people, 'lost' people, people who for one reason or another have become detached from their ancestral root.

Turning now to a reconstruction of Karembola circumcision ritual, we find ourselves hampered by the kinds of historical material that are available. While we have several detailed descriptions of circumcision practice in southern Madagascar (e.g., Decary, 1933: 91–94; Frère, 1958: 150–151; Grandidier & Grandidier, 1928: 402–410)— though nothing comparable to the rich primary sources that enabled Bloch (1986) to trace the history of Merina circumcision ritual over almost two centuries—the problem is that these descriptions seldom, if ever, specify the particular group(s) or region(s) to which they refer.

---

[4] In the literature the term *hazomanga* is often glossed as denoting the timber stakes at which sacrifices are performed. For Karembola, it covers the practice of sacrifice *in toto*—its offices, its rituals, its taboos—everything that makes up the work of 'pleading for the soul' (*mangatake fiay*). Informants emphasised that the stakes themselves—what Astuti (1995: 101) terms the *hazomanga*-object—were never that important, being always less potent than the sacred knife (*vylava*). The *vy*, they say, was what made the *hazomanga* (i.e., the *sacrifice*) efficacious.

For this reason, the following account is based almost entirely upon descriptions I collected from Karembola men and women who as children or young adults had witnessed the last performance of the rites. It is by no means a detailed reconstruction of 'traditional' Karembola circumcision ritual but more an outline of its key features as Karembola now *remember* it.

The first thing Karembola were keen to impress upon me, whether they had witnessed the rites in person or had only heard their elders talk of them, was that 'we Karembola were circumcised during the funeral/at the tomb' (*zahay Karembola nisavatse an-dolo*). That is to say, Karembola circumcision ritual was an integral part of mortuary ritual. It was embedded in the funeral of the *mpisoro*, the clan or lineage priest. Secondly, and more specifically, my informants emphasised that the defining moment of circumcision ritual had involved the initiates walking over their late *mpisoro*'s tomb. Indeed, circumcision (*savatse*) is more often known in the vernacular as *mandika lolo* (to step over, to walk across, to tread upon the tomb/corpse), and when Karembola remember the circumcision ritual their ancestors practised, this singular action overshadows all else. Tomb-walking is part of their identity, what made them Karembola; it is part of the history they as Karembola bear.[5]

To understand why initiates should have carried out this curious action, let us listen to Fihatoa describing what happens when a priest dies.

When a great priest dies, Fihatoa explained, he is very angry, sad beyond belief. He hates the idea of dying, and is intensely jealous

---

[5] This close association with tombs and funerals certainly appears atypical of circumcision practice in Madagascar. For while it is common to find an extensive symbolic cross-referencing between circumcision ritual and mortuary ritual (e.g., Bloch, 1986; Lambek & Walsh, this volume; cf. Barley, 1981), most Malagasy peoples seem at pains to keep the two rituals apart. 'Chez les Antemoro et Antambahoaka [south-east],' for instance, 'on ne peut annoncer la mort d'une personne avant la fin de la circoncision. Le corps est enterré surepticement, et après la fin de la circoncision, on peut annoncer la mort et faire un *andry faty*' (Ph. Beaujard, pers. comm., 17th December 1995). Whether Karembola circumcision ritual was as singular as Karembola claim is less clear, however. Decary (1933: 91–94) and Frère (1958: 150–151) both record that among certain 'Tandroy' groups circumcision sometimes took place during the priest's funeral, and Frère (*ibid.*) goes on to describe initiates stepping over his corpse, if not his tomb. Since, however, the Karembola are often classed as 'Tandroy,' and neither author indicates to which 'Tandroy' group or region they refer, they may actually be describing Karembola practice here.

of those who still live. Because of this, he comes bothering the living, with all kinds of demands, never wanting to let go. If thwarted,
he soon becomes vindictive, sending misfortune, sickness, even death.
In this, the dead priest is basically no different than all *lolo* (the
recent, 'unsocialized' dead).[6] And yet his spirit is infinitely more spiteful and more potent (*masiake*) than that of other *lolo* because the
whole *foko* (lineage) once was his. As its owner-priest, he is especially
jealous of his successor. Even if the man is entitled 'to hold the
hazomanga,'[7] that is, own the *foko* and make sacrifices on its behalf,
the late *mpisoro* cannot help but be hostile for he regards him as
usurping *his* power and *his* glory.

It was to contain this fearsome anger, which, as Fihatoa now indicated, threatened the very survival of the descent-group, that Karembola
groups previously made the practice of abandoning their *hazomanga*
for a period of between three and five years when their *mpisoro* died.
All the sacra—the sacred knife (*vylava*), the bowls, the baskets—were
taken from the village, wrapped in cloth, brought into the forest,
and put in a tree. They were, in effect, treated rather like the corpse.
During this time, no-one dared approach the 'toppled' *hazomanga*; all
were in mourning for their priest. Finally, however, assuming that
the *foko* had been assiduous in its mourning, everything, including
the dead man's anger, was supposed to become cool enough for a
new owner to re-establish (*mañoriñe*) the *hazomanga* and lay claim to
(*mandova* lit. 'inherit') the *foko*.

Whenever Karembola talk of this 'difficult,' extended mourning,
they explain that the *mpisoro* is a 'great person' (*ondate be*) demanding 'great homage' (*fiasiañe be*) of those he owns. It is clear, however, that the 'homage' Karembola made to their dead *mpisoro*
contained the same elements of parody that pattern Karembola funerals generally (Middleton, l995a). For even as they continued to honour him as their 'owner,' the 'root' and 'source' of their being, they
actually made a mockery of his *asy*, his sacred efficacy, his erstwhile
power to give them life. This is because so long as people belong

---

[6] Karembola configurations of the relationship between the living, the recent
dead, and the ancestors differ significantly from the well-known deme-tomb-ancestors
complex of the Merina (see Middleton, 1995b).

[7] Each lineage has its *mpisoro*, ritual master of the people and the herds. According
to the *lilin-drazañe* ('the ways' or 'commands of the ancestors'), succession is adel-
phic, i.e., the office passes between 'brothers,' before devolving to the generation
below. Hence, we are not talking of a 'priestly' or 'royal line.'

to a *dead* priest, a *lolo*, they behave as though they 'too were dead' (*fa lolo ka*). They picture themselves as a dirty, stricken people, tied to a man whose *hazomanga* has fallen and whose body is a stinking corpse. So long as they remain in his charge, they are *anadolo*, literally 'children of the dead.' Now the point to note about *anadolo*—for Karembola a deeply resonant term—is that they are literally cut off from the ancestors (*razañe*) and their blessing because it is taboo to make sacrifices on their behalf (*tsy azo asoroñe anadolo fa faly*). Or rather, the only person who can make 'sacrifices' for *anadolo* is the *tsimahaiveloñe* (lit., 'one who knows not the living'). The *tsimahaiveloñe* is a man, normally a political dependant, an uxorilocal groom, who 'stands for the dead person' and who 'is of the dead,' and Karembola are reluctant to see his 'slaughters' as proper *soro*, that is, sacrifices that make them feel 'loved by the ancestors.'[8] *Anadolo*, then, are 'outside ancestry,' beyond the ancestors' reach, which, of course, is precisely why, throughout the period that the *foko* mourns its late *mpisoro*, the *hazomanga* is out of play. Things of the *lolo* and things of the *razañe*, Karembola say, are 'taboo to one another' (*mpifaly*). 'They know not how to mix or share.' In effect, the ancestral cult—the practice of *soro*—is suspended for the duration, and the *foko* behaves as though it is only with the instatement of a new priest and the raising of his *hazomanga* that it will live again.

I noted that circumcision ritual is known in the vernacular as 'stepping over the dead' (*mandika lolo*). In its most literal sense, this expression means simply that on the eve of their circumcision, the initiates walked across their late *mpisoro*'s tomb. (According to many informants, this coincided with the eve of the *efa-pate*, the rite that celebrates the completion of the tomb: the boys walked the tomb in the night, and were circumcised at dawn.) At the same time, the term *mandika* ('to step over') also carries the sense of transgression. For instance, to *mandika faly* (lit., to overstep a taboo) is to breach sexual prohibition, to commit incest. This points to the second meaning of the boys' action: the initiates were 'breaking taboos' (*mañota faly*) when they trod upon their *mpisoro*'s tomb. And indeed the taboos they broke were multiple for to begin with, here as throughout Madagascar, it is a very grave offence to climb or walk upon a tomb

---

[8] A full description of the *tsimahaiveloñe* is to be found in Middleton, *The In-Between People*, Chapter 8.

(*tsy mañanike kibory fa faly*), and in addition, it is forbidden to stand when the *mpisoro* is sitting or lying, or to step across his legs (essentially, people must grovel, bent double, around their priest). Noting that the priest's corpse, also termed *lolo*, lies beneath the tomb, we see that the bodily act that constituted the defining moment of traditional circumcision ritual involved initiates in a powerful, compounded form of transgression against their late *mpisoro* and upon his tomb.

This brings us to the third meaning of the boys' actions which is to be found in the expression *mandika fate* (lit., 'to over-step the corpse'), meaning 'to deny' or 'to bring kinship to an end.' Funerals are held to be times of reckoning when those who have quarrelled must either settle their differences or forever go their separate ways; Karembola often talk of people 'stepping over the dead body' if, by the time of the *efa-pate*, they remain estranged. Yet if Karembola funerals seek to reconcile the living, they are also times when the living must 'break with the deceased' (*fanarahañe ama ty lolo*) for Karembola believe that the bereaved can only know the continued flow of ancestral blessing by repudiating their association with the dead person and the tomb (Middleton, 1995a, 1995b). Pulling together these myriad meanings, we see that the patterning of traditional circumcision ritual echoes the overall dynamic of Karembola mortuary practice when what begins as an extended parody of the dead man's power over the living is brought to a dramatic end as the initiates break many of the key taboos relating to his authority. Indeed, tomb-walking probably constituted the most powerful way Karembola could imagine of 'breaking with their dead owner-priest.' It was literally a case of 'stepping over' his dead body to bring his reign to an end.

By now it will be obvious that circumcision was embedded in an interregnum, between the end of the 'rule' of one *mpisoro* and the beginning of the next. The rite was an integral part of the symbolism of succession; it was the bodily enactment of the process of repudiating the old order in order to instate a new, living priest. Accordingly, the ritual culminated in a ceremony in which all the people of the *foko* 'conveyed the power of sacrifice' (*manese soro*) to their new priest, and were blessed in turn by him. For Karembola, then, as for most Malagasy peoples (e.g. Bloch, 1986), circumcision ritual plays a key part in imagery of continuity and succession, of the links that bind the living to the ancestors, the present to the past.[9] Informants were eager that I should grasp the intense sense of regeneration Karembola once experienced as, in the course of one ritual cycle, they re-established their *hazomanga*, reclaimed the sacred knife from the forest, put death and the tomb behind them, made allegiance to a new *mpisoro*, and circumcised their boys. In this way, as Karembola remember circumcision, they picture the past as one endless, unbroken process of succession, as generation upon generation of new-born Karembola reclaimed their link with life and the ancestors by stepping over the bodies of their dead priests.

Serial Killings and Fallen Stakes

By the time I came to work for the first time among the Karembola in the 1980's, they no longer 'walked the tombs.' It was, they said, a 'very long time' (*fa ela be*) since they had last performed the traditional circumcision rite. Piecing together all the individual and clan oral histories I collected, it would appear that the rituals had come to a halt during the 1930's. As a result, several generations of Karembola men had grown up uncircumcised, and Karembola had become 'a people who do not circumcise' (*ondate tsy misavatse*). Since the *vazaha* came into this land (*vazaha* 'foreigner,' 'stranger' is a category in which Karembola include *not only* the French colonial administration *but* also agents of the post-colonial Malagasy state), informants explained, we have been unable to follow our ancestral ways. 'We are a people who remain sitting' (*mitoboke avao*, i.e., no longer stand up and defend ourselves). Foreigners own the land today, so when they speak, we simply nod our heads (*mañeka avao zahay*).

Indeed, according to my informants, the coming of *vazaha* had brought about not only the decline of circumcision ritual but a total collapse of the *hazomanga* cult. We Karembola, they often told me, no longer have *hazomanga*. 'We gave up our *hazomanga* when the for-

---

[9] Today, the element of 'tradition' figures strongly in the *performance* of circumcision ritual in many parts of Madagascar: for example, foreigners and photographers may be excluded from the ceremony, and local women can approach only if their hair is plaited in the traditional style (cf. Bloch, 1986). This suggests that for some Malagasy peoples circumcision is the objectification *par excellence* of 'ancestral time.'

eigners came' (*le niavy ty vazaha, finoy ty hazomanga'ay*). 'Today we only asperge with water' (*mitsipe rano avao*); 'we just pray at the house' (*mitata an-trano avao*). Actually, these statements, I soon discovered, are not all to be taken at face value. For a start, it is not the case that Karembola nowadays 'only asperge with water': all without exception continue to make blood sacrifices regularly. These statements are rather to be understood as metaphors by which Karembola try to express a sense that their practice of *soro* and thus their *asy*, their life-giving efficacy, has weakened in modern times. The notion of asperging with water, of course, gives particularly strong expression to this feeling because the blessing or *asy* it engenders is always held to be less potent than that engendered in blood sacrifice. It is also an act associated with *anadolo*, children of the dead, because, as I noted, so long as a person is in mourning, it is taboo for anyone (other than the *tsimahaivelone*) to perform a sacrifice on their behalf. Kin wishing to bless *anadolo* must use water, not blood.

Despite the strong element of metaphor that figures in Karembola discourse on the practice of *soro*, however, the cult has undergone some important changes. One is that Karembola no longer use the *vylava* to cut the throats of cattle; another is that they no longer make their sacrifices at the *hazomanga*-stakes. What happened to bring these changes about? In addition to the general explanations that Karembola give which are couched in idioms of foreign domination, Karembola also have a set of more specific narratives, of which I give two examples here.

The last great *hazomanga*-stake of the Lavaheloke-Maromenake lineage at Tranovaho now stands in a thicket of 'foreign cactus' (*raketa vazaha*, newly introduced types of Opuntiae), to the north of the present site of the village, hardly visible at all.[10] After Fiaiña, its master, died (around sixty-five years ago), the people of Tranovaho, in keeping with the custom, had abandoned the *hazomanga*, put the *vylava* in a tree, and mourned their dead priest. After three years, however, when they supposed their mourning to be completed, they had proceeded to reestablish the cult (*nanorine soro*). Clearly, though, they

---

[10] A great disparity of age appears to have existed among co-initiates as a result of circumcision being keyed to the *mpisoro*'s death. To my knowledge, initiation was not linked to the creation of formal age-sets, as found, for instance, in parts of East Africa.

were mistaken for the man who tried to succeed Fiaiña as *mpisoro*
died shortly after his instatement, completely without warning (*mate
tampok*), within three days of his essay. Three other men tried to follow, all rightful successors in their turn; but each had died rather
suddenly before the week was out. 'On account of these deaths,'
Mitsangana told me, 'people dare not touch the toppled *hazomanga*;
they leave them lying where they fell. Today Menakena by rights
should be the owner but he will not try. To save his skin, he simply prays for his people at the house. Fiaiña was the last to hold
the *hazomanga*, the last to circumcise us' (*ty nitampaha'ay*), Mitsangana
summed up.

    The people of Ivane told a similar story. Here the last to hold
the *hazomanga* had been Tsikalafo. When Tsikalafo died, the *hazomanga*
had been abandoned, following the custom, and the knife had been
put high in the tree. When time came to re-instate the *hazomanga*,
however, there was a problem because the rightful successor had
'gone abroad' (*nandeha andafy*, i.e., left Karembola land). 'Then perhaps we should have held it,' explained Tsilañoa'e, 'but we were
afraid. For what would happen if they or their children were to
arrive, and we had set it up? Things of other people are not to be
handled. To take on the work of *mpisoro* when it belongs to another
is like 'stealing' (*mangalatse*), like breaking taboos. In some Karembola
villages, people had tried to set up the *hazomanga* in the absence of
the rightful owner, and many had died as a result. So we left the
hazomanga where it was, and simply asperge ourselves with water
whenever we need to pray for our souls.'

    All the narratives I collected were essentially variants on these two
protypical stories, and to this extent the Karembola clans presented
a remarkably consistent picture of when and how their *hazomanga*
came to fall. Indeed, each narrator typically ended his particular
story by declaring that the same holds true for all the Karembola
clans: 'from Anjedava to Marovato, whosoever is Karembola, not
one has a *hazomanga* standing today.' There are, of course, problems in treating these narratives, with their serial killings and unap-
peasable anger, as straight-forward historical accounts, although they
do, in fact, exhibit a remarkable consistency on dates and, as we
shall see, bear a strong relation to historical events. Reading them
for the moment, though, more as a kind of discourse on Karembola
identity, as constituted in the present by their experience of the past,
they are clearly all stories about the impossibility of realizing suc-

cession in the 'modern' age.[11] Either the dead will not relinquish their hold upon the living (their anger will not cool) or the rightful owners of the cult are living but are absent because they have 'gone abroad' (*andafy* i.e., to a foreign land). In either case, whenever Karembola had tried to set up their fallen *hazomanga*, the outcome had been the same: another still owns the *foko*, is jealous of his *fiasiañe* ('homage'), and kills the 'pretender' within the week. As a result, Karembola stopped trying to instate proper *mpisoro*, make full-powered *soro* or circumcise their boys. The *vylava* remained in the forest, the practice of *soro* weakened, and circumcision came to an end. The Karembola literally got stuck in the interregnum: they became *anadolo*, 'children of the dead,' not for the interim, but for all time. Their uncircumcised bodies epitomize this sorry history for it is the bodily condition of a people who have been unable to bring the interregnum to an end.

In her work on the Bemihisatra dynasty of northwestern Madagascar, Feeley-Harnik (1991) explores the nature of Sakalava responses to colonial rule. Prior to the C19th, she argues, the authority of Sakalava rulers derived primarily from the possession of relics embodying the royal ancestors; these relics, in association with spirit possession in the *doany* (royal capital), were the foci of royal services. Sometime in the C19th, however, as first the Hova (Merina) and then the French began to meddle in Sakalava affairs, there was a radical shift in the centre of power from the *doany* to the *mahabo* or royal cemetery (p. 95). This radical transformation of ancestors from relics into tombs was then exacerbated in the colonial period when the French prevented royal followers from completing the funeral by forbidding them to rebuild the royal tomb. 'People in northwestern Madagascar,' she writes, 'have been preoccupied with ancestors over

---

[11] If Karembola were consistent about their interregnum, they would live in the perpetual charge of *tsimahaiveloñe* making slaughters that do not really make people live. However—and this means that the decline of Karembola circumcision ritual cannot be read simply as encoding a breakdown in traditional authority or lineage cohesion—Karembola continue to instate *mpisoro*. Only they are weak *mpisoro*, 'only children,' splashing water (metaphorically) instead of making authentic *soro*. What we have, then, is a complex, multi-layered discourse on 'tradition' and 'modernity,' in which Karembola seek to articulate a sense of alienation with a continuing desire to live. The same appears to be true of the (symbolic) interregnum described for the Sakalava Bemihisatra by Feeley-Harnik (1991), for as Lambek observes (pers. comm, 26th October, 1996) 'even in Analalava there was always succession and the existence of the monarchy.'

the past century and a half because they have not been allowed to
bury their dead and reassert the leadership of living rulers who would
bring [the] long interregnum to an end' (p. 4). In an earlier paper
(1984), Feeley-Harnik coins a striking expression for this development: 'the political economy of death.'

The parallels between the Karembola narratives and the Sakalava
material are striking. All the key Sakalava motifs—the rise in death
and tomb-based symbolism developing in popular response to the
intrusion of strangers, the sense of being caught in an interregnum,
and of belonging to 'dead kings'—are evident here. Like Sakalava,
Karembola talk of living in a 'dead and foreign land' (*tane vazaha,
tane mate*) and, like Sakalava, they have given this imagery ritual
expression, in their case by moving away from the ancestors-in-the-
hazomanga into possession of the *lolo*-in-the-tomb.[12] Indeed, Feeley-
Harnik's notion of 'the political economy of death' expanding in
response to foreign power has a resonance in the Karembola context far beyond the performative around the decline of circumcision
ritual. For the one domain of Karembola cultural practice that grew
in the colonial period, and has expanded ever since, is that of ritual centred around the dead. The coming of strangers has seen a
positive florescence of mortuary ritual: the building of massive, stone
tombs, of funerals that even for ordinary people now last a year or
more, accompanied by the staging of highly elaborate ceremonial
exchanges that draw in hamlets from right across Karembola land.
While it is beyond the scope of this paper to explore this 'ritual
economy' in any detail, we can say that Karembola today have made
mortuary performative the focus of their lives.

But to return to the issue in hand, if Sakalava were responding
to the intrusion of Merina and then French power, to what were
Karembola responding when they put themselves in the interregnum? Why did they see themselves as 'living in a dead or dying
land'? And why should this sentiment have become so overwhelm-
ing in the 1930's? The time has come for us to move out from the

---

[12] Feeley-Harnik's broader claim, viz., that '[c]ontemporary Malagasy preoccupations with ancestors, attributed to age-old tradition, are a relatively recent development' (1991: 3) would require rephrasing in the Karembola context, for it is the
realm of the *lolo*—the-dead-in-the-tombs—rather than the realm of the *razañe*—the
ancestors-in-the *hazomanga*—that has expanded over this century. To put it another
way, the cult focusing on angry, cruel spirits has been elaborated at the expense
of ritual around resocialized, generative ancestors.

specific narratives told by Karembola to explore the wider historical context of their experience of French colonial rule.

The End of Cactus Times

In the early months of 1902, French colonial troops began to close
in on the Karembola in a kind of pincer action mounted from north,
east and west. Assisted by a terrain in which they were at a very
great advantage, the Karembola clans put up a strong resistance, to
which the French in turn responded with an extensive series of puni-
tive reconnaissances.[13] A period of repression then followed, during
which, to keep the people under surveillance, the French first reset-
tled them in larger villages, often in unsuitable land, and then obliged
their subjects to carry water, to labour on roadworks, to pay taxes
or surrender their cattle, to grow peanuts and other crops for export.
Such policies had a harsh impact upon a people, who, on account
of their marginal environment, are in any circumstances hard pressed
to survive, and their impact intensified during the Great War (Gontard,
1968). Even so, the evidence, both from the narratives I collected
and from the colonial records I consulted, is that the Karembola
continued to practice circumcision ritual for the first three decades
of colonial rule.

A more profound sense of rupture with 'ancestral time' (*faharazañe*)
came later, towards 1930, with what can only be described as an
environmental intervention of a most extraordinary scale. Early emissaries of French imperialism had described how the deep south of
Madagascar was covered by dense stands of prickly-pear cactus,
armed with fierce, long spines, forming hedges 4–5 m high and up
to 50 m thick (Grandidier, 1928). Introduced some centuries earlier,
this non-native plant had become especially invasive in the dry
climate and limestone soils of the Karembola, which was consequently dubbed the 'region cactée' in military reconnaissance maps.
That this vegetation, together with the scarcity of water, posed
problems for the occupying forces is very obvious from the military
reports. Forming impenetrable labyrinths around the villages, it ruled

---

[13] The literature on indigenous resistance in the deep south to the imposition of
colonial rule (e.g., Gontard, 1968; Esoavelomandroso, 1975) focuses almost exclusively on the Sadiavahe movement (1915–19), and overlooks the strong resistance
put up by clans like the Karembola during the preceding fifteen years.

out military operations of a conventional kind. Later, long after
'pacification,' colonial administrators continued to protest that the
plant made it impossible to carry out proper surveillance of this wayward region of the colony. Thus, prickly pear soon became a metaphor for the 'anarchy' and 'impenetrability' of the deep south
(Middleton, in press).[14]

For the indigenous populations, however, and the Karembola especially, this plant was of vital importance. Put plainly, the fruit—the
prickly pear—was a useful supplement in the human diet, bridging
gaps in the seasons when people were waiting to harvest crops, and
becoming a basic foodstuff in times of scarcity and drought. During
true famines, people would also eat the cladodes (*ravinbaketa*, the fleshy
'leaves'), along with native roots and tubers. The plant was also valued as a source of water: a sweet if tasteless drink could be extracted
by grating the fruit on rough bark, and when the *ranovato* ran dry,[15]
water could also be obtained by pounding and pressing the cladodes or even the plant's fleshy trunk. This made the plant especially
valuable in the arid land between Cap St. Marie and the Menarandra
(i.e. the Karembola) where waterpoints are few and far between
(Decary, 1930: 252). At the same time, prickly pear had become a
mainstay of the pastoralist economy because, once their spines had
been burned off, the cladodes could be used to feed the cattle when
other fodder became scarce or non-existent.[16] Such, then, was its all-
round importance in the Karembola that it would be no exaggera-
tion to say that this plant often kept both people and their cattle
alive. Indeed, it is undoubtedly the case that its introduction and
naturalization in the Karembola had allowed higher densities of
bovine and human populations to develop there than ever could
have been sustained by the 'natural' carrying capacity of this arid

---

[14] *Raketa* was seen as an obstacle to the rational exploitation of land and labour.
For a discussion of colonial discourses on *raketa*, see Middleton, in press.

[15] *Ranovato* are created from deep natural crevices in the limestone. Once full of
rain-water, they are covered by stones and branches to prevent evaporation in the
hot sun.

[16] Decary (1933: 152) records a local saying to the effect that the Tandroy and
the cactus are kin, a saying which, he feels, expresses the symbiosis that existed in
the Androy between man and plant. While I never heard Karembola use this particular expression, their manner of employing the terms *tamy raketa* ('cactus time'),
faha razañe ('ancestral time'), and *faha gasy* ('gasy time') almost synonymously, conveys much the same sense.

land. For Karembola, then, *raketa* ('cactus') or *raketa gasy* ('Malagasy cactus') as it is now known, had shaped and now sustained their lived world. Thus, the consequences were far-reaching when in the late 1920's a kind of cactus pest (most probably, *Dactylopius tomentosus*, a strain of the wild cochineal) attacked and killed all the Opuntiae within five years.

How this cochineal came to southern Madagascar is neither the accident nor the mystery some suppose, for the insect had been introduced to Tongobory, near Tulear (in south-west Madagascar), in full knowledge of its destructive habits, specifically in order to assist a French settler to clear his land of prickly pear. Beyond and behind this specific motive, however, lay a broader dream of rewriting the landscapes of the deep south: in ways that would not only strengthen political control of this wayward region but also transform the indigenous economies from ones oriented to subsistence and exchange values into one that would better serve the needs of the colonial economy. This dream, which the cochineal was expected to help realize, involved 'developing' the land with European settlers, driving the local peoples into wage labour, and finally gaining access to the 'inestimable' cattle-wealth that they had long supposed 'lay sleeping' behind the prickly bush (Middleton, in press).

The most immediate effect of the introduction of the cochineal was upon the physical landscape. Some idea of the dramatic scenes Karembola would have witnessed can be gleaned from a series of photographs documenting the cumulative effect upon Opuntia forests of Australia of similar campaigns of biological control (Dodd, 1929). First, the insects begin to cluster on the cladodes, multiplying rapidly until thousands cover each one. Under attack, the tall trees begin to tumble, until finally a year later they lie in shrivelled heaps upon the ground. It would be difficult to overestimate the psychological impact such scenes had upon the Karembola, 'living in and of the cactus,' to borrow an expression from Pouchepadass (1993: 8). For, as has been observed many a time of the Irish potato famine, there is nothing like visible pestilence, resulting in famine, in a once familiar environment to engender a sense of alienation, of decline and moral ruin, of being under attack by foreign elements, of being forsaken by the ancestors or by the God(s) (Woodham-Smith, 1991; see also Ranger & Slack, 1992). As the once proud, green cacti forests were reduced to piles of brown, crushed thorns that crackled underfoot, the land had become not only 'a dead land' (*nanjary tane mate*) but also 'a foreign land' (*nanjary tane vazaha*!), alien, unrecognizable to the very people whose ancestors had lived there.[17]

Within two years, famine was widespread in the region. Deprived of their fodder, around 100,000 head of cattle are reckoned to have died in the Androy as a result (Bérard, 1951). As for the villages, they are described as 'emptying overnight.' In the course of one year (1931) Tsihombe District had lost half its population, down from 60,000 to 32,000, and in some parts of the Karembola the decline was sharper still. The 1926 census for the cantons of Beloha and Andempopale (where I was later to do my fieldwork) had shown 12,574 and 7396 inhabitants respectively. Five years later, the population of the canton of Beloha had fallen to 5533 and that of Andempopale to 2440. It is probably now more or less impossible to determine exactly how many people died, whether directly or indirectly, because of the destruction of the cacti. As Deschamps (1959: 70) notes, some died; some went away; others went away and later returned. To claim, however, as some have, that the greater part of the population emigrated is to be less than frank. The number of deaths among the Karembola was certainly far higher than the figures recorded. The French military officer in charge of Beloha District himself wrote to his superior that the canton heads were too frightened to register the full toll (Decary, 1931: 13).

Perhaps the essential point, however, is that the devastation worked upon the Karembola landscape and its people by the 'foreigner's insect' (*biby vazaha*) was symbolic of conquest. 'This land here,' Dareke remembered, 'looked just as it had when the Maroseraña armies ransacked it several centuries before: our herds were devastated, people everywhere were in flight, corpses lay unburied on the way. Foreigners again had laid the land to waste' (*mandrotsake ty tane toy*). One notes the mirror imagery: if for members of the French colonial regime, *raketa* had become symbol and metaphor for all that was impenetrable or lay beyond their control, for Karembola, both at the time, as the colonial archives bear witness, as still today, its decimation symbolised their own defeat.

'Famines gather history around them' (Vaughan, 1987: 1), and

---

[17] This experience perhaps helps explain why I never heard Karembola quote the 'Malagasy' proverb, viz., that the land is constant, fixed or unchanging unlike people who move (cf. Lambek & Walsh this volume p. 156).

this is certainly true here. The famine of 1930 was not the first famine Karembola suffered nor would it be the last—on average, *kere* (hunger) comes to this arid land every four years—but it acquired a special place in Karembola historical narratives, partly because 'the moment when the cactus died' (*lehe mate ty raketa*) came to stand for their experience of conquest and foreign imperialism, and partly because this particular famine was the first to define modern relations between the national economy and the local economies of the deep south. Colonial reports had long remarked upon the unexpectedly high densities of population in this arid region; what these same reports found irksome was the fact that colonial plantations in other parts of Madagascar were crying out for labour while these 'lazy' people apparently satisfied all their wants by feeding on prickly pear. Up until the demise of cactus, the Karembola, like the Tandroy, had been very reluctant to leave their homeland, despite intense labour recruitment drives. Now, however, even if colonial reports made out that more people had emigrated than had really, famine, poverty, and general social dislocation certainly caused an unprecedented number of people to 'volunteer' to 'work abroad'. This then set the pattern for the years remaining until Independence and beyond: the deep south was essentially maintained, at minimal input, as a pool of cheap, unskilled but physically strong labour for export to other parts of Madagascar. The aridity, which in the event made the Karembola useless for 'development,' had been turned against its people, who, deliberately unschooled, were periodically driven into the cash economy by famine.[18]

For all these reasons, we can well understand why Karembola experienced the thirties as the moment when 'ancestral time' (*faha razañe*) ended, and 'foreign times' (*tamy vazaha*) began. The decimation of the cacti was a watershed: it marked the end of 'Malagasy time' (*fahagasy*), that is, of the world they knew, definitively, as did no other single event. Given this history, it is also not difficult to understand why, abandoning circumcision ritual shortly after, Karembola began to keep the memory in their bodies of themselves as a 'broken people,' living in a ruined land. Indeed, it is precisely because circumcision carries such powerful meanings of ancestral blessing, of succession and continuity, of being in a state of grace, that made

---

[18] Other work typically done by 'Tandroy' migrants to the towns of Madagascar is that of night watchmen (gardiens) and pullers of 'pousse-pousse' (rickshaws).

the *un*circumcised body such a potent symbol for alienation and loss. To be uncircumcised *is* to be impotent, to be cut off from the ancestors, to be in a state of *hakeo*, unresolved blame. It *is* the mark of a 'dead' people, a people who 'can only nod their heads,' a people 'akin to slaves' (*sahala ondevo*). And indeed Karembola felt exactly like a people uprooted against their will and taken to live in a 'foreign land,' 'a land that strangers now owned.'

One criticism that is often levelled at earlier 'reaction-to-conquest' type explanations of the decline of traditional ritual is that they falsely construe the 'colonized' as passive and impotent subjects of the 'colonizer.' Another is that they overestimate the *actual* power of colonial regimes. Critics argue that administrative discourses should not be confused with what happened in practice (Cohn, 1987; Cooper, 1994; Denning, 1988; Stoler & Cooper, 1989; Vaughan, 1991); and that even within the colonial apparatus there were often different and competing notions about the purpose and methods of colonialism (Comaroff, 1989; Stoler, 1989). Certainly, the French colonial administration in Madagascar was no more monolithic than colonial administrations in other parts of the Empire, and its power in practice was limited by divisions among its own local administrators and by the agency of Malagasy themselves (e.g. Fremigacci, 1981). Indeed, it would be quite wrong to portray the French colonial administration as thinking and acting as one body on the question of cactus—there was, in fact, intense conflict of opinion within its ranks—and in normal circumstances the dream of rewriting the landscape to suit the needs of the colonial economy—would have remained just that—a dream formulated by one faction but subverted both by dissent within the colonial apparatus and by Malagasy resistance (Middleton, in press). What made the difference in this instance was the virulence of the cochineal. A fortuitous specism endowed the actions of a few key *vazaha* with the power to stage an event that had an impact upon the destiny of a people, completely transforming their lived world. Seldom in the history of empire, has a colonial 'ideology' been made so effective in practice, and at such little cost. To Karembola, the *biby* introduced by foreigners made an extraordinary and incontrovertible display of 'colonial power.' It literally dismantled their cultural landscape overnight. Against this embodiment of the foreigner's malice (*hasia'e*), Karembola were impotent: they had no means to stop its advance. Even if the authors of this event subsequently failed to realize many of their political and economic objectives, the event itself had succeeded in what one apologist for Empire has declared to be the chief purpose of French colonialism: 'pour insérer profondement leur marque sur le sol des pays and dans le cerveau des peuples conquis' (Pelletier & Roubaud, 1931).[19] Perhaps then if Karembola responded by portraying themselves 'as a people who have been robbed of their capacity to act on the world' (Comaroff & Comaroff, 1993: xiv), they had better reason than most.

Withstanding Trials

I have shown how the decline of circumcision ritual makes sense when read against a series of historical events that gave Karembola good reason to think that 'the time of the ancestors' had ended and that they were now 'living in dead and foreign land.' At the same time, I have indicated how in responding to these events Karembola drew on metaphors which had long dominated their political discourse: the difference between 'kinds of people,' between 'living' and 'dead' ancestries, between freemen and slaves. Thus, those who once practised circumcision in order to have a history, to have an ancestry, to be people of worth, now remained uncircumcised to express their sense of impotence and defeat. Even in discontinuity, then, there was continuity between past and present, as Karembola drew on familiar cultural symbols to express their sense of rupture with ancestral time. Indeed, as Connerton notes (1989: 9), a rite revoking or expressing a break with a former social order can only make sense by invertedly recalling what went before.

Clearly, though, we are not talking here of the mechanical articulation of ritual transformation with political or social factors—one could never say, for instance, that circumcision ritual *had* to stop because of what happened—but rather of the interpretation Karembola

---

[19] The power of the cochineal became one of the things like aeroplanes or motor-cars that Karembola cite as demonstrating the extraordinary, supernatural, power of *vazaha*, both immensely potent, yet alien and alienating (Comaroff & Comaroff, 1993: xxiv). Karembola characteristically express wonder at anything done or said by *vazaha*, by shaking their heads and putting their hands to their mouths, saying 'Foreigners! Strange, dangerous creatures, to their very core' (*vazaha! Biby, vata'e!*). It is worth noting that a plane was flown for the first time over Androy shortly after the *raketa* perished (19th August, 1931), followed a month later by three more (Decary, 1933: 246). Whether by chance or design, these displays could not have been timed to better effect upon a people already demoralized by events.

made of events. This century, sadly, has provided enough examples
of dislocation, persecution, tragedy, and suffering to prove that personal and collective responses to trauma, however intense, differ
greatly, and that it is, above all, a question of self-interpretation and
self-presentation (e.g., van Onselen, 1972; Werbner, 1991; Antze &
Lambek, 1996). Thus, even if the decline of circumcision ritual makes
sense when set against the killing of Malagasy cactus, we need to
recognise that Karembola did more than abandon a ritual. In putting
themselves in the interregnum, they were seeking to make sense of
what had happened; they were telling a story about themselves. To
say this is not to minimize the impact this environmental intervention had upon Karembola nor to deny the fact that in important
ways it set the parameters for Karembola lives. It is simply to underscore the need to read the decline of Karembola circumcision ritual as a kind of ritual performance in and of itself.

A comparison with the well-known *Ramanenjana*, a popular millenarian movement which occurred in 1863 in the highlands of
Madagascar, points up some interesting aspects of this performative.
A number of studies show how a time of great economic and political uncertainty engendered a similar sense of alienation from the
ancestors, when the king Radama II was believed by many Merina
to have surrendered the kingdom to foreigners. In this instance, however, people sought to oblige the king to *restore* the link with the
ancestors by carrying out the state circumcision ritual which he had
abandoned (Raison, 1976; Raison-Jourde, 1991; Bloch, 1986, 1992).
Among the Karembola, a sense of the intrusion of strangers produced the opposite performative: they abandoned circumcision ritual, claiming that they could no longer follow the ways of the ancestors
because foreign elements had penetrated them to their very core.
Possessed by their dead kings and queens, Merina began to made
preparations for circumcision. Possessed by *vazaha* and indeed by
their dead *mpisoro*, Karembola stopped circumcising their boys.

I am reminded here of an essay by Bloch (1992, Chapter 3)
suggesting that there are basically two kinds of response to the kind
of sickness or malaise that is caused by the intrusion of alien elements. The first response involves resistance: the cure seeks to restore
the person to well-being by expelling the intrusive elements. The
second response, normally proceeded to when the former cure proves
ineffective, is to seek accommodation with the intrusive forces by
actively taking them into the self. Could one say that the *Ramanenjana*

epitomizes the first response to foreign conquest—'resistance'—while the Karembola 'interregnum' has more in common with the second response? That is to say, three decades of both active and passive resistance were followed by an experience in which Karembola were so overwhelmed by foreign power that they saw no other remedy than to acknowledge defeat by actively taking death into themselves. In another essay, though, Bloch (1992, Chapter 6) applies his model directly to the *Ramanenjana*, producing a rather different interpretation of its symbolism. Here he argues that it is significant that the participants proceeded only as far as the first part of Merina circumcision ritual, that is, they gave up their vitality and behaved 'as if dead' (1992: 90). From this perspective, the *Ramanenjana* looks more like Karembola and Sakalava responses to the intrusion of strangers: for, far from proclaiming a return to ancestral blessing, it too becomes a ritual performance expressing a sense of living in a dead and foreign land. Indeed, the participants *are* in a kind of interregnum, because they literally behave as though they were in the possession of dead kings and queens.

The extended comparison leads me to make a very important point about Karembola responses to the killing of Malagasy cactus, which is that they appear to have involved no 'millenary' elements, comparable to those of the *Ramanenjana*, in which participants refuse reproduction in this life altogether, for example, by abandoning agricultural tasks, especially forward-looking ones such as sowing and planting (Bloch, 1992: 90). While Karembola certainly gave ritual expression to a sense of giving up on life and becoming 'as dead,' there is no evidence to suggest that they ever carried such symbolism over into everyday life. On the contrary, the evidence is that Karembola responded to the fracturing of their lived world with remarkable practical ingenuity and resilience. Within five years, for instance, they had replanted their land with *viha*, a kind of agave, to replace the hedging and the cattle-fodder that had been lost (Decary, 1933: 110). This, then, was a people who, even as they acted out a picture of themselves as a dead or dying people, were determined to make themselves live.[20]

---

[20] Karembola mourning taboos normally include a prohibition on agricultural activity: the bereaved are forbidden to 'handle hoes' i.e. to cultivate crops, precisely because they are 'like the dead.' Thus, the fact that the Karembola ignored this taboo underscores the point that they are a people whose ultimate desire in and through mortuary practice is to make themselves live.

Such 'this-life' orientation does not surprise me for this is a people whose primary values of ancestry, duration, and continuity, are oriented, not to some other imagined world, but to the here-and-now (Middleton, 1995b). It does imply, however, that the story Karembola tell about themselves in the narratives around the decline of circumcision ritual is only half the story or rather only one of many stories they might tell. Certainly, my sense of Karembola formed over two periods of fieldwork is hardly of a broken people: rather, it is of a forthright, optimistic, rather defiant people, who love to play and joke. These are a people who, somewhat contradicting the picture of themselves as a 'ruined' people, 'living in a dead land,' actually pride themselves on 'withstanding trials' (*mahatante ty hasarotse*) that would break other folk. 'When the grip of the "iron belt" slackens on our bellies,' Pengelina told me, 'we simply busy ourselves with the work of making ourselves live. We are like cladodes of Opuntia that break from the plant, fall to the parched earth and against all expectation root again.'

And if the pictures Karembola present of themselves and of their history pull in contrary directions, then in a sense dualism is rooted in their experience of the world. For a start, two parallel worlds are dramatized in the semi-desert landscape where the 'xerophilous bush—spiny, twisting, and silver grey—suddenly brighten and green after two or three days of rain' (Olson, 1984: 174). Then again, there is the alternation of years of drought with years of plenty: in bad years when the land is hungry and crops wither on the stems, people starve and cattle die; but in good years when the rains have come, the people and their cattle eat well of crops harvested from the land *they* own. Above all, dualism characterises the political domain. For these people who 'only nod their heads when *vazaha* speak' are also those who live far from the reach of the bureaucratic nation state. Here, in a land so arid that it has *in the event* escaped both European colonization and settlers from other parts of Madagascar, the Karembola have been able to reconstruct their own autonomous domain. Arguably, the very isolation of this region, equidistant from Fort-Dauphin and Tulear, the two major urban centres of the south, together with the relative lack of polyphonies that characterise modern Madagascar, enhanced in turn by the local institutional weakness of formal schooling and the Christian Churches,[21] has meant that its people have

---

[21] Little touched by missionary activity, the events I describe took place in a very

been able to retain many of their traditions, again belying the sense Karembola project in their discourse of themselves as a people who, more than other Malagasy peoples, follow foreign ways. Indeed, it is this evident sense of autonomy and cultural continuity which has led earlier writers (e.g. Hoerner, 1990) to completely overlook the utter disruption wrought upon the social order by the destruction of the cactus, and to talk of the people of this region being 'peu colonisés' or of their 'imperméabilité à toute pénétration d'ordre politique ou économique' (e.g. Guérin, 1977; Hoerner, 1990).

In their introduction to *Modernity and its Malcontents*, the Comaroffs sketch out their vision of an historical anthropology that, among other things, 'acknowledges—no, stresses—the brute realities of colonialism and its aftermath, without assuming that they have robbed African peoples of their capacity to act on the world' (1993: xiv). Balancing these contradictory values in analysis is always difficult, as the present ethnography testifies (cf. Ortner, 1995). While it is easy to understand why Karembola came to see themselves as 'a people lost to the ancestors,' 'a people of a dead land,' a people robbed 'of their capacity to act upon the world,' it is not possible to accept this self-definition as a full and proper assessment of their history and their lives. As Borofsky observes, coherence may be an important element in the formation of cultural constructs regarding a people's history and their accounts of their present selves; indeed, '[s]omething about the structure of memory seems to lend itself to a story with a plot' (p. 359); but this coherence is often achieved only by ignoring the ambiguities, the contradictions, and the discrepancies that are present in real life (Borofsky, 1987).

But is it simply a case of Karembola projecting an over-coherent image of themselves as victims in the stories they tell about the decline of circumcision ritual? Or is it possible to see the decline of circumcision itself as a kind of resistance, even if the people themselves present it as the metaphor for their powerlessness? To explore this possibility, I want now to consider Lambek's (1992) argument around taboo.

---

different cultural milieu than the *Ramanenjana* movement in C19th Imerina where the Bible had become part of the social fabric fifty years before colonization (Raison-Jourde, 1991).

Taboo and Bodily Memory

In his essay on taboo as Malagasy cultural practice, Lambek (1992) suggests that the observance of taboo is a kind of performative act with moral consequences and significance in the constitution of personhood and society. 'At the heart of Malagasy identity,' he writes, 'lies implicit affirmation by means of denial' (p. 245). Cole (1996) too explores the important role taboos play in the Betsimisaraka imaginary as bodily ways of 'practising,' that is, of 'remembering the past.' The link between these particular interpretations of taboo and more general anthropological understandings of the importance of bodily performance in 'how societies remember' (Connerton, 1989) hardly requires underlining here.

If, however, taboos are far from static proscriptions—rather, as a kind of cultural practice, they will change, mutate, and be re-invented as people redefine their identities and their perceptions of the past,— then such fluidity to my mind in turn suggests that it may not always be clear at a particular moment what precisely constitutes the taboo. For example, when Karembola reflect on their contemporary practice, they say that by not setting up the *hazomanga*, by not practising circumcision, by not doing as their ancestors did, they are *breaking* all the ancestral taboos (*mañota faly*). Yet in a sense it would be more accurate to say that Karembola have made the practice of ancestral custom itself subject to a set of taboos. For they die if they try to make themselves full-blown *mpisoro*; they die if they try to make proper *soro*; they die if they try to set up the stakes. Small boys would die today if they tried to walk the tombs. Though I have never heard Karembola themselves class the *practice* of ancestral practice in 'modern times' as *faly*,—they see themselves as breaking, not keeping taboos—they have in effect made ancestral custom behave exactly like taboo. All the stories they tell about what happened to the *hazomanga* cult underscore this message, that to do as the ancestors did before them has effects identical to taboo-breaking: people either fall sick or are struck dead.

To put this point in another way, the sense Karembola have of the sacred, of the intrinsic potency of 'ancestral things,' has not diminished in or because of 'foreign' (i.e. modern) times; rather they have drawn upon the power that once made them effective to engender the fear that now makes them taboo. The *hazomanga* shrouded in thickets of *raketa*, the *vylava* suspended in the trees,—all the things that have the potential to express continuity, to restore Karembola to their ancestors, to re-forge the link with 'ancestral time,' remain sacred but have been put away from use. To handle any of these things in *vazaha* times 'would prove fatal' (*le mate teña*); thus, to touch them is taboo. Indeed, given that the things of *lolo* and things of the *razañe* are taboo to one another, it is clear that by putting themselves in the interregnum, Karembola have made 'ancestral time' taboo.

In a curious way, *keeping* these misrecognised taboo-analogues has actually become the way of realising the prime and enduring value of Karembola culture: 'of sustaining themselves in life' (*mahaveloñe anteña*). Again, this is not a thing Karembola would ever admit freely but tabooing the things of the ancestors has become a way of surviving in a 'foreign land.' Thus, what presents itself explicitly in idioms of defeat, impotence, and ruin, is implicitly a means for their continued survival as a people. And of course this strategy makes cultural sense when we think about how Karembola behave in funerals, warding off the anger of the *lolo* which threatens their very existence, by tabooing all the things of the ancestors and pretending that they too were dead. It is Karembola cultural practice to mimic death in order to make themselves live (Middleton, 1995b).[22]

At one level, this means that Karembola have reworked the conventional set of mourning taboos to create a set of bodily behaviours that, by inscribing their own *vazaha*-ness, befits 'foreign' times. As Karembola today go about the business of 'holding onto life' (*mitaña ty havelo*), they must not try to be too like the ancestors because they 'live in a foreign land'. They can only be pale imitations of the great men who went before them: asperging themselves with water, instead of anointing themselves with blood; praying at the house, not daring to approach or set up the timber stakes. It is as if the ancestors and foreigners can no more mix than can the living and the dead. From a certain perspective, then, it would seem that for Karembola taboo has become, *pace* Cole (1996), a way of *not* practising the past.

---

[22] The 'political economy of death' which developed in Analalava evidences a similar tension, being both the place in which the Bemihisatra Sakalava expressed their sense of impotence in the face of foreign power *and* a place of cultural innovation, in which they asserted the value of alternative labour, thus signalling their resistance to the colonial economy (Feeley-Harnik, 1991). This kind of ambiguity seems absent from Zionist practice which is more explicitly concerned with rebirth (Comaroff, 1985, 1992).

Yet at the same time, all these negatives—the fallen *hazomanga*, the uncircumcised bodies, the sacred knives suspended in trees— make a powerful remembrance of the past. Fashioned by taboo into memory-objects, they re-present 'ancestral time' upon the contemporary landscape but in a way that underscores Hartley's oft-quoted observation, viz., that the past is a foreign country; they do things differently there. For wherever Karembola walk, wherever they pick *raketa*, wherever they collect firewood or food, whenever they urinate, they are made to recall 'ancestral time' by the existence of taboos. At every turn taboos provide objectified 'traces' (memories) in the present of the alienated past ('ancestral time'), but always incorporated into the present in such a way that points up the difference (the distance) between the present and the past. Looking at the way these taboos shape bodily practice in the lived world today, it would be difficult to deny that, far from becoming *vazaha* to their very core as they claim, Karembola remain very firmly rooted in their history and their past. Being Karembola today may be constituted less in the act of performing ancestral custom than in *not* performing it or performing it as incompetents, but a series of negatives constantly focuses Karembola attention on imagery of a remembered (imagined) ancestral time. Indeed, what is striking is the extent to which Karembola have managed to encompass 'modernity,' the experience of living in a 'foreign land,' not in foreign idioms at all, but in idioms drawn from their own cultural heritage. They have made the interregnum the context within which the transformation of their world may be acknowledged and addressed (Comaroff, 1992).[23]

This encompassment of the 'modern' within the familiar, even while marking out the difference between the present and the past, is evident in the contemporary landscape where cacti grow once more. Like their ancestors before them, Karembola today rely heavily on Opuntiae to keep themselves and their herds alive, although the plants do not as yet form the dense impenetrable labyrinths of former times, and to this extent, we can say that Karembola have more or less reconstituted their broken world, if again as a pale

---

[23] While Karembola culture offered a very strong set of idioms in the form of the interegnum and the *lolo*'s malice for the interpretation of misfortune and change, I should note that Karembola also register and rework their historical experience in non-conventional idioms, such as *tromba* possession cults brought from west and north-west Madagascar by returning migrants.

shadow of its former self. This landscape is, however, emphatically marked as 'modern,' because it grows 'foreign cactus' (newly introduced types of Opuntia), not 'Malagasy cactus' (*raketa gasy*), the authentic cactus of the ancestors. Moreover, Karembola have used this 'modern,' 'foreign' cactus to block access to 'ancestral time,' by deliberate planting around the fallen *hazomanga*, where it now forms dense hedges both warning and preventing people from breaking taboos by coming too close. In this way, the landscape carries the memory of a past divided into two epochs, managing both to commemorate a profound rupture of the social order—by recalling that there was a time before the *vazaha* came, a time before the *raketa* died,—while also working 'ancestral time' into the present as a basic parameter of their lived world.

Nowhere is this paradox more evident than in the uncircumcised body itself. For, on the one hand, this bodily condition epitomizes a people alienated from their past. It proves that Karembola cannot do as their ancestors did before them; but must do as *vazaha* bid. And yet being uncircumcised is also about being owned by dead priests. As a bodily performance, it has its roots in mourning practice. It is about being unable to sever links with yesterday's people (*ondate taolo*), to put down the burden of memory, to remake bonds of ownership and rootedness in order to begin again. To bury *lolo* properly, to bring mourning to an end, would be to silence their voices forever, to allow the past to slip away.[24] Thus, even as Karembola express a sense of becoming *vazaha* through idioms of belonging to *lolo*, they refuse to forget the past. Hence, the paradox that, although the uncircumcised are held to be men without history or ancestry, in this instance it means refusing to accept that the links which bind Karembola to the time of the ancestors are gone for good.

'Ancestral time' is also present as a negative—an imagined other— in Karembola funerals. For each time the corpse of an uncircumcised man comes to be buried, Karembola must perform a 'symbolic' circumcision on the wood of the coffin. I say 'symbolic' because

---

[24] Many of the people who witnessed the last circumcisions and the demise of the *raketa* were still alive in the 1980s and 1990s. It will be interesting to see how these events are remembered by future generations, especially as Karembola ethnopsychological theories of memory place some emphasis upon a three-generation span.

Karembola themselves class the action as *oharañe avao*, meaning 'to provide (only) an example,' 'to symbolise,' 'to stand for another or more general thing.' The curious thing about this practice of corpse-circumcision is the way it too relates present to the past: like their ancestors before them, Karembola still carry out circumcisions during funerals at the tomb, but this 'modern,' 'purely symbolic' circumcision also turns 'ancestral practice' upside-down, because instead of circumcising boys who are about 'to enter into life' (Decary, 1930: 87), Karembola now 'circumcise' the coffin just before lowering it into the grave. Bloch (1986: 102) indicates that Merina circumcisions are at least partly concerned with creating a sexually functional body, as evidenced 'in the celebration of the child's future erections'; among Karembola, who apparently value the living body as the site of ancestral blessing more highly than do the Merina, a cultural concern with making bodies 'able to do the work of the living' is even more pronounced (Middleton, 1995b). To circumcise a coffin, then, even 'symbolically,' is a nonsense. As Karembola say in other contexts, what's the point of trying to secure blessing for what is already dead? No wonder that Iavimasy was prompted to comment, 'We Karembola have forgotten all our customs. We lost them when the foreigners came. We're people of a dying land.'[25] And of course the point is that Karembola have not actually forgotten their customs: handling the uncircumcised body in mortuary ritual both makes them aware of how estranged they have become from the ancestors *and* serves as a mnemonic of the ancestral custom they no longer keep.[26] Articulated to both past and present, the 'symbolic' circumcision provides the *ritual* complement to their uncircumcised bodies. It is a commemorative performance, prompting parents to explain to their children how Karembola once stepped over corpses, and why they no longer do.[27]

---

[25] The practice of circumcising coffins (*hazo*, 'sacred wood') may also make an oblique reference to the *hazomboto* ('sacred wood-penis'), the wooden stakes that were erected, one for each initiate, during traditional circumcision rites (cf. Decary, 1933: 92). If so, it would be telling that the 'penis-wood' today not only takes the form of a coffin but is supine rather than erect.

[26] Given the argument Astuti (1995) makes about the Vezo of west Madagascar being 'kinded' only or finally in the tomb, circumcising coffins might be considered a very Vezo-type of thing to do. Karembola ideas of kindedness are, however, very different than those of the Vezo because they believe themselves to be kinded in life (Middleton, 1995a). Thus, to circumcise a coffin is to show just how cut off from the ancestors they, the living, have become.

[27] We could say that the bodily memory 'is conveyed and sustained by ritual

This, then, is what Connerton (1989: 14) terms a 'theology of memory,' in which the present is not severed from the past (see also Stoller, 1995). For as Karembola circumcise coffins, and tell their stories of what happened to would-be priests, they keep alive the communal memory of both the historical events that have formed their community and the 'ancestral traditions' they are supposed to have lost. To be *un*circumcised, then, is to remember, to make the past actual. To be a 'people who once practised circumcision but now no longer do' is to commemorate what it means to be Karembola, to be a member of a particular historic group today.[28]

The Work of Time

In her monograph *A Green Estate*, Feeley-Harnik (1991) seeks to complete the circle started years earlier in her essay on the 'Political Economy of Death' by showing how the Sakalava were eventually able to 'restore their independence' by completing the royal funeral, thus not only putting an end to the interregnum but moving out into a new history by 're-burying colonial rule.' What Feeley-Harnik describes for the Sakalava Bemihisatra of Analalava is typical of the 'resurgence' (re-invention) of 'traditional' ritual that has characterised the post-colonial era in Madagascar, as its various peoples have sought to give expression to both a sense of newfound independence and their essential 'Malagasyness.' By the 1970's, the Merina, for example, were showing a new-found enthusiasm for elaborate circumcision rituals as part of a revival of 'Malagasy' things (Bloch, 1986: 155; see also Raison-Jourde, 1983; Sharp, 1993). It is here that Karembola part company with their compatriots: for the *hazomanga* still lie toppled, the *vy lava* remain unclaimed in trees, and Karembola boys still grow up uncircumcised.[29] Indeed, far from restoring

---

performance' (Connerton, 1989: 71) for arguably, the traces which the past has left in the men's bodies would be invisible, were it not for the practice of coffin-circumcision, which by evoking the master narrative retrieves the meaning of being *un*circumcised.

[28] A similar case for the uncircumcised body carrying profound meaning might be made for the Tsimihety of northern Madagascar, many of whom are not circumcised because, it is said, they reject all symbols of monarchist authority (Wilson, 1992: 113–115).

[29] At the time of fieldwork Karembola made little, if any use, of the clinic at Beloha. A few boys were circumcised by an itinerant circumcizer in the cool season, 1983.

'independence,' Karembola claim to have become even more entangled in funerals since Independence. The dead, they say, are more
numerous than ever. They can no more see an end to mortuary
work than they can circumcise their boys.

One can suggest all sorts of reasons why Karembola should have
remained suspended in history, caught like *anadolo* in an interregnum, still belonging to foreigners and dead men. One must lie in
the droughts and famines that afflict Karembola with increasing reg-
ularity, making it difficult for them to imagine that they might ever
put this 'dead,' broken land behind them and return to the time of
the ancestors. Or to put the same point another way, it probably
makes better sense to continue to blame foreigners for the signs of
the times than to expose the ancestors and authentic priests, by moving out of the interregnum. Another reason why Karembola continue to dramatize imagery of alien domination—and this takes us
far beyond our remit here—lies in an age-old discourse around the
proper articulation of authority and autonomy, a discourse which
was intrinsic to the pre-colonial Karembola polity, but which acquired
a new currency in the colonial context, and which Karembola have
now reworked yet again to express their relationship with the Malagasy
State. But perhaps the greatest motive for remaining in the 'political economy of death' is to be found in the immensely rich, densely
textured experiences it *now* provides. The sheer capacity of contemporary mortuary ritual to meet people's multiple aspirations—for cultural meaning and aesthetic pleasure, for risk-taking and prestige
fulfillment, for self-aggrandizement and public display, for writing
personal and collective narratives,—helps explain why Karembola
leave the *hazomanga* in the thickets of foreign cactus, and the *vylava*
to rust in the trees.

Looking at this 'political economy of death' today, it is difficult
to credit the political impotence, the moral decline, and the cultural
impoverishment that Karembola claim it evidences. For it is clear
that, in and through their mortuary performative, Karembola have
fashioned a world from which foreigners are excluded, an imagined
polity to which only Karembola belong. Nonetheless, the fact remains,
as indeed Karembola seek to remember, that the story of the decline
of circumcision ritual and the expanding realm of the dead is anchored
in a set of historical circumstances which Karembola experienced as
victims, and to which they responded by portraying themselves as
victims. This case-study, then, underlines not only the complexity

and fluidity of ritual expression, its potential to yield new, often unforeseen, meanings and forms; but also suggests that some of the criticisms now made of earlier 'reaction-to-conquest' type explanations of ritual transformations in the colonial period may have failed to take proper account of the work of time. As Borofsky (1987) shows in his exemplary study, where there are differences between the accounts written of one culture but at different periods, reconciling them may be less a case of judging one ethnographer right and the other wrong, than of recognising that time brings its own changing perspective.

REFERENCES

Antze, P., and M. Lambek (eds.)
    1996   *Tense Past. Cultural Essays in Trauma and Memory*. New York, Routledge.
Astuti R.
    1995   *People of the Sea: Identity and Descent among the Vezo of Madagascar*. Cambridge, Cambridge University Press.
Barley, N.
    1981   'The Dowayo Dance of Death,' in S.C. Humphreys and H. King (eds.) *Mortality and Immortality: the Anthropology and Archaeology of Death*. London, Academic Press.
Bérard, H.
    1951   'Le Problème Agricole du Ravitaillement des Populations dans L'Extrême Sud de Madagascar,' *L'Agronomie Tropicale*, VI (3–4): 146–399.
Bloch, M.
    1986   *From Blessing to Violence: History and Ideology in the Circumcision Ritual of the Merina of Madagascar*. Cambridge, Cambridge University Press.
    1992   *Prey into Hunter. The Politics of Religious Experience*. Cambridge, Cambridge University Press.
Borofsky, R.
    1987   *Making History. Pukapukan and Anthropological Constructions of Knowledge*. Cambridge, Cambridge University Press.
Cohn, B.
    1987   *An Anthropologist among the Historians and other essays*. New Delhi, Oxford University Press.
Cole, J.
    1996   The Necessity of Forgetting: Ancestral and Colonial Memories in East Madagascar. Unpublished Ph.D. thesis, Department of Anthropology, University of Berkeley.
Comaroff, J.
    1985   *Body of Power; Spirit of Resistance: The Culture and History of a South African People*. Chicago, University of Chicago Press.
    1992   'Bodily reform as historical practice,' in J. & J. Comaroff *Ethnography and the Historical Imagination*. Oxford, Westview Press, pp. 69–91.
Comaroff, J.
    1989   'Images of Empire, Contests of Conscience: Models of Colonial Domination in South Africa,' *American Ethnologist*, 16: 661–685. Reprinted in

J. & J. Comaroff, 1992, *Ethnography and the Historical Imagination*. Oxford, Westview Press, pp. 181–213.

Comaroff, J. & J. Comaroff
1991   *Of Revelation and Revolution*. Chicago and London, University of Chicago Press.
1993   Introduction. J. & J. Comaroff (eds.) *Modernity and its Malcontents: Ritual and Power in Postcolonial Africa*. Chicago, University of Chicago Press.

Connerton, P.
1989   *How Societies Remember*. Cambridge, Cambridge University Press.

Cooper, F.
1994   'Conflict and connection: rethinking colonial African history,' *American Historical Review* 99 (5): 1516–1545.

Decary, R.
1931   *Rapport sur la famine en Androy pendant la saison chaude 1930–31*, 1931, Fonds Decary (3076), Bibliothèque centrale du Muséum National d'Histoire Naturelle, Paris.
1933   *L'Androy (Extrême Sud de Madagascar). Essai de Monographie Régionale. II. Histoire. Civilisation. Colonisation*. Paris, Société d'Éditions Géographiques, Maritimes, et Coloniales.

Denning, G.
1988   *Islands and Beaches: Discourse on a Silent Land: Marquesas 1774–1880*. Chicago, University of Chicago Press.

Deschamps, H.
1959   *Les Migrations Intérieures Passées et Présentes à Madagascar*. Paris, Berger-Levrault.

Dirks, N.
1992   *Colonialism and Culture*. Ann Arbor. University of Michigan Press.

Dodd, A.P.
1929   *The Progress of Biological Control of Prickly Pear in Australia*. Commonwealth Prickly-Pear Board, Brisbane, Government Printer.

Esoavelomandroso, F.V.
1975   'Les Sadiavahe: Essai d'interprètation d'une rèvolte dans le Sud de Mada-gascar (1915–1917),' *Omaly sy Anio*, (1/2): 139–179.

Esoavelomandroso, M.
1980   'Le Temilahehe et ses Femmes,' *Cheminements*, ASEMI, XI, 1–4.

Feeley-Harnik, G.
1984   'The Political Economy of Death: Communication and Change in Malagasy Colonial History,' *American Ethnologist* 11 (1): 1–19.
1991   *A Green Estate: Restoring Independence in Madagascar*. Washington, Smithsonian Institution Press.

Fremigacci, J.
1981   'Protectorat intérieur et administration directe dans la province de Tuléar (1904–1924),' *Revue Française d'Histoire d'Outre-Mer*.

Frère, S.
1958   *Madagascar. Panorama de l'Androy*. Paris, Aframpe.

Gontard, M.
1968   'Les Troubles dans le Sud de Madagascar pendant la première guerre mondiale,' *Bulletin de Madagascar* (Dec.): 1148–1155.

Grandidier, A. & G.
1928   *Histoire Physique, Naturelle, et Politique de Madagascar*, Vol. IV Ethnographie de Madagascar, Vol. III. Paris, Imprimerie Nationale.

Guha, R. & G.C. Spivak (eds.)
1988   *Selected Subaltern Studies*, New York & Oxford, Oxford University Press.

Guérin, M.
    1977   *Le Défi: L'Androy et l'Appel à la Vie*. Fianarantsoa, Librairie Ambozontany.
Heurtebize, G.
    1986   *Histoire des Afomarolahy (Clan Tandroy-Extrême-Sud de Madagascar)*. Paris, Editions du Centre National de la Recherche Scientifique.
Hoerner, J.-M.
    1990   *La Dynamique Régionale du Sous-Developpement du Sud-Ouest de Madagascar*. Perpignan, Cahiers No. 1 du Groupe d'Etudes des Régions Chaudes—Iles Francophones Australes.
Lambek, M.
    1992   'Taboo as Cultural Practice Among Malagasy Speakers,' *Man JRAI*, 27 (2): 245–266.
Middleton, K.
    1995   'Tombs, Umbilical Cords, and the Syllable *Fo*,' in S. Evers and M. Spindler (eds.) *Cultures of Madagascar*. Leiden, International Institute for Asian Studies, Working Paper Series 2.
           'Tomb-work, Body-work: Body-as-Leib in Karembola Birth and Death Ritual,' Paper presented to the 1995 Satterthwaite Colloquium.
    In press   'Who Killed "Malagasy Cactus"? Environment, Science, and Colonialism in Southern Madagascar (1924–1930),' *Journal of Southern African Studies*.
Mitchell, T.
    1988   *Colonising Egypt*. Berkeley, University of California Press.
Olson, S.H.
    1984   'The Robe of the Ancestors. Forests in the History of Madagascar,' *Journal of Forest History*, (Oct): 174–186.
Ortner, S.
    1995   'Resistance and the problem of ethnographic refusal,' *Comparative Studies in Society and History* 37: 173–193
Pelletier, G. & L. Roubaud
    1931   *Images et Réalités Coloniales*. André Tournon, Paris.
Pouchepadass, J
    1993   'Colonisations et Environnement,' *Revue Française d'Histoire d'Outre-Mer*, 80, 298 (1): 5–22.
Raison, F.
    1976   'Les Ramanenjana. Une mise en cause populaire du christianisme en Imerina, 1863,' *ASEMI*, 7 (2–3): 271–293.
Raison-Jourde, F. (ed.)
    1983   *Les Souverains de Madagascar: L'Histoire Royale et ses Résurgences Contemporaines*. Paris, Editions Karthala.
Raison-Jourde, F.
    1991   *Bible et Pouvoir à Madagascar au XIXe siècle. Invention d'une Identité Chrétienne et Construction de l'État (1780–1880)*. Paris, Editions Karthala.
Ranger, T.O.
    1972   'Missionary Adaptation of African Religious Institutions: The Masasi Case,' in T.O. Ranger and I.N. Kimambo (eds.) *The Historical Study of African Religion*.
    1992   'Plagues of beasts and men: prophetic responses to epidemic in eastern and southern Africa,' in T.O. Ranger and Slack, P. (eds.) *Epidemics and Ideas: Essays on the Historical Perception of Pestilence*. Cambridge, Cambridge University Press.
Ranger, T.O. & I.N. Kimambo (eds.)
    1972   *The Historical Study of African Religion*.

Ruud, J.
    1960   *Taboo. A Study of Malagasy Customs and Beliefs.* Oslo, Oslo University
                    Press.
Sahlins, M.
    1985   *Islands of History.* Chicago, University of Chicago Press.
Sharp, L.
    1993   *The Possessed and the Dispossessed: Spirits, Identity and Power in a
                    Madagascar Migrant Town.* Berkeley, University of California Press.
Stoler, A.L.
    1989   'Rethinking colonial categories: European communities and the
                    boundaries of rule,' *Comparative Studies in Society and History* 31(1):
                    134–161.
Stoler, A.L. & F. Cooper
    1989   'Introduction: tensions of empire: colonial control and visions of
                    rule,' *American Ethnologist* 16(4): 609–621.
Stoller, Paul
    1995   *Embodying Colonial Memories.* New York and London, Routledge.
Van Onselen
    1972   'Reactions to Rinderpest in Southern Africa, 1896–97,' *Journal
                    of African History,* XIII (3): 473–488.
Vaughan, M.
    1987   *The Story of an African Famine.* Cambridge, Cambridge University
                    Press.
    1991   *Curing Their Ills: African illness and colonial power.* Palo Alto, Stanford
                    University Press.
Werbner, R.
    1991   *Tears of the Dead: The Social Biography of an African Family.* Edinburgh,
                    Edinburgh University Press for the International African Institute.
Wilson, P.J.
    1992   *Freedom by a Hair's Breadth: Tsimihety in Madagascar.* Ann Arbor,
                    University of Michigan Press.
Woodham-Smith, C.
    1991 [1962]   *The Great Hunger: Ireland 1845–1849,* Penguin.

Plate 10. Now that their *hazomanga* have 'fallen', Karembola perform their sacrifices very simply, 'just at the house', 1983. The *mpisoro* (priest) is seated on the threshold of his dwelling (left); his adjunct anoints family members with the blood of the slaughtered ox. Photograph: Karen Middleton.

CHAPTER NINE

THE CONSTRUCTION OF HISTORY AND
CULTURE IN THE SOUTHERN HIGHLANDS:
TOMBS, SLAVES AND ANCESTORS

SANDRA EVERS

This chapter describes a process of personal and group identity formation based on the selective construction and interpretation of history and culture, in which tombs and ancestors are crucial idioms.
It is well-known that tombs and ancestors are the primary parameters of human interaction and social alignment in the Highlands,
and that both Merina and Betsileo demonstrate their social status
through family tombs. In this chapter I seek to deepen our understanding of these processes of identity construction in everyday life
by focusing on Betsileo and Merina who do not have family tombs.
By studying the dynamic interaction between established groups and
outsiders in a number of contexts, I also address key issues around
slavery, stigmatization, and the dichotomous classification of people
as 'pure' and 'impure'.

   The data on which this chapter is based result from my doctoral
study of the socio-economic dynamics of Betsileo communities in the
Southern Highlands. This study is a synthesis of archival research
conducted at the French Colonial Archives (Archives d'Outre Mer)
and a two-year (1992 and 1996) period of field work in rural and
urban settings in the Southern Highlands. In this chapter, I draw
on my research in the rural region between Ambalavao and Ankaramena (about thirty miles to the southwest of Ambalavao) and the
town Ambalavao itself. I shall highlight the important aspects of my
data through comparison with Maurice Bloch's model of tombs and
ancestry in Merina society. First, however, I will define some of the
concepts I use.

   I understand identity formation to involve an interplay between
endogenous and exogenous factors. The individual construes his identity by taking on certain roles, and these modes of self-representation
are accepted or denied by society in a psycho-social interaction
between the ego and his environment. In this process of identity

construction and affirmation, the role repertoire that is available to the individual depends on the context in which he lives. In settings with a high level of face-to-face contacts, the individual is restricted in his choice of roles simply because certain roles will not be accepted by society. In this chapter, I describe the socio-cultural position of Merina and Betsileo migrants who settled in different parts of the Highlands, with special reference to those migrants upon whom others imposed slave origins either because they do not have a family tomb or have only recently established one. These individuals are stigmatized on the basis of an ascribed identity, an identity initially created by the dominant group. I define stigmatization as a social process whereby one group confers upon another a negative qualification based on characteristics, real or fictive, attributed to the stigmatized group. The stigma, once created, then forms the basis for a group's inferior social position in, or even total exclusion from, community life.

Elias and Scotson term stigmatization as 'a collective fantasy of the establishment' (1985: 27). In their study of the tensions and power relations between two working class districts of an English town, they conclude that those who had lived for generations in a particular area stigmatize newcomers. The established perceive migrants as outsiders to whom they ascribe all manner of stereotypical characteristics and exclude them as their subordinates. Elias and Scotson define this relationship between the 'old' residents of one district of the town and the 'new' residents of another as an 'established-outsiders configuration' (1985: 8–12).

The most striking established-outsiders configurations in the Highlands of Madagascar operate on both inter- and intra-ethnic level. I consider an ethnic group to be a people with an identity based on actual or fictive kinship and a territory, or region of origin. Ethnic identity is a social identity that differs from other social identities in that it invokes actual or imagined shared descent and cultural heritage. The ethnic composition of the Northern Highlands is dominated by Merina, while in the Southern Highlands Betsileo form the majority. I utilise the concept of intra-ethnic descent to refer to the different social strata within an ethnic group. In Merina and Betsileo society these strata consist of kin groups of noble descent, free origin, and slave descent.

Established-Outsiders Configurations in the Highlands

The terminology Merina and Betsileo employ to conceptualize social stratification differs slightly. Among Merina, people of noble descent are called *andriana* whereas among Betsileo they are either *andriana* or *hova*. For Merina, however, *hova* refers to people of free descent without a noble ancestry. My Betsileo informants of noble descent claim that this difference in designation dates from the 19th century Merina hegemony over the Betsileo. Not wanting to share the same noble (*andriana*) title with Betsileo nobles, the Merina rulers called them *hova*: the free. When Merina political dominance was broken during the French colonial period (1896–1960) some Betsileo restyled themselves *andriana*.[1] The claim of noble Betsileo that their *andriana* title already existed before the Merina invasion is remarkable, however, since *andriana* is a Merina term. Dubois who published an impressive monograph (1500 pages) on the Betsileo in 1938 never mentions the utilization of the term *andriana* in Betsileo society, either before or after Merina rule. He states that Betsileo nobility is called *hova* (Dubois 1938: 551–600). It seems that Betsileo of noble descent in the Southern Highlands borrowed the *andriana* title to construct their current superior social status. I will elaborate on this process of identity formation later in this chapter.

---

[1] My *andriana* informants explained to me that not all former *andriana* could reclaim their noble name during the colonial period. This was supposed to be something which was decided by their ancestors: when someone of a former *andriana* (noble) family died and a little worm would come out of his backbone, the ancestors had 'spoken'. The eldest of that particular family would then take it to the river where the little worm would grow into a crocodile. While the crocodile represented the reincarnation of one of their ancestors, the worm symbolized the ancestors' decision that the family could reclaim its *andriana* status. This myth was explained to me at the beginning of my 1992 field work; its significance only became obvious to me three months later when I made a near escape from a crocodile in the river. People told me that the crocodile I had encountered was the reincarnation of the grandmother of a noble family in the village where I lived at the time.

David Graeber also refers to myths of reincarnation in his chapter in this book. He states that *mainty* ('black') Merina often claim to be of Betsileo origin. After death they are supposed to have the ability to transform, first into a worm and later a snake (*fanany*). Whenever a *fanany* appears in a Betsileo family, the family members ask whether it is one of their ancestors. By nodding its head the snake confirms or denies its presumed identity. Although the mythical stories recorded by Graeber show remarkable similarities with what I heard, the most striking difference is that in my research area Betsileo of noble descent declare that only they can transform into a worm and later into a crocodile, whereas Graeber asserts that according to his informants all *olona mainty* ('black people') of Betsileo origin have the potency to reincarnate.

Today Betsileo of free descent are called *olompotsy*, but *hova* and *andriana* also are *olompotsy* since the term refers to all persons of free descent. In both Merina and Betsileo society, people of slave descent are called *andevo*, a term which in former days referred to slaves but nowadays is used to designate their descendants.[2] Merina furthermore are divided between *fotsy* ('white') and *mainty* ('black'). *Fotsy* refers to Merina with an Asian physiognomy, who claim to be of free descent. The ancestors of those now called *mainty*, described as negroid, were for the most part slaves who were captured in other parts of Madagascar. They worked for the Merina king or for landowning *fotsy* families. Because both *fotsy* and *mainty* lived in the same kingdom of Imerina they were all Merina just as the generations after them. Currently, being 'black' does not necessarily mean that someone is of actual slave descent since free Malagasy have also migrated to Imerina. Moreover, most Merina do not fit into the *fotsy* or *mainty* category since they are not clearly 'white' nor 'black'. In fact, most Merina are part of the *fotsy-mainty* dichotomy, not on the basis of their physiognomy but according to whether or not they have a family tomb. *Fotsy* are those Merina who have a family tomb and *mainty* are those who have none or who have only recently established one.

In Betsileo society the distinction between *fotsy* and *mainty* is not made. To understand why, we need to go back to the pre-colonial period again: when the Merina king Andrianampoinimerina and his successor Radama I conquered the Southern Highlands in the early 19th century, they utilized the existing power structure within Betsileo communities. Land mostly was in the hands of a few families (*tompon-tany*, 'masters of the land'). The king appointed the *tompon-tany* as village governors and local representatives of the Merina monarchy. They extracted tribute, a part of which they could keep for themselves and the remainder they gave to the Merina royal house. To increase production, fallow ground was put to use by *tompon-tany* and the less affluent villagers worked these fields as corvée (*fanom-poana*) labourers. The poorest villagers were deprived of their liberty and were forced to work in the rice paddies of their free fellow-villagers or were sent to cultivate the rice fields of the Merina royal house (Solondraibe 1986: 149–167). Thus, their relationship with

---

[2] In this chapter the term *andevo* refers to people who are called *andevo* by others. This does not necessarily mean that they are of actual slave descent.

the local landowning *tompon-tany* suddenly changed to one of slave and master.

Slavery had existed among the Betsileo before Merina dominance but had been restricted to the local Betsileo royal houses. Merina presence intensified the practice of slavery to such an extent that landowning families (*tompon-tany*) also acquired slaves (Dubois 1938: 557). But whereas in Merina society the slaves were 'black' (*mainty*), in Betsileo society they were not recognizable by their physiognomy: their colour was the same as the free. Today, more than hundred years after the abolition of slavery (1896), they nevertheless are still defined as a specific group.

In the next part I address the Merina model of tombs and ancestry as developed by Maurice Bloch. This model will form the point of comparison for my discussion of Betsileo socio-cultural organization and intra-ethnic established-outsiders configurations.

Kinships, Tombs and Ancestry: a Model of Merina Socio-Cultural Organization

In his book *Placing the Dead: Tombs, Ancestral Villages, and Kinship Organization in Madagascar* (1971), Maurice Bloch presents a model of the socio-cultural organization of 'white' (*fotsy*) Merina families in the region that is now called Antananarivo province.

Demes are the basis of traditional *fotsy* Merina socio-cultural organization. Bloch defines the deme as a territorial unit of kinship organization, whose members share a common eponymous ancestor and have a family tomb (*fasana*) in their area of origin, called *tanindrazana* ('ancestral land'). Demes may be divided into various sub-demes based on descent from a common ancestor. These smaller families (*fianakaviana*) nevertheless all demonstrate their kinship origin through their family tomb in the *tanindrazana*. In the past all deme members lived in their *tanindrazana* and married endogamously (*ibid.*: 41–50).

Nowadays most Merina live away from their *tanindrazana* due to demographic pressure on the ancestral lands, economic ventures in other regions of the Highlands, or professional obligations elsewhere. These migrants, called *voanjo* ('seeds'), founded new villages and reshaped their lives away from the *tanindrazana*, but their homeland remained a crucial point of reference since *fotsy* Merina prove their rank through their *tanindrazana* and family tomb. In the Merina cognitive map, the socio-cultural position of kinship groups, organized in territorial demes, is well-known. This knowledge dates from before the colonial period when the Highlands were ruled by Merina kings: the various demes were ranked according to their closeness to the monarch. Even today Merina identify themselves and others through this ranking system. So whenever Merina meet, they immediately inquire about each other's *tanindrazana* in order to place each other socially (*ibid.*: 105–108).

The *tanindrazana* is not only the Merina's first point of reference in interactions with others. It is also the place where they ultimately will return. The return to the *tanindrazana* is a major preoccupation in the Merina's existence. They consider life on this earth only a period of transit to another 'life' after death which only can be entered through the family tomb. Their tombs are solid cement buildings while the houses of the living often are in a deplorable condition: people generally spend more money on their tomb than on their house (*ibid.*: 112–115).

Tombs unite the dead and the living since people through their *tanindrazana* belong to a certain family or deme. However, not all members of the deme are actually buried in the family tomb in the *tanindrazana*. Merina have various options, despite patrilinear preferences. A male Merina, for example, may chose to be buried in the tomb of his mother (if she is from another deme), or in the tomb of his wife's maternal or paternal family. People decide at an early age, normally after their marriage, in which tomb they want to be buried. This is important since they have to participate in the maintenance of a tomb in order to activate the right to be buried in it (*ibid.*: 122–124).

Having elaborated on Bloch's model of tombs and ancestry in 'white' Merina society, one wonders whether slaves (*mainty*) were organized in the same way. Did they also have *tanindrazana* and family tombs? While Bloch stresses in *Placing the Dead* that he only deals with 'white' (*fotsy*) socio-cultural organization, he nevertheless mentions the exceptional position of the slaves: 'The fact that they had no legal standing meant that they were not involved in the major territorial and kinship organization of the state but were only legal extensions of their masters' (*ibid.*: 71). Slaves lived dispersed in Merina society and were isolated from each other. Moreover, their masters did not allow them to establish permanent tombs. Instead, they were obliged to bury their dead in simple graves. This meant that they did not have a place in the continuing social structure (ibid.: 165), which leaves the question of whether ex-slaves were able to integrate in the social structure by creating their own family tombs after the abolition of slavery in 1896.

When the French freed the slaves in the first year of the colonial period, no measures were taken to ensure their socio-economic emancipation: they were left with no means of subsistence. Some ex-slaves returned to their native region, although only sporadic use was made of this option probably because they had lost contact with their kin. Others began cultivating in areas in the Highlands where land was still abundant. A third group decided to remain on, or near the property of their former masters where they continued to work the small plots of land that they had been given during their enslavement.[3] Liberation did not improve their economic prospects or increase their prosperity because while rights to land use could be transmitted from father to son, the land remained the legal property of the former slave master (Bloch 1980: 103–106, Savaron 1932: 294–296). As they often only rented land, most of these ex-slaves were precluded from establishing ancestral land and a permanent family tomb. Even when they moved away from their former master, they still were recognized as ex-slaves:

> The slaves only had perishable tombs in old Imerina and, many of them have built new permanent tombs in the new area and not in the old where their inferior status is remembered. This aspect should not, however, be overestimated since there are many other ways in which 'free' descent can be demonstrated. Most important of these is the fact that physical appearance is usually sufficient indication of slave descent (Bloch 1971: 136).

So whereas not having a family tomb implied that one was a non-person (Bloch 1980: 120), creating a tomb did not mean that the *mainty* could free themselves from their ancestors' past: their physiognomy made them instantly recognizable as *andevo*, people of slave descent. Even today *mainty* live on the fringes of society since many 'white' Merina still consider them inferior[4]

---

[3] Sometimes these former masters allowed their ex-slaves to establish a tomb. Its location however symbolized the inferior position of the ex-slaves: '. . . ces tombes d'affranchis devaient être construites au Sud de celles des anciens maîtres, suivant le principe de la place de chacun dans la société merina et respecté encore de nos jours' (Rabearimanana 1997: 297).

[4] Rabearimanana, Rajaoson and Randriamaro deal with this subject in the publication of the proceedings of an international Seminar entitled: 'L'Esclavage à Madagascar. Aspects historiques et résurgences contemporaines', 1997.

The interaction between people of free and slave origin in Merina society will be discussed later when I compare the positions of Merina and Betsileo *andevo*. First, I describe the position of Betsileo *andevo* in the rural region between Ambalavao and Ankaramena in the Southern Highlands, and ask how people of slave origin are identified since in Betsileo society they are the same colour as people of free descent. In order to analyze the current socio-cultural configuration of this region, a bird's eye view of the local history is required.

Tombs as Identification Symbols

Throughout the 18th and 19th centuries the *efitra*, the no-man's-land between the rice-growing Betsileo in the Southern Highlands and the cattle-raising Bara and Antandroy to the south, was settled by people fleeing wars between the 'Betsileo' principalities and, at a later stage, Merina hegemony. In addition, runaway slaves, mostly from the Northern Highlands, came to the region hoping to build a new life for themselves. Refugees who did not originate from the Betsileo region—the area between Ambositra and Ankaramena—took over the 'ethnic' title from those already occupying it.[5]

Up until the end of the 1960s newcomers arriving in the region between Ambalavao and Ankaramena were able to settle and culti-vate land that was still available. Occupying this land gave the refu-gees the opportunity to become autochthonous since in both Merina and Betsileo society possession of land and a family tomb are mark-ers of family authenticity in a particular region (Bloch 1971: 106–108). So for ex-slaves wanting to leave their past behind them, building a family tomb upon their own land would make them autochtho-nous. These migrants who came before 1970 nowadays form the established group in the zone between Ambalavao and Ankaramena. They call themselves Betsileo and stress that they are the autochthons of the region and have a free origin. They may very well be of slave

---

[5] The name Betsileo, which can be translated as 'the many unbeatable', was given to them in the 19th century when they initially fiercely resisted Merina expan-sion (see also Sick 1984: 185–200). Merina domination over the people in the South-ern Highlands created ethnic consciousness among the Betsileo (Kottak, 1980: 4–5); but Betsileo only became an ethnic title as a result of political manipulations of the French colonial government (1896–1960). When Betsileo nowadays migrate to other parts of the country they keep their 'ethnic' (Betsileo) name: their family tomb in the home-area fixes their 'ethnicity' in time and space.

descent, but because of their newly created ancestral land and family tomb they were able to identify themselves as autochthons of free descent.

I tried to verify whether the migrants who became autochthons were of actual free origin. Most were willing to tell me where they originally came from, and some of their claims I checked. I visited seven villages which were supposed to be the *tanindrazana* of seven 'autochthon' families in the region between Ambalavao and Ankaramena. I found their relatives but it was difficult to tell whether the villages really were their *tanindrazana*. Often these relatives also turned out to be migrants, who had themselves only recently become autochthons by establishing a family tomb on their newly acquired land. Moreover, I was restricted by the fact that questions about descent are surrounded by a *fady* ('taboo', 'forbidden'). People of free descent mostly do not have a problem discussing their family tomb; indeed, they are proud of it and demonstrate their social status through it. People of slave descent, however, feel that by talking about ancestral land and tombs they might reveal either that they do not have a tomb or only a recently established one. Because of the *fady*, finding out peoples' actual origin turned out to be a hazardous adventure. After several long trips (ranging from 10 to 30 miles on foot) to places that people named as their *tanindrazana*, I decided that it would be more fruitful to look at what people perceive or claim. Although *tompon-tany* free origin might have been instrumentally created, their tombs legitimize their current status as autochthons of free origin. The key issue is not authenticity but what kinds of identities are created or stressed in particular contexts to organize human interaction.

The crucial point is that a migrant can only become an autochthon in the region between Ambalavao and Ankaramena if he is able to acquire land. It is precisely this that posed problems for migrants who came after about 1970. These later migrants came for three main reasons. First, there were Antandroy, Bara and Betsileo escaping the terror of the cattle thieves to the south. Secondly, there were people, including those of slave origin, who wished to break with the past and to start afresh by moving to another region. A third group of migrants came for economic reasons; the area between Ambalavao and Ankaramena is renowned for its manioc harvests.

It was difficult for these groups to start a new life in the region because by the end of the 1960s all the available land in the *efitra* had been claimed by the so called autochthons. These *tompon-tany* ('masters of the land') are now very selective in accepting migrants in their villages. Malagasy who are not Betsileo are rejected outright. To justify this, the *tompon-tany* stereotype them as 'different', as outsiders. Migrants of non-Betsileo origin are often the victims of prejudice but none more so than the Antandroy, who are referred to as *olona ratsy*, 'bad people'. The Antandroy are not only rejected in the Betsileo villages, but the *tompon-tany* also refuse to rent them land. In this way they hoped to see the last of the Antandroy. Yet the Antandroy remain to this day living in small hamlets where their basic means of livelihood is rearing cattle. Their zebus often trample and destroy the manioc fields of the autochthons, which only serves to reinforce their bad image and leads to further animosity.

A person can only become the 'Other' if he can be identified as such. On an inter-ethnic level, this happens when Betsileo claim that Antandroy speak, look, and act differently from themselves. On an intra-ethnic level, Merina make the division in their own society between *fotsy* ('white', free descent) and *mainty* ('black', slave origin). In Betsileo communities people of supposed slave origin also are defined as outsiders despite the fact that they are not instantly recognizable. This poses the questions of how and why they are identified as *andevo* and 'outsiders'. To understand the daily practice of this process I will describe one village in the region between Ambalavao and Ankaramena which I call Tanambao. Tanambao nevertheless represents other villages in the region in which similar established-outsiders configurations exist.

Identifying and Excluding the 'Other'

Every Betsileo migrant[6] who wishes to live in Tanambao must first report to the members of the *tompon-tany* village council, who always demand to know where the applicants' ancestral land and family tomb are located. Their aim is to gain an understanding of the origins of the newcomer. The *tompon-tany* immediately suspect any migrant who is vague about his descent of being of slave origin since all free-born persons in the Highlands have ancestral land and a

---

[6] These migrants claim to be Betsileo. The *tompon-tany* of Tanambao verify this statement by checking whether the ancestral homeland and family tomb of these migrants actually are in the Southern Highlands.

family tomb in their native region. *Tompon-tany* refer to Betsileo who cannot identify their *tanindrazana* as people who 'do not have a history' *(tsy misy tantara)*. For the *tompon-tany* it is simplicity itself to exclude newcomers 'without history' because their past has given them no status or claim to recognition.

Over the last few decades, the *tompon-tany* have only allowed migrants thought to be of slave origin to settle in Tanambao on the condition that they are prepared to live in the western periphery. Migrants of free origin, meanwhile, have been allowed to establish themselves in the eastern part of the village. In this way, the *tompon-tany* have laid the foundations for the lasting stigmatization of the people of the western part. Anyone now living in the west of Tanambao is considered by other villagers to be a member of an inferior group. In Merina and Betsileo ideology, the west is associated with everything bad or evil and is also seen as impure (Mack 1986: 40). No Betsileo of free descent would live in the western periphery. As a consequence the western areas of Betsileo settlements are occupied by people who are referred to as *andevo* ('slave' or 'of slave descent').

One needs to note that the *andevo* stigma is imposed upon the newcomers by the *tompon-tany*. The fact that migrants were unable to prove their free descent by means of a family tomb and ancestral land does not necessarily mean that they are of actual slave descent. Sometimes their place of origin and family tomb are too far away for the *tompon-tany* to be able to verify their claims. In such a case the *tompon-tany* leave the newcomers with two options: either to depart or to establish themselves in the western part. Most migrants accept to live in the western area of the village.

Having learned my lesson trying to verify the roots of those who currently call themselves *tompon-tany*, I knew that checking the actual origin of the migrants in western Tanambao would serve no useful purpose. Once again social constructions, externally ascribed or personally achieved, take on lives of their own with the prejudice against migrants in western Tanambao further reinforced in the cultural idioms employed by the elite. The *tompon-tany*, and above all those *tompon-tany* who claim noble descent *(andriana)*, call the migrants in the western periphery *olona maloto* ('impure' or 'dirty people'), while they address each other as *olona madio* ('pure' or 'clean people').[7] These

---

[7] Rasolomanana refers to the pure and impure dichotomy in his article *L'intégration*

abstracts, taken from my field work diary (1992), show the impact that these labels have upon migrants who dwell in western Tanambao.

> 22nd March: Lalao, a woman of thirty, is married to Patrice who is thirty-two. They live in south western Tanambao in a little hut of poor quality. The hut is divided into two parts by a piece of cloth. On the right side they cook on a wood fire and on the left side Lalao and Patrice sleep with four children: three girls between the ages of four and seven and a little boy of almost one year. Patrice is not the father of the three girls. Lalao says that they were conceived before she knew Patrice; the fathers are 'unknown'. The family moved to Tanambao in 1988.

> Patrice: 'When we came to the village I went to see the village elder; his name is Joseph Andriana. I told him that we really would like to live in Tanambao. First, he asked me with how many we were. I told him four, my wife was pregnant with another baby. His second question concerned our *tanindrazana*. Well, I answered him that we came from a village near Fianarantsoa but he wanted to know the name. I just could not remember.[8] He replied that he could not accept us and that we had to leave. But we could not leave, Lalao was very pregnant. He said that he had to consult his ancestors on this matter, we waited three days, we slept at the riverside. His son came to see us and told us that his father had received a dream in which the ancestors had spoken. We were allowed to live here. We had nothing. We had to build the house ourselves. Nobody helped. We also could rent some land from a family who has a lot of land in Tanambao. I try to cultivate it now but it is far away, near the mountains, and there are too many stones in the ground. I have nobody to help me.'

> Lalao: 'The house was not even finished when I got my baby. I was alone, nobody came to see her. I could not understand it. It was not clear. I was very sad.'

> Patrice quickly continues: 'Later someone told me that we live in the wrong part of Tanambao, the *maloto* part which is reserved for peo-

---

du phénomène d'esclavage vue à travers les proverbes: cas d'une région du Nord-Betsileo. Unfortunately he does not elaborate on this issue. He writes: '. . ., une femme "*tsy madio*" (ayant du sang *andevo*) qui voulait à tout prix s'intégrer dans le groupe des descendants s'acheminant vers le tombeau ancestral, a été enlevée par un tourbillon subit, pour ne plus être retrouvée!' (1997: 333).

[8] Most people who were labelled *andevo* by the *tompon-tany* refused to speak about their *tanindrazana* or said they could not remember where they came from. They seem ashamed of their origins; this might mean that they are of actual slave descent but may also be due to other reasons such as having had social conflicts in the area they migrated from. But whatever the real reason, it is remarkable that they do not wish to talk about their *tanindrazana* since most Betsileo declare proudly where their ancestral land is.

ple who do not have a *tanindrazana* and a family tomb. That is why people speak ill of us. I went to see the village elder again and told him that we do not belong here but he thinks we do.'

When I discussed the position of the people of western Tanambao with the other villagers, I was often confronted with gossip about the supposed behaviour of the so called *andevo*, just as Patrice states. 'Talking bad' about *andevo* usually concerns their 'misdeeds', but insinuations about alleged contacts between *olona madio* and *olona maloto* also result in many discussions within the village. The *tompon-tany* use gossip both as a mechanism of social control over their fellow autochthons and as a way of holding the *andevo* in their inferior position. Thus, gossip sharpens the social divisions of Tanambao. On the one side are the autochthonous *olona madio* who claim social recognition as the established group. On the other side—literally as well as figuratively—are the *olona maloto* whom the established group portray in scurrilous terms.

The case of Patrice and Lalao clearly illustrates the isolation of people in western Tanambao. Other villagers do not wish to socialize with them. Social exclusion is articulated through the anxiety people of free descent have of being polluted by *andevo*. Autochthons not only feel superior to 'impure' people, but they also keep a great physical distance from them. Villagers who come into contact with *olona maloto* immediately become 'impure', and this pollution can only be removed by being ritually cleansed by the oldest member of the former royal family, who lives about ten miles from Tanambao. Under the motto of 'prevention is better than cure' most villagers try to avoid the *andevo* at all cost.

Thus, social inclusion and exclusion in the region between Ambalavao and Ankaramena are primarily based on descent as it is perceived or ascribed by the *tompon-tany*. *Tompon-tany* deny non-Betsileo migrants access to their villages. As for Betsileo migrants, those who can 'prove' their free descent are allowed to join the established *tompon-tany* group. But those Betsileo migrants who are unable to demonstrate their free descent are defined as outsiders and stigmatized as *andevo* and 'impure' people. They live apart and are denied participation in community life. In their newly created classification system, *tompon-tany* shaped the identities of newcomers. These identities have become part of the world with which migrants have to deal, and even part of their own conceptual scheme, as I shall now show.

Perpetuating Established-Outsiders Configurations: Marriages and Land

Marriages and land are key factors in established-outsiders configurations in Betsileo villages in the Southern Highlands. I begin by
discussing the role of marriage politics in the process of excluding
andevo and people who maintain social relations with them before
turning to a consideration of the economic factors.

Not all *olona madio* ('pure people' of free descent) respect the rule
of not socializing with *olona maloto*. In fact, in Tanambao there are
seven couples of mixed origin.[9] By means of abstracts from my 1992
field work diary I will introduce a couple of mixed origin in order
to explore the practical consequences of the Betsileo ideology of
inequality.

> It is the third of June when I hear from my informant Rakoto, who
> lives in a village near Tanambao, that Joseph Andriana (he is the vil-
> lage elder of Tanambao) has an *andevo* in his own family.[10]
> Rakoto: 'he obviously did not check her out sufficiently. I know for a
> fact that the wife of his cousin is the sister of Thérèse.'
> Thérèse lives in western Tanambao with her husband and nine chil-
> dren (seven are daughters). I do not believe that Thérèse and the wife
> of the son of the deceased brother of Joseph Andriana actually are
> sisters since I have never seen them together.

> July 12th: Today there was a reunion of the elders from all the vil-
> lages near Tanambao. They discussed what should happen with Dama
> and Zanamavo. Dama is the cousin of Joseph Andriana and Zanamavo
> his wife; she is now openly acknowledged to be the sister of Thérèse
> and therefore seen as an *andevo*. So Rakoto seems to have been right
> after all.
> The elders decided that Dama and Zanamavo do not need to get a
> divorce, which is normally demanded when mixed couples are caught.
> They came to this decision because the couple already has two children
> together. Zanamavo and the two children, however, will not be allowed
> to enter Joseph Andriana's family tomb.[11]

---

[9] In this context the term 'mixed origin' refers to marriages between people of
free descent and slave origin.

[10] Statements like this were often made and must be considered along with gossip as part of the social interactive dynamic of claims and counter-claims of free/pure
and slave/impure descent.

[11] Dama obviously had close bodily contact with Zanamavo and therefore, in the
perception of the *tompon-tany*, had himself become impure. So how could he enter
Joseph Andriana's family tomb? When I asked Joseph Andriana about this, he said
that when Dama would die he would be ritually cleansed by the oldest member
of the former royal family before being buried in the tomb. I also wanted to know

July 16th: I saw Dama today at the river and I had the courage to ask him what he thought about the decision of the elders.

Dama: 'You probably think that I should be happy because they said that I do not have to divorce my wife. But my father is buried in Joseph Andriana's tomb and I want to be reunited with him when I die. But I cannot take my wife and children with me, they cannot enter. So I will be alone. This I fear; it is not good to be alone. I better try to find another wife and get children with her so I will not be alone, later . . . I did not know that my wife and Thérèse are sisters.'

This case shows the exclusion of *andevo* and the *tompon-tany*'s belief that it must continue in the hereafter. People of free descent told me that this is their ancestors' wish and that therefore marriages between people of mixed origin are forbidden (*fady*). Moreover, they think that Betsileo of free descent who marry *andevo* show tremendous disrespect towards the ancestors. Most importantly, however, anyone entering into marriage with an *andevo* is, and remains, polluted until the marriage is dissolved and he or she is ritually cleansed. Children who are born to these marriages are considered 'impure' and, more disastrously, can never rid themselves of the pollution. For the parent of free origin this is already reason enough to dissolve the marriage, although there is the more forceful argument stressed by Dama, namely, that upon their death, the 'impure' children and *andevo* wife/husband cannot be placed in the tomb of the free descent parent. Many informants told me that this means that they cannot 'live' as a family in the hereafter. This is a particularly efficient form of exclusion, enabling the *tompon-tany* to ward *olona maloto* off from their families by appeals to the supernatural.

Whereas *andevo* are defined as unsuitable marriage partners, migrants of free descent are accepted in *tompon-tany* families. *Tompon-tany* constantly conclude marriage alliances with them. Bloch describes this same process for Merina who live away from their *tanindrazana*. In the area of settlement these migrants had to establish new social bonds. They attracted family members to live with them but they also welcomed other migrants. In order to consolidate relations between kinsmen and non-kinsmen, the villagers concluded exogamous marriages in place of their traditional endogamy. '[A]s marriages between neighbours originate from the need to establish a

---

why it took so long for Joseph Andriana to discover that Zanamavo was of slave descent. His reply: 'You ask too many questions'. Discussion closed.

moral link to strengthen political and economic ones, the continuing and strengthening of that link comes from the need to have a permanent and long lasting political or economic alliance' (Bloch 1971: 209).

With these marriage alliances, *fotsy* Merina reproduced the traditional social structure of their *tanindrazana*, where people shared both kinship and economic means of subsistence. This created a new deme in the migration area, and after some generations this was sometimes followed by the creation of a new family tomb and thus a new *tanindrazana*. This did not mean, though, that migrant *fotsy* Merina were free to marry whomever they wanted. Bloch notes that while marriages between *andriana* ('noble descent') and *hova* ('free origin') are generally accepted, marriages with *mainty* ('black') are strongly disapproved. 'This disapproval is mainly explained in racialist terms and the *fotsy* often describe the *mainty* as ugly' (*ibid.*: 199).

Betsileo *tompon-tany* in the region between Ambalavao and Ankaramena also utilize tombs as identification symbols and consider migrants who cannot prove their free descent through a family tomb as *andevo*, but the discrimination is never made on racialist grounds because people of free and slave descent share the same colour. Their motives for excluding *andevo* geographically and socially are mainly couched in terms of the fear of being polluted by the *andevo* stigma. Although authors who have studied socio-economic relations between *mainty* and *fotsy* Merina do not mention the pure-impure dichotomy, from conversations I have had with Merina friends and from personal experiences, I assume that it also is a parameter in Merina concepts of inequality. Merina and Betsileo show remarkable cultural resemblance and share the same spatial symbolism, in which the west is perceived as impure. In her study of the descendants of former slaves (the *mainty*) in Antananarivo, Rabearimanana notes that in Merina villages they also live in the western parts (1997: 291).

Authors pay closer attention to the prohibition of marriages between *fotsy* and *mainty* Merina (Rabearimanana 1997: 291–310, Rajaoson 1997: 347–357, Ramamoijisoa 1986: 39–77). Merina who break this rule are excluded from the *fotsy* family network and their *andevo* partners and children are, just as in Betsileo society, not allowed to enter the family tomb of the *fotsy* parent (Bloch 1971: 199).

Bloch, Rabearimanana, Rajaoson and Ramamoijisoa all explain the *fotsy-mainty* established-outsiders configuration in terms of racial discrimination and economic competition. For example, Rabearimanana writes: 'Beaucoup manquent, en effet, de terres, ce qui les place dans une situation de dépendance par rapport aux propriétaires fonciers' (1997: 297). *Tompon-tany* dominance is also intertwined with the economic subordination of migrants in Betsileo villages in the Southern Highlands because newcomers depend upon the *tompon-tany* families for land. In effect, the established group monopolizes not only superior social status but also the basic means of subsistence. Stigmatization is not, in fact, a necessary condition for controlling people because all newcomers enter into a land contract with a *tompon-tany* who retains control of the land while gaining certain rights over the newcomer. The *tompon-tany* can, for example, demand his labour during harvest time. Stigmatization, however, provides *andriana* (*tompon-tany* of noble descent) with permanent workers the whole year round because *andriana* are able to demand the labour of *andevo* at any time. Often *andevo* are called upon to do the more demeaning and dirtier work. Gaining and maintaining access to this source of labour is one of the major motivations driving the noble *tompon-tany* families to define newcomers as *andevo*.[12] Thus, those labelled as *andevo* are *both* excluded from community life *and* a vital part of its socio-economic dynamics.

The fact that migrants rent all their land from *tompon-tany* means that they are unable to create ancestral land and a family tomb in the region. For migrants who can demonstrate their free descent through a family tomb in a *tanindrazana*, this represents no problem since they say that they will return to their homeland at death. Those stigmatized as *andevo*, however, do not go back to their land of origin. Some were willing to admit that they do not have a family tomb. Others said that due to financial limitations they are unable to bring their dead 'home'. In reality, they bury their deceased in graves near the mountains. Which happens in silence, mostly at night. Their practice of the *andevo* stands in sharp contrast with *tompon-tany* funerals. For *tompon-tany* the passage from this life to the hereafter is 'celebrated' in ceremonies lasting four days. These are attended by all villagers of free descent, including most recent migrants, and numerous family members from elsewhere. *Andevo* are not allowed

---

[12] Bonded labour based on descent is not mentioned in literature on the Merina but this may be due to the fact that no author has studied the socio-economic relations between *fotsy* and *mainty* in any depth.

to participate and so, once again, are confronted with their 'polluted' identity.

In daily life villagers expect the *andevo* to be obedient towards the *tompon-tany*. On account of their economic dependence upon the *tompon-tany*, the so called *andevo* have to comply. If those stigmatized as *andevo* behave in ways that contradict the expectations of the other villagers, they pay a high price: the *tompon-tany* reclaim the land or throw them out of the village.

The migrants in western Tanambao seem to be well aware of the risks involved in 'deviant' behaviour. This internalization of the *andevo* stigma is one of the most significant elements of the established-outsider configuration in Tanambao. It is most poignantly demonstrated by the *andevo* bowing to passing nobility, and in their self-imposed adherence to *olona madio* rules of avoidance. According to the *andriana* this confirms their inferiority. The autochthons constantly claim that the *olona maloto* deviate from the norms of Betsileo culture yet, were they to abandon their genuflexion and self-exclusion, then they would fail to meet the established's expectations of what constitutes deviant behaviour. As Goffman has noted: 'Those in a given category should not only support a particular norm but also realize it' (1963: 6).

To conclude, people of slave descent, or ascribed slave origin, are marginalized in both Betsileo villages in the Southern Highlands and Merina communities in Antananarivo province. *Fotsy* Merina and Betsileo *tompon-tany* benefit from *andevo* subordination. They therefore seek to perpetuate existing established-outsiders configurations through marriage politics and land control. But will those stigmatized as *andevo* remain willing to carry the burden of their imputed past into the future?

Breaking with the Past in order to Resist Subordination

In the region between Ambalavao and Ankaramena, where I carried out my 1992 research, *andevo* do not seem to resist their subordinate position. Their submissiveness toward *tompon-tany*, and their internalization of the *andevo* stigma, are intertwined with the fact that economically they are tied hand and foot to the landowning *tompon-tany*. This entanglement makes resistance futile.

Nevertheless, I found that young unmarried *andevo* men try to escape their stigmatized position by leaving the villages. Their departure is not only a form of resistance; it also is a gendered reaction. They want to accomplish the principal goals of every Betsileo man: to make money and to get married. *Andevo* girls are less mobile, and remain in the villages. They often remain unmarried since their fathers are unable to provide them with husbands. Instead they conceive children by 'unknown' fathers.

By turning their back on the villages *andevo* men liberate themselves from the control of the *tompon-tany*, but this does not necessarily mean that they can rid themselves of their stigma and construe another identity. In the countryside the chances of finding housing and land to cultivate are slight. In villages in the immediate vicinity their alleged origins are well-known and they are consequently unwelcome. In fact, however far they go, they will be unable to persuade inhabitants of other villages that they are of free origin because they have no ancestral land and family tomb. As a result, the *andevo* stigma is firmly fixed in the rural context.

This raises the question of whether the possession of ancestral land and a family tomb are factors in determining socio-economic status in an urban setting. In 1992 I had already noticed that *andevo* men migrated to the town of Ambalavao. So in 1996 I followed them, anxious to know how they lived there.[13]

Tombs and *Tanindrazana* in an Urban Setting

Ambalavao is located in the Southern Highlands and has almost 20,000 residents. It has been dubbed a 'Betsileo town' by the president of the 'Circonscription d'Ambalavao' because, he says, over two-thirds of its population is of Betsileo origin. Nevertheless, Ambalavao is also home to many migrants, who work mainly in the wine producing industries or as pedlars. In addition, there are many youngsters who move from the countryside to the town to pursue their education. Over half the population of the town is under the age of twenty.

Most migrants who come to Ambalavao already have family and friends in the town. In general they spend their first weeks with them while looking for work and a place to live. Relatives and friends

[13] This field work for my dissertation was financed by the Research School CNWS (Leiden University) and the Netherlands Foundation for the Advancement of Tropical Research.

play an important role in the social and economic integration of newcomers, housing them and informing them about the social facilities and formal organization of the town. My research shows that *andevo* who left the countryside for Ambalavao have no or only vague contacts. Their stigmatized position in the villages and their social isolation deprives them of the information and contacts required to facilitate their integration in the urban environment. The upshot is that most *andevo* have to create their own social network when they reach Ambalavao.

One might expect *andevo* to turn to each other for company and friendship. In his book *Stigma: Notes on Management of Spoiled Identity*, Goffman (1963: 20) concludes that people often organize themselves on the basis of a shared stigma. In Tanambao, and other neighbouring villages, however, the contrary can be observed. Through internalization of the *andevo* stigma, submissiveness and divided loyalties to the different *tompon-tany* on whom they depend for land, there is no solidarity between the so called *andevo*. Even in the town of Ambalavao, where they are not burdened by obligations towards *tompon-tany*, I did not find any bonds of friendship between them. Furthermore, it is difficult for *andevo* to find each other since they are all Betsileo and therefore do not share any physical characteristics which would make them instantly recognizable. So before they can come together on a shared issue, they have to make their stigma explicit by identifying themselves as *andevo*.

Young *andevo* men fail to realize their reasons for leaving the villages: unable to escape their stigma, they have enormous difficulties in finding work and getting married. The town does not turn out to be the anonymous environment in which they had hoped to rebuild their life. Their 'polluted' identity, which was created by the *tompon-tany* in the countryside, is re-activated by town dwellers to exclude them in the competition for scarce urban resources, especially jobs and houses. The revival of the *andevo* stigma in Ambalavao is possible because most town dwellers have relatives in the countryside; they seem to know about the migrants' dubious descent, and for this reason exclude them from their social network. Marriages with *andevo* are 'taboo' in the town just as they are in the villages between Ambalavao and Ankaramena.

In contrast to the isolation of the *andevo* migrants, ethnic cohesion in Ambalavao is highly conspicuous because most migrants identify themselves primarily as member of a certain ethnic group. They live together with friends and family, other migrants from the homeland. Antaimoro and Antandroy notably dominate certain parts of Amba-lavao. The ethnic groups maintain strong social relations in both informal and formal ways. For instance, every ethnic minority in Ambalavao has its own association whose members have to pay 1,000 FMG ('Franc Malgache') per month into a social fund. Traditional feasts and rituals are celebrated with this money. The association's most important function, however, becomes obvious when a member dies, and the association contributes to organizing and financing the return of the body to the *tanindrazana* in order to be buried in the family tomb. For most migrants, particularly those of Merina, Antandroy and Antaimoro origin, this reunion with the ancestors is fundamental and therefore an important reason to participate in their ethnic association. Even Betsileo migrants have these formal social arrangements. No *andevo* I met is a member. Many said that this was because they could not care less where they are buried. Only a few were willing to admit that they do not have a family tomb.[14] Their professed indifference to tombs is remarkable since almost everywhere in Madagascar ancestral land and tombs are crucial para-meters in contemporary socio-economic relations and moreover sym-bolize the symbiotic bond between the living and the dead. The following quotations illustrate how young *andevo* men in Ambalavao speak about tombs:[15]

> Soavelo (aged 22): 'My father always told me that it is very impor-tant to have a tomb. Neither my father nor mother has one. That is why we always moved from one place to another. But we never got a tomb because we never got our own land. When I was little, I often overheard my parents say that they were worried about not having a tomb, mostly shortly after we left a village to live somewhere else. My parents live in Tanambao now, they still do not have a tomb. I left them, I feel bad about it. I miss them but cannot go back. The son of Joseph Andriana, the most important *tompon-tany* in Tanambao, told me that I would be killed if ever I returned. Probably I will never see my parents again. He also told me that my father is sick now. What

---

[14] As noted *Andevo* in particular prefer not to speak about their place of origin (*tanindrazana*) and funeral rites (they might have to reveal that they do not have a family tomb). However, I have now known many *andevo* informants for over five years and there is enough trust between us to even tackle these sensitive issues.

[15] To protect their identities the names of the *andevo* men are pseudonyms, just as the name of Tanambao village is fictive. All three men were uncertain about their ages; the ages given are their estimations.

will happen to him when he dies? I have decided not to worry about a tomb. Thinking about today is difficult enough. What to eat and where to sleep. I do not have a job because nobody helps me. You know that I steal food. I know that you will not tell anybody because you are my friend. My father told me that if he did not get a tomb then I should work hard to get one. He said it would change my life for the better. My father was wise. I never will get a tomb, I am sure. I might die tomorrow or even today. I know that my life will be over soon. I do not care where I will be buried.'

Rakoto (aged 16): 'Soavelo and I left Tanambao about the same time, some years ago. I hardly see him here. We are both busy doing our own things. I left Tanambao when my mother died. We buried her near the mountains in the middle of the night. I felt sad because I do not know what will happen to her. You see, we do not have a tomb, I think you know. We have put her in the ground. It makes me sick when I speak about it. I am angry with everybody who has a tomb, they feel better than us only because they have one and we do not.'

François (aged 12): 'Did you visit my parents in Tanambao? How are they? I have not seen them since I left. A long time ago. Someone told me that my little sister got a baby?[16] ... She must have been buried near the mountains, just like all the other deceased of western Tanambao. My sister had a miserable life. She is dead now, maybe it is better like this. I remember that she always cried. I sometimes wonder what happens to people like her, I mean to people who do not have a tomb. Well, I do not mind where I will go when I die.'

The quotations reveal very mixed feelings about not having a family tomb. Although François and Soavelo claim that they are indifferent to where they will be buried, they are concerned about not knowing what will happen to them when they die. Tombs provide people with a defined place in today's society and also represent an entry to the hereafter. For *andevo* uncertainty about the hereafter is a psychological burden. This anxiety is seldom voiced in everyday life since discussing these subjects is *fady* ('taboo'). Nevertheless, I noticed that *andevo* do express their worries, especially when they get sick or old. And even young *andevo* men, as François, Rakoto and Soavelo, sometimes refer to this issue.

---

[16] When I spoke to François I had just spent a few weeks in Tanambao and knew that his sister had died shortly after the child was born. Her parents mentioned that she was only ten; they now take care of the baby. It was hard to tell François about the death of his sister, about which he seemed not to know. The three points in the quotation refer to my conversation with him about the death of his sister. I continue where François starts speaking about tombs.

Another clear difference between *andevo* and other migrants is that the latter generally remain in close contact with family members in the homeland. They send money to help the family and to contribute to the maintenance of the family tomb. *Andevo* rarely have contact with their families in the countryside; most say this is because they feel ashamed for having failed to achieve their goals of making money and getting married.[17] In addition, they claim that the *tompon-tany* of the villages they left would take revenge for their sudden disappearance. This assertion is difficult to verify since almost none of the *andevo* boys who left Tanambao, and villages in its vicinity, returned for family visits. I witnessed only one occasion, when a boy came to visit his sick mother in Tanambao. He came late at night and left before dawn. Many people noticed though. Joseph Andriana (the village elder) commented: 'The boy's visit was wrong. My ancestors will punish him.'

In the above quotation, Soavelo states that he has great difficulty finding work because he has nobody to help him. Most other migrants are guided by intermediaries from their homeland, who, for example, already work for someone and can introduce their friend or family member to the employer. My research shows that these contacts to have been of major importance to over 90 percent of employees in the wine-producing industries in Ambalavao. For *andevo*, this road to finding work is blocked since they lack the social contacts. Most *andevo* try to make a living by buying and selling products and food on the streets. Although this generally provides an inadequate income, *andevo* nevertheless consider their life in Ambalavao as an improvement since they are free to determine their own economic activities. In Tanambao village the *andriana tompon-tany* do not allow *andevo* to sell their labour freely. Thus, by leaving Tanambao the *andevo* liberate themselves from economic entanglement with the *tompon-tany*. However, their role repertoire remains defined by others, frustrating their ability to construct another identity for themselves.

---

[17] Rabearimanana concludes from her research among *mainty* in towns in Antananarivo province that they have scarcely any contacts with their family in the countryside: 'Souvent ils n'entretiennent que peu de liens avec les parents restés au village, certains ne donnent même pas signe de vie pendant des années et les familles perdent pratiquement leurs traces' (1997: 300).

Conclusion

Kinship relations are primordial in the socio-cultural organization of Betsileo and Merina of free descent, and are materialized in tombs and ancestral lands. All Merina and Betsileo of free origin, even those living away from their *tanindrazana*, belong to a kin group through these parameters of identification. Most descendants of slaves were placed outside Merina society because they did not have the opportunity to establish ancestral land and a family tomb. And even when they were able to create a *tanindrazana* and family tomb, they remained 'outsiders' because the imagined history of their ancestors stayed visible in their 'black' (*mainty*) physiognomy. *Fotsy* Merina continue to exclude *mainty* from their family network by labelling them as unsuitable marriage partners.

In Betsileo villages in the region between Ambalavao and Anka-ramena, social fission and fusion are also based primarily on idioms of descent (real or ascribed). Those who nowadays call themselves *tompon-tany* were once migrants who were able to become autochthons through the creation of an ancestral land and a family tomb. It is possible that these *tompon-tany* were of slave descent but through the process of tomb construction they have constructed an identity as *tompon-tany* of free descent. This is accepted by more recent migrants. In fact, the status of the *tompon-tany* is taken for granted because they have shifted the onus of proving origin onto the newcomers. Since the more recent migrants depend on the *tompon-tany* for acceptance in the villages and land, the *tompon-tany* have the power to place newcomers in their newly created classification system. They reject Malagasy of non-Betsileo origin by describing them as outsiders and portraying them in antagonistic terms, and they stigmatize as *andevo* migrants of their own ethnic group who are unable to prove free descent by means of a family tomb and ancestral land. Daily affirmation of their social inferiority by the established *tompon-tany* leads to the internalization of the stigma by the people concerned. Even when they move to the town of Ambalavao, villagers stigmatized as *andevo* find it difficult to escape their inferior status due to the family networks of people of free descent.

Thus, 'white' Merina and Betsileo of free descent claim the position of established groups through family tombs, and marginalize migrants on the basis of the selective construction and interpretation of their culture and history. Socio-economic elites have re-activated the ideology and terminology of slavery in the modern era. Terms from the past such as *andevo* and *andriana* remain in use with all their cultural connotations, and villagers suspected of slave origin are still considered to be people of inferior status, just as in former times. So called *andevo* today are socially isolated and economically exploited although their *andevo* identity has been constructed in the present by the socio-economic elites. Merina and Betsileo of free origin seem to have forgotten that the slaves were liberated in 1896 and that under the Malagasy constitution everybody is deemed to be equal. They prefer to say that in their culture everything is determined by the ancestors and that they are obliged to execute the ancestors' demands by keeping 'tradition' alive.

BIBLIOGRAPHY

Bloch, M.
    1971   *Placing the Dead: Tombs, Ancestral Villages, and Kinship Organisation in Madagascar*. London: Seminar Press.
    1980   Modes of production and slavery in Madagascar: two case studies. In: Watson J.L. (ed.), *Asian and African Systems of Slavery*. Oxford: Basil Blackwell.
    1986   *From Blessing to Violence: History and Ideology in the Circumcision Ritual of the Merina of Madagascar*. Cambridge: Cambridge University Press.
    1989   *Ritual, History and Power: Selected Papers in Anthropology*. London: Athlone Press.
    1989   The symbolism of money in Imerina. In: Bloch M. & Parry J. (eds.) *Money and the Morality of Exchange*. Cambridge: Cambridge University Press.
Dubois, H.M.
    1938   *Monographie des Betsileo*. Paris: Institut d'Ethnologie.
Elias, N. & Scotson, J.L.
    1965   *The Established and the Outsiders: a sociological enquiry into community problems*. London: Cass.
    1985   *Gevestigden en de buitenstaanders: een studie van de spanningen en machtsverhoudingen tussen twee arbeidersbuurten*. Den Haag: Ruward.
Evers, S.J.Th.M.
    1995   *Hedendaagse Ideologie en Terminologie van Slavernij. 'Slaven' op de Zuidelijke Hoogvlakte van Madagascar*. Amsterdam: CASA, Working Papers Series.
    1995   Stigmatization as a Self-Perpetuating Process, *Cultures of Madagascar: Ebb and Flow of Influences*, S.J.T.M Evers and M.R. Spindler (eds.). Leiden: IIAS, pp. 157–189.
    1996   La stigmatisation des descendants d'esclaves, *ISTA*, Antananarivo: Institut Supérieur de Philosophie et de Théologie de Madagascar.
    1997   Solidarity and Antagonism in Migrant Societies in the Southern Highlands, *Actes du Colloque International sur l'Esclavage*, Antananarivo: Institut de Civilisations/Museée d'Art et d'Archéologie, pp. 339–347.
Goffman, E.
    1963   *Stigma: Notes on Management of Spoiled Identity*. Harmondsworth: Penguin.

Kottak, C.P.
  1980 *The Past in the Present: History, Ecology and Cultural Variation in Madagascar.* Ann Arbor: University of Michigan Press.
Kottak, C.P., Rakotoarisoa, J., Southall, A., Vérin, P. (eds.)
  1986 *Madagascar: Society and History.* Durham: Carolina Academic Press.
Mack, J.
  1986 *Madagascar: Island of the Ancestors.* London: British Museum Publications.
Portais, M.
  1974 *Le bassin d'Ambalavao. Influence urbaine et évolution des campagnes (sud Betsileo Madagascar).* Paris: ORSTOM.
Rabearimanana, L.
  1997 Les descendants d'*andevo* dans la vie économique et sociale au XXᵉ siècle: le cas de la plaine d'Ambohibary Sambaina, *Actes du Colloque International sur l'Esclavage*, Antananarivo: Institut de Civilisations/Musée d'Art et d'Archéologie, pp. 291–303.
Randriamaro, J.R.
  1997 L'émergence politique des *Mainty* et *Andevo* au XXᵉ siècle, *Actes du Colloque International sur l'Esclavage*, Antananarivo: Institut de Civilisations/Musée d'Art et d'Archéologie, pp. 357–383
Rajaoson, F.
  1997 Séquelles et résurgences de l'esclavage en Imerina, *Actes du Colloque International sur l'Esclavage*, Antananarivo: Institut de Civilisations/Musée d'Art et d'Archéologie, pp. 347–357.
Rasolomanana, D.
  1997 L'Intégration du phénomène d'esclavage vue à travers les proverbes: cas d'une région du Nord-Betsileo, *Actes du Colloque International sur l'Esclavage*, Antananarivo: Institut de Civilisations/Musée d'Art et d'Archéologie, pp. 319–339.
Ramamoijisoa, J.
  1986 'Blancs' et 'Noirs', les dimensions de l'inégalité sociale, *Cahiers des Sciences Sociales*, 1: 39–77.
  1993 Une thèse qui nous interpelle, *Lakroa* 24–10–1993, pp. 5–6.
Savaron, C.
  1932 Mes souvenirs à Madagascar avant et après la conquête (1885–1898). *Mémoires de l'Académie Malgache.* Tananarive.
Scott, J. C.
  1985 *Weapons of the Weak: Everyday Forms of Peasant Resistance.* New Haven: Yale University Press.
  1990 *Domination and Arts of Resistance: Hidden Transcripts.* New Haven: Yale University Press.
Sick, W. D.
  1984 Die Socioökonomische Differenzierung der Volksgruppen in Madagaskar, Kultur und Naturgeographische Hintergründe, *Paideuma* 30, pp. 185–200.
Solondraibe, T.
  1986 Traditions orales et histoire: La région de Ranomafana-Ifanadiana, *Omaly sy Anio*, 23–24, pp. 149–169.

CHAPTER TEN

SOCIAL COMPETITION AND THE CONTROL OF SACRED PLACES IN RURAL IMERINA: THE CASE OF ANKADIVORIBE

FRANÇOISE RAISON-JOURDE

During the First Republic attempts to study Merina ancestral cults met with considerable reticence. I wanted to gain access to these cults on account of my main research project which concerned the establishment of Christian churches in the Highlands. The first phenomenon appeared to me to be the reverse—the hidden face— of the second, much more official reality. I hoped to work back to the colonial period when the encyclopaedia *Firaketana*, recounting the character and history of even the smallest Merina villages, indicates that numerous ancestral cults existed. In this way, I expected to be able to show how certain *sampy*, protective talismans of the mon- arch or certain individuals, and certain cults, for example, those upon the sacred hills, went underground. At the time, I assumed that an element of continuity was indispensable to the authenticity of these cults. A former research assistant in sociology at ORSTOM had just been appointed to work in the History Department of the Uni- versity at Antananarivo; I benefited from the knowledge he had acquired in making enquiries in several cult localities, among them Namehana and Ankadivoribe. What I discovered from looking at the contemporary practice of the cults in 1970 was disconcerting for me as an historian. The villagers made incessant references to history, but these references sustained a historical fiction that served to legit- imize contemporary roles and power in the village. However aber- rant this historical 'bricolage', it found meaning in the current context.

Twenty years later, having completed my work on the establish- ment of Christianity,[1] I wanted to know what had become of the

---

[1] F. Raison-Jourde, *Bible et pouvoir à Madagascar au XIXᵉ siècle. Invention d'une iden- tité chrétienne et construction de l'État*, Paris, Karthala, 1991, 840 p.; 'Mission LMS et Mission Jésuite face aux communautés villageoises merina', *Africa*, 1983 (53) 3, pp. 55–72.

cult of Andraisisa at Ankadivoribe. I returned there in the company
of Thomas Solondraibe, who held a doctorate in History from the
University of Paris VII.[2] My perspective had been modified by reading Hobsbawm and Ranger's work, *The Invention of Tradition*. I now
perceived the powerful, well-argued resistance local elites made to
the hegemony of Christian churches and the double recalcitrance
of social minorities, especially the *mainty* as descendants of slaves,
vis-à-vis both the churches and the country land-owners who remain
masters of the land even if they are no longer masters of men.[3] I
detected that a historical narrative, drawing on worldly signs to invoke
the magical and the mythical, was being used to construct identities
that had changed markedly over the intervening period of only twenty
years. What had happened during this period that corresponded to
the duration of the 'revolutionary' Second Republic?

Far from its audience and its renown expanding, the cult of
Andraisisa had closed in on itself. Its functions were now purely
local, serving the interests of one family whose members had worked
between 1970 and 1990 to secure this outcome. Was the case of
Andraisisa unusual? It appears not for in the context of the revival
of *andriana* (nobility) values and identity that marked the late 1980s,
other cult-places that, under pressure from President Tsiranana of
the First Republic,[4] had been open to pilgrims of every geographical and social origin also underwent retraction, becoming cult-places
for lineages or *foko* (demes). At a time when identities throughout

---

[2] I was helped in 1991 by the parallel research of Chantal Andriantseheno, who
has subsequently written master's degree in Archaeology on the sites of Vakinisisaony,
under the direction of M. Rafolo Andrianaivoarivony, and by the investigations of
Thomas Solondraibe, specialist in oral history, whose premature death was greatly
regretted amongst historians. The project was funded by the French Ministry of
Research.

[3] The terms are defined in the following ways. *Andriana*: the king; nobles (a debat-
able translation made by European authors). *Hova*: free men. *Mainty* ('Blacks') formerly designated one moiety of society in opposition to *fotsy* ('Whites'). In the 19th
century it designated royal servants and more broadly the most ancient elements
of the population that had settled the borders of Imerina. After the abolition of
slavery in 1896, the term *mainty* was extended to *andevo* (slaves and descendants of
slaves).

[4] The First Republic, which saw teachers from secular schools come to power,
deliberately kept a distance from the Christian churches as well as from the ancestral cults, which were tolerated but not encouraged. However, many *mainty*, who
were followers of these cults, voted for President Tsiranana. The Second Republic,
socialist and revolutionary, encouraged 'cultural authenticity', that is to say, adherence to Malagasy cults, in order to undermine the authority of the churches, until,
that is, 1986, when it reversed its policy and sought reconciliation instead.

Imerina were being reworked, these cults became closed to the rag-bag of pilgrims, and were harnessed to the social aspirations of a few families.

I. *The 1970 enquiry at Ankadivoribe*[5]

Ankadivoribe lies fourteen kilometres to the south-west of the capital of Madagascar. From its heights on a dry, clear July day, one could easily imagine that the Hilton hotel lies within arm's reach, so close does it seem. Yet this village, which was very prosperous during the 19th century and the colonial period, paying its taxes very regularly and the first in the district to acquire a small hospital with its own generating unit, is now isolated at the end of two roads across dykes pitted with fearsome holes. The local teacher reckons that it is a case of deliberate withdrawal in the face of a capital that no longer gives anything to its environment. As a result, Anka-divoribe has been spared the urban sprawl that has developed along the roads to Tamatave and Antsirabe, and stands firmly with its heritage intact.

This heritage is by no means slight. The village appears in two reference works of fundamental importance to historians: the well-known *Tantara ny Andriana*, which is the collection of oral traditions and manuscripts assembled by Father Callet, and the encyclopaedia *Firaketana*. Andraisisa is mentioned for two periods. To begin with, this wooded hill was known as Marololo ('many spirits').[6] A Vazimba prince, Rafandramanenitra and his wife, Rafaramahery, lived close by, at Ampandrana. They had two children: Rangita, who later reigned at Merimanjaka and who figures in the royal genealogy, and

---

[5] Ankadivoribe has the advantage of having been studied on three separate occasions, by R. Cabanes, author of a highly original article on the cults in 1972, then by myself. Numerous other cult-places are examined in a collection of essays now in preparation relating to royal spirits, territorial settlement, and the social imaginary in Imerina (M. Rakotomalala, F. Raison, S. Blanchy). It is important not to confuse Merina cults of royal or princely spirits, of which two forms are studied here, with those of Sakalava royalty where possession is integrated into the exercise of power, or with the Betsimisaraka *tromba*, analysed by G. Althabe as a way of contesting post-colonial Malagasy power.

[6] This place-name is somewhat disturbing. *Lolo* are 'evil spirits that one fears' ('esprits malfaisants *qu'on craint*,' Dictionnaire Malzac). Ill-defined and anonymous, they afflict the living with sickness or madness. The dead who have not been ancestralised become *lolo*.

Ratsiseranina who, on making his submission to his elder, was allocated Marololo to live. The reference to Rangita places this episode in the 16th century.

During the 17th century, the reign of Andriamasinavalona was marked by a serious famine. Despatched to the countryside, royal servants met Andriandrivotra, a rice-cultivator and cattle herder, who gave them rice to bring back. They returned with a canoe full.[7] Andriandrivotra and his three brothers, all *hova*, lived in the region between Ambohitraina and the bottom of the valley. Andriampanarivo, one of the four brothers, married the daughter of another group (probably noble) and wanted to raise sheep and cattle, which others feared would destroy their crops. He insisted and his descendants, subsequently humbled, became known as Zanamihoatra ('those who go too far').

To express his gratitude, the sovereign gave the descendants of Andriandrivotra the privilege of impunity (*tsimatimanota*, 'do not die [when they] transgress') and allowed the village to remain relatively autonomous (*mahadidy tena ary tsy hanimbodihena*). Marololo was renamed Andraisisa by the king. In fact, Ankadivoribe has the reputation of being a very prosperous rice-producing region. It is, however, doubtful that this village alone could have met the needs of the king and the capital, or, *a fortiori*, that it might have supplied rice to all Imerina, as the narrators boast. The reputation is above all symbolic.

In the 19th century, the village sent several illustrious persons to the capital,[8] and obtained a primary school during the reign of Radama I. Like many villages in the south of the plain, it subsequently underwent a political eclipse under Ranavalona I and Ranavalona II, when the military chiefs, including the Prime Minister Rainilaiarivony in power between 1864 and 1895, favoured the northern part from which they stemmed. The site does not figure among the twelve sacred hills. Yet Andraisisa, overlooking the later site of Ankadivoribe lying closer to the rice fields, has all the characteris-

---

[7] Further details of this event are given: the servants carried round piastres, symbols of royalty (and more highly valued than cut silver) and pearls in order to buy rice. Refusing any payment, Andriandrivotra gave them seven baskets of ripe rice, seven baskets of green tender rice, and fourteen baskets of meat. The story has given rise to a number of sayings, including one that figures in the popular game of Fanorona: *Hany vary Andraisisa* (Andraisisa, the only place where rice is to be found).

[8] Notably Rabetrano, summoned by Ranavalona I to write a History of Madagascar.

tics of an ancient settlement surrounded by a ditch (*hadivory*), and is still marked by a very visible tomb. The *Firaketana* tells us that people regularly climbed the hill to practise a cult. It refers to them pejoratively as *mpanompo sampy* (idolators practising the cult of talismans).[9] Every festival of Alakaosy, they came in large numbers to address Ratsiseranina who was buried in the tomb.[10] The text, dating from December 1939, provides a useful land-mark in reconstructing the history of this cult.

Even so, we do not know whether the cult dedicated to Ratsiseranina is very old, whether the tomb was much frequented under the monarchy. After the official conversion of the Queen to Protestantism in 1869, local people insisted on demonstrating their loyalty to the monarch by mass attendance at the Protestant church. From then on, anyone frequenting the ancient tombs, labelled *vazimba* tombs (in effect, unknown ancestors and wild nature spirits were linked together and confused) attracted suspicions of paganism. The site does not figure among those listed by the LMS as providing refuges for clandestine and obscure rituals. All the sources agree on one point: Ratsiseranina had no direct descendant. This explains how, during the colonial period, the tomb could be seen as a 'public place' where anyone might come to pray without fear of appearing to seize hold of other people's ancestors.

The early years of the colonial period were difficult for the great families. The *Andriana*, very few in number, left the region following the general emancipation of the slaves in 1896 and migrated towards the Betsileo[11] where they hoped to restore their fortunes. They had long-standing ties there with the producers of *lambamena* whose merchandise they bought to sell in the capital. As a result, *hova* monopolise access to land, although their numbers from the

---

[9] For discussion of the talismans, fragments of wood protected by cloth, fragments of metal set into a horn encircled with a band of pearls, etc. . . see G. Berg, 1979, J.P. Domenichini, 1985.

[10] The ninth astrological month of the Malagasy year, Alakaosy, was both opposed and complementary to the first month, Alahamady, time of the royal fete. Alakaosy involved celebrations in honour of the popular *sampy*. Following the disappearance of the royal festival under colonization, the Alakaosy celebrations became a clandestine affair attracting many 'practitioners'. Today its importance has faded, save on the Ankaratra, on account of the revival of celebrations focused on Alahamady.

[11] Formerly, Andriamasinavalona had been established in the region by central authority. The only *andriana* still alive in 1970, we were told, was the wife of M. René Depuis who owned a large store at Tananarive.

outset included numerous officials, appointed to posts outside Imerina and awaiting comfortable retirement, while their rice fields are worked by share-croppers.

Focused on Ankadivoribe, this enquiry has a broader frame of reference, extending more than 5 or 6 kilometres beyond the village to take account of other cult localities situated just below the ridge of Ambohitraina and Ifandro. We shall return to their role later in this chapter. On account of their altitude they have no close connection with any rice lands. They are, moreover, frequented and guarded by *mainty*, that is to say, descendants of those who, prior to 1896, were slaves and royal servants. Designated *vazimba* cult places, they provide a negative point of reference for the *hova* of Ankadivoribe, a foil, as it were, against which they can elaborate the so-called 'royal' tomb of Andraisisa and its guardian.

1. *Traditional cult roles and their social devolution*

Here we must introduce the person central to the enquiry: Davidson R. A *hova*, *zanak'Andriampanarivo*, this man is well-known in the village on account of the public duty he performs. This is because at the time he held the *ody havandra* ('hail medicine'), a talisman to be found in every rice-producing region of the Highlands. The *ody* is a staff, which is brought out whenever hail threatens.[12] While his assistant pronounces the ritual incantation, Davidson holds out the staff threatening to puncture the heavens or, more exactly, the white cloud bringing the hail. Sole user of the *ody*, Davidson keeps it hidden in his tall brick house with its straw roof, situated below Ankadivoribe on a kind of mound in the middle of the rice fields. The place is known as Ambolomborona. However, his work also takes him above the village to the ancient site where the tomb of Ratsiseranina, oriented on a north-south axis, head to the north, shows through level with the surface of the earth, flanked by standing stones and a hearth.

His task is to stop rain waters flowing into the tomb by making sure that the clay surround that seals the stone border remains waterproof. The earth he uses for this purpose is held by all to be pure and precious because he fetches it from Ambohimanga, the ancient

---

[12] According to one elderly informant, whom we interviewed in 1990, 'the "conjuror" begins by showing his arse to God' (*misongoloka*), that is, to the sky, and works himself into a rage against the clouds.

capital and holy city to the north of the plain. Without it, holes would appear (*goaka ny fasana*) that will prevent the rain from falling. In this respect, we could compare the clay border to the wooden paling that surrounds tombs in many parts of Madagascar or to the concrete fence that often replaced it in Imerina in the late 1950s. Any rupture of the fence represents an attack on the sacrality of the place, and to the *andriana* buried there.[13] As everyone in the neighbourhood knows, this *andriana* gives rain to the land but may withold it if the inhabitants prove negligent. Catastrophic for the seasonal flooding of the rice fields upon which the harvests depend, such an eventuality may, however, interest the many brick makers in the plain, who, during the dry season from June to September, remove the damp surface soils of the rice fields and make bricks with earth taken from below, firing them in open air kilns that cannot function in the rains. In the taxis-brousse that run between here and the capital, the conflicting interests of these two occupations generate incessant speculation concerning changes in the weather and the ways in which certain parties can attempt by ritual means, at a local level, to bring about rain or drought. The brick makers are drawn from among *mainty*, while the owners of the rice fields are *hova* employing *mainty* share croppers. The antagonism of the two occupations is thus accompanied by a latent antagonism within the *mainty* milieu. As everyone acknowledges, Davidson holds in the *ody* and the tomb the two keys to climatic equilibrium and the rice harvests at Ankadivoribe. They also know that, on account of his symbolic means of intervention, Davidson also holds the play of social relations, relations of dominance on the part of the descendants of free men (the *fotsy*), and relations of domination in the case of the descendants of slaves (the *mainty*).

In 1970, Davidson's work could be roughly contrasted with another kind of activity in the service of men: that of Ral., known as *mpitaiza* or diviner-healer.[14] Living in Ankadivoribe, this old and almost blind man would accompany pilgrims wishing to go to the tomb, whose

---

[13] As Feeley-Harnik (1991) has shown in the case of Sakalava royal tombs, to reconstruct the fence that surrounds the tomb is to reconstruct the ancestors themselves.

[14] During the royal period, the term *mpitaiza* designated, in one of its senses, the tutor-counsellors of the princes (*mitaiza* = to protect). The term subsequently became more democratic, applying to the relationship between diviners-healers and their 'protégés'.

reputation extends far beyond the village, to the capital especially. After consultations in his house, he guides the supplicants to the tomb where he mediates on their behalf with the invisible world that he invokes. Possessed by Ravololona, a spirit identified with the ancient *sampy* (talisman) that was very powerful in these parts before 1868, he transmits the spirit's words, then treats his patients at his house with earth taken from the tomb[15] which they must swallow, mixed either with 'holy water' (*rano masina*), kept in bottles with labels indicating their origins, or with honey. At both tomb and house, he uses a plate containing water blessed by the addition of coins and pearls. The patients come because of family quarrels, physiological conditions that conventional doctors have been unable to treat, and, occasionally, infertility. Most often, they begin by consulting an urban diviner-healer, who, on the advice of royal spirits, recommends a pilgrimage to a tomb (historical or fictive), often accompanying the patient there.

Ral. represents his gifts as wholly personal, an opinion shared by the villagers we consulted in the market. He became *mpitaiza* in 1964. Having fallen ill, he consulted a *mpitaiza* who gave him a medicine from the ancestral pharmocopoeia, a *fanafody*, but forbade him to use it to care for anyone else. Pressed by his family circle, he had disobeyed and began to work as *mpitaiza* himself. So Ravololona made him blind but efficacious in the use of the gift. During consultations, he is shaken by the spirit who possesses and inspires him.

Davidson is opposed to Ral.'s activities because they take Ral. to the tomb, where 'he makes sacrifices with chickens, shedding blood at the tomb'.[16] Without doubt he is imploring the *Vazimba*, repulsive spirits, about whom Davidson as a good Christian will not speak. Thus, Davidson expels the *Vazimba* into the domain of devilish superstitions, associating himself, by contrast, with the holiness of kings and princes. Ral. for his part does not deny that Davidson's guardian-

---

[15] The earth is considered blessed, thus efficacious because sanctified by contact with the royal or princely remains.

[16] To back up his separation between pure and impure, Davidson cites the existence of an ancient ditch (*hadivory*) around Andraisisa as evidence that it was the original site of habitation, subsequently abandoned for Ankadivoribe. 'When Andrianampoinimerina passed through Ankadivoribe, he asked that a ditch be dug out around Andraisisa . . . "I understand why you hesitate," he said, "as there are no *fahavalo* (brigands) but the danger comes from you, that you might climb this hill and do forbidden things, bringing anger upon this *tany masina* (holy ground). We must protect the *hasina* of this hill."'

ship of the tomb is useful. He stresses the complementarity of his own work. He has received the gift to serve as a medium for the spirit of Ravololona. Possessed by his spirit, he is entitled to frequent the place where Ravololona has been hallowed over several centuries.

The fierceness of Davidson's remarks reveals a passionate contempt for Ral., a very poor *mainty*, who 'dishonours the royal cult' not only by his practices but also on account of his 'impure' nature as a man outside the community of free men. Only freemen, *hova* or *andriana*, are fit to practice a cult at the tomb. This belief is never stated overtly but is insinuated in conversation. He lets it be understood that the facts are already known by the speakers: no point then in talking of it. This view is not shared by all villagers, however. At market opinion is divided. Some think that the *mpitaiza* are charlatans who make money through their activities. Others cite cures obtained in their own families thanks to *mpitaiza*. 'I do not believe in *tapakazo*' ('pieces of wood', that is to say, quackery), they say, 'but the tombs of kings are sacred, they are holy places'. The most common view is that 'the tomb is for everyone' because it is so old and because no direct link can be traced between the inhabitants (*hova*) of the district and the person buried there. The problem appears to be that Ral., a familiar figure, practices on this ground. Even those villagers who are sympathetic to him recognise that, to make an invocation, it is better to go elsewhere. This kind of cult is possible provided that it is not practised where one lives and where one is known as a parishioner, be it Catholic or Protestant. Ral. therefore bothers some villagers because his activity takes place on communal ground.[17] In their eyes, the price to pay for full acceptance in parish life is, among other things, a separation in the localisation of practices *vis-à-vis* the world of invisible Malagasy protectors.

But our enquiries also uncover uneasiness about Davidson. There are more than slight differences between what the villagers tell us of him and how he presents himself. He presents himself as descended from a long line of tomb guardians, thus legitimizing his work by rooting it firmly in the past. The villagers, however, cannot remember whether Davidson descends from those once in charge of the local *sampy* or from the ancient guardians of the tombs.

---

[17] Some of them, quoting the aphorism 'A prophet is never recognised in his own country,' go to distant sites and *mpitaiza*. They prefer not to be observed by the village community.

2. *Selective amnesia and recycling scraps of history*

The situation is therefore paradoxical. The historical references are very numerous and are coupled to the villages or even to the tombs, making them places of memory. On the other hand, an old royal talisman is mentioned (on occasion) but its cult never localised. The families once supposed to have held the ritual functions are forgotten. Only the line of pastors survives, engraved on a plaque at the Protestant church. This place, situated at the heart of Merina history until at least the mid 19th century, and which even then continued to supply notables and elites, appears struck by amnesia regarding the rituals of times past. This trait, particularly marked at Ankadivoribe (we propose some hypotheses on this subject below), is widespread in Imerina, a region where history is invoked in all manner of contexts to legitimize arguments in socio-political disputes, a region where a deliberate, perhaps inevitable, amnesia pervades the question of politico-religious activities during the period prior to the conversion.[18] The novice researcher should be warned from the outset: oral enquiry at least in history will result only in disillusion. Historical documents and archaeology may allow us on occasion to reconstitute and reassemble elements, which, transformed long ago, first, by the royal conversion of 1869, then by colonization in 1895, came to provide carefully chosen props for new roles. Today these elements are set into rather different arrangements.

For a start, what became of the *sampy* Ravololona, mentioned by only one villager, other than Ral.? Is the forgetfulness on this subject deliberate? Or put on solely for the benefit of strangers to the village? It appears not. Only the most famous *sampy* of the kingdom (Kelimalaza, Ramahavaly) are still objects of reference in village memory. According to the *Tantara ny Andriana*, Ravololona, bequeathed to the inhabitants by *ranakandriana* spirits, that is to say, by Vazimba, who are held to be the first occupants of Imerina, was offered to King Ralambo as protector of the kingdom.[19] The King installed the *sampy* to the south of Ampandrana, that is, on the heights overlooking Ankadivoribe. 'It is old, many go there to consult it', say the *Tantara ny Andriana*, assembled after 1865. Prior to this, it is men-

---

[18] Cf. Babadzan, 1982, for a similar type of amnesia in French Polynesia, converted to Protestantism by the LMS. For the deliberate, indeed obligatory, character of the amnesia, see F. Raison-Jourde, 1991, pp. 625–626.

[19] *Tantara ny Andriana*, I, pp. 340–341.

tioned in the *History of Madagascar* collected by W. Ellis (1838, p. 413), who also refers to Randranovola and Randranomena, forgotten today. With the royal conversion to Protestantism in 1869 and the decision of local Malagasy authorities to break with the *sampy*, the *sampy* disappears, like all those of the south that were collected and collectively burned. P. Finaz, a Jesuit present at the time of their destruction, witnessed the trauma that the actions of the royal officers, charged with the 'auto-da-fé', caused amongst the population. As a result of this act of symbolic violence, comparable to those perpetrated in America by the conquistadors and missionaries several centuries earlier, the *sampy* was said to have been destroyed. Everyone hastened to the Protestant church, from fear of being suspected, or even (though in fewer numbers) to the Catholic church, the latter being an oblique and subtle way of signalling discontent. But, as Ral. the *mpitaiza*, puts it so well:

> the *sampy* were not destroyed, for what we hold is only the exterior manifestation (*famantara hita maso*, sign seen by eyes).[20] If they were to be destroyed a hundred times, a hundred times they can be reconstituted. For the spirits show themselves in dreams . . . I am a Protestant and I keep *ody* in my house. For me there is no contradiction. Both advise me of good things. People tell me: 'You cannot serve two masters'. I reply: 'The ways (*fomba*) of serving *Zanahary* are different but there is only one *Zanahary* (creator God). Malagasy who believe that their ancestors served the Devil's *sampy* are people colonized to their very core'.

Perhaps the *sampy* encompassed rain-making and hail prevention among its many functions, or perhaps not.[21] It has become impossible to know on account of the transfer of agrarian functions, held to be essential to the plain's survival, from the *sampy* (destroyed and forbidden on official orders) to the *ody havandra* (perceived as more trivial and harmless), that took place after 1869. The people hid these activities from the authorities, who in turn prefered to shut their eyes and say nothing to the missionaries. Perhaps the *andriana* enjoyed his reputation for rain-making for far longer, or perhaps the tomb, venerated for being contemporaneous with the period of

---

[20] It is very possible that this expression might be taken from the Catechism of the Sacraments in the Roman Catholic church!

[21] The *sampy* often had an agrarian base to which were added other powers, therapeutic, commercial, political, etc. . . .

transition from *vazimba* chiefs to the first *Andriana* kings, provided a new mooring for ritual concerning the rain?[22]

The reasons for the amnesia are therefore tied to the 'conversion' for which we possess very few autobiographical accounts, as though it were simply a mass phenomenon and hardly a matter of personal choice involving convictions.[23] While taking account of the official obliteration of the *sampy*, we can also see how this link has remained active in possession, albeit in an individual rather than collective capacity. Becoming possessed as he works as *mpitaiza*, Ral. 'raises up' the succession of keepers of the agricultural *sampy*, who in a state of possession once carried the *sampy* across the rice fields. This took place during the annual festival of Alakaosy, when the '*sampy* of the people', concerned with promoting fecondity and well-being (as distinct from the royal *sampy* with more political functions), were carried all around the countryside. The *sampy*, and possession as the proper means by which the *sampy* manifest themselves, are the elements that have been abandoned and are subject to Christian denial today. The same is true of the link to the *Vazimba*, spirits of the first occupants of the land. On account of the general adoption of Christianity, Imerina is the only region of Madagascar where these spirits, demonized, are the object of denial.

II. *The irresistible rise of Davidson, guardian of the tomb and holder of the hail talisman*

To situate Davidson better, we shall have to take a long detour, passing by way of witnesses from other groups or notables whose ancestors were rivals of his own.[24] The official archives of both the Jesuit mission and the French Protestant mission, immensely rich on the intense religious conflict that marked the year of General Gallieni's installation (1897), confirm their statements.[25]

---

[22] One probably could go to the tomb only in the most serious cases when drought held sway. In this case, a *volavita* cow (of royal colour, notably a cow with white markings on its head, back, tail, and feet) would be sacrificed at the tomb.

[23] On the contrary, we have very precise accounts of the minority conversion (resisted under Ranavalona I) of the first generation of Protestants during the first half of the 19th Century.

[24] I benefited in this rather delicate investigation from all the information recorded by R. Cabanes during the ten months he spent researching in Ankadivoribe with V. Raharimanana.

[25] The list of archives consulted is given in the appendix.

1. The tribulations of one notable hova *family from the royal period to colonization*

Davidson's father was a butcher at Tananarive. His mother was descended from an officer of the royal era who was Governor at Ankadivoribe until 1890 when he was ousted from the post by a competitor: Rabarijaona, son of Rainibarijaona, the Protestant pastor, himself son of the founder of the parish, Rainimiandrisoa, a wealthy merchant trading in *lamba* from the Betsileo and owner of many slaves.[26]

The eldest of Davidson's maternal great uncles saw in the arrival of the French troops an opportunity to change the local balance of power. He thus tried to oust Rabarijaona by denouncing him, together with his father the pastor, on a charge of concealing guns, which were then 'discovered' in their house after a search. The French officers soon realised that the affair had been motivated by jealousy, and Davidson's great uncle was imprisoned. In the meantime, however, the Jesuits were offered the Protestant church by the soldiers and, taking advantage of the confusion, installed their small Catholic community there. Terrorised by these two events, many of the *hova* Protestants left the village for good, hoping to make a new life in the Betsileo further south, towards Ambositra and Ihosy. Davidson's family also dispersed, but not before putting an association of descendants, the TeradRabetrano, in place around the tomb of Rabetrano[27] so as to be able to keep close links on the occasions of important ceremonies, burials and above all *famadihana* when corpses are removed from the collective tomb and rewrapped.

Shunted from side to side, and far from his natal village, Davidson was seven or eight years old when he left with his maternal aunt for Mananjary, where he attended primary school, before entering the regional school at Fianarantsoa and finally Le Myre de Vilers École supérieure. Appointed a state surveyor, he was posted to Tamatave on the East coast in 1922. Returning to Tananarive in 1928, he expressed no desire to live in the village. It was only on retiring after forty years in the service of the French administration that he returned to take charge of his family lands, previously deserted and cultivated by *mainty*. Purchasing land with his pension, by the start

---

[26] For the foundation of this Protestant church, see Raison-Jourde, 1991, pp. 547–549.

[27] This is situated at Andriampanarivo, in a different district than Andraisisa.

of the First Republic he had become one of the six largest land-
owners in Ankadivoribe.

Parallel to his recovery of land rights, he captured two ritual functions. First of all, he took charge of the *ody havandra*, the hail medicine, whose use appears never to have ceased and to have been
vested in his family for several generations. Until Davidson's return,
however, it had been held by his cousin, Ik., a poor countryman, a
descendant of the elder branch of the family. Several incidents and
setbacks recounted by villagers help to provide a rational explanation of the transfer.[28] One anecdote concerns the years 1948–49
when Davidson was working in the capital and visited the village
from time to time. Hail threatens. Ik. wants to use the *ody* but cannot
find the key to the room where it is kept. Hail destroys the crops.
The Deputy Mayor tells us of another incident sometime between 1950 and 1958. Ik. is widowed. After his wife's burial, he suddenly remembers that the *ody* should never come into proximity to
a corpse, then he discovers that it has disappeared. It is found again
several days later, stuck on the wall of the house opposite. Finally,
Davidson, having returned for good to the village, discovers one day
a sizeable hole in the surrounds of the tomb. Ik., bribed by the brick
makers, is held responsible. Davidson forbids him ever to climb to
the tomb again. He begins his work as tomb guardian at an initial
consecration in 1958, the year that the Malagasy Republic was pro-
claimed. It is very probable that until then the tomb had never had
a permanent guardian and that we are witnessing an 'invention of
tradition' that enables Davidson to present himself as inheriting a
long-standing tradition. The work is defined primarily in negative
terms: it involves defending the tomb against those who make holes
in the stone surround, and against those who profane the site. The
indesirables in the first category are identified with the faction of
brick makers, keen to see the rains delayed as long as possible so
that their industry can continue beyond late Autumn.

The second field in which Davidson defines his social utility involves

---

[28] The *ody* is efficacious only if one respects a number of *fady* (taboos). Vegetation
should not be taken from the rice-fields to the hills during the time between the
pricking out and the harvest. Neither sunshades nor umbrellas should be brought
into the rice-fields. One must not fire bricks in the interval between pricking out
and harvest. The cousin bakes bricks in an open air kiln. Discovering that those
at the centre of the furnace are insufficiently fired, he fires them again although
pricking out has begun.

defending the tomb against those who would profane it, notably, Ral. and the *mpanasina* who follows in his suit. He claims that they treat the tomb as a *vazimba* tomb, bringing red cocks, chickens whose throats they cut and whose feet they plant on sticks before the tomb. The royal cult, however, demands distinctive things, 'white rice, the grilled fat of a cattle hump, pure water',[29] that is to say, the kinds of offerings that once were made on the twelve sacred hills surrounding the capital, among which Ankadivoribe did not figure.

Finally, his guardianship of the tomb is held to be legitimated by hereditary transmission: generation after generation, our ancestors, he says, have been the *andriana*'s right hand. Not hesitating to make Ratsiseranina a woman, although several sources designate her as a man, and indulging in a sizeable 'ascending anachronism', he explains that the princess had no children (like the last three Merina queens) and that his own ancestor was 'her right arm'. Like Rainilaiarivony, he played the role of Prime Minister. Like him, he was husband to the childless Queen but had children by another woman. Thus, the function of tomb guardian is a heritage, like the site of Ampandroana, very close to the family home, where the Queen once bathed. Afterwards she would dry herself on a small island at the spot where his house stands today.[30]

2. *How the vocation of tomb guardian was born*

Davidson also describes himself as 'called' to a 'vocation', in this way countering Ral.'s 'gift'. His work is not simply functional; it has a place in the God-given destiny of the whole island. This mission has been revealed to him little by little. Hiding the misfortune suffered during the installation of colonial power, he reads the hand of Providence in a life, overturned, as we saw, by the arrest of his great-uncle and the dispersal of his family, viewing all its negative aspects in a positive light, reversing the severance he experienced as child. Raised in Mananjary by his mother's sister, he is told little of his ancestors. His father returns to Tananarive after a visit,

---

[29] It is not the *Vazimba*, he says, who are holy, but the kings. The *Vazimba* are not good, they kill and drown people. If Andraisisa had been inhabited by a *Vazimba*, neither Andriamasinavalona nor Andrianampoinimerina would have come there. Davidson either does not know or glosses over the fact that the tombs of historic *Vazimba* chiefs (at Anosisoa, near to Ambohimanga) were greatly honoured by the kings.

[30] An identical schema is to be found at Andranoro, near to Ambohimanarina.

announcing that he is not to be counted on (sub-text: to maintain the traditions, but ... which ones?). However the *masina* (literally, the saint, that is to say, the spirit of the prince or princess) wants to choose a member of the family to take over. 'The *masina* was always with me.' At twelve years of age, he believes he hears someone calling him, a shade speaking to him. 'But I cried as I did not understand.' The incident recalls the passage in Samuel, 1–31, describing how the very young prophet Samuel was called by Jehovah three times before he understood. Davidson, a Protestant who studies his Bible, is probably familiar with this passage. At Mananjary, people cooked eels and pork together. It turns out that he can eat neither this nor chicken. Eels are taboo to those who have a relationship with a spirit, whether recognised or still latent. Thus, a *fady* (taboo or prohibition) is revealed, a *fady* which Davidson subsequently keeps and which leads him to identify the spirit desiring to be known. The voice tells him that he is called to exercise an important responsibility. He can only reflect. 'I have had an European education,' he says, 'and it is despite myself that I have done a complete turnabout'.

Returning to Tananarive in 1928, he loses two sons within two months and then falls ill himself. An Andriamasinavalona (noble) from Ambohitrandriamanitra, to the east of the plain, a hill that is well known for its ancient and unbroken links with the spirits, is called. By then, the patient is on extended sick leave and knows that he suffers from albumin. 'All those with this illness are dead'. As a result of the consultation, eels are declared *fady*, and Davidson learns that one of his own ancestors, a great *masina*, 'lives' in him *(mipetraka)*. It is then, he says, that he decides to devote himself to guarding Andraisisa. His health improves, a son is born. But the administration offers him a post at Maroantsetra in keeping with the 'coastal tour' required of bureaucrats during the colonial period. An ordinary event in the life of a surveyor, this appears to Davidson to be invested with supernatural meaning because it will take him to the place where his ancestors arrived in Madagascar. He will retrace their steps as a kind of ritual initiation while working as a surveyor. 'Such is the *razana*'s wish.' He will also discover Ambohidratrimo Anala ('where the ancestors halted') after leaving Maroantsetra, then Ambatomirahavavy 'where they found the land too restricted'. God wished to lead them further, to the region of Ampandrana, cradle of the royal dynasty, at the gates of Ankadivoribe.

He passes over the twenty odd years he spent in the capital without taking any initiative in his natal village but dwells on his subsequent consecration following his retirement in 1958. With all the family present, he asks the *masina* to give a sign that he is 'chosen'. On the eve of the ceremony, the great stone that stands at the head of the tomb is found toppled. 'The ancestors were asking that I set it up again.' Plenty of *toaka* (local alcohol) is drunk at the celebration.

3. *Some suggestions for deciphering this account*

Davidson's account can be deciphered from three angles: the call and his response, the journey, required by his career, which becomes a passage of initiation, and his insistence on the distinction between royal cult and *vazimba* cult.

The call matches numerous accounts collected among Merina *mpitaiza*. Davidson speaks of voices heard, of signs given, followed by sickness, as stages leading to the revelation of ancestral spirit. He never mentions possession. He classes himself with people inspired by an interior force, by dreams whose practice involves a higher, more purified relationship with ancestral spirits,[31] in contrast to that of Ral. His own initiation involves no agitation, no noise; the body is not privileged.[32] It is to be noted that, while the consultation of 1928 confirmed that a spirit lived in him, he changed nothing in his life,

---

[31] The *Tantara* (I, 338) distinguish possession, which characterizes the people's relationship to the supernatural, from dreams or interior inspiration, which characterize the *ombiasy*, guardians of the royal talismans, that is to say, the diviners who advise royalty.

[32] As historical research shows, this distinction is bound up with the kind of knowledge favoured by the school and the Protestant church, both places where literacy is essential and where the body is totally mastered. Although I share P. Larson's (1997) view that Merina from various social backgrounds took an interest in missionary efforts from the outset, and sought to assimilate aspects that interested them, I think that he underestimates the submission of subjects to royal power in this matter. Moreover, I consider the break between a culture based on literacy and culture based on orality, which became more pronounced throughout the 19th century under the impetus of several missions, to be important. Myths, oratorical contests in the form of *hainteny*, funerary songs exalting sexuality were largely downplayed, above all by the LMS, in contrast to proverbs, which were instrumentalised. From the very first generation, the literate were careful to cultivate and elevate the art of writing. Thus, P. Rainitsiheva, leader within the first congregation at Tananarive, condemned claims made by Rainitsiandavana, guardian of a *sampy* who had converted to Christianity, to preach on biblical passages that he knew by heart and to prophesy with the help of the Holy Spirit, by the intermediary of his *sampy*. These two antithetical figures prefigure Davidson and Ral.

other than respecting a food taboo. Leaving for Maroantsetra, even his family have the impression that he is going away for good. He assumes his functions thirty years later, in 1958, when retirement not only makes the transition convenient but very likely stimulates a desire for self-affirmation and public recognition.

At the time, this required political functions: to be a local PSD official (the party of President Tsiranana), to be mayor. Davidson's long absence made this difficult. Cultural innovation seemed a more certain route, given that the *ody havandra* is already in the family. It was precisely during the years 1956–60 that cults based on the royal tombs of Imerina began to spread openly. Linked with the protection of agricultural activities, taking charge of a tomb can be presented as a service to the community, even if it is a form of individualised social climbing. The poorest villagers say that he never comes to collect their subscriptions (in rice) to support the work of the *ody havandra*. From this, they infer that it helps to have a rich man in the job.

Davidson himself talks as though education and wealth counted for little in recruiting the guardian. 'One is either called by the ancestors or not.' But he counts the wealth he acquired while working for the state, the purchase he has made of rice fields and the successful restoration of the tomb, as proof of God's blessing. 'I have lands at Ankadivoribe, a great plot at Ankadikely from my mother, Ambatolampy also belongs to me along with rice fields at Ampandroana, making 700 square metres in all. This proves that if one is held in regard by an ancestor, he helps you in life. In return, the wise should become head of the family [to employ a euphemism, for he had in fact 'taken over' from his poor cousin]. A person who practices the cult of the ancestors can be recognised by the interest he shows in agriculture, in the land . . . My aim is to develop my *tanindrazana* (ancestral land). This is my vocation'.

The way of the ancestors
Called from his childhood, confirmed in his ritual functions by lasting wealth, Davidson broadens our vision by linking the chance journeys of his career to the paths taken by the ancestors who first disembarked on the coasts.

> It is stupid to say (like foreign historians) that the people of Malaysia departed without purpose. They were destined by God to come here. Did they simply leave to go on an excursion carrying their *farantsa*

(piastres) with them? Their ship was not wrecked. They built it solidly for they expected to return home. 'But God subsequently guided them through the outlying points of the coast. 'He compelled the king to the place where he might establish his kingdom over the whole island, that is to say, to the centre of the land (*ka dia nentiny ho aty ampovoan-tany izy*).

Thus, Davidson has been guided 'without any doubt' by God to retrace the steps of the migrant Princes towards the Centre from where they could, according to God's will, dominate the princes of the four cardinal points. Taking up the theme of the journey of the Hebrews to the Holy Land, the story undergoes malgachisation: what is at stake is the domination of the whole island according to a very old geo-political schema that holds that the prince of the centre is called to dominate the others.[33]

Davidson rebels against Grandidier, Malzac and all the other European authors who invoke hypothetical shipwrecks in order to explain the arrival of 'Asiatic' immigrants. This hypothesis, according to him, had been repeated by a local man, a certain Rabenjamina, who had surely read these European authors and erroneously accepted what they said.[34] Davidson's discourse, shored up by very few arguments, provides for a historical reconstruction whereby the Merina rediscover a dominant role and can again count on Providence to guide their steps as in the past: it bears the hallmark of a discourse elaborated in the years following Independence.

Silence on immediate ascendants

By anchoring his career in the Merina 'myth of origin', Davidson is able to mask the paucity of detail concerning his own ancestors. He never refers to the painful incidents which brought about the denunciation of the pastor to the French by one of his ancestors. He mentions his father on several occasions, without going further

---

[33] Cf. J.C. Hébert, 'La cosmographie ancienne malgache, suivie de l'énumération des points cardinaux et l'importance du nord-est', *Taloha*, 1965, 1, pp. 83–195. This schema of Indonesian origin is also found in the identification of the Andriambahoaka sovereign, of Itasy, as king of the centre, as well as in that of Ibonia, hero of the principal myth of sovereignty of the Highlands (cf. P. Ottino, 1978).

[34] This probably refers to Rabenjamina Androvakely, a man from south of Tananarive who is known for his mastery of oral history. Davidson is familiar with western hypotheses on the Asiatic origin of the Malagasy on account of his time at the regional school. History was no longer taught in primary school following the discovery of the VVS plot in 1915.

back, while other sources in the village provide names for several ancestors, all royal officals, on the paternal side. To the question of what was the name of your great ancestor (contemporary of Ratsiseranina) he replies: ' I do not remember, I do not know' (*tsy tadidiko intsony izany, ary tsy fantatro*). He acknowledges that he cannot be buried in the tomb at Andraisisa for 'we are not descended from *andriana*.' 'When the Queen [Ratsiseranina] died, this great ancestor took her piastres, money brought by her father from Malaysia, for it is not by chance, in journeying around, that he arrived at Maroantsetra but he was brought here by God. The piastres are used to make a silver canoe in which Ratsiseranina is buried'.

This providential discourse clears away another difficulty: the land where the tomb is situated appears not to have belonged to the family. Under colonization it was state land, where people went to celebrate the children's festival, launched by Gallieni, the last occasion being in 1949. The Protestant school also celebrated its anniversary there. At these times, a temporary barrier was put around the tomb to stop participants trampling upon it. For the tomb to be considered part of Davidson's patrimony, the villagers' tacit accord at least is still required. Davidson has sought to register the land in his name, bringing him into dispute with a certain Ranj. who had been recognised as the owner. The seemingly insoluble character of the conflict resulted in the whole hill being attributed to the State. But when hail and violent winds struck Ankadivoribe three years later, the *fokonolona*, acknowledging an 'error' had been made, demanded that the tribunal restore the land to its 'rightful' owners. A fresh enquiry of the land tribunal decides to attribute the land to Ranj. and the tomb to Davidson.[35] In short, it is very likely that the tomb was not maintained prior to the late 1950s. In making this innovation, Davidson invents a tradition that simultaneously offers reassurance to the villagers and proves vital in ratifying his own status as a notable. The new cult finds acceptance because it reinforces a Malagasy identity without breaking with the Christian cult.

---

[35] Enquiries at the Land Registry have had little success so far. The archives of the travelling land tribunal are difficult to track down.

III. *Installation of an ancestral village cult, ritual disqualification of the* mainty

1. *Some identical critiques on the subject of Christianity*

How does Davidson reconcile his responsibility with his status as communicant at the Protestant church and as *diakona* (deacon) elected by fellow communicants? He argues passionately:

> Christians who believe that in honouring the ancestors, one is committing sin, are all mistaken. The ancestors are neither *sampy* nor *Vazimba* but saints. Are European saints considered to be *sampy*? No, certainly not. Saint Joseph was a living being like us. . . . Everywhere God has created man.

One notes that Davidson avoids invoking Protestantism, which condemns the customs tied to the tomb. He draws on the cult of saints, these mediators analogous to the ancestors, who find a place in Catholicism:

> The ancestors are not Andriamanitra but they find favour with God. The ancestors helped me to become better, thus a better Christian. It is the colonizers who put the idea into our heads (and it was very obvious) that only their *razana* (ancestors) were to be respected and ours to be rejected. If God created humankind, he must also have created the Malagasy. Therefore he has also created Malagasy saints . . . I, Davidson, I have been told that Saint Davidson, who was English or American, protects me.[36] I do not believe this at all. It is my own ancestors who protect me.

Thus, blessing follows inevitably the flow of life from generation to generation. It is reserved for descendants, that is to say, all those whose remains are collected on the shelves of the ancestral stone tomb. Vision typically *hova*:

> Saint Alfred and the European saints will never sustain us but they will sustain their own descendants first of all. Therefore they are not made for everyone. But we have our own saints who should also be respected. All the saints of humankind are alike, but if we do not begin by honouring our own, no-one will honour them. People who say that the Malagasy saints are *sampy* ('idols') do not know what they are talking about.

---

[36] Ironically, Davidson is the namesake of a LMS missionary whom he assimilates to a patron saint on the Catholic model.

Ral. holds almost identical views on what seems to him to be the excessive symbolic imposition of strangers. He too argues from within a self-ascribed Christian identity, while wishing to modify the terms that oppose his Malagasyness. His prayers are more closely modelled on those heard in Catholic churches. He receives us at home with a prayer addressed on our behalf to the north-east corner of the room (the corner to which prayers to the ancestors are made), but addressed to Andriamanitra, the Christian God. 'Finding ourselves here, in this house of sinners, we thank you with all our heart. . . ., with all our soul. We trust in your eternal kingdom.' Also he denies praying to *Vazimba* and becomes ironic on the very superficial understanding Europeans have of the *sampy*. 'The sampy were not destroyed (when burned as in 1869), for what we hold is only a visible sign'. He talks of the ancestors as saints, using a language very like Davidson's:

> I should like to agree that the foreign *masina* are God's *masina*. But that does not mean that my *masina* are not intermediaries between men and God. God is the creator of the whole universe and if there are saints, it is thanks to Him. This is why one says: God the holy of holies and the king of kings. If I climb to Andraisisa, it is to come closer to my ancestors who are the intermediaries between God and myself. I do not renounce the saints of the Church. I accept that they are saints but no more do renounce the holiness of my own saints.

He invokes exactly the same reasoning concerning the universality of saints (Malagasy and European) for a second time in connection with the *masina* buried at Andraisisa. He does not understand the appropriation of the tomb:

> It is not good. The *masina* (saints) belong to all men just as do those of the church. Davidson has no right to forbid people to go to the tomb. He is jealous of me, claiming that I practice the *fanompoan-tsampy* (the cult of idols), whereas I myself have seen him with chickens and even a red cock. He does the same as me (that is to say, a cult in *vazimba* style).

As for his own activities, Ral. presents an interesting account. 'You can go completely alone to Andraisisa, he explains, but if you wish to communicate directly with the *masina*, you have to go and see me or another, those of us who are possesssed by the *masina*.' Likewise, when *mpanasina* come to fetch earth from the tomb, they receive it from the *mpitaiza*, whose 'hand, belonging to one in whom the saint dwells, can bestow a certain life upon the earth for you to use at home'.

The separation between the two men can be understood in the terms of the cleavage noted by the *Tantara* between *Alahamady* and *Alakaosy*, between royal and popular *sampy*, between inspiration or dream and possession. Interested in his own power, Davidson creates a great gulf between the practices that are in fact very close. He never stops discrediting the ritual status of a man whose lowly origins he calls into question.

2. *The breach: keeper of the* hova *tomb and* mainty *diviner-healers of public* doany *cult*

Davidson insists upon the opposition between the *vazimba* cult and the royal cult. 'It should not be thought that the ancestor buried there is a *Vazimba*,' he repeats, 'this holy place is not like the others where *vazimba* cults are celebrated'. Here he is alluding to ten or so sites close by, evidently known to him though he claims never to frequent them. When finding out how to guard the tomb, he did not consult the guardians of these places, some of whom were probably already in place or in the process of installation but travelled to Merimanjaka to ask its elderly guardian for advice.[37] The latter is famous for its sacred pool in which, according to tradition, the viscera of Queen Rafohy were immersed and from which the holy water used in the circumcision of princes was subsequently drawn. No doubt he also gathered information at Ambohijanaka, a nearby village, where the tombs of the *andriana*, surmounted by *trano manara*, a privilege reserved for nobility of the highest rank, must be maintained with great care. Should a hole appear in the roof, the rain will not fall. These are the people of Alasora who, according to the tradition recorded in the *Tantara*, alone were skilled at this work. In the absence of a *trano manara* on the tomb, Davidson transposed the problem onto the clay sealing the surround.

From now on he fetches soil from Ambohimanga, the most prestigious of places. He claims never to sacrifice chicken, or to make invocations to *Vazimba*. This is somewhat paradoxical since Rangita,

---

[37] She always uses sand taken from under the water because it has not been polluted. She tells him 'The gaps in the tomb are best plugged with soil taken from the edge of an abyss where people never walk.'

Ratsiseranina's sister, and Rafohy are referred to as *Vazimba* princesses of the dynasty. In them a cult to royal *and vazimba* spirits might be merged. But Davidson insists upon their complete separation in order to affirm that in all other respects he is a true Christian. Bowing to foreign missionaries, the *Vazimba*, spirits of the land, the water, plants and trees, also unknown ancestral spirits associated with unidentified tombs, are designated as evil spirits, subjects of idolatrous cults. Demonised, they cannot be invoked. To recognise them is to be revealed as adhering to superstition. Consequently, their rejection must be constantly and brutally reaffirmed so as to promote the royal cult as the true cult, pure and legitimate. But the hostility is also directed at the person of Ral. and the pilgrims he accompanies to the tomb. Just as the identity of *Vazimba* is ill defined, so Ral. is a landless *mainty* whose social respectability is doubtful. Owning no property, he is suspected of trading on the cult.

The remarks Ral. in turn makes about Davidson and his role are very restrained. He does not attack him: he complains only of being misunderstood. Curiously, their histories share much in common: the experience of sickness, the calling of a spirit to whom they become bound, but they then diverge to the point where the two men turn their backs on one another. The one, possessed by a demonized spirit, in theory, chased from the Christian world of Imerina, looks after people of modest means, many of whom are strangers to the village, coming from the capital, for example. In attracting this broad clientele, Ral. wants to make the site into what is known as a *doanimbahoaka*. Borrowed from the Sakalava, *doany* is the term currently used to designate a cult-place; *vahoaka* designates a public cult, open to all, as when one speaks of a state school. In fact, many of the cults of the royal period were restricted, being forbidden to slaves. This was the case for Andranoro, for the tomb of Andriambodilova or Anosimanjaka, to the north of Antananarivo. In the latter case, President Tsiranana intervened in financing alterations to the tomb of Ranavalonatsimitovy and in exchange asked for it to be opened to *mainty*.

Inspired by an 'ancestor,' Ratsiseranina's fictive 'spouse,' Davidson has established a kind of monopoly over the tomb, delights in his worthy role, makes 'the rain and fine weather', and is determined to chase out intruders. A series of anecdotes, conferring a certain reputation on the sites, helps him in this end. After bathing at Ampandroana, Ratsiseranina used to climb the hill to dry herself, which accordingly became a holy hill. Her servants (*mpanompo*) could not go there without risking death. Today, these sacred powers still operate in the land. The proof is that in 1929 or 1930, a certain Raini.climbed the hill, drawn by the dazzle of pieces of silver, and died upon coming down. In 1965, Rakoton., from below the village, having also climbed up, became very weak, with his mouth pulled to one side, behaving as though he had had a stroke. People had to come searching for him. The tomb is in effect the means by which Davidson mediates his relations with the villagers. He is not concerned with people from outside the village. They can go to the 'Devil'.

And where might this be? Looking at the pattern of settlement in the region, the sites seem to form a staircase, according to their relative age. Theoretically, Ambohitraina is the most ancient site. From there the settlers descended to Mangabe, half-way down, before reaching the valley bottoms, where they settled at Andraisisa and Ankadivoribe. The location enjoyed by Ankadivoribe is rather similar to that of Anosimanjaka, in the northern part of the plain. It is fine rice-producing land, accessible by dykes, difficult to reach at times in the rainy season when partly under water. The battle over the tombs has taken place here because it is situated at the level of rice. Higher up, the ancient sites have been abandoned. Although some have tombs which represent the 'sources' of the dynasty, they are cut off from the rice fields. They attract *mainty* to the extent that these, doing battle with their *hova* owners, marginalised economically and socially, are also ousted from the cults of the plain that the latter jealously guard. In effect, they have little choice but to go to the *doany* which, maintained by *mainty* guardians installed in the late 1950s, have become *doanimbahoaka*. These are all located in the hills on the right bank of the Sisaony, along the western and southern slopes of Ambohitraina and on the northern slope of Ifandro. Situated well above the rice fields, at an altitude of around 1600 m, and accessible only on foot, this zone, where contraband *toaka* (local rum) was manufactured, where the Menalamba rebels once used the network of little paths and short cuts, constitutes a kind of refuge for a cult based on *sampy* which hides under other names. It is to this hinterland that Davidson intends to drive Ral. and his clients, far from the ricelands and the tomb. To drive them in the first instance from the hill, towards Ambohimasimbola, reckoned by villagers to be the seat of *sampy* Rafanenitra (the *doany* is protected in

the middle of a wood), towards the site half-way up the hill where
Rafaramahery, sister of the siren Ranoro who lived in the northern
of the plain, is installed, and on to Andranoro, where Rabesatroka
(the man with the big hat) lives.[38]

3. *Twenty years on: yet another historical bricolage*

What had happened twenty years later? Did Davidson succeed in
restricting the tomb cult to the people of Ankadivoribe and more
precisely to *fotsy*? Did the *mainty* give way to his objurgations? Had
the pilgrims from elsewhere disappeared?

In 1991, the hegemony of the *hova* groups was still pronounced.
Six families owned at least three-quarters of the land. They considered that they alone controlled the district. Very distrustful of outsiders, other than their own descendants who arrived each weekend
to attend the Church service and returned to the town carrying pro-
visions, they were blocking repairs to the two secondary roads. The
mainty and the poor *hova* seek emancipation but lack the necessary
means. It requires regular contact with the capital to sell market
garden produce or the ability to arrange for one's children to be
educated to a good level. The owners support the *Sakelimihoajoro* association[39] which sprang up among *hova* in response to the associations
that formed among *andriana* of the plain, according to the different
hills of their origin. The *andriana*, with the wind in their sails, seize
the slightest opportunity to draw attention to their ancient role,
emphasizing their particular aptitude to manage the common good
on account of the close ties they held to the sovereigns and their
personal heritage of *hasina*. Suddenly, one of the few most prestigious notables originating in the village but living in the capital and
good professionals, judges that the moment has come to erect a
trano manara on his family tomb and declare himself Andriamasinavalona. Everyone knows that he is not entitled to do this but nothing is said. It is easier to forbid the hill of Andraisisa to the *mainty*

---

[38] If Rafanenitra is described by the people of Ankadivoribe as *sampy*, Rabesatroka
seems to me to be a mythical *Vazimba*. Twenty years later, both of them have been
transformed into princes by members of these cults, at the cost of historical accu-
racy on account of the condemnation of *Vazimba* that still exists today.

[39] This movement, inaugurated by Ramelison Désiré, known as Ngovitra, a well-
known diviner in the Ankazobe region, has spread to Imerina and the Vakinankaratra.
Organizing marches and demonstrations of strength, replete with fascist-style ges-
tures, and providing a channel for the distribution of very cheap rice, it was among
the supporters of D. Ratsiraka during the presidential elections of 1989.

than to tell a powerful *hova* that he is making a fool of himself. The climate of suspicion in a disunited *fokonolona* is obvious, tales of sorcery incessant.

The cult of Andraisisa is more jealously guarded than ever. Although still presented as vital to the prosperity of the region, it has become a strictly family affair. The tomb regulates the rain; the *ody havandra*, the hail. Davidson and Ral. are dead, but the former transmitted his dual functions to his son. The son, who spent almost 12 years away studying in the USSR, returning with a diploma in engineering, now performs the rites. His sister, educated by the Sisters of Cluny, plays the role of well-to-do farmer. Around Ankadivoribe cult places have proliferated, as the map drawn by Thomas Solondraibe shows. They are visited by *mpitaiza mainty* and their clients, of whom a high proportion are also *mainty*. For Davidson's descendants, the task of assuring their identity in the midst of the *fotsy* is more imperative than ever. The *hova* are closing ranks on account of their rivalry with the *andriana*, who are reconstructing their genealogies and their networks of control and staging an increasing number of picnics on the sacred places of the plain.

The importance of the *fady* (taboo) on goats at Ankadivoribe is now impressed upon us. This is a new development, never mentioned in 1970; there had been a goat-pen at Ampahitrosy, to judge by the toponymy. The *fady* suggests, informants explain, that Ankadivoribe was once a royal site.[40] They are certain that Davidson's lineage is 'noble' (*tena fianakaviana andriana*), because, they argue, the family has charge of the tomb. A retired state inspector explains to us that '*Andevo* (slaves, sic) cannot climb to the tomb because an *andriana* is buried there and in the past the place was restricted to *fotsy* for the *fanasinana* (cult)'. But this elderly man knows full well that the guardian is not *andriana*. The sister of Queen Rangita, Ratsiseranina, married a *hova* and thereby lost her rank (*nandrorana izy*), he says. Davidson may be her descendant but it is also said that she had no children, in which case he would be descended from a *hova* of her retinue, that is, a man without noble blood.

The greatest surprise comes from Davidson's daughter: H. Ras. According to her, the site of Andraisisa dates back two hundred years. Ratsiseranina is presented as a noblewoman, Andriamasinavalona (thus

---

[40] Cf. J.P. Domenichini 'La chèvre et le pouvoir. Première approche historienne d'un interdit', *Omaly sy Anio*, (January–June 1979) 9: 79–126.

assuring with the greatest clarity the break with *vazimba* identity
while situating prestigiously her descendants since there are a fair
number of Andriamasinavalona among the leaders of the political
class today). As a result, she must make the tomb younger than it
is. Ratsiseranina would have had two brothers, Andriampanarivo
being one. Their descendants are buried at Ambohimanga (2nd to
4th generation), at Andraisisa at the 5th generation (4 adults, including Andriampanarivo, and one child are buried there). Davidson,
the retired surveyor, figures in the 7th generation. 'We are the children of this man'. The problem appears no longer one of distanc-
ing themselves from a *mpitaiza mainty* but of supplying a genealogy
to support their claim to be of *andriana* origin, thus breaking with
the *hova* mass—at a time when *andrianité* confers prestige. She also
knows what objects accompany *andriana* to the tomb: a *valiha* (bamboo zither), a small silver chair, and a silver canoe. This is all the
more surprising as no *famadihana*[41] appears to have taken place.

The objects listed as buried in the tomb of Andraisisa accentuate
the classification of Davidson's descendants as *andriana*. The *ody havandra* is closely linked to the tomb for, we are now told, it derives from
Rakotovohitra, Ratsiseranina's other brother, and was brought from
Ambohimanga or more precisely from the nearby magical forest of
Andringitra. 'When some *hova* wanted to use this *ody*, it refused to
work. They therefore gave it to our ancestor who brought it here. It
is an *ody havandra* of *andriana*'. As for the tomb, no rituals properly
speaking are carried out because 'that would attract blame (*tsiny*). We
just stick to cleaning, maintaining the land, and to asking for rain.
Andraisisa is absolutely vital to people's agricultural lives'. Other kinds
of request are ruled out in principle, turned away to the numerous
sanctuaries in the neighbourhood dedicated to Andriamandazoala,
the Sakalava king, to Rafaramahery, Rakotomaditra, etc . . . to so-
called *vazimba* sanctuaries where the *mainty* go en masse. Ankadivoribe
is proud of its specificity. Only Davidson's descendants are entitled
to care for the tomb, ensuring that rain will come. His daughter
puts it strongly: 'The people depend upon his descendants to sanc-
tify the ancestor' (*no teren'ny vahoaka hanasina eny*). She adds: 'We have
inherited the power to go to Andraisisa'.

---

[41] The *famadihana*, rewrapping of the mortal remains in silk cloth, involves opening the tomb, making it possible to know what objects were once deposed to accompany the dead.

In conclusion, Ankadivoribe, rich rice-producing lands, dissociates itself from the cults on the heights of Ambohitraina overlooking the plain. To be sure, anyone is free to go there in their individual capacity but, as far as the rice fields are concerned, symbolic mastery of the water and climate is managed locally. The village presents a striking example of the seizure of the mediation between heaven and earth by a club of comfortable land-owners for whom the past serves as a straightforward tool to promote their own interests. Floating elements of historical accounts are used at every opportunity to legitimize very pronounced socio-economic differentials and discriminatory status differences.

A tomb provides a point of anchor for these narratives, as so often happens when relations between a community and land are involved. Davidson knew how to seize the appropriate historical moment for a cultural restoration. His descendants have survived the Second Republic without mishap, shrugging off the Marxist preoccupations of the regime, which says a great deal about the latter's artificial character. Two steps from the capital, in a world turned in on itself to an astonishing degree, possession is a 'democratic' issue, allowing ordinary people to rub shoulders with people born in the town or originating on the coast but resident in Imerina, thus transcending social divisions based on status or distinctions of wealth. Possession enables social minorities like Ral. to speak and to have some chance at last of being heard.

SOURCES

Archives

Archives Nationales, Section d'Outre-Mer. Aix-en-Provence (ANSOM): Série F (Cultes):

- –F 2:   Culte catholique, 1857–1938.
- –F 6:   Constitutions de temples, 1902–1925.
- –F 124: Correspondances de militaires avec Gallieni au sujet des querelles entre catholiques et protestants, 1897–1898.

Archives des Missions Évangeliques, Paris (DEFAP): Correspondances entre B. Escande et le général Gallieni, 1895–1897.
Archives historiques de l'Archevêché, Ambatoroka, Tananarive (ATAH): Diary of P. Finaz, n° 23. L'autodafé des *sampy*, letter from P. Jouen, C48^c, 20 September 1869.

BIBLIOGRAPHY

Anonymous
1935–1967   *Firaketana ny fiteny sy ny zavatra malagasy*,[42] Tananarive.

Babadzan, A.
1982   *Naissance d'une tradition: changement culturel et syncrétisme religieux aux îles Australes (Polynésie française)*, Paris, ORSTOM, Travaux et Documents 154, 313 p.

Berg, G.
1979   'Royal authority and the protector system in nineteenth century Imerina,' in R. Kent (ed.) *Madagascar in History*. Albany, Foundation for Malagasy Studies, pp. 102–122.

Bloch, M.
1968   'Tombs and conservatism among the Merina of Madagascar,' *Man*, 3 (1): 94–104.
1991   *Prey into Hunter. The Politics of Religious Experience*. Cambridge, Cambridge University Press, 117 p.

Brown, P.
1984   *Le culte des saints. Son essor et sa fonction dans la chrétienté latine*. Paris, Le Cerf, 184 p.

Cabanes, R.
1972   'Les cultes de possession dans la plaine de Tananarive,' *Cahiers du Centre d'Étude des Coutumes*, Faculté de Droit et Sciences Économiques, Tananarive, 9: 33–66.

Callet, F.
1953 to 1978   *Histoire des rois d'Imerina*, translation by G.S. Chapus and E. Ratsimba, Académie Malgache, Tananarive, 5 volumes.

Domenichini, J.-P.
1985   *Les dieux au service des rois*. Paris, CNRS, 718 p.

Ellis, W.
1838   *History of Madagascar*. London, 2 volumes. 517 and 537 p.

Feeley-Harnik, G.
1991   *A Green Estate. Restoring Independence in Madagascar*. Washington, Smithsonian Institution Press, 627 p.

Feierman, S.
1990   'Peasant intellectuals. Anthropology and History in Tanzania.' University of Wisconsin Press, 340 p.

Halbwachs, M.
1971   *La topographie légendaire des Évangiles en Terre Sainte. Étude d'une mémoire collective*. Paris, PUF, 171 p.

Hobsbawm, E. and T. Ranger (eds.)
1983   *The Invention of Tradition*. Cambridge, Cambridge University Press, 320 p.

Larson, P.
1997   '"Capacities and modes of thinking": intellectual engagements and subaltern hegemony in the early history of Malagasy Christianity,' *The American Historical Review*, 102 (October) 4: 969–1002.

---

[42] Begun in 1935 by a committee which included notably Ravelojaona and Rajaonah, this encyclopaedia of language and history stops at the start of the letter 'M'.

Ottino, P.
    1978   'La mythologie malgache des Hautes Terres. Le cycle des Andriambahoaka,' in *Dictionnaire des Mythologies*. Paris, Flammarion, II, pp. 30–45.
Raison-Jourde, F. (ed.)
    1983   *Les souverains de Madagascar*. Paris, Karthala, 476 p.
Raison-Jourde F.
    1989–1990 'Individualisation sociale et production d'identités dans la société merina au XIXe siècle,' *Omaly sy Anio*, 29–32: 173–187.
    1991   *Bible et pouvoir à Madagascar au XIXe siècle. Invention d'une identité chrétienne et construction de l'État*. Paris, Karthala, 840 p.
Rakotomalala, M. Raison, F. Blanchy, S.
    1999 (sous-presse) La légende dorée des ancêtres. Modes d'enracinement et invention sociale en Imerina. (Madagascar). Paris, l'Harmattan, 360 p.
Savaron, C.
    1928   'Contribution à l'histoire de l'Imerina,' *Bulletin de l'Académie Malgache*, n.s., 11: 61–81.
    1933   'Note sur les tombeaux royaux merina (Alasora et Imerimanjaka),' *Bulletin de l'Académie Malgache*, 16.
Vincent, J.-F., Dory, D., Verdier, R. (eds.)
    1995   *La construction religieuse du territoire*. Paris, L'Harmattan, 379 p.

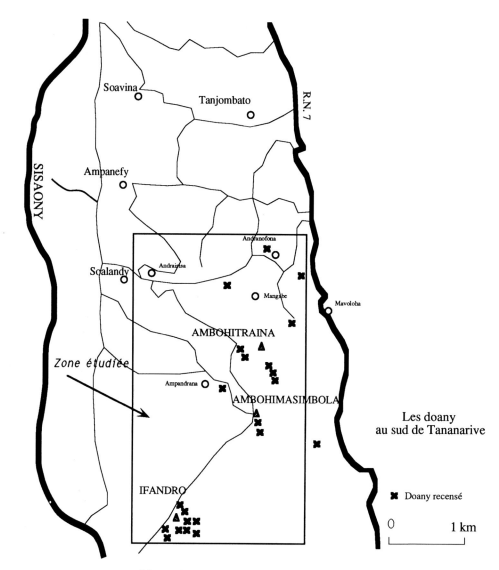

Map 5. *Doany* in the region south of Tananarive

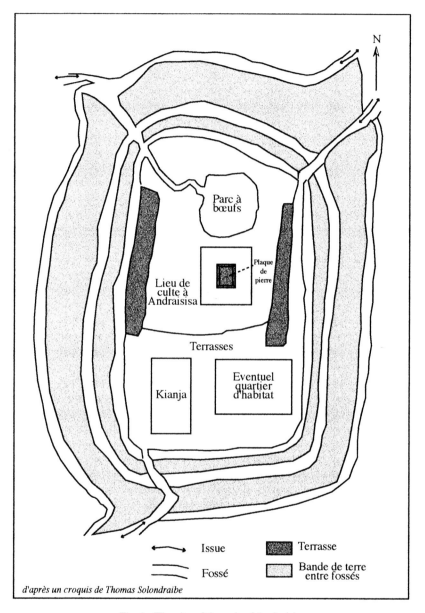

Fig. 3. The site of the cult of Andraisisa

Plate 11. The tomb of Ratsiseranina at Andraisisa. Photograph: Françoise Raison-Jourde.

Plate 12. Landscape of hills and ricefields, central Highlands. Photograph: Roger Turley.

Plate 13. Family in mourning, central Highlands. Photograph: Roger Turley.

Plate 14. Musicians at a *famadihana*, central Highlands. Photograph: Roger Turley.

Plate 15. Women dancing with the corpse during a *mainty famadihana*, central Highlands. Photograph: Roger Turley.

CHAPTER ELEVEN

PAINFUL MEMORIES*

DAVID GRAEBER

In this essay I would like to talk about people who lost everything.
Imerina (the traditional name for the northern half of the central
plateau of Madagascar) is a place where people attach enormous
importance to the memory of their ancestors and the lands on which
their ancestors once lived. History, in Imerina, is largely a matter
of placing the living in an historical landscape created by the dead.
About a third of the Merina population, however, is made up of
the descendants of slaves, and in Madagascar, slaves are by definition
people without ancestors, 'lost people' (*olona very*) who have been
ripped from their ancestral landscapes, left unanchored to any place.
These were people who had been literally stripped of history. Even
today, almost a hundred years after emancipation, most 'black people' (as their descendants are called) remain in a kind of historical
limbo, unable to make a real claim to the territories in which they
live and are buried.

The question I want to ask is: what forms does historical memory take for such people? What forms can it take?

It has become a commonplace, nowadays, to argue that historical consciousness is ultimately about identity. Memories of the past
are ways of defining who one is in the present—and perhaps too,
of defining what kind of action one is capable of, of enunciating collective projects (e.g., Connerton 1989; Friedman 1992). Clearly, this
would leave the historical consciousness of slaves more than a little
problematic. Slaves' identities were created by events their descendants would not wish to commemorate, events which not only annihilated any link to their previous histories, but left their victims
generically incapable of producing new ones. Not surprising then
that most descendants tried their best to avoid having to admit to

* I should thank Bruce Applebaum, Jennifer Cole, Jean Comaroff, Nhu Thi Le,
Stuart Rockefeller, and Hylton White for their many helpful comments and suggestions.

their ancestry. It was embarrassing. Almost all the stories I did manage to cull about the 'days of slavery' centered on the insidious
means masters used to ritually pollute their slaves—rubbing excre-
ment on their heads, making them sleep alongside pigs—and so
destroy their *hasina*, a word whose meaning in this context falls about
halfway between 'state of grace' and 'power.' The ultimate message
was often quite explicit: it was only by destroying their ability to act
for themselves that masters were able to keep slaves in subjugation.
But it is telling that these were just about the *only* memories of slavery I ever heard recounted. It was as if, having explained how slaves
were rendered people who did not have the right to act, or even to
speak, for themselves, there was nothing left to say.

The experience of slavery could not be directly told, as history,
if only because admitting to such a past deprived one of the authority with which to speak. It was inherently shameful. Of course, the
feeling that one is not entitled to have an opinion, or a history, is a
common phenomenon among the dispossessed of any society (Bourdieu 1984). However, what I am going to argue in this paper is that
Merina slaves did, in fact, develop a ritual idiom with which to
reflect on their history and their condition, and even to speak to
others with the voice of authority. It was, perhaps, somewhat veiled
and indirect. But here too the ability to speak was inseparable from
the ability to act; it was through the very process of seizing the
authority to speak that the descendants of slaves, in so many cases,
began to take back for themselves the capacity to act as historical
agents in their own right, actors as well as narrators, and so perhaps to begin to recuperate a little bit of what they had lost.[1]

Merina slavery

From around 1820 to sometime around 1850, hundreds of thousands of people were taken prisoner by Merina military expeditions
and carried back to the central highlands of Imerina. The Merina
kingdom's army, armed and trained by its British allies, made common practice of massacring all the adult males of 'rebel' villages,
and carrying off everybody else to be sold as slaves. Sometime around
1855, Queen Ranavalona I's secretary Raombana wrote of these
campaigns:

---

[1] I would like to thank Nhu Le for first suggesting this connection.

As to the miseries which these continual wars brought to the provincial people, that is indescribable, for by fighting, but more deceit, that is, the offer of life and pardon if they yield and submit, thousands and thousands have thus been murdered in cold blood, and their numerous wives, children and cattle seized and reduced to slavery.

Mothers are separated from their tender offspring and other relations, as they are divided and distributed amongst different masters, and are thus taken into different parts of the country where they never discover one another again, with very few exceptions.

An officer who is a real Christian informed me that the pains in hell could not be more than the pains suffered by these unfortunate people in being separated from one another to be taken away to their different masters. Their cries, their weepings and their lamentations, said the above Christian, is such as almost sufficient to raise the dead from their graves for to take their parts. . . .[2]

It is important to remember that for its victims, the very first thing slavery meant was a complete rupture with everything that had made their lives meaningful: of all the ties of love, kinship, shared experience that had bound them to a home, to parents, friends, lovers, to everyone and everything they had most cared for. It was in this sense too that slaves were 'lost people,' alone, in an alien place among people who did not know them.

It is even more important, perhaps, to emphasize that this situation did not end once a captive had been sold and settled in Imerina. It was extremely difficult for slaves to create any kind of enduring ties, either to people or to places. Free Merina lived in permanent towns or villages on hilltops; slaves, in makeshift settlements in the valley bottoms, near the paddy fields. These hamlets were mostly structured around a handful of older men or women; most younger slaves had no fixed abode at all but circulated between several hamlets in different parts of Imerina, often between different masters, as well as between scattered family, friends, and lovers. Many slaves managed to win a remarkable degree of independence from their masters; they came to make up the majority of both Imerina's petty merchants and its petty criminals, as well as almost all wage laborers; but the mobility which made this possible also ensured their uprooted condition remained permanent.[3]

The most obvious symptom of slaves' placelessness was their lack

---

[2] Raombana's 'Annals,' A2, no. 5: p. 74 (693–696). Raombana wrote his history in English; in part to ensure that no one else at court could read it.

[3] My generalizations about slavery are based partly on European sources (e.g., Sewell 1876, Cousins 1896, Piolet 1896) but even more on my readings of 19th

of proper tombs. For free Merina, tombs were—as they remain today—the ultimate link between people and places, the anchors of group identities (cf. Bloch, 1971). It is through collective stone tombs that each descent group is fixed to an ancestral territory; one may spend one's entire life far from one's ancestral lands, but one nonetheless expects to be buried on them when one dies. To be buried in a magnificent tomb, to be remembered there by one's descendants, and to be periodically rewrapped in beautiful silk shrouds called *lambamena*, is the ultimate aspiration of any important man. But the ideal is hard to achieve; to guarantee one will not be forgotten, one has to acquire enough land to settle a large number of descendants around one's tomb. For slaves, all this was nearly inconceivable. Most slaves were not buried in proper stone tombs at all—many were buried in simple graves or improvised pit-tombs near their settlements,[4] usually with people of very different ancestries buried together. It was only after emancipation (which came in 1896, a year after the French conquest of Madagascar) that most of those former slaves who chose to remain in Imerina[5] began to create solid and substantial tombs of stone like those of free people. Usually, a number of families would have to pool their resources to do so. To acquire the land to keep one's descendants around was even more difficult. Almost all 'white' Merina claim their ancestors forbid them to marry or sell their ancestral land to the descendants of slaves; when they make exceptions, it is only for vastly inflated prices. In the village of Betafo, where I did my fieldwork, for example, almost every 'black' (*mainty*) family that had managed to establish itself over time had only been able to do so because of some exceptional windfall: a gift of land from former masters (for whom they were also obliged to work as sharecroppers), a military pension, an unusually

---

century Malagasy documents preserved in the National Archives, notably court cases and the AKTA series (état civil).

   [4] I never found anyone in the present who recalled how slaves were buried, though some pointed out that there were a few, exceptionally generous masters who set aside a shelf within their own family tombs for slaves; others built modest slave-tombs near their own.

   [5] Most of the slaves emancipated in 1895 abandoned Imerina entirely. Some returned to their former homes—if those places existed and they still had any memories of them. Many others moved to lands newly opened up for farming to the west. Even among those that stayed, only a handful remained in their former villages. Some moved to towns like Arivonimamo, working as porters, merchants, laborers; others moved off to found their own settlements in depopulated corners of Imerina; many sought work in the capital.

advantageous marriage. . . .[6] The majority still spent their lives traveling between places which were not really theirs; for most, lives of endless striving ended only in failure and oblivion, to be buried in the tomb of a distant relative in a land where they had likely never lived.

There is an irony here, because the very difficulty of creating tombs and ancestors meant they came to take on a very different meaning for the descendants of slaves than for the other two thirds of the Merina population. As I have argued elsewhere (Graeber 1995), attitudes of 'white' Merina towards ancestors are profoundly ambivalent. People do wish to be remembered as ancestors when they die; but in part for that very reason, the memory of existing ancestors is seen as an imposition on the living, supported by the constant threat of punishment for lapses of memory or neglect of ancestral restrictions. Memory itself is felt as a kind of violence. As a result, the *famadihana* rituals in which the bodies of the dead are periodically removed from the tomb to be rewrapped in new *lambamena*, have a dual meaning too. While represented as ways of remembering the dead, their covert purpose is to make it easier to forget them: reducing ancestral bodies to dust so their names can be forgotten; then, locking them inside the tomb. For the descendants of slaves, on the other hand, it was not the pressure of history and memory that was felt as a kind of violence, but the very lack of it, and for that reason, ancestors took on a far more benevolent countenance. It is hard to be certain, but I did find that descendants of slaves were much more likely to insist that ancestors really did provide concrete benefits for their descendants, and I had a strong feeling that, while the form of mortuary ritual was the same, the content was slightly different; that there was an honest piety in 'black' attitudes towards the dead often lacking in their 'white' neighbors.

The first story I have to recount, in fact, is largely about how difficult it is for 'black people' (*olona mainty*) to lay claims to Merina mortuary ritual.

---

[6] When several black families did manage to get a foothold in some village, their kin would usually follow, and often this would lead to a kind of 'white' flight: the more the children of the *mainty* prospered, the more the children of the *fotsy* would move out, so that after a generation or two none of the villages' former inhabitants were left.

The story of Rainitaba

The community of Betafo, the focus of my own fieldwork which I conducted between 1989 and 1991, consisted of something like 13 settlements and perhaps 400 people, occupying a stretch of rolling country about forty minutes' walk to the north of the town of Arivonimamo. It was a community divided between the descendants of an *andriana*, 'noble,' descent group, and the descendants of their former slaves. The latter made up about a third of the total population.

The main reason they were there was because shortly after emancipation, members of the wealthiest *andriana* families had given their former slaves a large grant of land to encourage them to stay on. Almost all of it went to two men, who were, at the time, the chief men of a hamlet called Antandrokomby which sat, like most slave settlements, on the edge of a stretch of terraced rice fields. Both men built substantial tombs and kept large numbers of descendants around them; in fact, most 'black people' in Betafo were descended from one of them in some way or another. Betafo was also a somewhat anomalous community because on the whole, its 'black people' were doing rather well: partly because with their greater acclimatization to wage labor, they had been better able to adapt to the economic crisis that had hit rural Madagascar since the late 1970s; also, because some of the families that had not originally received grants of land had been able to capitalize on their reputations as astrologers and magicians to acquire enough money to buy land from their increasingly impoverished *andriana* neighbors. On the whole, in fact, Betafo's *mainty* were, by the late '80s, doing rather better than the *andriana*; certainly that was the *andriana* perception of the matter. But there were some *mainty* families who held on more tenuously. One of the most famous was made up of the descendants of a certain Rainitaba, a man who had, apparently, also lived in Antandrokomby, but who had already died, leaving behind only a single daughter, before the land was distributed in 1896.

It had never been a prosperous family, and most people I knew in Betafo were convinced that it had entirely died out. Nonetheless, everyone had heard Rainitaba's story.

The story goes like this:

When Rainitaba died, his children wrapped his body and buried it in the tomb, but when they opened the tomb to rewrap him, the body had disappeared. Only an empty cloth remained. Later, Rainitaba appeared in a dream to his daughter and told her he had taken the form of a snake and abandoned the tomb, becoming a *Vazimba* spirit in the waters to the east of the village of Betafo.

Some would repeat the story with amusement, others with a trace of scandal. But almost always, the narrator would then go on to point out the course of Rainitaba's meanderings since death. First he descended to the waters around the spring to the east of the village—a secluded spot, full of shade trees and quiet pools, where people used to be afraid to take children after night lest ghosts seize them and they waste away and die. Later, he followed the waters that flowed by the rice fields to the north of Betafo downstream until he reached the ruins of Antandrokomby—by then long since abandoned. Near the ruins was a reedy pool, and there he was supposed to have resided for some time, before again disappearing. No one was quite sure what happened to him since, but most were sure he was not in Betafo any more.

Now, there is every reason to believe that a man named Rainitaba did indeed live in Antandrokomby in the 1870s or '80s;[7] his daughter, Rabakomanga, was still living there with three sons of her own when she died (probably at the age of 45 or 50) in 1912. She was apparently the one who had the dream in which her father revealed that he had left his tomb, but, after that, almost all of her descendants were said to have had dreams of him, and sometimes unrelated people, too. I was told Rainitaba would always appear whenever one of his descendants conceived a child, and would often give advice about how to ensure a healthy birth.

It was only after I had been working in Betafo for some time that I discovered that there were still several descendants of Rainitaba living in Betafo or, anyway, quite frequently around. The most notable was Razanamavo, an old, poor woman who spent most of her time doing odd jobs for her slightly better-off neighbors in the *mainty* quarter of Betafo, or seeking work in town. She didn't really have a house in Betafo, but lived in an outbuilding—little more than a shed really—which a man named Armand had given her as an act of charity. Most people in Betafo did not have any idea of her ancestry; ordinarily, most tended to forget she existed at all.

---

[7] French documents from the second decade of the twentieth century say that he was Rabakomanga's father, and that she was born in Antandrokomby in the 1860s.

I first met Razanamavo in town. Armand—who was a good friend of mine—kept a room in the town of Arivonimamo, from which he conducted a small business selling bananas; people from Betafo often used to gather there, or drop by seeking news. Once I happened by while Razanamavo was visiting, and Armand's wife, Nety—always helpful in tracking down bits of Betafo history for me—immediately seized the opportunity to see if we could get her to tell us something about her famous ancestor.

Actually, Nety had previously wondered whether Razanamavo would be willing to talk to me at all: 'she might consider it embarrassing, having an ancestor who was a *Vazimba*.' But at first she seemed quite happy to tell us. Rainitaba, she said, was originally a nobleman from Betsileo. 'Back then, you know, people would be bought and sold' she said. 'And that was the origin of Rainitaba. He was a lost person.' He had been captured and sold into slavery in Betafo. The fact that people referred to him as a Vazimba did not bother her. What bothered her, she told Nety, was that people said he had turned into an animal. 'Rainitaba is not an animal,' she insisted, 'but a *Vazimba*—a person, a person like a *Kalanoro*.[8] Haven't you ever dreamed of him?' Nety hadn't. Well, Razanamavo said, many have; he used to appear to her grandmother and her father regularly. He had appeared to her, too, before the birth of her first child.[9]

Razanamavo had an oddly distant manner of speaking, somehow absent; she crouched wrapped in a yellow cloth staring off into the courtyard as she talked, as if looking at something far away, or perhaps nothing at all, and never once gazed at the other people in the room, even when she was more or less speaking to them. In part she was probably exhausted from an afternoon at work; but her manner seemed to complement the content of her discourse, which was much more evocative and dreamy than the usual, matter-of-fact style of historical narration. After telling her story, and answering a few of Nety's questions about her relatives, she seemed to just fade away, staring off as if so lost in thought that she didn't even

---

[8] Kalanoro are diminutive, human-looking creatures said to live in watery places; one often hears that they are living versions of Vazimba.

[9] Armand's brother Germain had gone much further: he had told me she hadn't ever had a child and then happened to pass by the stand of reeds where Rainitaba was, saw the animal, and immediately afterwards found she had conceived a male child.

notice anyone was talking to her, until after a little while, we gave up and started talking about something else.

> *Razanamavo*: He, you know—our grandmother said that when he was about to die, he said: 'I am about to die now, so take me to the north of the village, to the dam. And as for me' he said, 'don't bury me in a tomb but just release me in the current of the river. And get a *lamba arin-drano*'[10] he said, 'like you would for burying a son-in-law.'
>
> And they said: 'maybe we won't put you in the river, because we'd be embarrassed.'
>
> 'No, don't be embarrassed,' he said, 'because you'll receive a great blessing if you do it that way.'
>
> But they didn't do it. They just buried him normally and left him there.

> *Someone*: This was Rainitaba?

> *Razanamavo*: A little hole like that they buried him in—there was no tomb, no entry to the west. Later they got ready to do a *famadihana* [to move him into a proper tomb], and looked for the cloth, and they set the cloth around him nicely.
>
> 'If you do this thing, then a great blessing will come to you.' Then the water flooded . . . he was dead. 'I don't like *lambamena*' he said, 'but *lamba arin-drano*, and . . .' those were to be the mourning clothes. 'So your children will never become poor, nor the generations of your descendants to come . . .' This is something they all dreamed, all of them absolutely. But we didn't get the blessing because we didn't do it. They put him in the center of the top shelf to the north of the tomb, and he still hasn't been moved to this day.
>
> Once, there were a good number of descendants, but there are few left any more.[11]

---

[10] A kind of silk cloth from Betsileo, marked by bands of bright color set between black and white stripes, worn during Betsileo funerals, but also on festive occasions.

[11] MV: *Izy manko efa ho faty izy, hoy izy izany ilay renibenay, 'izaho izao efa ho faty' hoy izy, tsy maintsy tonga aty avaratanana io, an-baragy io. Dia izaho hoy izy aza alevina ampasana fa alefasao hanaraky an'io renirano io. Dia hovidiana lamba arin-drano hoy izy, ohatra an'ilay alevina vinanto-lahy izany, dia hoe 'angamba tsy nandefany an'iny renirano iny, fa menatr'olona izahay. 'A-an, tsy menatra ianareo hoy izy io, fa hahita fahasoavina be ianareo raha vitanareo izay.' Dia tsy nanao izy, fa nalevina ihany dia izay lasa izay. ?: Rainitaba io?*

MV: *I-e, lavaka kely ohatra an'izao no nilevenany, tsisy fasana miditra eo, amin'ny atsi- nanana. Dia nanao an'anona hamadika an'ilay olona dia nitady lamba dia nijanona tsara ilay lamba. Izy naka.*

Raha vitanareo iny zavatra iny dia ho avy aminareo fahasoavina be. Dia nitondraka ny rano—maty izy. 'Izaho tsy tia lambamena,' hoy izy, 'fa lamba arindrano, dia. . . . Ireny ilay lamba fisaona ireny izany.

Fa tsy manjary mahantra ny zanakareo, olona farana mandimby sy ny olona any ivelany izy. Zavatra efa vao tsinjony daholo daholo mihitsy. Fa tsy nahazo fahasoavina izahay fa tsy nanao. Apetraka amin'ny avaratra indrindra amin'ny afovoany sy mbola tsy afindra hatramin'izao. Taloha, taranany betsaka ihany fa efa vitsy izy izao.

She too told how he had moved from the pool to the east of the village to the one near Antandrokomby. She wasn't sure where he had gone after that, but she suspected he had finally returned to his original home in Betsileo.

The 'little hole' she refers to was a temporary grave—it seems that when he died, his daughter simply buried him—as was often done by slaves—until such time as a group of slaves could pool enough money to create a proper tomb. The opportunity only arose around 1910, when several 'black' families got together to build a collective tomb on a hill overlooking Betafo to the northeast. Rabakomanga contributed some money to the effort, and when the tomb was done had her father's body wrapped properly in cloth, and then transferred it to one of its most prominent shelves. It was after this, the first time they returned to perform a *famadihana*, that they found the body gone.

At the time, Rabakomanga was by no means penniless; she had apparently received a small amount of land from her former own-ers, which she had passed on to her sons.[12] Her sons apparently were not able to hold on to much of it. What land there was was sold or mortgaged off. Those who remember her sons, Ingahivelona and Rakotonanahary, remember them as landless laborers, and des-perately poor. In fact, the history of Rainitaba's family was always represented as one of loss, poverty and dispersal. They never received the blessing that they were offered. They scattered; now they're gone. In fact, it is one of the ironies of their history that it took me a long time to realize that the lineage had been really quite prolific: most of Rainitaba's grandchildren had numerous sons and daugh-ters. Some died in infancy; others were fostered by relatives in other places. Almost all of them would leave Betafo before they were thirty, there being no property to speak of or reason for them to stay. When once or twice I tried to make lists of their names, I found it was impossible: people would just shrug and said something to the effect of 'oh, there were lots of them. Who remembers? None of them live around here any more.'[13]

---

[12] When she died in 1913 this land was estimated to be worth about 152 francs; actually somewhat above the average legacy for Betafo as a whole. (Though this might simply be because none of the land had been parceled out in advance among her sons.) Her husband, who had died in 1912, appears to have left no property at all to his descendants, which is apparently the reason he has been entirely forgotten.

[13] Ingahivelona stayed in Andrianony, the *mainty* quarter of Betafo, most of his

About Vazimba

Unrealized promises, currents, dispersal, disappearance . . . the traditions surrounding Rainitaba seem to echo the sense of loss and displacement inherent to the experience of slavery, and to make it a figure for the lineage's own eventual dispersal, its withering away as a presence in Betafo. In fact, it is a very complicated story, which draws together a series of very old ideas and images—some Merina, some Betsileo—into a narrative so powerful that it has gone from an obscure piece of family history to an essential part of the historical consciousness of the community, a story everyone could repeat.

Part of how it could do this was by seizing on the richness of the term 'Vazimba,' a word which can be used to refer to ancient aborigines, lost ancestors, or dangerous spirits of the water—categories which tend to overlap considerably. It might be helpful to explore some of the term's meanings: not least because it has become something of a notorious issue in the scholarly literature.

The so-called 'Vazimba problem' has, in fact, generated a very long and (in my opinion) largely pointless intellectual history. It all started in the 19th century, when early missionaries heard stories about dark, diminutive Vazimba spirits lurking in wild places, and concluded that they must reflect the memory of an ancient 'aboriginal race' that had occupied the highlands of Madagascar before its present-day inhabitants (see Berg 1975, 1977). The logic seems to have been this: the people of Imerina tended to have straight hair and more Asian features than most other Malagasy. Therefore, they had to be the descendants of recent immigrants from the Malay archipelago.[14] The Vazimba, then, would have to be the people already living in the highlands when they arrived: backward,

---

life, as did his daughter Rabakolava, now remembered mainly because of her unusual height. She had a number of children who either married away or, reportedly, moved to town—though I never managed to track any of them down. In her old age she lived by herself and like most solitary old women was widely rumored to be a witch. Her brother Pascal only died in 1985, but his children too have also since disappeared.

[14] The first settlers of Madagascar undoubtedly came from somewhere in this area: this is why Malagasy is an Austronesian language. But no one has ever managed to come up with any evidence (linguistic, archaeological or otherwise) for such a second migration. Despite this it appears to remain unchallenged in the literature, it apparently never occurring to anyone that, if the first inhabitants of Madagascar came from Indonesia, and people had been coming from Africa ever since, the inhabitants of the most isolated central highlands would be likely to look the most like the original inhabitants.

dark-skinned savages, originally from East Africa. For English and French missionaries working in Imerina, this soon became a matter of simple common sense. There was some speculation the Vazimba might have been pygmies; others argued that the 'race of pygmies' (called Kimosy) was an even earlier strata the (perhaps pastoral) Vazimba drove out, before they were in turn put to flight by conquering Malays.

Needless to say, no evidence was ever produced to back up any of this, and there would be little reason to go into it were it not for the fact that this picture of Malagasy history has become entrenched in schoolbooks and, therefore, that anyone who has been to school has been exposed to it. When the descendants of free Merina call themselves 'white people' today, in contrast to the descendants of slaves, who like people of the coast are called 'black' they draw on this picture of Malagasy history.[15] On the other hand, popular conceptions of Vazimba themselves seem to have changed little from the ones Gerald Berg (1977: 7–12) documents for the early 19th century—the stories that missionaries first seized on and misinterpreted.[16]

First and foremost, Vazimba were ancestors whose bodies had been lost. If a man or woman drowned or died in a far-off country and their body was not recovered, they were often said to have 'become a Vazimba.' This could be a simple figure of speech; one did not necessarily mean anything more than that the person would never become a proper ancestor, never be wrapped and placed inside the tomb. But, more often, the term Vazimba was applied to the ghosts of such unfortunates, dangerous spirits, angry because they were cut off from proper relations with their descendants.[17]

---

[15] I am not suggesting that terms like *fotsy* and *mainty*, 'white' and 'black,' are simply the products of missionary influence: they go back to 19th century social classifications which, however, originally had a very different meaning. For further exploration of this point, see Graeber, 1996a.

[16] Occasionally, people I asked about Vazimba would reply with something to the effect of 'well, you have to understand that the Vazimba were really an entirely separate race' (always using the French word, *race*); and then go on to cite things they had read in books about Malagasy history, or heard professors discussing on the radio. Even Armand (who had been to college) did this the first time I asked him about Vazimba; but it was a one-time thing, a kind of bow to the authority of scholarship which seemed to have nothing to do with anything else he had to say on the subject thereafter.

[17] The word *razana*, normally translated 'ancestor,' actually means both 'ancestor' and 'corpse.' Vazimba were most definitively not *razana*. When people chanced

For all they lacked bodies, Vazimba were always identified with a specific place. Most often, their ghosts inhabited marshy places far from human habitation: little springs or pools between the rice fields, grottoes often marked by the presence of red fish or red crabs, knots of bamboo, reeds and rushes, sometimes, in certain kinds of tree. One might occasionally encounter a Vazimba by a rock or spring on an isolated hillside or even amidst the crags of a mountain, but it was unusual to find them far away from water.

I heard a lot of speculation about the origin of such ghosts. One medium from Arivonimamo told me they were usually ancestors whose descendants no longer 'took care of them.' If descendants stopped conducting *famadihana*, stopped keeping up the tomb, eventually the ancestor's *fanahy* or soul would leave the crumbling tomb entirely to settle in watery places, having become a fierce creature full of resentment towards the living. Others suggested most Vazimba were the spirits of travellers from other parts of Madagascar—Bara, Sakalava, Betsileo—who happened to die while passing through, and were buried hastily on the spot by whoever found them there. Others would point to the existence of Kalanoro: small human-like creatures rumored to live in distant lakes and marshes. Vazimba, they suggested, were the ghosts of Kalanoro. Finally, some (for instance, Betafo's schoolteacher, or one of its former pastors) did speak of Vazimba as if they were a former population, long since driven away, and therefore, whose ancestors no longer had any descendants to remember them.

Many refused to even speculate. The important thing about Vazimba, Armand's brother Germain once told me, is that you don't know what they are or where they come from. They are by definition mysterious, invisible, a kind of unknown power:

> *Germain*: Vazimba are a kind of thing that isn't seen. They don't show their bodies like, say, people do, or the divine spirits who possess mediums and cure people. If you carry pork to a place where one is, then that night, as soon as you kill the light you look and there's this hand moving towards you. As soon as you light the candle again, it's gone. Or, say you're washing your face in you don't know what . . . and likely as not your face will swell up hugely like this, and it absolutely

---

upon forgotten skeletons in their fields or wild places, for example, they often speculated that they were the remains of witches or lost travelers; but even if they ended up propitiating the spirit of the deceased, they never referred to them as Vazimba; Vazimba lacked bodies by definition.

won't go away until you burn incense over it. You take it to someone who will make offerings, and then you're cured. But that's all you
know—you have absolutely no idea what was in the water.[18]

As this quote makes clear, when people thought about Vazimba, it
was usually not as a matter for abstract historical speculation but as
one of immediate practical concern. One discovered that a place
was haunted by Vazimba because someone had taken ill. A child
playing in the fields had drunk some water from a reedy pool, or
taken fishes that they shouldn't have, or they had been tending pigs
or taking some other polluting substance to the place where a Vazimba
was. Such children would often fall into a fever, or parts of their
body would swell up; usually, they would be tormented by dreams
or apparitions. Vazimba were normally invisible; when they did
appear, it was almost always in the nightmare visions of an adoles-
cent or a child. Normally they appear either as horribly mutilated—
fingerless, noseless—reaching out to snatch the children, or else,
especially with older children as extremely attractive members of the
opposite sex, trying to lure them into their watery domains. The ritual for expelling Vazimba was similar to rituals for expelling hostile
ghosts: the curer would burn things, there would be incense, smoke.
But one would usually also leave offerings at the place, almost exactly
those one would give to ancestors at *famadihana*: rum or honey, can-
dies, ginger, suet, bananas, bread. If nothing else, these rituals would
'clean' the place of the pollution that had offended the creature and
made it 'fierce,' to soothe it, placate it, and at the same time, ensure
it remained confined there.[19]

Some places thus develop reputations. I knew at least seven in the
eastern half of Betafo alone where there were rumored to be Vazimba;
I wouldn't be surprised if there were more. Often it was not entirely
clear, because people differ on whether there is still a Vazimba in

---

[18] GR: *Ny Vazimba aloha dia karazana zavatra tsy hita. Izy tsy miseho vatana ohatry ny
hoe olona sa Zanaharin'ilay mitsabo olona Zanadrano ireo. Raha toerana misy azy, dia ohatra
hoe mitondra hena kisoa io, izany hoe dia nentina izany tsy maintsy atao na ... vao maty ny
jiro dia hitanao misy tanana manatona anao; efa vao mirehitra ny jiro dia tsy hita. Izany hoe,
ianao misasa tarehy, tsy fantatra na inona. Dia mety lasa vonto be ohatra an'izany koa, dia tsy
afaka mihitsy hono raha tsy evoahany—misy fanevokan'ny olona azy. Anateran'ilay olona fanasina,
izay vao afaka. Dia izay no tena hoe misy ... tsy fantatra mihitsy na inona na inona no ao
anatin'ny rano fa izay fotsiny.*

[19] In this, the basic underlying logic was not all that different than that of *famadihana*, which as I've argued elsewhere (Graeber 1995) was largely about the con-
tainment of ancestors.

a given spot, or if there is, whether it is still *masiaka*, 'fierce,' still a force to be reckoned with.

For present purposes, what is really important is the relationship between Vazimba and slaves. This relationship appears to be long-standing. Many of the captives brought to Imerina quickly developed ritual ties with local Vazimba.[20] It makes a certain sense that they should feel an affinity, since Vazimba were themselves figures of loss and dispersal. The one common feature in all stories about Vazimba is that they involve people being uprooted, cast out of their proper place. Vazimba are people who have been driven from their homes, ancestors whose descendants have dispersed and forgotten them, who have themselves left their solid tombs to enter confused, watery places. Like slaves, then, their defining feature is that they are lost; they embody the complete negation of those ties of descent that bind the living to ancestors buried in ancestral soil.[21] If slaves were people wrenched from their ancestors, Vazimba were ancestors lost to their descendants. It is not difficult, then, to understand why slaves might have seized on these images as a way of capturing their own experience—and in many cases at least, translating it into a source of power with which to restore some of what they'd lost.

Nymphs and Mediums

The only well documented example of how such ritual ties first developed is a story preserved in the *Tantara ny Andriana*, a collection of 19th century Malagasy texts (Callet 1908: 240–243; Dahle and Sims 1984: 197): about a woman originally from Betsileo, who became the medium for a Vazimba spirit named Ranoro.

First, a word about Ranoro. Ranoro remains, even today, probably the most famous Vazimba in Madagascar (Domenichini 1985:

---

[20] The connection probably would have made perfect sense to Europeans who assumed that Vazimba were themselves the remnants of an African population; slaves, after all, were mainly drawn from the coastal populations of Madagascar, who were assumed to be equally African. But clearly, this had nothing to do with Malagasy attitudes. I certainly never heard anyone refer to Vazimba as 'black.'

[21] This indeed is the gist of most previous analyses. Gerald Berg (1977) for instance notes that in Merina king-lists, the earliest rulers are referred to as 'Vazimba' because unlike later kings they were not buried on solid ground; their bodies were thrown into lakes. Likewise Bloch (1982, 1985, 1986) draws an opposition between ancestors identified with ancestral land and Vazimba identified with water.

416–445; Rajaofera 1912; Aujas 1927: 16–17; Peetz 1951; Haring 1982: 358–359; see Bloch 1991).[22] She is considered one of the most ancient ancestors of a large and historically significant descent group called the Antehiroka, whose territory is just to the north of the capital. The Antehiroka are sometimes described as 'Vazimba' themselves—if only because they were the original inhabitants of the hill on which Antananarivo, the Merina capital, was later built, displaced when it was taken over by an early king.

According to the story the Antehiroka ancestor Andriambodilova was strolling by the banks of the river Mamba one day when he chanced on Ranoro, a beautiful water nymph (*zazavavindrano*), sunning herself on a rock. He proposed marriage. Ranoro was not necessarily disinclined, but she warned him that marriage with supernatural beings was difficult; there were always all sorts of taboos. If he wished to marry her, he would have to agree, among other things, never to use salt or even to pronounce the word.

Some versions explain the reason for this unusual demand. Ranoro knew that if she abandoned the waters to marry a mortal man, it would mean never again seeing her father, whose name was Andriantsira, 'Lord Salt.' Therefore, she made him promise never to say or do anything that would remind her of him. He agreed, the two married and had children. But one day many years later, during a domestic argument, he spat it out in anger, calling her 'daughter of salt.' No sooner had she heard the word than she turned her back on him and walked to the banks of the river, dived in, and was never seen again. The place where she disappeared, a rocky grotto by the river, has been a place of worship ever since, and her present-day descendants continue to maintain a taboo on salting food—in fact, many versions add that any salt that comes near the grotto immediately dissolves.

The taboo on salt is the main claim to fame the Antehiroka had among people I knew in Arivonimamo: it was considered the most difficult taboo anyone had ever heard of. And salt does seem the key to the story. In fact I suspect the whole story is a kind of play on a Malagasy proverb: *sira latsaka an-drano, tsy himpody intsony*, 'like salt fallen into the water, it will never again return to its previous

---

[22] Her fame—or at least her documentation—is in part due to the fact that her grotto is located less than an hour's drive from the center of the capital.

form.' As with Rainitaba, a broken trust leads to a very literal dissolution: what was once a single object becomes an infinity of tiny things which flow away in all directions.

Already in the 19th century, Ranoro's sanctuary, like her husband's tomb, had become a place where people came from far and wide to make vows, and ask for favors; Ranoro is still famous for helping infertile women to conceive.[23] But in the 19th century, these were places which slaves were not allowed to enter. The presence of slaves was considered to be polluting, in much the same way as pork. This makes it all the more surprising that the most famous disciple of Ranoro of that century was, in fact, a slave—she was a woman originally from the Betsileo country in the southern highlands of Madagascar. During the reign of Ranavalona I (1828–1861), this woman—always herself referred to as Ranoro—began periodically to fall into trance and be possessed (*tsindriana*) by the Vazimba's spirit. Her fame began to spread after she cured a woman who had been struck blind for having sullied Ranoro's grotto; soon, even free people were beginning to frequent her, seeking advice and cures. According to the story preserved in Callet (1908), the news eventually reached the Queen, who ordered the woman to be put to the poison ordeal. When she survived, Ranavalona recognized her claims to be legitimate and granted her an honorary guard of thirty Merina soldiers.

The mortal Ranoro appears to have become a figure of some fame and influence—despite her continued status as a slave. She is said to have slept on an elevated bed suspended from the rafters, to have walked across the room on a tightrope when possessed, and performed other remarkable feats. For her last miracle, she went to Ranoro's grotto and dived into the water; it was only three days later, according to the story, that she emerged. In the interim, she told her followers, she had lived with Vazimba in the bottom of the cave, who fed on raw fish and raw crabs. They tried to make her join them in their meals, but the food repelled her, and having refused them, she was returned to the surface. The spirits had rejected her. Claiming her contact had thus been broken, the woman left and went back to find her father, who she believed was still alive somewhere in Betsileo.

---

[23] An interesting parallel with Rainitaba.

In her case at least—and hers was clearly very unusual—it was possible to use access to Vazimba as a way of restoring the severed bonds of descent.

Fanany: people who come back as snakes

It is worth exploring the connection to Betsileo in more detail, since most 'black people' in Imerina today claim Betsileo origins.

Betsileo is the name given the country directly to the south of Imerina, including most of the southern part of the vast plateau that forms the center of Madagascar, as well as to the people who live there. In the 18th century, they were divided into a number of independent kingdoms; in the beginning of the 19th, Betsileo was conquered by the Merina king Andrianampoinimerina. From the point of view of present-day Merina, the Betsileo are a bit of an anomaly. On the one hand, like all other Malagasy they are considered 'black people'—if only because they are much less likely to have straight hair. However, in almost every other way, they are indistinguishable from Merina. Their way of speaking is similar; so are their houses, clothes, and ritual practices. If any differences are widely remarked upon, it is that Betsileo tend to be more open and easygoing than Merina (those from Ambalavao are widely held to be the most talkative people in Madagascar), and are much more sophisticated farmers: their skill at irrigation and terracing, for example, is famous throughout Madagascar.

Nowadays, descendants of slaves in Imerina almost always claim to be Betsileo (I met dozens, in fact, who insisted they were descendants of the famous Betsileo king Andriamanalina). There are any number of reasons why the identity might seem appealing.[24] Not only were Betsileo also 'black people' who were otherwise indistinguishable from Merina, they also had a renown as migrant laborers. During the '50s and '60s, thousands used to cross Imerina every year, following the rice replanting and the harvest; many ended up marrying local people and stayed on. Since local attitudes towards Betsileo migrants were so strikingly more accepting than they were

---

[24] Pier Larson (personal communication) has pointed out to me that in the 18th century, most Merina slaves were, in fact, Betsileo. Later this was not the case, but since no single group ever gained the same numerical dominance Bestileo once had, the identity might well have lingered.

being was utterly annihilated. The result, as Raombana's friend himself observed, was a trauma so intense that no mere physical pain could possibly surpass it.

All this does not mean that memories of such a moment are likely to become a part of historical consciousness. In fact they are just the sort of events that would not; that one would normally suspect survivors would prefer never to have to talk about. Certainly the memory of them is not preserved in oral histories of the present day. But if for slaves and their descendants, that one moment, when worlds dissolved away, seems to have reverberated endlessly, it is because such experiences did not stop. Dispersal, families drifting apart, people uprooted from their memories: for most, it was repeated with every generation.

It also took place within a cultural milieu which placed an extraordinary emphasis on the politics of memory. The manipulation and transformation of such memories—particularly, women's memories of their parents and ancestral homes—was a constant theme of Merina ritual. In marriage negotiations, for instance, the suitors' family offered a series of cash payments which compensated either for the nurturance and care the girl's parents had provided her—such as the *valim-babena*, the 'answer for having carried an infant on one's back'—or services the daughter herself would no longer be able to provide—the *akana kitay*, 'gathering firewood,' or *alana volo fotsy*, 'pulling out white hairs.' In the latter case especially, an image so intimate of a daughter poring over her father or her mother's head, searching for white hairs to pluck out, evokes a whole world of domestic sentiments: protective affection, the fear of aging and resultant loss, the pain of ruptured domesticity when the woman moves away. The money, officially meant to 'ask for the parent's blessing' for the marriage, can equally be seen, I think, as compensation for that pain. In *famadihana* the evocation of emotionally-charged memories becomes even more explicit. When one places the corpses of women's relatives on their laps, the effect is to break the power of women's most vivid, intimate memories of people that they loved. It evokes that entire world in order to efface it, to free the living from their attachments to the dead.

For women who had been carried into slavery, evocation of such memories could only serve as a reminder of acts of such irreparable violence, that the entire world of those memories had been brutally destroyed. It is hardly surprising that the Betsileo woman should have felt such an affinity with the figure of Ranoro. Ranoro was a woman who could not bear to hear her father's name; the memories it evoked for her would be too painful. It was a story about salt dropped in water, things that could never be brought back together or attain their previous form. In this one case, of course, the story may have taken on a different level of poignancy because the woman possessed by Ranoro believed her father was still alive—at least, in the end she managed to win her freedom so as to try to find him. Though one cannot help but wonder whether the dream of finding her father was really as much a projection of her imagination as Ranoro herself had been.

Containment and Redemption

At this point, let me return briefly to the question with which I began: about stories that can, and can't, be told.

Students of working-class history have noted that it is relatively easy to cull oral histories of periods of successful strikes, political advances, in which workers had some control of their destiny; much harder for periods of massive retrenchment or defeat. When Italian workers told the stories of their lives, for instance, the two decades of fascist rule often seemed to drop out entirely (Passerini 1987). In a fascinating essay, Michel Bozon and Anne-Marie Thiesse (1986) asked: what happens, then, to workers who have never known anything but defeat? Their research focused on farm laborers from the countryside near Paris, people who had begun their lives at the bottom of the social heap and then moved down steadily: made redundant by mechanization, set to scrabbling for endless miserable jobs wherever they could get them. They discovered that, indeed, most found it impossible to give any account of their lives since childhood; many found it painful to even try. Instead, they tended to fall back on quasi-ethnographic descriptions—'how we used to do things in the old days'—and anecdotes about their own experience of famous historical events—mainly, of France's wars. These anecdotes, however, were in almost every case and themselves little images of loss and dispersal: peasants fleeing before unearthly German horsemen, the government fleeing Paris by balloon. . . . It was as if, having been told all their lives they had no right to speak of or for themselves, they could only do so through the borrowed authority of 'national' history.

Malagasy understandings of what history is, and what gives one the authority to tell it, are rather different. Histories are, indeed, matters of privilege,[30] but they are also intrinsically tied to places— where ancestors lived and are buried, where famous events took place. And there is a very deep-seated feeling that only those who live near a place can really know its history. Even the wealthiest and most powerful descendants of Betafo's noble families would look mildly irritated when I asked them about the histories of their illustrious forbears, unable to speak about the place because their families had long since relocated to the city. Several ended up referring me to the descendants of their former slaves, who still lived there. In this sense what Vazimba pools provide is not just a way to conceptualize a history of pain and dispersal, but the right to speak of it: after all, most of these pools were in wild places in the valley bottoms, the very places to which slaves too were once exiled.[31]

Even if what they spoke of was, ultimately, their own sense of loss, their own disempowerment, the ability to speak about such things itself opened up possibilities of taking action and beginning to reverse the situation. In the case of Ranoro this was fairly obvious; less so, perhaps, in the case of Rainitaba. But histories keep changing, and Vazimba provide endless possibilities of moving from speech to action.

One of the last descendants of Rainitaba everyone remembered, for example, was an old man named Pascal, a landless laborer who had died several years before I came, when, while working a neighbor's field, he had an epileptic fit and fell on his own shovel. Pascal, I was told, was haunted by a Vazimba, who would periodically possess him. Some said it was Rainitaba himself; others insisted it was a different, nameless spirit, that he had first encountered while swimming in a pool to the north of the village. All though remembered how Pascal would periodically announce he felt the Vazimba beginning to move in him, and how practically the entire population of the *mainty* quarter of Betafo would set out across the fields to the

---

[30] In fact, the word for 'history,' *tantara*, could be used to mean 'privilege' as well.

[31] Though almost all these ancient hamlets had long since been abandoned, the slaves on liberation having moved further up the hills.

The almost ritualized invocation of Betsileo origins might also be interpreted as serving as a kind of authorization to speak. In many rural communities I found that even old Merina men would push the descendants of Betsileo migrants forward to tell me local histories, despite the fact they had been born elsewhere, just on the basis of their greater ability to talk.

north of the village, and then gather to sing and clap, encouraging the spirit to emerge. The sessions would always end the same way. After some time, the Vazimba would come to him, and Pascal would bolt off randomly into the surrounding woods or waters, whereon everyone would chase after him, to bring him back again—in an endless drama of dispersal and retrieval.

These gatherings were organized with the help of another man— one I will call Rainibe. Unlike Pascal, Rainibe was an experienced medium. This is not how people around Betafo put it, though. Rainibe, people would tell me, 'had' a Vazimba. Many insisted that he had moved out from his old home in Betafo to found a new hamlet at the end of a long valley to the northeast just to be closer to the field where it was. Every night when there was a new moon his whole family could be heard out there, clapping and singing to bring it out. Rainibe himself never admitted any of this to me—in fact, he denied that he even worked as a curer. But this sort of coyness was typical of people who had Vazimba, because being too close to a Vazimba is a morally dubious thing: such spirits can not only help one in curing, they can also take vengeance on one's enemies, making one little better than a witch. Most people in Betafo were very careful not to pick a quarrel with Rainibe, and from the money he got from curing and the fear he inspired he had managed to acquire quite a bit of land, and to keep a very large number of his children and grandchildren around him in his little hamlet by the fields. This was the main thing that struck me when I would visit him in his hamlet, occupied entirely by his own descendants. He was always surrounded by children.

Rainibe did not entirely deny his links with Vazimba. His grandfather, he said, had many years before been mysteriously pulled into the waters underneath the dam to the northeast of Betafo, and wasn't seen for days. When he finally re-emerged, he told little, except that the spirit was an old man with a long beard, dressed all in red, surrounded by endless numbers of tiny children. He had stayed there for three days in all, and all he had to eat was crabs.

'Raw crabs?' asked my companion, an *andriana* from Betafo.

'I have no idea if they were raw or they were cooked.' Then, deciding this might be a bit too coy: 'well, I guess there wouldn't have been cooked ones.'

'Because you know what they say' (everyone, apparently, knew this story): 'if you eat those, then they become your friend for life. But if you refuse, they might even kill you.'

'Yes,' he smiled. So they say.

Just so as to show that anything is possible, let me end by noting that towards the end of the time I was in Betafo I discovered there was another of Rainitaba's descendants living there. He was one of Razanamavo's sons, a man in his thirties named Tratra. Tratra too claimed to be a medium. Nobody I talked to took these claims particularly seriously: most considered him a drunken blowhard, and a bit of a buffoon ('if you *really* have spirits,' Armand told me, 'you don't go around telling everyone.') But a few years before he had built a little house near the ruins of Antandrokomby, just a few meters away from the reedy pool Rainitaba is said to have inhabited before he disappeared. He couldn't afford to be around very often; most of the time, like his mother, he was off looking for work. But it at least suggests the possibility that, were one to come back in twenty years, Rainitaba might have acquired a new and entirely different history.

BIBLIOGRAPHY

Abinal, A.
    1885   *Vingt ans à Madagascar: colonisation, traditions historiques, moeurs et croyances.* Paris.
Aujas, Louis
    1927   *Les rites du sacrifice à Madagascar.* Tananarive: Mémoire de l'Académie Malgache, fasc. II.
Berg, Gerald
    1975   *Historical Traditions and the Foundations of Monarchy in Imerina.* Doctoral Dissertation, University of California, Berkeley.
    1977   'The myth of racial strife and Merina kinglists: the transformation of texts.' *History in Africa* vol. 4, 1–30.
    1980   'Some words about Merina Historical Texts.' In *The African Past Speaks: Essays on Oral Tradition and History* (J.C. Miller, ed.). London: Dawson, pp. 221–239.
Bloch, Maurice
    1971   *Placing the dead: tombs, ancestral villages, and kinship organization in Madagascar.* London: Seminar Press.
    1978   'Marriage amongst Equals: An Analysis of Merina Marriage Rituals.' *Man* (n.s.) 13: 21–33.
    1979   'Slavery and Mode of Production in Madagascar: Two Case Studies.' In *Asian and African Systems of Slavery* (L.J. Watson, ed.). Berkeley: University of California Press, pp. 123–45.
    1982   'Death, women and power.' In *Death and the Regeneration of Life* (M. Bloch and J. Parry eds.). Cambridge: Cambridge University Press, pp. 211–230.
    1985   'Almost Eating the Ancestors.' *Man* (n.s.) 20: 631–646.
    1986   *From Blessing to Violence: history and ideology in the circumcision ritual of the Merina of Madagascar.* Cambridge: Cambridge University Press.
    1994   'The Slaves, the King, and Mary in the Slums of Antananarivo' in *Shamanism, History and the State* (N. Thomas and Caroline Humphrey eds.), Ann Arbor: University of Michigan Press, pp. 132–145.

Bourdieu, Pierre
    1984   *Distinction: A Social Critique of the Judgement of Taste.* Cambridge: Harvard University Press.
Bozon, Michel and Anne-Marie Thiesse
    1986   'The Collapse of Memory: the Case of Farm Workers (French Vexin, pays de France).' *History and Anthropology* 2: 237–259.
Cabanes, Robert
    1972   'Cultes de possession dans la plaine de Tananarive.' *Cahiers du Centre d'Études des Coutumes* 9: 33–66.
Callet, F.
    1908   *Tantara ny Andriana eto Madagascar,* Antananarivo: Imprimerie officielle.
Connerton, Paul
    1989   *How Societies Remember.* Cambridge: Cambridge University Press.
Cousins, William
    1896   'The Abolition of Slavery in Madagascar: with Some Remarks on Malagasy Slavery Generally' *Antananarivo Annual and Malagasy Magazine* 21: 446–50.
Dahle, Lars and Louis Sims
    1984   *Anganon'ny Ntaolo, Tantara Mampiseho ny Fombandrazana sy ny Finoana Sasany Nanganany.* Antananarivo: Trano Printy Loterana.
Delivré, Alain
    1974   *L'Histoire des Rois d'Imerina: interprétation d'une tradition orale.* Paris: Klincksieck.
Delord, J.
    1958   'Note sur la croyance en la réincarnation des princes betsileo sous la forme d'un serpent.' *Bulletin de l'Académie Malgache* 47: 155–170.
Domenichini, Jean-Pierre
    1985   *Les Dieux au Service des Rois: Histoire orale des Sampin' andriana ou palladiums royaux de Madagascar,* Paris, CNRS, 716p.
Dubois, Henri
    1938   *Ethnographie des Betsileo.* Paris: Institut d'Ethnographie.
Ellis, William
    1838   *History of Madagascar.* 2 vols. London: Fisher & Son.
Faublée, Jacques
    1954   *Les esprits de la vie à Madagascar.* Paris: Presses Universitaires de France.
Feeley-Harnik, Gillian
    1982   'The King's men in Madagascar: Slavery, citizenship and Sakalava monarchy.' *Africa* 52: 31–50.
    1986   'Ritual and Work in Madagascar.' In *Madagascar: Society and History* (C.P. Kottak, J.-A. Rakotoarisoa, A. Southall and P. Vérin, eds.) Durham: Carolina Academic Press, pp. 157–174.
    1991   *A Green Estate: restoring independence in Madagascar.* Washington D.C.: Smithsonian Institution Press.
Friedman, Jonathan
    1992   'The past in the future.' *American Anthropologist* 94: 837–59.
Graeber, David
    1995   'Dancing with Corpses Reconsidered: an Interpretation of Famadihana (in Arivonimamo, Madagascar).' *American Ethnologist* 22: 258–278.
    1996a   *The Disastrous Ordeal of 1987: Memory and Violence in Rural Madagascar.* Ph.D. dissertation, University of Chicago.
    1996b   'Beads and Money: Notes Toward a Theory of Wealth and Power.' *American Ethnologist* 23: 1–32.
    1996c   'Love Magic and Colonial Labor Policy in Central Madagascar.' *Gender and History* 8.

Haile, John
    1893   Malagasy Village Life: Pen and Ink Sketches of the People of Western
            Imerina. *Antananarivo Annual and Malagasy Magazine* 18: 1–20.
Haring, Lee
    1982   *Malagasy Tale Index.* Folklore Fellows Communications no. 231. Helsinki:
            Suomalainen Tiedeakatemia.
Jully, Antoine
    1894   'Funérailles, tombeaux et honneurs rendus aux morts à Madagascar.'
            Anthropologie 5: 385–401.
Larson, Pier
    1992   *Making Ethnic Tradition in a Pre-Colonial Society: Culture, Gender, and Protest
            in the Early Merina Kingdom, 1750–1822.* Doctoral dissertation, University
            of Wisconsin-Madison.
Meillassoux, Claude
    1991   *The Anthropology of Slavery: The Womb of Iron and Gold.* Chicago: University
            of Chicago Press.
Passerini, Luisa
    1987   *Fascism in popular memory: the cultural experience of the Turin Working class.*
            Cambridge: Cambridge University Press.
Patterson, Orlando
    1982   *Slavery and Social Death: a Comparative Study.* Cambridge: Harvard University
            Press.
Piolet, J.-B.
    1896   'De l'Esclavage à Madagascar.' *Le Correspondant (Paris)*, 10 February 1896,
            447–480.
Raison-Jourde, Françoise
    1991   *Bible et pouvoir à Madagascar au XIXe siècle.* Paris: Karthala.
Rajaofera, Henri
    1912   'La culte d'Andriambodilova.' Tananarive: *Bulletin de l'Académie Malgache*
            10: 189–198.
Ramamonjisoa, Janine
    1975   'Etude du village d'Ilafy.' *Annales de l'Université de Madagascar, Série Lettres
            et Sciences humaines*, no. 8–10. Paris: Cujas.
    1984   'Blancs et Noirs,' les dimensions de l'inégalité sociale. Documents socio-
            linguistiques.' *Cahiers des sciences sociales (Antananarivo)* 1: 39–75.
    1986   'Ilafy: terre et parenté.' In *Madagascar: Society and History* (C.P. Kottak,
            J.-A. Rakotoarisoa, A. Southall and P. Vérin, eds.) Durham: Carolina
            Academic Press, pp. 229–244.
Raombana
    N.d.   *Annales.* Manuscript preserved in the archives of the Académie Malgache,
            Antananarivo.
Razafintsalama, Adolphe
    1983   'Les funérailles royales en Isandra d'après les sources du XIXe siècle.'
            In *Les Souverains de Madagascar* (F. Raison-Jourde, ed.) Paris: Karthala,
            pp. 193–210.
Renel, Charles
    1910   *Contes de Madagascar.* Paris: E. Leroux.
    1920   'Ancêtres et dieux.' *Bulletin de l'Académie Malgache* (n.s.) 5: 1–261.
Richardson, John
    1885   *A New Malagasy-English Dictionary.* Antananarivo: London Missionary
            Society.
Ruud, Jørgen
    1960   *Taboo: A Study of Malagasy Beliefs and Customs.* New York: Humanities
            Press.

Scarry, Elaine
    1985   *The Body in Pain: The Making and Un-Making of the World.* New York: Oxford University Press.
Sewell, Joseph
    1876   *Remarks on Slavery in Madagascar.* London: Elliot Stock.
Shaw, George
    1878   'The Betsileo: Religious and Social Customs.' *Antananarivo Annual and Malagasy Magazine* 4: 312–334.
Sibree, James
    1880   *Madagascar: the Great African Island.* London: Trübner & Co.
    1896   *Madagascar Before the Conquest: The Island, the Country, and the People.* London: T. Fisher Unwin.
Van Gennep, Arnold
    1904   *Tabou et Totémisme à Madagascar.* Paris: Ernest Leroux.
Vig, Lars
    1977   *Croyances et Moeurs des Malgaches* (2 volumes). Antananarivo: TPFLM.

INDEX*

---

* Page numbers in *italics* refer to illustrations.

STUDIES OF RELIGION IN AFRICA

SUPPLEMENTS TO THE JOURNAL OF RELIGION IN AFRICA

1. MOBLEY, H.W. *The Ghanaian's Image of the Missionary.* An Analysis of the Published Critiques of Christian Missionaries by Ghanaians, 1897-1965. 1970. ISBN 90 04 01185 4
2. POBEE, J.S. (ed.). *Religion in a Pluralistic Society.* Essays Presented to Professor C.G. Baëta in Celebration of his Retirement from the Service of the University of Ghana, September 1971, by Friends and Colleagues Scattered over the Globe. 1976. ISBN 90 04 04556 2
3. TASIE, G.O.M. *Christian Missionary Enterprise in the Niger Delta, 1864-1918.* 1978. ISBN 90 04 05243 7
4. REECK,D. *Deep Mende.* Religious Interactions in a Changing African Rural Society. 1978. ISBN 90 04 04769 7
5. BUTSELAAR, J. VAN. *Africains, missionnaires et colonialistes.* Les origines de l'Église Presbytérienne de Mozambique (Mission Suisse), 1880-1896. 1984. ISBN 90 04 07481 3
6. OMENKA, N.I. *The School in the Service of Evangelization.* The Catholic Educational Impact in Eastern Nigeria 1886-1950. 1989. ISBN 90 04 08932 3
7. JĘDREJ, M.C. & SHAW, R. (eds.). *Dreaming, Religion and Society in Africa.* 1992. ISBN 90 04 08936 5
8. GARVEY, B. *Bembaland Church.* Religious and Social Change in South Central Africa, 1891-1964. 1994. ISBN 90 04 09957 3
9. OOSTHUIZEN, G.C., KITSHOFF, M.C. & DUBE, S.W.D. (eds.). Afro-Christianity at the Grassroots. Its Dynamics and Strategies. Foreword by Archbishop Desmond Tutu. 1994. ISBN 90 04 10035 0
10. SHANK, D.A. *Prophet Harris, the 'Black Elijah' of West Africa.* Abridged by Jocelyn Murray. 1994. ISBN 90 04 09980 8
11. HINFELAAR, H.F. *Bemba-speaking Women of Zambia in a Century of Religious Change (1892-1992).* 1994. ISBN 90 04 10149 7
12. GIFFORD, P. (ed.). *The Christian Churches and the Democratisation of Africa.* 1995. ISBN 90 04 10324 4
13. JĘDREJ, M.C. *Ingessana.* The Religious Institutions of a People of the Sudan-Ethiopia Borderland. 1995. ISBN 90 04 10361 9
14. FIEDLER, K. *Christianity and African Culture.* Conservative German Protestant Missionaries in Tanzania, 1900-1940. 1996. ISBN 90 04 10497 6

15. OBENG, P. *Asante Catholicims.* Religious and Cultural Reproduction Among the Akan of Ghana. 1996. ISBN 90 04 10631 6
16. FARGHER, B.L. *The Origins of the New Churches Movement in Southern Ethiopia, 1927-1944.* 1996. ISBN 90 04 10661 8
17. TAYLOR, W.H. *Mission te Educate.* A History of the Educational Work of the Scottish Presbyterian Mission in East Nigeria, 1846-1960. 1996. ISBN 90 04 10713 4
18. RUEL, M. *Belief, Ritual and the Securing of Life.* Reflexive Essays on a Bantu Religion. 1996. ISBN 90 04 10640 5
19. McKENZIE, P. *Hail Orisha!* A Phenomenology of a West African Religion in the Mid-Nineteenth Century. 1997.
    ISBN 90 04 10942 0
20. MIDDLETON, K. *Ancestors, Power and History in Madagascar.* 1999.
    ISBN 90 04 11289 8